Principles of Retailing

D0234767

To be strong candidates for careers in retail, one of the biggest and most important sectors in today's economy, graduates need a solid knowledge of its core principles. The *Principles of Retailing*, Second Edition is a topical, engaging and authoritative update of a hugely successful textbook by three leading experts in retail management, designed to be a digestible introduction to retailing for management and marketing students.

The previous edition was praised for the quality of its coverage, the clarity of its style and the strength of its sections on operation and supply chain issues such as buying and logistics, which are often neglected by other texts. This new edition has been comprehensively reworked in response to the rapid changes in the industry, including the growth of online retail and the subsequent decline of physical retail space and new technologies that improve customer experience and help track consumer behaviour. Brand new to this edition are sections on e-tail logistics, retail security, corporate social responsibility, green logistics and the fashion supply chain.

This edition is also supported by a collection of online teaching materials such as mini cases, multiple choice questions to complement review questions, and lecture slides, to help tutors spend less time preparing and more time teaching.

John Fernie is Emeritus Professor of Retail Marketing at Heriot-Watt University and Honorary Professor at the University of St Andrews. He was Director of the Institute for Retail Studies at Stirling University prior to becoming Head of the School of Management & Languages at Heriot-Watt, UK.

Suzanne Fernie has developed, led and taught retail programmes at all levels in the further and higher education sector. She developed and examined MBA modules in retailing and services marketing at Edinburgh Business School and has taught retail classes at Adam Smith College, Heriot-Watt University and the University of St Andrews, UK.

Christopher M. Moore is Professor, Chair in Marketing and Assistant Vice-Principal of Glasgow Caledonian University, UK. He is Director of the British School of Fashion. He consults to leading international fashion and retailer brands, including Marks & Spencer, and has visiting professorships in the UK, Japan, the USA and Europe.

Principles of Retailing

Second edition

John Fernie, Suzanne Fernie and Christopher M. Moore

Routledge
Taylor & Francis Group

LONDON AND NEW YORK

Second edition published 2015
by Routledge
2 Park Square, Milton Park, Abingdon, Oxon OX14 4RN

and by Routledge
711 Third Avenue, New York, NY 10017

Routledge is an imprint of the Taylor & Francis Group, an informa business

First published 2003 by Butterworth-Heinemann

Every effort has been made to contact copyright holders for their permission to reprint material in this book. The publishers would be grateful to hear from any copyright holder who is not here acknowledged and will undertake to rectify any errors or omissions in future editions of this book.

British Library Cataloguing in Publication Data
A catalogue record for this book is available from the British Library

Library of Congress Cataloging in Publication Data
Fernie, John, 1948-
   Principles of retailing / John Fernie, Suzanne Fernie, and Christopher Moore. –
Second edition.
       pages cm
   Includes bibliographical references and index.
   1. Retail trade. 2. Retail trade–Management. I. Fernie, Sue. II. Moore, Christopher,
1937- III. Title.
   HF5429.F38 2015
   658.8'7–dc23
                   2014041922

ISBN: 978-1-138-79194-7 (hbk)
ISBN: 978-1-138-79195-4 (pbk)
ISBN: 978-1-3157-6243-2 (ebk)

Typeset in Perpetua
by Taylor & Francis Books

In memory of our parents, Jim, Sophia, Averil, John and Teresa who passed away since the first edition of the book was published

Contents

List of Illustrations

Figures

Tables

Boxes

Preface

When the first edition of *Principles of Retailing* was written at the turn of the millennium, the retail environment was very different from that of 2014. The economy was buoyant with low inflation, strong economic growth and low unemployment. These healthy economic indicators resulted in a boom for consumer goods, and retailers enjoyed a period of rapid growth that would take many of them from small family-owned companies to large public global corporations. By the end of the decade, however, the market environment had changed. The collapse of the sub-prime mortgage market in the USA precipitated the financial crisis of 2007/08 and plunged global markets into a recession from which they are only now beginning to show signs of recovery. Ironically, much of customer expenditure and retail growth were fuelled by debt and access to available credit predicated on continuing economic growth. With low or no growth, high unemployment, inflation well above wage rises and banks cautious in their lending, consumer confidence waned with a change in spending patterns. Price/value for money became the focus of consumer attention, although it should be noted that the boom in luxury goods consumption continued unabated after a minor dip in 2008/09. The rich apparently continue to spend while others review their spending habits.

Retailers faced severe challenges in this new market environment and the period 2007–June 2014 saw 308 UK companies enter administration (Centre for Retail Research, 2014). High-profile cases included Woolworths, Comet, HMV, Allied Carpets, JJB Sports and Focus DIY. In the USA, the filing for bankruptcy of well-known retailers such as Circuit City, A&P, Borders and Mervyns also highlighted problems facing many traditional retailers which had already been facing competition initially from 'big box' formats, but now also from online players, most notably Amazon. It is interesting to note that Amazon only reported its first annual net profit in 2003, when this book was first published. This was the beginning of online stability after the dot.com boom-and-bust period of the late 1990s and early 2000s, when online sales did not reach 1 per cent even in receptive markets such as the UK.

So at the time of the first edition of *Principles of Retailing*, most retailers' strategies were firmly focused on growth through the building of more stores, internationalizing formats and establishing an online presence. The world's two largest retailers, Walmart and Tesco, only began their major international expansion in the 1990s, with Tesco laying the basic foundations for its dominance in the online market in the UK and abroad in 1996. In the UK the 'race for space' was a feature of the major grocers' locational strategy as the best sites for large-scale formats were becoming scarce. With the changing market environment, however, this strategy was flawed. The idea of 'big box' formats was to exploit the better margins of a non-food offer but consumers increasingly began to shop online for such goods. The beleaguered CEO of Tesco, Philip Clarke, prior to his removal in July 2014, had commented that the company was the most competitive in online and convenience store retailing but was hampered by its legacy of Tesco extra hypermarkets.

The post-financial crisis era has led retailers to review their strategies and reappraise their capital investment plans. Most attention has centred upon the restructuring of their organizations to accommodate omni-channel retail so that customers can shop anytime, anywhere, receive deliveries and return goods to reception areas of their choice. The speed of change has been dramatic, with most markets achieving double-digit growth figures in terms of online sales and the UK share of sales rising from under 1 per cent to around 13 per cent since the first edition of this book was published. As sales migrated online, traditional store networks were scaled down to achieve a balanced portfolio of shopping options. This has led to major problems for traditional shopping malls and high streets, where vacancy rates have reached record levels.

Overseas markets were the engine for growth for the larger retailers in the 1990s/early 2000s, with the big four – Walmart, Carrefour, Tesco and Ahold – reshaping the global market. No sooner was the book published, than Ahold was involved in an accounting scandal in the USA which ultimately led to a withdrawal from most of its overseas markets apart from the USA and Europe. The other three companies have refocused their attention on markets that offer best rates of return, especially as shareholders have been concerned about their relatively poor performance in their home markets.

It is clear from this brief précis that much has changed over the last decade. However, our ideals remain the same as before, in that 'The challenge was to produce a book which was readable to a wide audience, students and practitioners alike, but to have academic authority based on the teaching and research experience of the authors' (Preface to the first edition). We have tried to keep as much of the underlying framework of the previous edition as possible, but instead of having four main sections, we have streamlined this into two parts: one on strategic direction, the first six chapters, followed by a further six chapters on the supporting functions to implement strategies. The main change is the reallocation of chapters on internationalization and e-commerce from the end of the previous edition under a section on 'Managing the future', to earlier in the new edition (Chapters 5 and 6). The future is here and, as outlined above, internationalization and online initiatives have been at the forefront of many retailers' strategies.

The early chapters are similar to the previous edition. 'The retail environment' has the same structure but has been extensively updated to incorporate how the new economic environment has impacted upon consumer attitudes, retailer responses and government initiatives with regard to competition and land-use policies. Despite these changes, the 'Theories of retail change' chapter has had fewer amendments than most chapters, primarily because cyclical, environmental and conflict theories remain the same; only the examples need revision.

In the first edition we had a chapter on 'Retail strategy' followed in a different section by 'The development of retail marketing'; these two chapters have been incorporated into two new chapters: 'Strategic retail marketing 1: the strategic planning process', and 'Strategic retail marketing 2: market segmentation and the service marketing mix'. In the first edition there was a degree of overlap in content with regard to the strategy process. Now Chapter 3 discusses corporate strategies, objectives and mission statements prior to evaluating tools for determining a retailer's strategic capability – environmental, competitive and resource audit analyses in order to evaluate the choice of strategic options available, from, for example, new product development to international expansion. Chapter 4 looks more specifically at how markets are segmented, the positioning within markets, retail branding and the implementation of the marketing mix. The content from the earlier 'Development of retail marketing' chapter has been extensively revised, with case study examples of Tesco's Clubcard and customer profiling, Aldi's marketing communications strategy in the UK, and the segmentation of luxury fashion brands. Also the 'location strategy' section, originally in the 'Retail strategy' chapter of the first edition, is now incorporated and updated as part of the marketing mix section of this new chapter.

As highlighted above, Chapters 5 and 6 are the repositioned 'Internationalization of retailing' and 'Electronic commerce and retailing' chapters. The internationalization chapter retains the same structure as before, drawing upon conceptual models developed for the retailing sector in the late 1990s and early 2000s. Considerable updating of content was required, however, in view of the restructuring of global operations of the main players as they have divested from some markets to focus upon countries offering the best investment potential. The e-commerce chapter has been extensively updated to reflect upon the rapid pace of change over the last decade. Much of this has been driven by Web 2.0 developments which have allowed greater consumer–retailer interaction and therefore the ability of retailers to exploit the 'long tail' through social media and viral marketing. To be successful in an e- and m-commerce environment, retailers have to embrace similar attributes to those of store choice – convenience, product range, customer service and price – and therefore build brand loyalty in a multi-channel environment. Despite such changes, similar challenges are faced by retailers in delivering to the customer, with solutions to the 'last mile' problem now focusing more on 'click and collect' to complement traditional delivery slots.

The second half of the book is a revision of the previous edition's sections on 'Managing the retail supply chain' and 'Managing retail operations'. Considerable restructuring of material has occurred in addition to the inclusion of a new chapter on 'Offshore sourcing and corporate social responsibility (CSR)'. The first chapter of this section brings together elements of the buying and merchandising chapters of the previous edition into a new chapter entitled 'Product management'. The conceptual framework is similar to before, but the digital revolution has meant that buying cycles are more frequent and commitment to buy is deferred as late as possible. The new chapter on offshore sourcing follows as Chapter 8. Most non-food products are sourced offshore primarily because of low labour costs. However, the complexity of global networks has led to significant challenges for retailers as they balance issues of cost, lead times, flexibility and ethical standards. The fashion sector is the focus of much of the chapter to highlight the conceptual models used to explain sourcing strategies and how retailers try to implement CSR initiatives. Sri Lanka is used as a case study to illustrate good management practice through the government's 'Garments without Guilt' programme.

Chapter 9, 'Retail logistics', covers the final chapter on the retail supply chain. The structure of the chapter remains the same but the content required considerable revision in the wake of changes in the fashion market discussed in the earlier chapters and the online revolution. There is added material on the fashion supply chain, supply chain models, the implementation of efficient consumer response (ECR) initiatives and an update on e-fulfilment and the 'last mile problem', building on the discussion in Chapter 6.

The final three chapters focus upon retail operations. 'Adding value through customer service' retains the same structure as the previous edition but has been substantially revised to update existing (Nordstrom) and new (Apple) case material. The content also reflects the use of digital technology to enhance the customer service experience. Chapter 11 has been restructured to incorporate 'visual merchandise' from the 'Merchandising in retailing' chapter of the earlier edition, into a new chapter on 'Visual merchandising and retail selling'. There is a strong relationship between customer service, retail selling and customer satisfaction. The early part of the chapter deals with the 'silent salesperson', namely the use of visual merchandising techniques to stimulate sales in-store prior to focusing upon the role of selling in relation to the merchandise on offer and the customer segment that is targeted. The final chapter, 'Retail security', links strongly to the previous two chapters in that the layout of merchandise can minimize theft, as indeed can staff loyalty and good customer service. This chapter has been substantially revised as research into shrinkage has become a more international phenomenon with the advent of the European, then latterly the Global, Theft Barometer. With these surveys, however, problems of definition and difficulties in comparing data sets have arisen. Furthermore, the advent of online buying has led to migration of retail crime from store to e-crime, and problems of some stolen goods appearing on online auction sites. The recession also led to high unemployment levels and increased crime levels at a time when retailers were under pressure to reduce levels of staff that can be used as a key preventative measure to combat crime.

Reference

Centre for Retail Research (2014) *Who's Gone Bust in Retailing 2010–14?* Newark, NJ: Centre for Retail Research.

Abbreviations

ABC	activity-based costing
AIDA(S)	awareness, interest, desire, action, (satisfaction)
B2B	business-to-business
B2C	business-to-consumer
B2G	business-to-government
C2C	consumer-to-consumer
CAD	computer-aided design
CAM	computer-aided manufacturing
CCTV	closed-circuit television
CDP	collection and delivery point
CEO	chief executive officer
CMT	cut, make and trim
CNP	card not present
CPFR	collaborative planning, forecasting and replenishment
CRM	customer relationship management
CSR	corporate social responsibility
CTN	confectionery, tobacco and newsagents
DC	distribution centre
DCPN	Development Control Policy Note
DIY	do-it-yourself
DPP	direct product profitability
DSD	direct store delivery
EAS	electronic article surveillance
ECR	efficient consumer response
EDI	electronic data interchange
EDLP	everyday low pricing
EPOS	electronic point of sale
ETI	Ethical Trading Initiative
FGP	factory gate pricing
FMCG	fast-moving consumer goods
FOC	factory outlet centre
FDI	foreign direct investment
ft	feet

G2B	government-to-business
GDP	gross domestic product
GIS	geographical information system
GNP	gross national product
ICT	information and communications technology
ISP	Internet service provider
IT	information technology
JIT	just in time
LBO	leveraged buy-out
LSP	logistics service provider
PAT	Policy Action Team
PEST	political, economic, social, legal factors
PESTLE	political, economic, social, technological, legal, environmental factors
POSCCTV	point-of-sale closed-circuit television
PPC	pay per click
PPGs	Planning Policy Guidelines
PPS	Planning Policy Statement
QR	quick response
RBT	resource-based theory
RDC	regional distribution centre
RFID	radio-frequency identification
RI	retail internationalization
RPM	resale price maintenance
SBU	strategic business unit
SCM	supply chain management
SEO	search engine optimization
SIRE	strategic international retail expansion
SKU	stock-keeping unit
SME	small and medium-sized enterprise
SPELT	social, political, economic, legal, technological factors
sq.	square
STEP	social, technological, economic, political factors
SWOT	strengths, weaknesses, opportunities, threats
USP	unique selling proposition
WMC	warehouse membership club

1 The retail environment

Learning objectives

After studying this chapter, you should be able to:

- Identify major demographic, socio-economic and lifestyle trends, and discuss their influence on consumption of retail goods and services.
- Evaluate how retailers have responded to the changing consumer in terms of:
  - retail innovation;
  - concentration of retail ownership; and
  - locational shift.

- Comment upon the waves of retail decentralization.
- Understand how government influence can shape retail development through:
  - legislation;
  - competition policy; and
  - planning policy.

1.1 Introduction

> In essence, retail change has been driven in the past by the interaction of consumer, retailer and government: in the 1990s and 2000s the role of technology became increasingly important as an agent of change.
>
> (after Fernie, 1997, p.384)

To understand the retail environment it is important to understand the interrelationships between the factors illustrated in Figure 1.1. In this chapter, we shall consider how changes in the consumer environment – demographic, socio-economic and lifestyle trends – have impacted upon retail change. At the same time, government has been a major agent of change. Retailers are regulated by an array of laws and ordinances which impinge on their operations. This can be on licences to operate, which goods to sell, hours of operation,

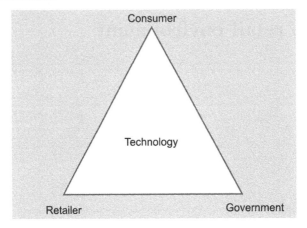

Figure 1.1 Factors influencing change

health and safety matters through to planning ordinances on where to locate the business. The types of merchandise on sale and the formats developed are a response to such interactions. However, retailers do influence consumers and government on product choice and format development. For example, the UK slowdown of the introduction of genetically modified foods was driven by retailers' refusal to stock these products. Also high-profile retail entrepreneurs (Archie Norman for Asda, Lord Sainsbury for Sainsbury's, Philip Green for Arcadia) have lobbied and advised successive UK governments. Political decisions such as refusal to join the European Monetary System and introduction of the minimum wage have had economic repercussions that influence retailers. UK tax credits have supported low-paid retail workers; government funding supports staff training in the skills academies of high-profile retailers.

The role of technology is not discussed at length here as it embraces most chapters of the book, especially those on logistics, marketing and online retailing. It should be acknowledged here, however, that technology should be seen in its widest sense. For the consumer, technology has freed up time as capital goods replace labour in the home. Communications in both a physical and information sense have given access to wider geographical markets. Retailers rapidly embraced the IT revolution through sharing data with their suppliers and communicating with their customers, especially those with loyalty card schemes. New technologies have been applied throughout the supply chain to ensure that products can be designed/tested, manufactured and distributed quicker and at a lower cost than ever before. Markets and companies have grown due to the links between innovation and technology. The example of the evolution of chilled foods in the UK was used in the previous edition of this book. In response to the demand for ready meals, two businesses, Northern Foods and BOC Transhield, grew to supply Marks & Spencer and other supermarket chains with these product lines.

The most significant change over the last decade, however, has been the growth of online technology. In the early 2000s online sales were barely 1 per cent of overall retail sales in the UK; a decade later this had risen to 10 per cent, with prospects of strong growth for the foreseeable future. The UK is a market leader in online uptake by consumers but it is the nature of online communications that is changing the face of retailing. Advances in smartphone technology have heralded an anytime, anywhere consumer culture that poses significant challenges for retailers. Deloitte (2013) claim that the future of retail has arrived and the winners in this new environment will be the companies that can deliver a seamless customer experience across all channels. As Deloitte claims we are in the midst of a consumer revolution, it is necessary to track the evolution of consumer trends.

1.2 The changing consumer

In order to discuss the changing consumer in more depth, we shall look at:

* demographic trends;
* socio-economic trends; and
* lifestyle trends.

1.2.1 Demographic trends

The structure of a country's population and its rate of increase over time will impact upon the growth of the economy and the nature of a consumer's savings. Europe had been viewed as the battleground for retail competition because of the launch of the euro and the enlargement of the European Union (EU) to 28 members and a population of 505 million by 2013. Despite the size of this market, the structure of the population in most European countries will experience dramatic changes in the next half century. Lower fertility rates and increased life expectancy will result in a 'greying population'. In 1997, around 23 per cent of the population in each member state was less than 20 years old (in Ireland it was 33 per cent) and the proportion of older people, those 60 and over, was 21 per cent and increasing. It is envisaged that by 2030, the latter figure will increase to around 30 per cent for most countries.

The increasing number of old people is changing the nature of household composition in Europe. For example, in 2008, 32 per cent of the EU population lived alone compared with 8 per cent in 1981. This is reflected in the increased number of single households across Europe and the number of people in a household declining in every one of the early EU members since the early 1980s. Indeed, the figures for one-person households would be higher if the more recent EU members were excluded from the data (see Iacovou and Skew, 2011). The classic image of a nuclear family of two adults plus 2.4 children in a household is the exception, not the rule. Also, divorce rates are at record levels, which has led to a breakdown of the traditional family household. On average, there were 2.4 people per household in the EU in 2008. In the UK there was a major decline from the 3.45 of 1951 to the EU average in 2008. Table 1.1 also gives a more detailed breakdown of housing types in the UK. Although one-family couples are the largest category, there is a reduction in the proportions of households in this type from 58.7 per cent to 56 per cent, whilst other types have increased, most notably one-person and lone-parent households with 11 per cent and 29 per cent, respectively, of total households.

Table 1.1 Changing household types in the UK, 1996–2012 (millions)

	1996	2012
One-family household couple	13.9	14.8
One-family household: lone parent	2.3	2.8
Two or more unrelated adults	0.7	0.8
Multi-family households	0.2	0.3
One person	6.6	7.6
All households	23.7	26.4

Source: Office for National Statistics, 2012.

1.2.2 Socio-economic trends

Clearly there is a strong relationship between demographic trends and the labour market. Over two decades ago there were great fears that the changing structure of the population would lead to a demographic 'time bomb' producing labour shortages as numbers of 15–29-year-olds entering the labour market began to decline (historically, unemployment rates were highest within this age group).

In reality, the nature of the labour market changed in line with the growth of high-tech 'sunrise' manufacturing industry and the service sector at the expense of traditional 'sunset' industries. This saw the rise in female participation in the workforce, more part-time/ casual working and the rise in self-employment, often as a result of early retirement or redundancy. In Europe, there has been a marked increase in the number of women in the labour force, and there is no longer a significant fall in the rate after the age of 30, implying that women are not stopping work after having children. In the UK, women comprise a higher proportion of the labour force than men; they are flexible (often by necessity), are often better educated, and have a wider range of skills for the service economy, of which retailing is a part. By contrast, men have seen their role in society change considerably, especially in areas of high unemployment, where 'light' industries and service jobs have replaced traditional male-dominated manufacturing work. The house-husband is now common, and the male head of household as the sole breadwinner is rapidly disappearing.

These trends in the labour market occurred during a period of strong growth in most 'developed' economies in the 1990s and early 2000s that witnessed a period of low inflation and low unemployment levels. Cyclical changes in the economy have a major impact on discretionary purchases, in that in an upturn in the economy, consumers tend to spend more on non-essential purchases or those that can be deferred if uncertainty exists about employment opportunities or interest rates. In the UK, 'real' disposable incomes grew throughout the 1990s and early 2000s, although it is important to note that many of the factors that fuelled consumer expenditure were unique to the UK. The main distinguishing features pertain more to the housing market and the size and structure of personal debt than households in other European countries. Much of this debt was mortgage debt, which tends to be short term and variable rated, exposing households to changes in short-term interest rates. The reason for the size of mortgage debt is that the rate of owner-occupancy in the UK is much greater (around 70 per cent) than in other countries: for example, the comparative figures for France and Germany are 55 and 50 per cent, respectively. This also means that changes in house prices would impact on personal sector wealth and thus consumer demand to a much greater extent in the UK than elsewhere.

The combination of these factors in the housing market meant that British homeowners were much more sensitive to changes in interest rates or tax relief on mortgages than their continental neighbours in the 1980s to the mid-2000s. In the late 1990s Oxford Economic Forecasting (1998) estimated that a 1 per cent drop in short-term interest rates would lead to consumer expenditure growth of 0.5 per cent. Although UK interest rates were already at historic low levels in the late 1990s, the government cut them even further to encourage spending in an attempt to ward off recession towards the end of the first decade of the 2000s.

Many of the trends discussed above are borne out by official UK government statistics. For example, retail sales from the 1980s have accounted for a decreasing percentage of total consumer expenditure. At the turn of the millennium UK households spent 16 per cent of their weekly expenditure on housing, 15 per cent on motoring and 12 per cent on leisure services. The categories for statistical analysis of household spending vary over time, but by 2011 expenditure on non-essentials such as culture and recreation, hotels, meals and communication accounted for a quarter of household expenditure – about the same proportion as spent on essentials for living such as housing, fuel, power and food (Office for National Statistics, 2011). The UK consumer spends much more on 'services', rather than traditional retailing goods. The consumer has 'traded up' to own their own home, plus one, two or three cars, and is taking more overseas vacations. Most UK households have access to a car and are willing to be much more mobile in search of employment, retail and leisure opportunities. People seek better-quality environments in which to live and work, and this is reflected in the general shift away from metropolitan to smaller-sized communities. Of course, this trend is evident in many developed economies, especially in North America, where suburbanization, urban sprawl and an automobile-orientated society alerted European planners to curb the excesses of this type of development, despite increasing pressure from housing and business development companies.

The most significant economic series of events to impact upon consumers and the retail sector were the global financial crisis of 2007/08 and subsequent recession in the main Western economies, which continues to lead to sluggish growth at best in some markets and major economic problems in the eurozone, especially in Greece, Spain and Portugal. In May 2013 EU unemployment stood at 11 per cent, but in Spain and Greece the level was 27 per cent. Youth unemployment (under 25) was worse, with rates of 56 and 63 per cent in Spain and Greece, respectively. The collapse of the sub-prime mortgage market in the USA had a ripple effect through the global financial market, with the demise of Lehman Brothers in 2008 and the subsequent UK government bail-out of many of the British banks. This led to much tighter restrictions on consumer borrowing and a stalled housing market. It is interesting to note that the Forum for the Future had pointed to this potential scenario occurring in their report in 2007. They had painted this rosy picture of UK gross domestic product (GDP) growing by 45 per cent from 1991 to 2006, with household disposable income growing even faster; however, they noted that 'personal debt is increasing: the average adult owed over £28,000 in 2006, up by more than 10% in a year ... and leading many to spend ever higher proportions of their income on mortgage payments. A decline or crash could leave many thousands facing negative equity' (Forum for the Future, 2007, p. 15).

1.2.3 Lifestyle trends

The combination of demographic and socio-economic trends has resulted in a complex set of values associated with consumer behaviour. A range of paradoxes exists. We are a more affluent society, yet there is a growing underclass of poor people in the UK who are long-term unemployed and cannot be regarded as conventional consumers. After the recession in the first decade of the 2000s, the proportion of young people out of work grew in particular, while high debt levels and graduate unemployment also soared. Clearly the situation is much more acute in other parts of Europe, as indicated above. The 'grey' consumer, however, is not the austere customer of 30 years ago, but is likely to be relatively wealthy and 'young' in attitude to health, sport and fashion. There is now a blurring of social activities so that people no longer perceive aspects of life in discrete compartments. Sport, fashion and music overlap so that while the clothing market stagnates, the sports market grows, mainly by selling clothes.

Christopher Field in 1998 identified some characteristics of 'new consumers' that are still evident today:

- they no longer conform to traditional stereotypes – they are demanding, fickle, disloyal, footloose, individual and easily bored;
- they are better informed and more sophisticated, and are prepared to complain when they get poor service;
- they have less time for shopping;
- they feel greater uncertainty about future personal prospects;
- they express a growing concern for the environment; and
- they have lost faith in traditional institutions such as the police, church and state.

The low turnout at the British general election in 2001, 2005 and 2010 illustrates this indifference. The decline in membership of collective organizations from trade unions and religious bodies through to political parties is further evidence of the individualistic nature of today's consumer in the UK. Webb (1998) pointed out, however, that at the same time individuals express the need for security and solidarity by coming together in 'tribes'. He used the examples of football supporters, local Neighbourhood Watch groups and PC user clubs. A more recent illustration is online social networking: in only a few years, half the UK population was reported to have signed up as members of Facebook while a quarter of the population used Twitter.

Although it is becoming increasingly difficult to segment consumers into discrete categories, this does not stop market researchers from producing segmentation models to categorize them. The younger generation has been the focus of much attention because of their influence on adult spending and the fact that they become 'consumers' much earlier than previous generations. In the previous edition of this book we showed how Carat, the media buying agency, analysed the post-children, young people generation. As indicated earlier in the chapter, attention has also focused on the relatively wealthy 'silver seniors' (see Thomas and Peters, 2009). It is perhaps more appropriate here to show the main general changes that have occurred in consumer shopping habits in the last 30 years, and how recession and social media have transformed attitudes more recently.

The roots of lifestyle changes go back to the 1960s and 1970s, when a counterculture questioning the status quo began in the USA with increased dissatisfaction of the young with the rampant materialism and traditionalism of their parents' generation. The Beat Generation of poets and writers was small in number but had a major influence in the USA at a time of general discontent with race riots and the Vietnam War. Writers such as Vance Packhard, Rachel Carson and Ralph Nader illustrated the negative aspects of eco-nomic growth in their cases of misleading advertising, despoliation of the environment and product safety, respectively. This was also expressed in a more promiscuous society fuelled by drugs and a new rock and roll music scene with the Beatles' and Rolling Stones' entry to the US market. The aftermath of these major societal changes saw the birth of the green consumer and its political expression in John F. Kennedy's speech to Congress in 1962 on consumers' four basic rights: to be safe, heard, informed and to have choice. These rights were eventually embodied into consumer and environmental legislation that has provided the foundations for consumers' present-day concerns over, inter alia, global warming, cli-mate change, the beef supply chain or ethical production standards. Consumers are now much better informed on what they eat and wear, where these products are sourced from and the nature of the ingredients/materials contained within the product.

It can be argued that with globalization consumers have much greater choice than pre-vious generations. Access to global markets and the quest for new tastes and fresh ideas have led to mass production of cheaper food and the 'democratization of fashion' (Tungate, 2008; Lopez and Fan, 2009) to bring fashion show styles to the high street. It is debatable, however, if fast food and fast fashion are positive lifestyle changes, with obesity levels rising in younger generations in the USA and UK, whilst disposable fashion leads to question marks over waste in the environment and ethical issues pertaining to global sourcing.

A more immediate concern is how consumers balance the ethical/environmental issues with price in a recession. In an extensive survey of shoppers' purchasing behaviour in 17 countries in 2009/10, Caret/Microsoft began to glean a picture of the post-recession, digital-age consumer. They show that consumers were seeking better value, undertaking more advanced purchasing research, using alternative channels, visiting stores less fre-quently and using word-of-mouth post-purchase reviews to aid decision making. Reading online forums, blogs and peer reviews indicates the strong influence of social media in addition to the increased use of Internet shopping for purchases.

The recession and the resultant poverty in many countries has led to a rise in the number of food banks as charities try to provide consumers with a basic level of food. Even in the richest country in Europe, Germany, the number of food banks has risen dramati-cally from 675 in 2006 to 906 in 2012. In the USA 14.5 per cent of households (17.6 million) were food insecure in 2012, with 5.7 per cent (7 million households) experiencing very low security (Coleman-Jensen *et al.*, 2013). Food insecurity is defined by the US Department of Agriculture as access to food being inadequate because of a lack of money and other resources.

For many food consumers the recession has changed purchasing habits. Affordability has become an increasingly important factor for some US grocery consumers. Watson (2013) has shown that price sensitivity is less about value for money and more about satisfying a particular need as cheaply as possible. Consumers may only have a fixed amount of money to spend until their next pay cheque and are only able to buy what they need for that money. This behaviour is characterized as 'knapsacking' and involves fitting the optimal amount of an entity into a fixed-space, subject to some constraint, in this case money. In the UK there is some evidence to show that the traditional bulk shop supplemented by a convenience store top-up is changing. Consumers are becoming more aware of food wasted, so shopping online precludes some impulse shopping, and the rise of the German discounters such as Aldi and Lidl have offered more choice in the marketplace. Thus it has been the more middle-market retailers that have been performing more poorly compared with discounters and more upscale retailers.

In the clothing market the middle market has also suffered as poorer consumers gravitate to thrift/charity shops and low-cost, low-price operators such as Primark in the UK. Somewhat paradoxically, the other segment of the clothing sector that has exhibited most growth during the recession has been the luxury fashion sector. The rich continue to spend, albeit much of the growth has occurred in the Chinese market where annual growth rates have been as high as 35 per cent in the 2000s.

1.3 The retail response

The retail response to these changes in consumer behaviour has made the retail sector one of the most dynamic in modern economies. Innovations in format development and operating practices have enabled retailers to compete or even survive in a changing retail environment. Three key responses will be discussed: retail innovation, concentration of retail ownership, and locational shift.

1.3.1 Retail innovation

Many retail innovations emanate from the USA. Ideas and 'know-how' have been sourced from the USA by retailers to their home markets for many years. A UK example is Marks & Spencer, whose executives did fact-finding missions to the USA in the 1920s and 1930s to refine operating practices at home. Similarly, Alan Sainsbury introduced self-service and the shopping basket into J Sainsbury stores in the 1950s after sojourns to the USA. More recently, formats such as warehouse clubs and factory outlet centres have reached these shores with varying degrees of success.

It is interesting to note that particular retail formats (formats are operating styles of retailing such as supermarkets, hypermarkets, convenience stores, mail order, online shops and so on) are often associated with a company or country of origin. The **hypermarket**, developed in France in the 1960s, was the forerunner of 'big box' retailing, which is a feature of the global retail scene today. The French began to restrict the development of the hypermarket at home in the 1970s in the wake of the Royer bill (see pp. 21–22), and companies such as Carrefour (meaning 'crossroads' in English) became synonymous with the international spread of the format. The Americans originally rejected this format in the

1970s, and it was revived only with the growth of Walmart in the USA and its development of the supercentre format in the 1990s.

Other innovative formats that have strong country-of-origin effects are 'hard' discounting and mail order in Germany. German mail order companies were world market leaders (Otto Versand) and the German market is the largest in the world after the USA. Why? The reason is historical. At the end of the Second World War there was a severe shortage of retail space in Germany, and mail order provided an alternative form of retailing. Also, German consumers were relatively poor at this time and could receive goods on easy payment terms. This explains why home shopping is a major feature of German consumer behaviour (much of their frozen food is home delivered, for example), and why this form of retailing impinges upon a wider cross-section of society than in other countries. By contrast, in the UK, the 'big book' catalogues were targeted mainly at lower socio-economic groups, invariably because it provided an avenue for cheap credit in the days before borrowing became easy.

Not only do German consumers shop from home more readily than other European consumers, but they are very price conscious. It has often been stated that there are three marketing tools in Germany: price, price and price. Thus, an alternative to the hypermarket was developed – the limited-line, no-frills 'hard' discounter, offering exceptionally low prices of frequently purchased packaged goods. This format, developed initially by Aldi and Lidl, has now spread internationally from its German base.

Again as a means of contrast, these discounters were initially less successful in the UK market, where consumers tended to polarize their grocery shop between a weekly 'trawl' and a convenience 'top-up'. Indeed, the main grocery multiples introduced their own limited-line offering to restrict defections of shoppers to Aldi, Lidl and Netto, the Danish discounter. The UK retailers have progressively segmented their store brands to range from basic lines to high-quality 'finest' ranges, and this unique shift from store to corporate brand has allowed them to diversify into other sectors such as banking (Burt and Davies, 2010).

In the clothing market, fashion entrepreneurs anticipated the lifestyle changes alluded to in the previous section. In the USA the shift to more casual attire led to the prominence of retailers such as Gap (the Generation Gap) and sports brands such as Nike. In Europe, Benetton, Zara and Hennes & Mauritz (H&M) not only brought affordable style to the high street but revolutionized lead times in a traditional four-season clothing supply chain. Time-based competition and the rise of fast fashion enabled these retailers to introduce new designs, and bring them into their stores in a matter of weeks compared with the months or even yearly cycle times of traditional retailers.

The evolution of retail formats is a response to the needs of specific country markets. The operation of retail formats also differs, however, because of different regulations and industry structures in such markets. For example, retailing in North America is not subjected to the same degree of government intervention as in Europe, and there is more development land and cheaper fuel costs. Thus, retailers in North America can trade successfully on much lower sales per square metre ratios than their European or Japanese counterparts. This also explains the evolution of logistical support networks to stores in these markets. It is not surprising that the UK has one of the most efficient grocery supply chains in the world, because of the high premium rates for retail sites. Taking inventory out of stores and other parts of the supply chain reduces costs and allows retailers to respond quickly to market changes.

1.3.2 Concentration of retail ownership

Fifty years ago, retailing was a fragmented industry. The 'giants' of the time were department stores with a nineteenth-century legacy of providing a range of departments for their customers. Sears and JCPenney in the USA, Marks & Spencer and Harrods in the UK, Galeries Lafayette and Printemps in France, and Karstadt in Germany were the high street brands of the time. Consumers have become more mobile and their behaviour has changed, as shown above. Retail entrepreneurs have risen to this challenge and transformed markets at home and abroad. Two of the largest retailers in the world today, Walmart and Tesco, were small family companies headed by enlightened entrepreneurs – Sam Walton and Jack Cohen, respectively. However, this trend is mirrored in other companies, especially in the speciality retail sector. The rise of Gap, The Limited, Zara and IKEA, for example, was the result of the vision of the founder to spot a niche in the market and grow the business. There are many diverse retail formats operated by retailers and large retail groups often operate a portfolio of retail formats in the guise of their different retail brands.

The retail marketplace was transformed in 40 years. Instead of classic proximity retailing, where consumers shopped at their nearest, most convenient store, the emphasis moved to destination retailing, where the consumer was willing to travel further to get the best choice at lower prices. While Walmart led the way in general merchandise/food followed by big box competitors such as Carrefour and Tesco, specialists or 'category killers' changed the nature of competition in many other markets. Home Depot in the USA and B&Q in the UK became market leaders in the home improvement market with major international aspirations. IKEA, Toys 'R' Us and Nevada Bob are good examples of international companies that specialize in a niche sector and operate destination stores. At the same time new proximity formats developed in the form of stores for operation in places where people congregated naturally, like forecourt stores, airport and other transport hubs. Consider, for example, the shopping malls linked to underground transport networks, or online retailers operating Facebook formats. Even the larger big box supercentre operators have been rethinking their locational strategy, with an increasing focus on smaller, proximity formats. For example, Tesco announced the ending of the 'space race' in the UK in 2012 by focusing on convenience rather than hypermarket developments; Asda, owned by Walmart, bought Netto UK in 2010 and has curtailed its opening of supercentres, the focus of its initial strategy after acquisition in 1999 (Sparks, 2011). Indeed, Walmart has even focused upon smaller stores in its home market.

Organic growth and acquisitions to spread fixed costs over larger sales volumes led to consolidation in most developed economies. No longer could the UK be classified as 'a nation of shopkeepers' when the retail sector was transformed from a large number of small independent retailers to relatively few, large and often publicly quoted corporations. The UK grocery market, which is even more concentrated, was subjected to a Competition Commission inquiry in the late 1990s and again in 2006 because of fears of abuse of market power. Nevertheless, concentration continued at national and regional levels to the extent that the top four grocery companies had 76 per cent market share (Kantar

Worldpanel, 2012), with most of the remaining grocery market share dominated by only five retailers. The French and German markets were also heavily concentrated among a few key players. Only the US market lagged behind, but greater consolidation occurred throughout the 1990s and into the 2000s, and the structure of the grocery market was affected by the entry of non-traditional grocers such as Walmart. Foreign-owned grocery companies also developed a significant presence in the USA during the same time period (Martinez, 2007).

Concentration, therefore, appears to be a feature of a maturing retail sector across both small and large countries where the climate of government regulation fosters consolidation. Wrigley (2001) termed this the **consolidation wave** in US food retailing. He showed how the top four firms (the CR4 statistic from the *Progressive Grocer*) have increased their share from a static 23 per cent to 37 per cent from 1992 to 1999. Wrigley explained these trends through the regulation of the industry until the 1980s and the financial re-engineering of the sector in the late 1980s. The enforcement of anti-trust laws dropped dramatically in the 1980s, but large-scale mergers did not take place because the US food retail industry got caught up in a spate of leveraged buy-outs (LBOs). The LBOs led to increased debt burdens for companies, which forced them to divest assets and cut capital expenditure programmes. Thus, throughout the 1990s as debt burdens were reduced, investments in technology, buying and distribution, along the lines of the Walmart operation, made these companies more efficient and hungry for growth to achieve further scale economies. Even by 2012, however, only 43 per cent of all grocery sales were controlled by four companies (Kroger, Safeway, SuperValu and Walmart). The US situation differs from many other mature markets in a number of ways. The sheer scale of the country has made it difficult for retailers, with the exception of Walmart, to be truly national in nature, even with deregulation. Furthermore, the US grocery/food market is more complex than most markets, with a high degree of channel blurring, for example 33 per cent of groceries are sold through non-traditional grocery stores, and food service providers take a high proportion of all food expenditure as 47 per cent of all such expenditure is on eating out.

1.3.3 Locational shift

When we take a leisure trip to any of the Disney theme parks, 'main street' features prominently as one of the key attractions. It is therefore somewhat ironic that the suburbanization of the US way of life and the resultant mushrooming of out-of-town shopping malls led to the decline of traditional main streets. The concept of the modern **shopping mall** can be traced to the Austrian architect Victor Gruen. Gruen fled the homeland of Hitler and began to develop blueprints of his utopian mall. His idea of an out-of-town mall was that it was to be the civic, social and cultural heart of the community, incorporating apartment housing and offices in addition to shopping provision. Although his 'ideal' mall never truly materialized, his concept of an all-year-round shopping environment quickly took root. The Southdale Center in Minneapolis was built in 1956 and became the prototype for thousands of others throughout America. Gruen reckoned that in the Mid-West you only had about 25 good shopping days a year. The development of the enclosed shopping mall with air conditioning and a constant temperature of 20°C changed all of that. It is perhaps no coincidence that two of the most popular malls in North America are in areas with extreme climates, namely the West Edmonton Mall in Alberta, Canada, and the Mall of America in Minneapolis/St Paul.

The classic mall attracted two key department stores as anchor tenants, with speciality stores linking them. For the next 30–40 years, geographers and realtors sought prime sites for new mall development. In the days before sophisticated geographical information systems (GIS), mapping of areas of population growth and interstate intersections offered the best sites for development as America became an automobile-orientated society. By the 1970s and 1980s, locational analysts began to use spatial interaction models to determine the success of one mall in relation to another, and to glean a picture of saturation compared with under-capacity in particular parts of the USA.

By the 1990s the out-of-town shopping mall had become a mature retail format in the USA and Canada. The rather monotonous, formulaic structure may have been fine for consumers in the 1960s and 1970s, but not for the more demanding consumer of subsequent decades. This enclosed environment was also a controlled environment with its closed-circuit TV and security guards. Whilst policing existed within the malls, invariably crime increased in the large parking lots outside.

The urban landscape began to be transformed by other smaller but 'themed' shopping centres or free-standing/clusters of big box formats. Already by the 1970s, many downtown areas of cities, especially those with historical landmarks, began to develop speciality centres based on restaurants and leisure attractions. The Californian coast from San Francisco to San Diego has numerous examples of old warehouses, canneries and piers that have been redeveloped using the waterfront as a key feature in urban regeneration. Former fashionable areas which declined with the growth of the traditional mall in the 1980s have been gentrified using their natural setting. Pasadena in southern California is an example of this type of development.

The growth in popularity in the USA of warehouse clubs, factory outlet centres, supercentres and category killers added to the pressure for new urban development. In several instances failed shopping malls were redeveloped for these new formats. The traditional mall is facing competition from not only other out-of-town developments, but the rise of e-commerce. Shopping malls have been closing at unprecedented rates since the onset of the financial crisis in 2007, and many others are exhibiting high vacancy rates. Several key tenants of malls have gone out of business (Mervyns, Circuit City, Borders and CompUSA), while other main anchors for malls have been reducing their store portfolios (Sears, JCPenney, Gap and Abercrombie & Fitch). The gravity of the mall situation is chronicled in a website entitled deadmalls.com.

The development of the shopping mall and various hybrids of the US prototype are evident in most countries of the world. In Europe, the shopping mall was not planned in such a laissez-faire, automobile-dominated manner. The preservation, and in many cases the rebuilding, of city centres in the post-war period was the main priority of governments. The eventual development of sizeable in-town malls, recreating the controlled environments of the US malls, took time because of difficulties in assembling land parcels with multiple ownership. Unlike the USA, development was focused towards city centres. In the UK, many schemes were small scale in most towns and cities, as the high street continued to maintain its pre-war dominance of shopping activity. The enclosed mall, when it was a large development, as in Eldon Square in Newcastle or the Arndale Centre in Manchester, did result in urban decay in city centre streets where major retailers vacated premises to move into new malls. Also, some of these developments, the Arndale for example, were heavily criticized for their lack of architectural quality.

It was not until the mid-1980s that the UK began to plan for US-style out-of-town shopping malls. The catalyst for such developments was Marks & Spencer, then the anchor store of many in-town shopping schemes. Marks & Spencer announced in 1985 that it was pursuing a dual-location strategy whereby it would invest in out-of-town developments in addition to traditional high street areas. Initially there were plans for between 35 and 50 schemes throughout the country, but the stock market crash of 1987, prolonged recession and changes in planning policy worked against any new out-of-town developments, reducing the number to a handful of large schemes. Nearly 30 years later only 16 out-of-town shopping malls had been built, although the number and size of open-air retail parks had grown substantially. The Bluewater scheme in Kent became the largest out-of-town shopping mall in Europe, accounting for 3 per cent of Britain's retail expenditure, attracting 28 million visitors annually and one of the largest employers in the county.

Although government policy is the subject of the next major section, it is worth noting that the development of these large shopping malls and other out-of-town developments became an element of the then government's policy on social exclusion and urban regeneration. Before this issue was high on the political agenda, the early schemes were also geared to a policy of regeneration. The Metro Centre in Newcastle was an enlarged retail park that had been built on former colliery wasteland, and Meadowhall near Sheffield was the site of former steelworks. More recent developments, such as Braehead in Scotland, were planned through partnerships between the developer and urban regeneration agencies. The Braehead complex is a massive (285-acre) mixed-use development encompassing retailing, leisure, housing and public parkland on the site of a former shipbuilding area on the River Clyde within the Glasgow–Paisley conurbation. Although there was considerable opposition to the scheme when it was first proposed, Braehead is now promoted as a growth area within the conurbation, and the development of the site represented a major opportunity for employment generation in nearby social inclusion partnership areas.

1.3.4 Waves of retail decentralization

Out-of-town shopping centres were classified as the third wave of retail decentralization in the UK. Schiller, writing in 1986, viewed Marks & Spencer's commitment to out-of-town investment as the 'coming of the third wave'. As we have seen, this wave has broken into a small number of large-scale developments. The two earlier waves of decentralization had a much greater impact upon the urban landscape. The superstore, pioneered by Asda in the late 1960s, became the predominant food trading format in the UK for the major multiple retailers by the 1980s. Unlike in France, where the hypermarket (over 50,000 square feet) was the main large-store format, the superstore (25,000–50,000 sq. ft) was the preferred model in the UK. Initially there was considerable opposition to these large-scale formats, and protracted planning enquiries were a feature of the 1970s. At this time Asda traded from sites where they could obtain planning permission, often disused mills in the textile regions of Yorkshire.

The acceptance of the superstore format by consumers, retailers and, somewhat reluctantly, planners saw the closure of small, in-town food stores and the construction of purpose-built superstores, invariably as anchor tenants in district centres. The fight for market share led to the so-called 'store wars' in the late 1980s/early 1990s as retailers scrambled for available sites. Throughout the 1970s and 1980s, discussion of saturation levels always featured prominently in the trade press, with figures of 600, 700 and 800 stores mooted and then passed. By the early/mid-1990s the position began to change. Some retailers, including Asda, became financially crippled because of their expansion plans, asset values for store properties fell, and fewer planning appeals at public inquiries were accepted for superstore development. The rate of growth slowed in the 1990s/early twenty-first century but the major companies continued to develop sites, especially in the wake of acquisitions by Walmart (of Asda) and Morrisons (of Safeway). However, the two main companies began to focus more upon the convenience market to sustain profitable growth. Tesco and Sainsbury's moved back into town centres with their Metro and Local formats, respectively, and as indicated above, the other two major companies belatedly entered this market in the 2010s.

The second wave of retail decentralization began in the late 1970s and quickly gained acceptance as an established trading format. Much of this can be attributed to the success of superstores. Just as consumers preferred the 'one-stop' shop for their bulky weekly groceries, they did not want to carry heavy DIY materials through town centre streets to car parks or bus stations. The forerunner to retail parks was the retail discount warehouse. Here the early pioneers of out-of-town non-food retailing traded from an assortment of makeshift, converted properties.

Thus, just as Asda was the pioneer for superstores, MFI championed the case for out-of-town furniture retailing, B&Q for DIY, and Comet for electrical goods. By the 1980s, **retail parks** mushroomed on the ring roads of most towns as planners acknowledged that industrial sites could not attract manufacturing jobs compared with those retail opportunities. By the mid-1990s, the pace of growth had slowed down and the composition of tenants in retail parks was changing. The original tenant mix was strongly based on the DIY, electrical, furniture and carpet warehouse format. New entrants appeared that were more associated with high street retailing. Clothing and sports retailers, and even that bastion of in-town retailing, Boots the Chemist, were represented. Retail parks grew in size and some large retail parks incorporated fast food restaurants and other leisure facilities. This trading-up of the original format made retail parks an attraction to consumers for comparison retailing to the extent that they could be classified as third-wave decentralization.

The conversion of a retail park to the Metro Centre illustrates the blurring of categories. This also occurred with Fernie's fourth wave of decentralization (Fernie, 1995, 1998). He argues that a new wave of retail decentralization began in the 1990s in the UK, based on a more upmarket, but value-for-money, retail proposition. The importation of two US formats to the UK – **warehouse clubs** and **factory outlet centres** (see Box 1.1) – was different from the third wave and coincided with the advent of other discounting formats in the UK in both food (hard discounters) and non-food (Matalan, New Look, TK Maxx).

Box 1.1 Factory outlet centres in Europe

Factory outlet centres (FOCs) were one of the fastest-growing formats in US retailing in the 1980s. They were developed initially as a profitable means of disposing of excess stock by manufacturers. The original formats were more like factory shops, but by the late 1970s/early 1980s purpose-built outlet malls were being constructed and managed in a similar way to conventional shopping centres.

By the mid-1990s, FOCs accounted for around 2 per cent of all US retail sales but the format was maturing, with around 350 outlet centres with an average size of 14,000 sq. metres. It was around this time that US developers sought growth opportunities in new geographical markets. Europe was a logical choice for market entry, as the main country markets of the UK, France and Italy had a tradition of factory shops.

The UK, however, was the initial target area for US developers, notably McArthurGlen, Value Retail, Prime and RAM Eurocentres. In 1992 and 1993, two small indigenous schemes had been developed at Hornsea and Street by companies that had gleaned some experience of US operations. The UK development of FOCs can be viewed in three distinct stages: 1993–96, 1997–99, and 2000 to the present. In the first phase, there were ambitious plans to build over 30 US-style FOCs within three-to-four years. Unfortunately for developers, these proposals came at a time when the government was hardening its stance towards out-of-town retailing, and planning permission was often refused or deferred. A notable landmark was the secretary of state's decision to reject RAM Eurocentre's proposal for Tewkesbury after a two-year deliberation (despite local council support). This resulted in a scaling-down of some developments and the withdrawal from the UK market by some US developers.

The 1997–99 phase witnessed a gradual acceptance of the format. Developers changed their strategies and either looked for sites that already had retail use designation for planning purposes or sought 'brownfield' regeneration areas. The acceptance of the format was reflected in the attraction of institutional investors to schemes, as some companies such as McArthurGlen sold equity stakes in existing schemes to fuel further expansion or initial developers sold out to property companies (C&J Clark to MEPC).

The most recent phase from 2000 to the present has led to the redevelopment or extension of some of the earlier sites. To differentiate from other FOCs and competing retail formats, new developments have had innovative designs (such as Ashford in Kent), or have stressed leisure-related activities (Gunwharf at Portsmouth, or Lowry Outlet, Salford). This approach was necessary as overcapacity led to the demise of smaller units in certain regions such as Scotland.

In theory, other European markets should be receptive to FOCs because of their culture of factory shops and, in the case of France and Germany, a strong price-led retail environment. Developments were slow to materialize, however, because of extensive lobbying by interest groups resistant to change in the retail structure. This did not deter developers from moving into Europe, having gained experience in the UK.

Most developers focused their attention on specific markets, notably:

- upmarket areas close to capital cities or cosmopolitan cities, for example Paris, Berlin, Vienna, Madrid, Barcelona, Munich, Florence; or
- near large catchment areas, often on cross-border routes, for example Mendrisio, Roermond, Zweibrucken, Maasmechelen (the latter two are brownfield sites).

By the 2010s there was considerable expansion in Europe as the format gained acceptance in France and Germany, in addition to considerable growth in Italy and newer markets further east such as Austria, Russia and Poland. In 2013 there were around 205 outlets in Europe.

The two companies that have strongly influenced factory outlet development in Europe are Value Retail and McArthurGlen. Both companies entered the UK market in the mid-1990s and were so successful that their initial sites (Cheshire Oaks and Bicester) have been extended. Furthermore, each company has successfully entered the European market, albeit with a slightly different approach. Value Retail has fuelled its expansion through internal growth and investment. It focuses on the luxury end of the market and prefers brands with strong control over their own distribution, a feature of the luxury market during the last decade. It only has one site in the UK but the Bicester development is probably the most successful outlet centre in the country. Its incremental approach is evident in that it only has eight more 'villages' in Ireland, France, Belgium, Italy and Germany. McArthurGlen, by contrast, has six outlets in the UK and five in Italy, with another nine sites in France, Germany, Greece, the Netherlands, Belgium and Austria. Its expansion has been financed through selling stakes in sites that it has developed. In 2013 it sold its only Scottish site in Livingston to a pension fund institution. Both companies now seek international expansion further afield. McArthurGlen opens a new outlet in Vancouver, Canada in 2015, developed in conjunction with the Vancouver Airport Authority and close to the SkyTrain link to downtown. Value Retail has been attracted to another continent and opened Suzhow village in 2014. This site is in an historical area, less than an hour by car from Shanghai. It was to be the same size as Bicester where the Chinese make up 38 per cent of the tourist trade (65 per cent of Bicester's visitors are tourists). This is only the first step into China, as the company has created a joint venture, Value Retail China, to explore the development of further sites in China's major metropolitan markets.

Warehouse clubs were originally envisaged to be represented throughout the country with 50–100 sites being developed, but by 2013 Costco, the only operator, had 25 sites open after 20 years of experience in the UK market. Planning problems can account for some of the slow growth, but the UK consumer, unlike its US counterpart, has neither the physical space to stock bulk purchases nor the appetite for shopping in limited-line discount sheds.

Factory outlet centres have fared much better and by the 2000s had become a mature retail format, with operators looking to the rest of Europe for expansion. It can be argued that the nature of UK developments differs from the original US model as developers have had to comply with changes in government policy (see Box 1.1). As with earlier waves, locational 'blurring' exists. The Galleria, a failed off-centre shopping mall, was successfully converted to a factory outlet centre, and the outlet centre at Livingston in Scotland is adjacent to a retail park and a superstore operator!

1.4 The role of government

The regulation of retail activity has shaped the structure of retailing in many country markets. Whilst most retailers have had to conform to national legislation with regard to 'operational' legislation, such as health and safety at work, hours of opening and employment law, the internationalization of retailing and the advent of the Internet have led to the establishment of legal frameworks across national boundaries. This is particularly relevant to the EU, where directives emanating from Brussels are implemented by national governments (see Box 1.2). Of course, one of the most significant changes to European retail business was the changeover to the euro for 11 member states in 2002, leading to short-term costs for retailers with changing prices in their stores, modification of IT support systems, and staff training to cope with the change. In order to avoid excessive detail on all aspects of public policy, the focus of this section will be on competition policy and retail planning.

Box 1.2 EU legislation relevant to retailers

Directive on the sale of consumer goods and associated guarantees (1999/44/CE)

The aim of this directive is to establish minimum rules of protection around which member states can adopt or maintain more stringent provisions. Consumers can now seek redress for the sale of a defective product within two years of delivery and receive a price reduction or their money back within one year. There were some problems with the implementation of this directive in the 2000s because of divergent regulatory provision between member states.

Directive 97/55/EC amending Directive 84/45/EEC concerning misleading and comparative advertising

This amendment now allows for comparative advertising as long as the advertising is objective, is not misleading, does not discredit a competitor's trade mark/name, and compares goods/services meeting the same needs or intended for the same purpose.

Directive 96/6 on consumer protection in the indication of prices of products offered to consumers 1998

This is better known as the unit pricing directive, in that it stipulates that the selling price of a product should be indicated as a price per unit to facilitate comparison of prices and clarify consumer information.

Directive 97/7 on the protection of consumers in respect of distance contracts

This directive aims to protect consumers from aggressive selling techniques by non-face-to-face methods, or by mail order or electronic retailing. It allows consumers the right to withdraw from a contract for up to seven days without penalty.

Directive 2000/31/EC was then established to provide a legal framework for the development of electronic commerce.

1.4.1 Competition policy

First we shall look at **anti-trust legislation** in the USA, because policy there has had some bearing on governments elsewhere in how they have tried to control companies that exhibit anti-competitive behaviour. Table 1.2 provides a summary of the key laws that have been enacted in the USA. The three main acts that provided the basis for subsequent modifications to anti-trust legislation were the Sherman Act of 1890, the Clayton Act of 1914, and the Federal Trade Commission Act of 1914. The Sherman Act prohibited contracts and conspiracies in restraining trade, and outlawed monopolies. The Clayton Act reinforced this legislation by further prohibiting price competition that lessened competition, and forbade tying clauses on exclusive dealing arrangements which would impede competition. In the same year it was deemed appropriate that an organization should be created to oversee the implementation of this legislation. The Federal Trade Commission (FTC) was created from the Act of the same name and was charged with stamping out 'unfair methods of competition'. This 'catch-all prohibition' was invariably left to the courts to decide, and the history of anti-trust legislation is inevitably bound to the interpretation of the law according to the political Administration of the time. As a rule of thumb, Republican administrations have a tendency to favour business; Democratic-majority administrations have championed consumer interests.

Table 1.2 Anti-trust legislation in the USA

Year enacted	Legislative act	Practices that impact on the retail sector
1890	Sherman	Resale price maintenance, illegal vertical integration and mergers, exclusive dealings, refusals to deal, resale restrictions
1914	Clayton	Tying contracts, exclusive dealings arrangements, dual distribution
1914	Federal Trade Commission	Price discrimination, dual distribution
1936	Robinson–Patman	Price discrimination, promotional allowances
1950	Celler–Kefauver	Horizontal mergers, vertical mergers
1975	Consumer Goods Pricing Law	Resale price maintenance

Regardless of the political dimension, most of the ensuing legislation tended to favour the small trader at the expense of the corporate giants. The landmark Robinson–Patman Act in 1936 made it unlawful for a company knowingly to induce or receive a discriminating price. This meant that sellers must charge the same price to all buyers for 'goods of like quality'. There were exceptions where price discrimination was allowed, most notably where there were differences in the cost of manufacture, sale or delivery resulting from different quantities sold. Hence 'quality discounts' were allowed for bulk purchases. This act also ensured that powerful buyers would not extract special promotional allowances from weaker suppliers.

Of more significance to our discussion on the history of US food retailing is the Celler–Kefauver Act of 1950, which responded to an FTC report that expressed concern at a spate of merger activity in 1948. Not only did this act reinforce anti-competitive activity as a result of horizontal mergers, but it brought into play mergers at inter-channel level, i.e. vertically integrated mergers. The final piece of legislation shown in Table 1.2, the Consumer Goods Pricing Law, brought resale price maintenance (RPM) under federal anti-trust legislation and closed a loophole that had allowed manufacturers vertical pricing arrangements with retailers in some states. RPM primarily sets a minimum price at which goods can be sold, to prevent retailers from using manufacturers' products as 'loss leaders' to attract customers into the store but undermine the suppliers' reputation for quality.

In section 1.3 on 'retail response', it was shown that consolidation in the US food retailing industry was slow until the 1990s because of the regulatory environment and the debt incurred by supermarket groups in the late 1980s/early 1990s. If we examine this more closely, it can be argued that the anti-trust legislation inhibited the growth of large supermarket groups from the 1930s until the 1980s. Indeed, Wrigley (2001) notes that by the early 1980s, the food retail industry was less consolidated than 50 years earlier, when A&P controlled 12 per cent of the entire US market. The Robinson–Patman and Celler–Kefauver Acts were very successful at protecting the small trader and inhibiting the growth of companies such as A&P by merger activity. The net result was that the USA had become structured into a series of regionally focused chains. In 1989, the chairman and chief executive of A&P contrasted the US situation with that of the UK: 'In the post-war years ... the US marketplace, because of Robinson–Patman, moved to a regional structure and the old large chains lost out ... [but] the UK without this disadvantage, moved to the consolidation route with the advantages of purchasing leverage driving the success of a few national chains' (Wood, 1989, p.15).

From the early 1980s, for over a decade, the Ronald Reagan/George Bush Sr Administrations began to loosen the regulatory net, allowing mergers to take place that might have been stopped in the 1960s and 1970s. The approach to horizontal mergers had been 'fix it first', whereby predators attempting to appease the FTC agreed to divest themselves of some acquired stores where horizontal market overlaps occurred at local levels. During the 1990s, however, there was pressure from food manufacturers and smaller retailer chains for the FTC to tighten its regulatory stance. Criticisms were levelled at the divestment process in that the acquiring company was allowed to 'cherry pick' the stores to be disposed of. This meant that weaker stores were sold to weaker competitors, allowing the predator to win back market share and increase consolidation of market power.

By late 1999/early 2000, the FTC took a tougher enforcement stance, especially on the divestment of acquired stores. The notable case was the proposed acquisition by the Dutch group Ahold, of the New Jersey Pathmark chain. Although Ahold was willing to divest a considerable number of its stores in the New York/New Jersey region, the FTC opposed the deal, which subsequently collapsed. Since 2003, mergers and acquisitions have slowed down because of regulatory constraints and internal consolidation efforts of the main companies. Nevertheless, the acquisition of Sainsbury's US business by Albertsons in 2004, which in turn was taken over by SuperValu in 2006, confirms the slow consolidation of the US grocery sector.

In Europe, competition policy is normally dictated at national government level unless an acquisition across national boundaries leads to the predator achieving a market share that would be deemed uncompetitive. In 1999, the German supermarket group Rewe notified the EU Commission that it intended to acquire the 343 outlets of the Julius Meinl chain in Austria. As Rewe was already represented in the Austrian market through its Billa subsidiary, the merger would give the combined group 37 per cent of the Austrian food retail market. In order to appease the Commission's objection to the bid, Rewe followed the US 'fix-it-first' policy and agreed to acquire only 162 stores, 45 of which were converted into drugstores.

In the UK, much of the focus on competition policy has been on **price competition** and the potential abuse of **market power** by large grocery retailers. It can be argued that the abolition of RPM in 1965 was the catalyst to greater concentration in British retailing. Until then, retailers were obligated to sell products at suppliers' recommended retail prices. The 1965 legislation allowed retailers to compete on price for all products except books and pharmaceuticals, which were allowed RPM until the late 1990s. It was pressure from the large supermarkets in the 1990s to give customers competitive prices, especially on over-the-counter drugs, which led to the removal of legal support for RPM in these last two product categories.

The growing power of retailers, especially the grocery multiples, has been a recurrent feature of competition policy during the last three decades. In the first half of the 1980s, food retailers came under the scrutiny of the Office of Fair Trading (OFT) through two reports, *Discount to Retailers* (Monopolies and Mergers Commission) and *Competition and*

Retailing (OFT). The latter report, published in 1985, assessed the nature of competition and the degree of profitability of food retailing from 1975 to 1983, whereas the Monopolies and Mergers Commission report in 1981 assessed whether volume discounts to large retailers were being passed on to grocery shoppers. In both cases the growing power of the multiple retailer was not deemed to be against the public interest.

In the mid-to-late 1990s, there was a further upsurge of discussion on retail power and competition. A series of research reports was published by the OFT from 1996 to 1998; the new Tony Blair government argued that the British consumer was being 'ripped off' by retailers, and it initiated an investigation into the competitive behaviour of the largest supermarket groups by the Competition Commission (published in 2001). After a lengthy review and a delay in publication, the commission did not find evidence of anti-competitive behaviour or that the British consumer was being 'ripped off'. Indeed, it argued that the higher British prices were partly related to higher costs, but mainly owing to the high pound and exchange rate fluctuations.

Throughout the 2000s the supermarket industry has been subject to further scrutiny by the OFT and Competition Commission as a result of Morrisons' takeover of Safeway, question marks over a lack of local competition, and the possible abuse of market power by retailers over their suppliers. The net result of these investigations has been a shift to a more US form of regulation (for example, Morrisons had to divest over 50 stores after its takeover of Safeway), the allowing of greater competition at local level and the initiation of a supplier code of conduct to moderate abuse of market power (Competition Commission, 2008; Elms *et al.*, 2010). Note that the OFT and Competition Commission were subsumed under a new regulatory body, the Competition and Markets Authority, in 2014.

1.4.2 Retail planning policies

Government planning policy also affects patterns of retail development. It is interesting to note in a comparison of UK and US competition policies that the UK government did not initially go down the route of insisting that the predator divest of stores in areas where local monopolies could occur as a result of an acquisition. By contrast, it is much easier in the USA to receive planning approval for new store development. The rise of the big box retail formats in the USA, and to some extent in Canada, can be attributed to the availability of land and the need to accommodate a car-orientated society. In its early decades of expansion, Walmart was welcomed to many small towns in Middle America as a sign of modernity and growth for the community. These communities even offered tax incentives to build! However, opposition to Walmart grew as evidence showed that small, traditional retailers closed down, unable to compete with the price discount format. Ultimately this slowed the process of acquiring and developing sites in North America, especially in California and New York where resistance to the retail giant has been strong.

The situation is different in Europe, as Walmart and other US retail chains discovered when they planned expansion outside their domestic market. Most planning legislation has been geared to protect traditional town centres and small-scale retailers from excessive out-of-town shopping developments. The international growth of multinational retailers such as Carrefour, Ahold and Delhaize can be attributed to restrictive planning regulations in their home market. For example, the Loi Royer, legislation designed to restrict the growth of hypermarkets, was introduced in France in 1973 after extensive lobbying by independent retailers that feared the growth of hypermarket development in the 1960s. In 1996, the Raffarin Law introduced further restrictions whereby developers have to apply for permits to open new or extended units over 300 sq. metres. Planning legislation was relaxed in 2009, allowing units over 1,000 sq. metres to open in towns with over 20,000 inhabitants.

In Germany, the Netherlands and Ireland similar trends have been discerned in that planning regulations are still strict compared with the USA, but some degree of relaxation of size and location restrictions has been imposed as the economic environment deteriorated. In Italy the government introduced the Bersani Law in 1999, which simplified the complex, multilayered system of approvals required, in addition to specific authorizations for product types sold. The categories are now food and non-food, and clearer rules have been initiated with regard to planning approval in relation to size of store and size of town. For example, to open a small outlet (150 sq. metres) in towns of fewer than 10,000 people, the local authority gives approval; for large outlets (over 2,500 sq. metres) in towns of over 10,000 population, permission must be sought from a committee representing the city, province and the district. Despite amendments in the 2000s, the Italian regulatory environment is still not attractive to large international grocery retailers.

Whereas the more mature retail markets of Europe have begun to liberalize their regulatory framework, countries subjected to international development by large retail groups have introduced tougher planning rules in an attempt to introduce Western European-style regulation to their markets. These markets include Eastern European countries such as Poland and some Asian markets, for example Thailand.

We now turn in more detail to **British retail planning policy**, primarily because it was seen to be more laissez-faire than policies in other parts of Europe, thereby attracting US companies to the UK to develop warehouse clubs, factory outlet centres and other large-scale formats. An outline of retail planning policy in the UK is given in Box 1.3. In essence, the first 20 years of planning policy were geared to maintaining the existing shopping centre hierarchy with a presumption against any type of development that was not zoned for retail use, i.e. in-town centres or district centres. From 1977 the government used a range of policy initiatives to attempt to strike a balance between the needs of consumers, retailers, developers and local authorities. In the 13 years of the Margaret Thatcher administration (1979–92), there was a considerable relaxation of planning controls. Advice to local authorities through Development Control Policy Notes (DCPNs) ensured that first- and second-wave operators could develop off-centre sites for food and non-food superstores.

Box 1.3 Retail planning policy in the UK

The basis for modern British retail planning dates back to the 1948 Town and Country Planning Act, when planning authorities had to produce plans to guide developers towards preferred locations for particular land uses. Regional authorities would provide broad structure plans, and lower-tier authorities developed local plans for their areas.

When the legislation was introduced, Britain was embarking upon a redevelopment of cities after the war. Local authorities were often the main instigators of these developments as they invariably owned much of the land in town centres. The focus of retail investment was therefore in these centres and in district centres in suburbia.

The so-called retail hierarchy was established at this time in that the land-use category for retailing was designated in central areas, and any development outside these zones would be deemed outside the local plan. It was the development of superstores in the late 1960s and early 1970s that challenged the status quo. Several high-profile public inquiries took place at this time as developers argued that bulk grocery shopping was better suited to edge-of-town sites, and that town centres would not lose the large amounts of trade predicted from such developments.

By 1977, the government acknowledged that some developments were better suited to edge-of-town sites because of their space requirements. This was embodied in advice to local authorities through DCPNs. DCPN13 opened the door for the rapid expansion of the 'second wave of decentralization', the development of retail parks throughout the 1980s. Although most shopping centre developments continued to be built in conventional downtown sites, the coming of the 'third wave' of decentralization in the late 1980s led to the government amending DCPN13.

By 1988, the government introduced Planning Policy Guidelines (PPGs). The relevant guidelines for retailers were PPG6 and PPG13. PPG6 sought to maintain a balance between the vitality of town centres and these new retail formats located in edge- or out-of-town sites. By 1996, PPG6 was substantially revised and amended to tighten the tests of acceptability for new out-of-town proposals. A sequential test was introduced whereby developers had to show that no sites were available in town centre locations for their form of development. It was in 1994, with PPG13, that the sequential test was first mooted in relation to the accessibility of sites by all forms of transport.

The change to a Labour administration did lead to a change in direction of policy. From 1997 until the late 2000s it was clear that a developer could expect to receive planning permission just because the proposed development was too large to be built in a town centre site. The assumption was that an element of 'downsizing' might be necessary. Furthermore, developers wishing to expand on existing sites also had to undergo the sequential test. Many developers, predominantly the large grocery retailers, tried creative ways to get round the legislation. Tesco and Asda, in particular, built mezzanine floors in their large hypermarket formats. By the mid-2000s, however, the government closed this planning loophole.

The most significant change for over a decade occurred in the late 2000s/early 2010s. The economic crisis of 2008 and its aftermath had a significant impact on the retail environment with high-profile failures (Woolworths, MFI, Comet) and store closures. The Labour government in 2009 introduced

Planning Policy Statement 4 (PPS4, which replaced PPG4); its very title, 'Planning for Sustainable Economic Growth', indicated that development would be allowed if economic regeneration was likely to be achieved. The Conservative-led coalition government was committed to relaxing planning regulations as a means to stimulate business growth in the 2010s.

It was the development of third-wave decentralization that prompted a revision of government policy through **Planning Policy Guidelines** (notably PPG6 and PPG13), introduced in 1988. PPG6 and its subsequent revisions aimed to give advice on achieving a balance between the vitality of town centres and new development; PPG13 sought to integrate transport and land use planning and, in the case of retailing, tried to ensure that new retail developments would be reached by public transport.

Until the early 1990s retailers had limited opposition to their plans, and market share could be achieved through the so-called store wars. Retailers would appease local authorities with sizeable donations to community projects to secure planning permission (the term for this was 'planning gain'). If a local authority rejected the application, the retailer appealed and had an 80 per cent chance of success at the subsequent public inquiry.

By the mid-1990s, policy was changing. PPG13 and PPG6 were revised in 1994 and 1996, respectively, and government ministers began to take a harder line towards new out-of-town developments, especially as an all-party House of Commons Select Committee in 1994 recommended that the 'tests of acceptability' in the PPGs should be enforced more rigorously.

The main thrust of the new policy was the sequential test, whereby a developer had to show that a proposed new out-of-town development could not be located in nearby town centres or district centres. Under the secretary of state at the time, a strict interpretation of the planning guidelines was introduced. This impeded development of factory outlet centres in the UK and encouraged developers to look for sites in Europe instead.

This shift in stance continued with the election of a Labour government in 1997. The sequential test was extended to include extensions of existing sites, and this firming of planning controls was reflected in the fall in success rates of those retailers taking a rejection of planning permission to appeal (20 per cent compared with 80 per cent a decade earlier).

A loosening of planning restrictions occurred later in the Labour government and after the election of a Conservative-led coalition government in 2010. The main catalyst for change was the economic recession and therefore a need to introduce measures that could facilitate economic recovery and growth.

Social exclusion was an important initiative of the 1997 Labour government, and Policy Action Teams (PATs) were established to formulate policy in this area. PAT13 reported on ways of improving access to shopping and financial services through eliminating 'food deserts' and facilitating urban regeneration in areas ravished by blight and disinvestment (Clarke and Bennison, 2004).

When it was difficult to secure planning permission in retailers' preferred out-of-town sites, those seeking new opportunities for growth began to explore the possibility of developing in-town sites in brownfield areas. It was shown earlier how factory outlet centre developers had reassessed their locational policies and began to develop sites in existing centres, many of which were in need of regeneration. Food retailers also incorporated social inclusion initiatives as part of their strategy for receiving planning permission in areas with social inclusion partnerships. The most-quoted case is the development of a Tesco extra store at Seacroft, Leeds, in 2000. Seacroft is one of the largest housing estates in Europe, and its district centre, built by the local authority in the 1960s, was largely derelict. Tesco redeveloped the whole site, trained and recruited the long-term unemployed in the area for its store, and provided lower prices, more choice and a better diet for local residents. Tesco planned seven more stores of this type using a similar regeneration partnership to that in Leeds.

It is worth noting that large-store development of this type was in conflict with PPG6, which advised local authorities not to release urban land for retail development if the land had potential for other employment opportunities. There are other inconsistencies in government policy. We have already shown that the government was keen to promote competition by investigating allegations of abuse of market power, but how could retailers offer low prices in suboptimal sites? Large-store formats benefited from scale economies, within the store and through supply chain efficiencies, which were passed on to customers. Companies that built large-store formats prior to the tightening of planning controls had a competitive advantage over late entrants, which either could not get sites or had to settle for a poorer location. This occurred in a haphazard way in the 1970s and 1980s, when local authorities seemed to be the determinants of competition policy rather than the retailers themselves. History repeated itself in that pre-1997/98 operators had 'open A1' planning consent, which allowed them to introduce any retail items in a store conversion. This approach was adopted by Asda in the introduction of supercentres.

Another area of dispute was the government's sustainability policies. Whilst PPG13 encouraged the development of sites with access to all forms of transport, large-store formats could have positive environmental benefits if developed on brownfield sites. Most developers of these formats had enlightened sustainability policies, and such formats were arguably better for the environment than town centre sites, which are difficult to access by customers and distributors of store stock.

Clearly the most significant problem facing government and local authorities has been the demise of the British high street. Initial planning policy initiatives highlighted above were to retain viable city centres in the face of the four waves of decentralization. However, the steady rise of online shopping, combined with the recession, has led to the collapse of some retailers and a considerable pruning of store portfolios by other retailers with a strong multi-channel presence. The dead mall syndrome identified in the USA earlier in the chapter is being played out on the British high street with one in every six units lying vacant.

The government response to this situation was to appoint a TV personality/consultant to advise on a plan of action. The Portas Review was published in December 2011, making 28 recommendations on how to reinvent the high street as a place for socializing, learning and creativity. Portas also suggested the creation of a fund to help towns that were particularly badly affected by the recession (Portas, 2011). The government responded to the review by allocating a £1.2 million High Street Innovation Fund to 12 pilot areas. Initial research indicates that some towns such as Margate and Bedminster have added units, whilst other towns such as Stockton-on-Tees and Nelson have had increased vacancy rates (BBC, 2013). There is no 'quick-fix' solution to reinventing the high street. Expensive parking and boarded-up shops are hardly encouraging a new generation weaned on Facebook/Twitter to socialize in traditional high streets. Some of the Portas recommendations on business rates have been reinforced through lobbying by the British Retail Consortium and the *Sunday Times* newspaper to demand fairer rates. Many retailers face business rates that are higher than the rents that they pay, but the government appears reluctant to change the status quo of rising rates in a time of falling demand.

1.5 Summary

The last section on retail planning policy illustrates the complexities of managing and regulating the retail environment. Overall, consumers are more demanding, affluent and mobile than ever before, but a sizeable segment of the population is poor and socially excluded from a range of services, including retailing. The recession has aggravated this trend between the 'haves' and 'have nots' with rising unemployment levels, especially in Greece and Spain.

Retailers have to respond to consumers' needs by providing a retail offer through appropriate formats. For many big box retailers and category killer specialists, this means large-store formats on out-of-town sites. In much of Europe, these developments were viewed by many governments as a threat to the viability of existing town centres, and planning regulations were developed accordingly. The rise of online retailing in the last decade and the recession of the late 2000s/early 2010s have overtaken concerns with such formats, many of which are suffering from online competition. The creation of regeneration partnerships to benefit areas deprived of retail investment was a positive step to address the issue of 'food deserts' and other accusations that large-format developments cater for the wealthier, more mobile segments of the population. However, the problem for most policy makers is how to respond to a situation where most markets are over-shopped. There are just too many units from a bygone era that will never be used for retailing again. The rise of desolate shopping malls in the USA and the decaying town centres of the UK are evidence of these trends in the last decade. The solutions to fill these vacant units do not appear to be forthcoming.

Review questions

1   Discuss the main consumer trends in the 2000s/2010s and the impact of these trends on retail provision.
2   Outline the four waves of retail decentralization in the UK and discuss the role in planning policy in shaping these developments.
3   Compare and contrast the regulation of retail markets in the USA and UK.
4   Discuss the role of planning policy in shaping retail developments in different geographical markets.
5   Evaluate the impact of online retailing and the recession of the late 2000s/early 2010s on shopping malls in the USA and high streets in the UK.

References

BBC (2013) 'Portas High Streets still struggling one year on', *BBC News*, 29 May.

Burt, S. and Davies, K. (2010) 'From the retail brand to the retailer brand: themes and issues in retail branding research', *International Journal of Retail & Distribution Management*, 38(11/12): 865–878.

Clarke, G. and Bennison, D. (eds) (2004) 'Special Issue on extending the food desert debate', *International Journal of Retail & Distribution Management*, 32(2): 72–136.

Coleman-Jensen, A., Nord, M. and Singh, A. (2013) *Household Food Security in the United States in 2012*. Washington, DC: US Department of Agriculture.

Competition Commission (2001) *Supermarkets: A Report on the Supply of Groceries from Multiple Stores in the United Kingdom*, three volumes. Norwich: The Stationery Office.

Competition Commission (2008) *The Supply of Groceries in the UK Market Investigation*. London: Competition Commission.

Deloitte (2013) *Global Powers of Retailing 2013: Retail Beyond*. London: Deloitte.

Elms, J. ,Canning, C., De Kervenoael, R., Whysall, P. and Hallsworth, A. (2010) '30 years of retail change: where and how do you shop?' *International Journal of Retail & Distribution Management*, 30 (11/12): 817–827.

Fernie, J. (1995) 'The coming of the fourth wave: new forms of retail out of town development', *International Journal of Retail and Distribution Management*, 23(1): 4–11.

Fernie, J. (1997) 'Retail change and retail logistics in the United Kingdom: past trends and future prospects', *Service Industries Journal*, 17(3): 383–396.

Fernie, J. (1998a) 'The breaking of the fourth wave: recent out of town retail developments in Britain', *The International Review of Retail, Distribution and Consumer Research*, 8(3): 303–317.

Fernie, J. (ed.) (1998b) *The Future for UK Retailing*. London: FT Retail and Consumer.

Fernie, S. (1996) 'The future for factory outlet centres in the UK: the impact of changes in planning policy guidelines on the growth of a new retail format', *International Journal of Retail and Distribution Management*, 24(6): 11–21.

Field, C. (1998) 'The new consumer', in *The Future for UK Retailing* (Fernie, J., ed.). London: FT Retail and Consumer.

Forum for the Future (2007) *Retail Futures: Scenarios for the Future of UK Retail and Sustainable Development*. London: Forum for the Future.

Iacovou, M. and Skew, A.J. (2011) 'Household composition across the new Europe: where do the new member states fit in?' *Demographic Research*, 25(14): 465–490.

Kantar Worldpanel (2012) 'Insights', www.kantarworldpanel.com/en/index.html#/Insights/Watch (accessed 28 February 2012).

Lopez, C. and Fan, Y. (2009) 'Internationalisation of the fashion brand Zara', *Journal of Fashion Marketing and Management*, 13(2): 279–296.

Martinez, S.W. (2007) *The US Food Marketing System: Recent Developments, 1997–2006*. Washington, DC: US Department of Agriculture, Econ.Res.Serv.

Office for National Statistics (2011) 'Family Spending 2011 Edition', www.ons.gov.uk/ons/rel/family-spending/family-spending/family-spending-2011-edition/index.html (accessed 24 February 2012).

Office for National Statistics (2012) *Families and Households, 2012*. Newport: ONS.

Oxford Economic Forecasting (1998) 'The economy', in *The Future for UK Retailing* (Fernie, J., ed.). London: FT Retail and Consumer.

Portas, M. (2011) *The Portas Review: an independent review into the future of our high streets*. Department for Business, Innovation and Skills, London.

Schiller, R. (1986) 'Retail decentralisation: the coming of the third wave', *The Planner*, 72(7): 13–15.

Sparks, I. (2011) 'Settling for second best? Reflections after the tenth anniversary of Wal-Mart's entry into the United Kingdom', *International Journal of Retail & Distribution Management*, 39(2): 114–129.

Thomas, J.B. and Peters, C.L.O. (2009) 'Silver seniors: exploring the self concept, lifestyles and apparel consumption of women over 65', *International Journal of Retail & Distribution Management*, 37 (12): 1018–1040.

Tungate, M. (2008) *Fashion Brands*. London: Kogan Page.

Watson, I. (2013) 'Internal reference price formulation in support of UK and US grocery retail price decision making', DBA dissertation, Edinburgh Business School, Heriot-Watt University.

Webb, B. (1998) 'New marketing', in *The Future for UK Retailing* (Fernie, J., ed.). London: FT Retail and Consumer.

Wood, J. (1989) 'The world state in retailing', *Retail and Distribution Management*, 17(6): 14–16.

Wrigley, N. (2001) 'The consolidation wave in US food retailing: a European perspective', *Agribusiness*, 17: 489–513.

2   Theories of retail change

Learning objectives

After studying this chapter, you should be able to:

- Discuss the major theories of retail change:
    - cyclical theories;
    - environmental theories;
    - conflict theory; and
    - combined theory.
- Analyse the response of existing retailers to retail innovation.
- Apply the various theories to explain the development of a range of retail organizations.
- Forecast future retail developments from a variety of theoretical perspectives.

2.1 Introduction

A number of explanations have been made about how retail organizations grow, develop, expand and succeed. Theories of retail change make sense of what has happened to retail organizations in the past and, more importantly, help retailers to foresee future scenarios for their business, and those of their competitors.

In this chapter the main theories of retail change are presented, explained and applied to current retail organizations.

There are three main categories of theory:

- cyclical theories;
- environmental theories; and
- conflict theory.

2.2 Cyclical theories

Cyclical theories are those that trace common patterns in retail development over time and include the earliest theories of retail change. There are three primary cyclical theories:

- wheel of retailing;
- retail life cycle; and
- retail accordion.

2.2.1 The wheel of retailing

This early hypothesis (McNair, 1958) attempted to explain the evolution of retail institutions as a wheel-like progression of three phases, as illustrated in Figure 2.1.

According to this theory, retail organizations enter the market with a low-cost, low-price, low-service format, using opportunistic buying and basic premises to undercut established competitors and establish themselves in the market. For those that succeed, there is a tendency over time to add product lines, upgrade stores and add services, which will tend to increase price levels for the merchandise. In stage three, retail organizations tend to operate at the high end of the market, offering quality merchandise and service at price levels that alienate their original customers, and increase vulnerability to innovative new market entrants.

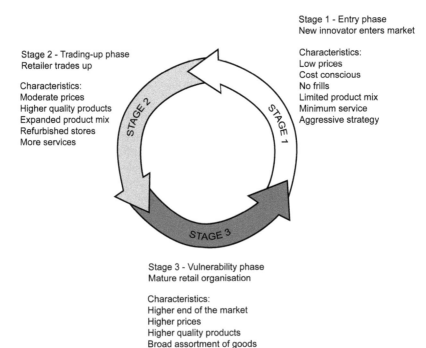

Figure 2.1 The wheel of retailing

In stage one, an entrepreneurial, opportunistic management style can lead to success, whether the organization is completely new to the market or a new format brought on-stream by an existing organization. As the organization/format grows, management strength is needed in terms of leadership and organization of the growing number of staff and units. Even organizations attempting to embed resolutely in stage one, such as value retailers Lidl and IKEA, have found it difficult to resist widening their merchandise range or adding services such as delivery.

According to Verdict (2002), 'scale will be a much stronger influence over the fate of retail companies', and opportunities for physical expansion are now limited in many areas due to market saturation and planning policy, so retail companies will have no alternative but to seek alternative growth strategies, such as merger and acquisition, or use of non-store-based retailing. IKEA, for example, experienced problems in UK expansion. Although 20 new stores in ten years were planned, site development was restricted (the Glasgow site took six years to open), and the organization had to resort to extending its existing stores to accommodate demand (David, 2002). In 2005, cost-focused, US-based global giant retailer Walmart, which had previously expanded its large-format box stores (a store format is a carefully designed style of retail outlet that can be replicated as the retailer expands; a box store is the type of store housed in box-like structures, common in retail parks on the edges of towns and cities), also developed a new, more stylish and upmarket format of store, incorporating wider aisles, less crowded displays and some more stylish goods. This was partly in response to the success of a more upmarket competitor (Target). Organic growth, merger and acquisition all tend to dilute the entrepreneurial style of management, and to make inevitable the characteristics evident in stages two and three of the wheel of retailing.

Without doubt, many retail organizations have developed in line with the wheel theory, for example department stores and variety stores such as BHS and Marks & Spencer, which have been challenged by former grocery retailers' expansion into fashion. Walmart has faced competition from discount retailers Dollar and Save-a-Lot (Gilmour, 2007). Internet retailing moved the same way, with discount pricing giving way to parity pricing in groups such as Dixons, for example. Delivery charges are the norm rather than the exception. Expansion of the merchandise range, adding to services and upgrading of virtual stores has occurred in successful online retailers such as Tesco.com and Amazon.com, although these retailers remain aggressive and innovative in exploiting the potential for tracking prices and customer behaviour to compete on price in the virtual market.

There have been many criticisms of the wheel theory. One major criticism is that it cannot be universally applied and is therefore not valid. Not all retail organizations enter the market at stage one; some enter as upmarket formats. Other retailers streamline their operations in order to retain their reputations for value for money while upgrading shops and services. Tesco, for example, has not traded up beyond stage two.

A second criticism is that the theory does not appear to apply to internationalization of retail formats, which often enter new, less mature markets as upmarket retailers and move downscale as they adapt to local environments. An example of this 'reversed wheel' effect is evident in the progress of factory outlet centre development in the UK. Upmarket developers such as Value Retail entered the UK market as an upscale, innovative format offering value branded merchandise, but domestic applications of the format such as those developed by Freeport were smaller, more downmarket versions (Fernie, 1996).

The wheel theory has also been criticized by post-modernists, who argue that time is linear rather than cyclical and therefore past patterns cannot be applied to future development (Brown, 1995). As the market environment is now too fragmented to apply concepts from 50 years ago, it is likely that new retail formats will be developed through the innovative combination of past, disparate retail practices.

The main utility of the theory is that it enables retailers to recognize their tendency to alter the characteristics of the format that has brought them success, and to be aware of organizational vulnerability in stage three. IKEA is a current example of a retailer that has developed its service range and raised some product prices to a level where they may become vulnerable in the future and can already be challenged by innovative partnerships like Habitat at Homebase, and other competitors with good online presence, such as Amazon, Argos and Tesco.

Organizations operating at the higher end of the market, offering quality, service and higher prices, are particularly vulnerable to innovation. Matalan and TK Maxx, entering the 'high street' fashion market in the 1990s, for example, shifted customer expectations for value/price in the fashion market. This upset the status quo in high street fashion retailing, which led to rationalization of high street stores by leading fashion retail group Arcadia, and contributed to the withdrawal of C&A from UK retailing.

2.2.2 Retail life cycle

This second cyclical theory of retailing, in common with demographic and product life-cycle theories, assumes that all retail organizations have a finite lifespan, during which they go through four phases of development:

- innovation;
- growth;
- maturity; and
- decline.

The theory assumes that retail organizations and retail formats will move through all four phases. The time dwelt within each phase will, however, vary widely, as will the total lifespan of the organization or format. Jenners, Edinburgh's traditional upmarket fashion department store, for example, is still going strong over 100 years after its launch (albeit in a format slightly diluted since its relatively recent takeover by larger department store operator House of Fraser), while the lifespan of many retailers is much shorter, and many new retailers enter and exit the market rapidly.

A new retail format will spend a short time, only a few years, in the **innovation** stage of the life cycle. Unsuccessful innovators will not enter the next phase, while successful innovators can take advantage of a lack of direct competitors to grow sales rapidly and develop retail unit numbers, entering the growth phase. Profits during this phase are low or non-existent due to investment in creation, infrastructure, expansion and promotion of the format. For example, Tesco.com planned for loss during its first few years of existence, investing in a national infrastructure for the online format.

During format **growth** the number of units is expanded rapidly, often with strong centralized planning and control. Both sales and profitability growth should follow. Investment levels will remain high, both due to the high cost of expansion and to the cost of developing a prime market position, because during this phase the number of competitors will also grow. The retail majors, often innovators in their own right, are also quick to exploit successful ideas. For example, when the hard discount box stores began to expand rapidly in the UK during the 1980s, the grocery retail majors successfully introduced basic retailer brands at discount prices alongside their normal merchandise. The growth phase normally lasts for several years before the format is established, or mature.

Maturity, on the other hand, will last indefinitely as long as the retailer is customer and competition orientated. A mature retail format will have many direct competitors and the rate of sales growth slows together with the level of profitability. In public limited companies, the delivery of continued growth to shareholders will drive growth of the format in untapped markets, through organic expansion, through acquisition and merger activity, or the development of new, innovative activities. The maturity of some of the UK grocery majors has driven expansion in areas of the UK with development potential such as Scotland and Ireland, and in international markets, as well as investment in town centre and forecourt formats.

The **decline** phase, when sales growth becomes negative and profitability is very low, can also last indefinitely. The declining format will have fewer direct competitors and more indirect competitors in the growth and maturity phases of the life cycle. Organizations with declining formats require active search and investment in format innovation or acquisition/ merger with organizations delivering formats in the innovation, growth or maturity phases of the cycle. For example, when Marks & Spencer moved into decline in the 1990s, it entered into a partnership with UK retail entrepreneur George Davies to develop the Per Una branded 'store within a store'. Entrepreneurial buying, expertise in both fashion and marketing together with strong publicity attracted a younger target market and helped to turn around the ailing retailer. There was a beneficial knock-on effect in terms of design, layout and branding within Marks & Spencer stores; this 'innovative maturity' did not last too long after George Davies left the partnership, however, and by 2014, Marks & Spencer was struggling again.

Life-cycle theory has been criticized because of the difficulty in defining the exact time when the organization, or format, moves from one stage to another. To be truly useful, a retailer would want to know exactly when the growth or maturity phase has ended, so that marketing objectives and strategies could be adjusted accordingly. However, in practice, it is not too difficult for a retailer with understanding of life-cycle theory to judge movement from one phase to the next in time to make innovations and format alterations. Figure 2.2 shows the estimated life-cycle phases for selected UK retailers in 2002. Check out this diagram and see where you think these retailers are now within the life cycle. Two of the names have disappeared – Safeway was acquired by Morrisons in 2004, while Somerfield was acquired by The Co-operative Group in 2009.

It is commonly agreed, however, that the time spent within each stage of the life cycle is becoming shorter. New retail formats are launched more frequently and grow to maturity

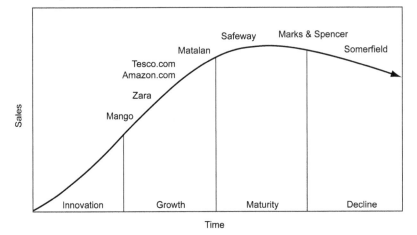

Figure 2.2 Estimated life-cycle stages for selected UK retailers in 2002

much more rapidly than in the middle of the twentieth century. Department stores as a format grew to maturity over decades, while the factory outlet centre format grew to maturity over a period of years. The Internet has generated rapid movement through the life cycle by some retailers. For example ASOS.com, the UK's largest independent fashion and beauty retailer, was arguably in maturity in that market within seven years of its launch when the company considered the development of physical stores (Berwin, 2007).

2.2.3 Retail accordion

The third cyclical theory is the retail accordion, which relates retail development over time to merchandise range. This theory (Hower, 1943) noted that there was a tendency for retail organizations to move alternately towards specialization and diversification over time. This US-based theory is rooted in its historical pattern of retail development. The earliest stores were general stores delivering a wide merchandise range, with narrow depth of category to small, dispersed communities. As urban areas grew, they could support speciality retailers with limited product assortment but depth of category, such as shoe stores, drugstores and clothing stores. The next expansion of the accordion brought the development of department stores offering a wide merchandise range and depth of category. The latest contraction of the accordion during the 1980s and 1990s brought more concentration of merchandise range in niche retailers such as Tie Rack and category killers such as Toys 'R' Us.

It is debatable whether this theory can be applied to future development of the retail industry. Certainly, the growth of scrambled merchandising among dominant grocery retailers, particularly in hypermarkets, is developing simultaneously with restricted line formats delivering to drivers, city centre workers or home workers. Nevertheless, it is evident at organizational level, in, for example, the expansion and retraction of store formats in Next and Arcadia during the 1980s and 1990s. According to theory, it is probable that the growth of formats in organizations such as Toys 'R' Us, which expanded into Babies 'R' Us, Kids 'R' Us, Imaginarium and Toysrus.com, would be followed by organizational rationalization, as will retailers such as Amazon.com that have become Internet portals offering an extremely diverse mix of merchandise.

Hart's (1999) study on assortment strategies in food and mixed retailing supported accordion theory, but concluded that this theory was more applicable to trends in merchandise assortment than to development of store formats. Noting that the number of lines in itself was not a sufficient measure of assortment width, she felt that an additional dimension was required to measure assortment 'coherence' or the real degree to which merchandise was scrambled. She concluded that if ranges were more clearly categorized within the width of assortment, then a more realistic picture would emerge of the extent to which product ranges were related to the core retail offer. Her study also found:

- Assortment and market diversification decisions are rarely supported by market research; some companies reverse these decisions after incurring high development costs.
- Inconsistent assortment additions can have an effect on the retailer's image.
- There is no clear dominance of generalist or specialist retailers.
- Food retailers, in adding new merchandise lines with service requirements unrelated to existing lines, followed a more risky strategy than mixed retailers, which tended to concentrate on their core business.
- These strategies are not based on customer requirements.

Where the retail accordion theory is useful is that historical patterns of retail development indicate that there is a distinct tendency for both small and large retailers to add new and unrelated lines, eventually blurring the focus of the organization to the level where specialization, or contraction, will inevitably occur. Indeed, the recent growth of home shopping formats and city centre limited-line grocery and convenience formats is an indicator that specialization is occurring in the food sector as a result of environmental forces and consumer desire.

In order to minimize the cost of faulty development, retailers should be careful regarding:

- the extent to which new, unrelated merchandise lines are added;
- the relationship between new merchandise lines and the core offering in terms of the benefits they offer customers, and the synergy offered in terms of service requirements;
- supporting merchandise diversification and specialization strategies with market research focusing on the requirements of their core customers and potential customers; and
- the effects that diversification or specialization strategies will have on corporate image.

2.3 Environmental theories

Environmental theories are concerned with the interplay between the external environment and organizational environment. The various influences of the external environment – political, legal, socio-cultural and demographic, economic and technological – on retailers change over time. Conditions can change slowly or rapidly, and only those organizations that can adapt to change and take advantage of the opportunities offered by the environment will grow, develop and thrive.

A range of examples supports environmental theories. Department stores would not have existed but for developing urban spaces, nor would out-of-town shopping centres but for the development of the road network, suburbanization and growth of car ownership. An organization's movement through innovation and growth to maturity depends upon successful response to changing environmental conditions.

There are two dominant environmental theories of retail change:

- evolution theory; and
- institutional theory.

2.3.1 Evolution theory

The theory of retail evolution is, naturally, linked to the theory of evolution observed by Charles Darwin in the nineteenth century – the process of natural selection in which the survival of organisms is based on their ability to adapt to changing conditions. In retailing, organizations that successfully adapt to changes in the external environment are those most likely to thrive.

Davies (1998) discussed evolution theory in the context of environmental 'design spaces' which offer opportunities and threats for the retail organizations operating within them. The viability or otherwise of the 'design space' is related to:

- the size and distribution of the population;
- the need structure for goods, which is related to demographic variables such as family size and income;
- regional income and income distribution;
- technology;
- government regulation; and
- social visibility of the design space.

According to this 'ecological' theory, changes in the environment will cause retail change, and therefore the structure of retailing at any point in time is the result of all previous retail management decisions, together with the political, social, economic and technological environment within which retailers operate.

One of the problems with this refinement of evolution theory is that it does not allow for the effects of retail organizations on the environment in which they operate, and these are many. For example:

- **Planning gain**: for instance, in order to secure a site a retailer may develop roads or leisure facilities, which will bring with them housing development, which will have effects on the economy.

- **Lobbying**: most of the largest retail groups have close political connections, which can have effects on locational policy.
- **24-hour opening**: expansion of opening hours has brought with it a rapid move to the 24/7 society; it has increased the propensity for part-time, flexible working, and has had a role in raising the proportion of women in the UK workforce to over 50 per cent. This in turn has affected marriage and divorce statistics, and, it could be argued, the rise of single-parent families.
- **Online retailing**: the growth of 'e-tail' (electronic retail) has contributed to the uptake of computers in the home, improving the technological skills of the workforce.

Ultra-Darwinism is a form of evolution theory that relates development not to survival of the fittest, but of the fittest's genetic material. In socio-cultural evolution, the equivalent of the gene has been called the meme, an idea, saying or ritual that propagates itself through a society in much the same way as the spread of a computer virus. Thus, technologies could be considered memes carried by organizations and replicated at different levels within an organization and beyond the organization. For example, the first-in, first-out practice in merchandising can be replicated in staff or management promotion practices as 'Buggins' turn', or at the organizational level in terms of early retirement. Another example might be where customer service through stock availability is replicated in staffing practices through flexible hours contracts, in organizational practices such as 24-hour opening, and beyond retail into road development and maintenance to maintain access to stores.

According to Davies (1998), there is a distinction between the development of firms and formats, the former evolving relatively slowly with the environment, the latter adapting more dynamically to meet the needs of local environments. Therefore, a retail organization can run a variety of successful formats which may or may not carry the memes of the parent organization. Davies also argues that when change is slow and predictable, firms and formats have a better chance of survival; conversely, when change is rapid and unpredictable, greater opportunism exists and the number and variety of formats and firms will change.

According to Hannan and Freeman (1989), within any design space there are two types of firms and strategies. **R-strategies** occur when the environment is rapidly changing and discontinuous, throwing up opportunities that are seized and developed by opportunist organizations, and resulting in the proliferation of new formats. These organizations could be said to be charting the new, emerging design space. As the pace of change slows again, organizations select the best of the new formats with which to occupy the new design space and the second type of strategy dominates. These **K-strategies** occur when the environment is relatively stable. Larger, dominant organizations converge on the successful formats, applying them with the efficiencies of scale and power on a wide scale.

Hence, the current position in e-tailing, in which the evolving virtual design space was charted by innovative dot.com organizations, which then failed or were absorbed by 'clicks-and-bricks' retail organizations, could have been forecast. Indeed, it should be expected that these K-strategy organizations and surviving R-strategy organizations such as Amazon.com should be well placed to take advantage of the refinement of Internet and digital TV technology in the future.

Kent (2007) turned attention to creative space, considering the links between design and the retail environment: 'the evolution of retailing towards stores as three dimensional experience spaces places new demands on retailer creativity and retailer ability to enable other stakeholders to co-create products, services and interactions that take place within the spatial configuration of the store ... mall and street' (Kent, 2007, p. 741).

This extends the notion of retail spaces as a theatre in which staff are actors, customers the audience, the physical retail domain the stage, and the selling process the play. The importance of the retail 'domain' lies in its centrality to culture – with retail spaces playing an increasing role in the culture of advanced economies. In societies that value creativity, therefore, there are opportunities for retailers not only to exploit creativity as a social and cultural event, but to engage various stakeholders (including customers) in generating the level and type of creativity needed (and expected in some sectors) to differentiate the retail 'brand'. Creative retail formats such as 'pop-up' guerrilla design-led fashion stores (temporary stores in unusual, edgy locations); Apple Stores, rooted in the company's technically innovative product design background and engaging customers in technological interplay; fashion stores such as Prada and Camper shoe stores, incorporating brand values into store and architectural design – these all achieve creative differentiation through the interplay between environment, company and customers.

A range of strategies are used by successful firms to ensure survival (Brockway *et al.*, 1988):

- **Experimentation**: this is widely used by successful retailers, which will test out unrelated merchandise or new systems in one or a few stores before rolling out successful innovations. Examples include Aldi selling a limited range of holidays, and Safeway (now Morrisons) testing then rolling out its self-scanning operation. Similarly, grocery retailers like Sainsbury's and Waitrose offered online shopping in a limited area before expanding online shopping provision.

- **Joint retailing**: two normally separate organizations combine to create a synergistic offer to their customers. Examples include the joint offering of Burger King, Little Chef and Travelodge, offering accommodation and a selection of fast food or full meals to travellers, and McDonald's restaurants in Walmart and Asda stores offering cheap food to people shopping for cheap merchandise.

- **Physical premises mutation**: the retailer changes its usual location or combines innovative activities under one roof. An example of both is the move out of town by the Co-op Travel Group, which, in a purpose-built unit five times the size of its normal outlets, combined travel agency with an Internet area, café and children's play area (Parker, 2002). Japanese retailer Uniqlo, for example, employed pop-up stores in shipping containers as part of their publicity before the opening of their New York flagship store.

- **Copycatting**: exploiting innovative systems or formats that have been developed by other organizations. Examples include provision for cleaning, photographic, pharmaceutical and financial services within grocery retail units.

- **Vertical integration**: retailers take over other distribution channel functions such as manufacturing or wholesaling in order to gain organizational power over supply of goods. This also operates in the opposite direction, with manufacturers entering the retail market to gain higher margins.

- **Horizontal integration**: retailers acquire control of other retail organizations in order to boost market share, gain market innovation or management/operational expertise. One example is Talk 4 All buying 30 stores from failing mobile phone retailer The Wap Store to build strength and share in the maturing mobile phone retail market. Another is the acquisition of Exito, the dominant Colombian food retailer, by French retailer Casino.

- **Micro-merchandising**: retailers involved in micro-merchandising make use of market segmentation techniques to focus on meeting the needs of a demographic or lifestyle group through creation of a suitable retail format. Girl Heaven and Claire's Accessories are two UK examples, targeting the 'tweenie' market of 7–12-year-olds with 'girly' toys, make-up, clothes and accessories.

Box 2.1 Retailer profile: Casino

The well-known, long-established French retailer Casino used innovation, and vertical and horizontal integration to grow, develop, internationalize and finally to compete in the global retail marketplace. The original shop was set up in a former casino – hence the name. One of the first European grocery retailers to introduce self-service into its stores, early expansion took place through horizontal integration – concentrating on neighbourhood stores. Casino also developed manufacturing subsidiaries, which contributed to the growth of its own-brand business. In 1999, it operated both a wine-bottling business and a meat-processing business. Casino was also an early entrant into the hypermarket format in the 1970s and is one of France's major retailers, with 10 per cent of the market.

The organization is itself majority owned by Rallye Group, which also owns the Groupe Go Sport chain in addition to having interests in a variety of other organizations. Casino operates a variety of food retail formats and fascias: Géant hypermarkets; Casino supermarkets, which have been developed into the Big C format in Thailand and Vietnam, and Extra Supermercado in Brazil; Petit Casino superettes; Franprix and LeaderPrice discount supermarkets; Spar and Vival neighbourhood stores.

The group developed through the 1980s, mainly through acquisition, and during the 1990s it continued this successful method of expansion abroad. For example, its presence in Latin America and Asia developed primarily through acquiring stakes in local retail groups. Although its domestic business dominated sales, in the early 2000s the group operated stores, or had acquired stakes in retail businesses, in:

- USA (United Grocers cash and carry)
- Poland (Polska and LeaderPrice)
- Argentina (Libertad and LeaderPrice)

- Uruguay (Disco and Devoto)
- Colombia (Exito)
- Venezuela (Cativen)
- Brazil (Pão de Açúcar)
- Thailand (Big C)
- Vietnam (Big C)
- Philippines (Uniwide Holdings)
- Taiwan (Far Eastern Géant)

The Casino group continued its global expansion plans through acquisition, particularly in the Philippines and South Korea, and as early as 2002 was also considering expansion in the Middle East. In 2010 Casino acquired Carrefour stores in Thailand, as Carrefour refocused its expansion on key overseas markets in which it had market leader potential. The company's current strategy is to develop presence and depth in high-potential markets.

In Europe, Casino operates company-owned stores, but also has a large number of franchised outlets in its Petit Casino, Spar and Vival fascias. The group acquired Franprix in 1997, which brought in a mix of franchised and own-operated outlets in Franprix (supermarkets) and LeaderPrice (discounters) formats. The company now operates discount fascias in Brazil (Assai) and Colombia (Surtimax).

In 2000, Casino acquired SLDC, the holding group for Auchan's convenience store network, and acquired a 50 per cent share in Monoprix. Like many large European grocery retailers there has been considerable focus on convenience formats, and Casino now operates about 20 convenience fascias across its international portfolio of stores.

The group also owned a chain of restaurants called Cafeterias Casino which has become Casino Restauration, developing over time into a series of formats from cafeterias, to themed restaurants and fast food outlets. Online it operates both grocery and non-grocery e-commerce sites in France and South America.

Innovation was the foundation for Casino's early growth – successfully importing the idea of self-service from the USA in 1948 and opening its first hypermarket in 1970. A very recent innovation is the Daily Monop urban fresh food format, where people can stop for a bite to eat. Casino has used horizontal integration to grow its retail business successfully, acquiring a variety of formats across the grocery sector from convenience store to hypermarket. The group also vertically integrated into manufacturing and cash and carry operations. By 2002, the group was the fourth largest in the French grocery market, with 10.6 per cent market share, and strengthened its position further in subsequent years to become the third largest retailer after Carrefour and Leclerc.

Source: www.groupe-casino.fr, 2002, 2014; Young, 2002; Retail Intelligence, 1999; Bord Bia, 2008; USDA, 2009.

2.3.2 Institutional theory

Institutional theory recognizes that the organization is an organic part of its environment and that there is a degree of interdependency between them (Arnold *et al.*, 2001). According to this theory, the decisions and actions of a retail organization reflect the economic and cultural norms of the environment in which it exists. These norms exist at task and institutional levels.

At **task level**, the organization responds to its environment through actions aimed at retail performance – from a customer perspective, these are linked to retail performance-related decisions on, for example, merchandise assortment, pricing strategy, inventory and location.

At **institutional level**, the retailer's actions are constrained or framed according to cultural and moral norms which will influence both the internal culture of the organization and its perceived role in the society in which it exists. For example, customers may expect it to employ and promote local talent, be active in the community and sell local products along with those that are sourced nationally or internationally.

The performance actions that retailers take can adhere to norms in an objective manner – for example, selling goods will be of consistent high quality. However, they can also take a symbolic form – for example, Sainsbury's 'Taste the Difference' range, or Tesco's 'Finest' range.

Likewise, symbolic institutional actions can reflect the organization's adherence to the norms of its socio-cultural environment – for example, Iceland's well-promoted purge of suppliers of goods with genetically modified ingredients in the 1990s, which responded to the upsurge of European concern regarding genetically modified foods, can be contrasted against the objective actions of organizations that source products deemed by various regulatory authorities to be safe or healthy to eat.

When a retailer's actions reflect the norms of its environment (termed isomorphism), this legitimizes the organization (and its institutional and performance actions) in the minds of the various institutional stakeholders (customers, shareholders, staff, suppliers). The institutional/environmental interaction is illustrated in Figure 2.3.

For example, the political climate of the 1980s and 1990s created destabilized unionism and high unemployment. This brought about the flexible labour market conditions that would bring the UK inward investment and allow organizations in the country to become more competitive, productive, profitable and adaptable. A retailer that exploits the labour market conditions by offering staff flexi-hours contracts, binding them to the organization for a variable number of hours each week, is therefore seen to be acting in an acceptable fashion, particularly in a sector that promotes efficiency as a means of keeping prices reasonable. The recession from 2008 allowed the proliferation of 'zero hours' contracts among retailers, in which staff were bound to the company but could be offered no work at all in a week in which they were not needed. These were justified in the pursuit of low prices to meet the needs of customers suffering high unemployment and reduced incomes in relation to inflation.

Socio-cultural norms are vague, variable over time and difficult to monitor. It is easy for a retailer's institutional actions to exceed what is acceptable. For example, in 2002, Sainsbury's acted in a manner regarded as 'mean' by many stakeholders when it fired managers

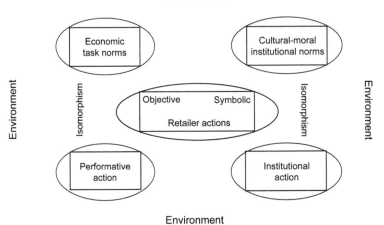

Figure 2.3 Institutional/environmental interaction

Economic task norms: the economic environment in which the organization operates and within which it frames its performance objectives and actions. Cultural-moral institutional norms: the organization's stakeholders create an institutional environment with cultural and moral requirements which reflect the norms of social conduct in the external socio-cultural environment. Performative action: performance levels and actions taken by the organization, e.g. pricing strategy, merchandising decisions. Institutional action: non-performance actions taken by the organization, e.g. community involvement, environmental policies. Symbolic actions: use of symbols such as slogans, signs and promotional literature which relate the organization's actions to its social and economic environment. Objective actions: actions taken to compete successfully within the economic task environment.

Source: Adapted from Arnold *et al.*, 2001; *Principles of Retailing*, Edinburgh: Edinburgh Business School.

in a morally dubious manner. This reflected the organization's 'meanness' in allowing store staff to work six hours with only a ten-minute break, seven hours with a 20-minute break, and eight hours with a 30-minute break. This compared poorly with the other grocery majors, which already were regarded as 'exploitative' by many staff, and contrasted with their transmitted image of quality and customer care.

Post-2008, the UK government simplified and reduced benefits paid to the country's poor and unemployed; the media focus on benefits highlighted the fact that numerous retailers were employing many staff on contracts that required the government to top-up their wages to what was considered a liveable amount. This was perceived as government subsidy of retailers, which was not regarded by many as socially acceptable, and pressure began to mount against use of these practices. There is a limit to the number of objective actions that a retail organization can take in the interests of successful competitiveness – but which transgress social norms of institutional conduct – without affecting perceived service quality and tarnishing corporate image.

A 2005 study attempted to determine the retail food store norm importance for Chinese shoppers and measure Walmart's retail norm performance. The study found that economic and socio-cultural norms for Chinese food shoppers differed slightly from those in the USA and UK; while similar importance was placed on store convenience (nearly 70 per cent of customers in the Shenzhen sample walked to the store they shopped at most frequently), more importance was placed on quality and trust and less on value prices. The study found that Walmart performed well across the spectrum of economic and socio-cultural norms relative to competing retailers, and in particular quality and trust, achieving a level of isomorphism that should be reflected in the stores' performance (Arnold *et al.*, 2006).

2.4 Conflict theory

Conflict theory addresses what happens when a new innovation or format challenges the status quo in a retail sector. As retail organizations adapt to each other in the competitive marketplace, new and different forms of retailing develop. This continual shift in operating forms is derived from a dialectic process that consists of action–reaction–synthesis.

As an innovator successfully enters the market through some competitive advantage (action), existing organizations will take actions designed to minimize that competitive advantage (reaction), which eventually lead to a modification of their operating methods. Meanwhile, the innovating organization will also adapt as it becomes established in the market (trading up according to wheel theory). The continual adaptation will bring the two differing types of trading closer and closer together until they are virtually indistinguishable (synthesis) (Maronick and Walker, 1974). The retail organizations that evolve deploy organizational elements (carry the memes according to ultra-Darwinist theory) of both innovative and established formats.

There are a number of examples that illustrate this theory in action. The latest is perhaps **Internet retailing**, in which many retailers faced the challenge of manufacturer/wholesaler-led dot.coms bypassing retail outlets, selling merchandise direct to customers at discount prices. In order to offer an effective service on a large scale, investment was required in warehouse, transport and customer service facilities in addition to an enormous marketing spend, which in most cases undermined their business viability. Meanwhile, major retail groups added Internet retailing to their existing formats and exploited their established brand names to embed their Internet offering with existing and new customers. At the same time, they made use of their logistics network to find solutions to delivery and returns problems. A second example is **forecourt retailing**, which is a successful 'merger' of petrol stations with convenience stores, which was partly fuelled by pressure for 24-hour retailing. A third example is the 'merging' of **retail and leisure parks**.

According to conflict theory, there are four stages of response to a retail innovation:

- shock;
- defensive retreat;
- acknowledgement; and
- adaptation.

Initially, retailers are hostile to the threat to their established role within the industry and distribution channel. Firm size, reseller solidarity, organizational rigidity and channel politics can all promote hostility towards the 'interloper'. In phase two, defensive retreat, established retail organizations will ignore or play down the possible effects of the innovation. As the threat of the innovation becomes more sustained and severe, there may be movement to block the progress of the innovation in phase three, acknowledgment, which, if unsuccessful, will give way to the final phase, adaptation.

In a study on the impact of warehouse membership clubs (WMCs) in the USA, Sampson and Tigert (1994) claimed that supermarkets are the primary targets of WMCs, with 43 per cent of customer supermarket spend transferred from the former to the latter. Nevertheless, it was only in the maturity stage of the WMC life cycle that food retailers acknowledged the threat to their viability and took defensive action through the reactive or proactive strategies outlined in Box 2.2.

Box 2.2 Response strategies of food retailers to the growth of warehouse membership clubs

1   Small section of warehouse club pack sizes at WMC prices put into stores.
2   'Power alley', with a larger number of stock-keeping units (SKUs) in club pack size at WMC prices.
3   Store-within-store warehouse club section, upwards of 200 SKUs at WMC prices.
4   Food-only warehouse club of 40,000 operating without a membership fee.
5   Food and drug-only warehouse clubs built in recycled supermarkets.
6   Petitioning against zoning applications by WMCs.
7   Petitioning against differing regulations on pricing on SKUs to create level playing field between WMCs and supermarket chains.

Source: Adapted from Sampson and Tigert, 1994.

Sampson and Tigert (1994) concluded that the proactive strategies aimed at synthesis were those which offered the established food retailers the greatest chance of success: food-only, or food and drug-only WMCs.

In terms of retailer response to the dot.com threat, it is interesting to note that those retailers that confronted the threat and adapted the earliest are among the most successful at gaining market share. In 2002, Tesco's online market share advantage over Sainsbury's was six times greater than in stores, and Argos' online share was three times greater than that of Woolworths. In addition to establishing market leadership, embracing change and investment in e-tailing has brought benefits in terms of the technical experience to refine online shopping, plus the ability to tap into and exploit the online movements of the growing number of technically proficient potential customers.

2.5 Combined theory

Having established that the development of a new retail format followed the principles established by the wheel, life-cycle and conflict theories, the links among these various theories as they drive retail change were also explored by Sampson and Tigert, who came up with a descriptive model for the evolution of new retail forms (see Figure 2.4).

Environment theory: environmental conditions enable the creation and development of the innovation. Political and economic conditions created negative growth in income for the majority of Americans during the 1980s, which, together with a car-based social environment, created conditions favourable for the growth of value retail formats such as factory outlet centres and WMCs. Internet use soared in the late 1990s, creating a technological and social environment that was successfully exploited by some retailers as a viable format and by many retailers to streamline their logistical efforts in a bid to drive down costs and increase competitiveness.

Cyclical theory: there are four main indicators retailers can use in establishing the life-cycle stage of their organization (or format). These are:

- price;
- product range;
- geographical expansion; and
- management style.

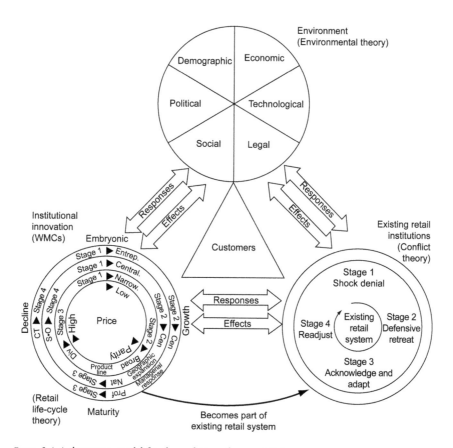

Figure 2.4 A descriptive model for the evolution of new retail forms

In Figure 2.4 these are portrayed as rings because each has its own separate stages, which may 'revolve' at varying rates according to external environmental forces. In the innermost ring, price varies from low to high, with higher prices generally associated with later stages in the life cycle. In formats reliant on price for their competitive advantage it is essential that low price levels are guarded from adverse environmental impacts, and this is the case with WMCs and factory outlet centres. However, the price advantage in online retailing can be less important. Customers pay for the convenience of home delivery, and in organizations operating several formats, price parity with bricks-and-mortar stores is regarded as advisable, partly due to the comparability of costs, but also due to the high cost of returns. Internet retailing offers experienced and maturing retailers the flexibility to price in relation to demand. The immediacy of the medium, the visibility of consumer interest and ease of tracking of demand has meant that creative use of pricing has been a fast-increasing feature of Internet retailing.

The second innermost ring is that of product range – as retail formats mature the trend is from narrow to broad and then to diversified product ranges. In WMCs this has been the case, as it has in factory outlet centres in the UK and in online retailing as major online retailers have developed into retail portals offering merchandise direct from manufacturers and other distribution organizations.

However, according to retail accordion theory there should come a point when a move towards specialization will occur, as a defensive measure against decline or an innovator. An example of the former is illustrated in specialized factory outlet centres, and of the latter in the food-only WMCs that have been set up by food retailers in the USA. In the UK Dixons, challenged by Tesco and Amazon retail portals offering electronic merchandise and 'white goods' such as cookers, has focused on its e-format, reducing the number of physical store outlets.

The second outermost ring represents geographical expansion. Retailers tend to expand outwards from their base location as they grow and mature, first into adjoining markets, then nationally and internationally. The last phase of expansion fends off decline as the national market is saturated, as has happened with both WMCs and factory outlet centres. It seems likely that online retailing will progress in a similar fashion as the market matures.

The outermost ring represents the most effective management style in each of the four life-cycle phases: entrepreneurial in the innovation phase, centralized during growth, professional during maturity, and caretaker during decline. Some retail organizations recognize this, and selected entrepreneurial managers take care of new start-ups.

A maturing retailer will become part of the established retail system as existing retail institutions acknowledge and adapt to accommodate them (conflict theory). Sampson and Tigert (1994) cite Source Club as an example of a new type of warehouse club with low membership fees, retail focus and supermarket-like atmosphere. McArthurGlen's factory outlet centre in Livingston, Scotland, is indistinguishable from a conventional covered shopping centre in size, atmosphere and location (in the town centre), and even its prices are matched by offsite competitors such as Matalan and TK Maxx. Many retailers have both absorbed online facilities into their bricks-and-mortar stores, and developed transactional websites – which shows a similar development in online retailing.

At the centre of Figure 2.4, customer needs, wants and desires drive all three parts of the model, because for a retail organization to succeed to the level of being absorbed into the existing retail system, it must operate in a manner that is acceptable and attractive to its customers.

2.6 Learning summary

Theories of retail change have been developed by studying past and current patterns of retail development, at format, organization and industry levels. There are three main categories of theory discussed in this chapter: cyclical theories, environmental theories, and conflict theory. A combined theory has also been presented which links all three categories.

The cyclical theories include the wheel of retailing, retail life cycle and retail accordion, all based on the thinking that there is a cyclical pattern in the evolution of retail institutions from which future business scenarios can be built.

Two main environmental theories have been outlined – evolution theory and institutional theory – both based on the effects of the external, uncontrollable environment on the retail industry and the organizations operating within it. Where evolution theory suggests that successful organizations adapt to survive and succeed in the changing environment, both the ultra-Darwinists and the institutionalists propose that organizations go beyond tactical adaptation to absorb into their fabric, design and organizational culture the 'technologies' and socio-cultural influences of the external environment.

Conflict theory is explained as a series of phases through which existing retail organizations pass when challenged by a retail innovation. After the initial shock, organizations engage in defensive retreat, which may involve an industry initiative to prevent the success of the innovator, then they pass through a phase of acknowledgement that the innovation is going to succeed, during which they engage various adaptation strategies. Meanwhile, the innovator is also adapting to survive and grow until a degree of synthesis exists.

Finally, a combined theory has been described, which integrates the various branches of retail theory. The main utility of theory is to predict outcomes, and research has indicated contradictory results for all the various theories presented. However, they remain useful tools for retailers to build alternative visions for the future of their organizations and their place within the changing retail industry.

Review questions

1 Critically evaluate the utility of the 'wheel of retailing' theory.
2 Apply one of the other main cyclical retail theories to the current status of a major fashion retailer. According to the theory, explain two likely future developments of the organization.
3 Ultra-Darwinism is a form of evolution theory which relates development to survival not of the fittest, but of the fittest's 'genetic' material. Explain what is meant by the term 'meme', and give an example of a 'meme' that has been replicated in retailing.
4 Explain what is meant by the terms 'symbolic' and 'objective' retailer actions.
5 Give an example of a symbolic action taken by a well-known retail organization and explain how it relates to the socio-cultural environment.
6 Give an example of conflict theory in action in today's retail market and explain how you believe the situation will develop, according to theory.

7   Explain what 'combined theory' entails. Apply combined theory to one retail sector and draw conclusions regarding the utility of this theory in explaining current sector developments.

Case study: Dixons – multi-channel retailing

Introduction

Dixons, a high street retailer for over 50 years, was first established by Charles Kalms as a photographic studio in Southend in 1937. As demand for photographic portraits surged during the Second World War, the business expanded to seven units, but by the time Sir Stanley Kalms took over the business as a teenager in 1948, only one London studio was left:

> Ours was the right industry at the right time. I was 16, with all the energy and enthusiasm of that age.
>
> (MacDonald, 2002)

From that time Dixons grew into a dominant retail group operating under a range of high street fascias, and proved a major force in the growth of online retailing in the UK. By the time Kalms retired as chairman of the group in 2002, the group was consolidating its presence in Europe and still innovating. Electro World, a new store type, was being tested in central Europe, and Dixons xL – an electricals superstore – was launched in the UK.

History

In 1962, Dixons had 16 stores, floated on the stock exchange and acquired 42 more shops; sales totalled £1.4 million. By 1967, the chain had grown to 90 units through further acquisition. Although photography remained the main focus, Kalms spotted opportunities for developing the product range into associated growth areas such as hi-fis, and own-brand products sourced from Japan allowed the retailer to compete on price. The acquisition of Currys in 1984 brought 613 new units and access to the related 'white goods' market.

Later, the growing market in information technology was successfully exploited. In 1993, the acquisition of Vision Technology (developed as PC World) gave access to the burgeoning home computer market, and in 1996 the first 'The Link' store opened. Dixons has been at the forefront in online retailing, and even set up the Internet service provider (ISP) Freeserve in 1998, which facilitated accessibility to the Internet within the UK – partly through the notion of a free access ISP, but also partly through the publicity achieved by its launch. Freeserve was one of the rare successes of the dot.com boom, launched in 1999 and floated on the stock exchange a year later.

By 2002 Dixons had over 1,100 stores in the UK, retailing under the brand names of:

- Dixons
- Currys
- PC World
- The Link

- PC World for Business
- Dixons Business Services

All of these brands also had online e-commerce sites.

Acquisition brought Dixons access to international retail markets, and the group had stores in Ireland, Denmark, Sweden, Finland, Norway, Portugal and Spain. The organization also had a stake in the market leader for electrical products in Greece, and operated Electro World in Budapest and Prague. There was a variety of associated businesses including Mastercare, an after-sales operation acquired along with Currys, and Codic, the European property division.

Dixons' changing customer

Although customers had more choice, income and opportunities to buy, there was also more competition for their leisure pound. Customers had more access to information – from the media, and increasingly from the Internet. In 2001, 7.5 million UK adults had Internet access, with 30 per cent of homes having at least one PC. Forty-five per cent of adults had accessed the Internet, and 2.3 million homes had unmetered Internet access (and this before the widespread uptake of broadband). Seventy per cent of 16–34-year-olds had used the Internet, with increasing access by older people and 'silver surfers'. Internet use was primarily for information search – 66 per cent of the time adults used the Internet to obtain information about goods and services, and 33 per cent of the time to acquire goods and services. (Internet and broadband soared in subsequent years, as did the ways in which people accessed the Internet and used it for social networking and purchasing goods and services.)

Many of the products sold by Dixons exploited Internet use, boosting sales. Consumers are presented with different types of buying situation according to the type of product they are buying. For example, purchase of a newspaper or sugar is usually a simple 'straight re-buy' situation involving little thought or search for information. Purchase of a cereal or beer may be a 'limited problem-solving' situation, with the consumer checking out new brands or versions of products. Electrical products, being more complex, present many customers with an 'extended problem-solving' situation, in which there are several stages:

- problem recognition;
- information search;
- alternative evaluation;
- alternative choice; and
- post-purchase.

There are clear benefits for the customer in condensing problem solving through Internet use, where information is easily accessible and comparisons with the offerings of other retailers but a click or two away.

Dixons recognized that customers were hard-working, cash-rich but time-poor with little time for leisure. Time deprivation meant that a growing number of customers researched and compared goods in catalogues and online, and in addition they also often phoned the store for information (for example, on availability) before coming in to buy – touching and trying goods is important to most people. Over 40 million calls a year were made to the stores in the Dixons Group.

As shopping increasingly became a leisure alternative to sport or entertainment, retail centres responded by offering a variety of quasi-retail leisure activities such as cinemas, food courts and play areas, and stores such as Dixons and PC World attempted to make purchasing electrical items in-store a more interesting, interactive experience.

Families tended to 'atomize' at home, pursuing individual leisure interests – for example, computer gaming, using the Internet, watching TV, listening to music, texting or tele-phoning – often in different rooms. For this reason, the market for electrical goods – which would once have been the province of family decision making – became disparate, and marketing to the individual was a way to boost sales.

Creating flexibility and choice for customers

Customers in the early years of the twenty-first century, therefore, lived in a high-tech, high-speed world and demanded instant gratification. Customers wanted to buy in the way that was most modern, efficient and convenient – and large retail organizations responded with the implementation of multiple-channel retailing.

Dixons offered customers its first new distribution channel as long ago as 1950, in the form of a mail order catalogue. By 2002 all the main Dixons fascias had online e-commerce sites, and the organization also ran PC City online in France. In addition to store-based shopping, Dixons' customers could buy products by mail order, telesales, TV, Internet and mobile phone.

Where there was so much information in an extremely competitive marketplace, mar-keting was used to fulfil customer needs and expectations. Communication was of prime importance, and over £100 million per year was spent on advertising to build the brand's strength and visibility. Clare (2000) believed that marketing communications had to be multi-channel, and preferably available on every channel. Examples of marketing communications included:

- advertisements in a range of media;
- sales promotions;
- full colour in-store guides (which can be taken home);
- brochures;
- online version of brochure;
- personal selling in-store; and
- online selling.

The post-purchase stage in the buying decision process was dealt with through provision of accessible and comprehensive information for customers, which was provided online, in-store and through the call centre. Many customers needed help to learn to work the appliances they bought, and managing ongoing relations with customers built loyalty. Dixons' call centre help lines operated 24/7, all year round to deal with after-sales support, warranties and product enquiries – eventually the centre would manage all telecommunications – leaving store personnel free to demonstrate and sell products.

Applying the 'martini principle', Dixons' customers could buy anytime, anyplace, anywhere through their range of retail formats, and multi-channel retailing was regarded as the means for providing that convenience and flexibility.

Integration of multi-channel systems was regarded as a key factor underpinning success in multi-channel retailing – £30 million was spent between 1999 and 2001 on systems that would provide support for e-commerce and stores. Integration of product information and pricing across channels was effected, and online sales integrated with stock management and order processing, creating the systems necessary for maintenance of product availability, dispatch and returns. With online retailing, returns were a significant part of the operation. An integrated operation also facilitated online customer tracking of orders, payments and delivery status, which reduced the customer support needed in terms of telesales and administration.

Conclusions

In just over 50 years Dixons developed from a single unit to a multinational, multi-channel operation. Customer focus and technology provided market opportunities that were exploited through entrepreneurial management and developed into a range of fascias for a variety of product markets. However, the expense of maintaining choice requires investment in efficient systems. Development of flexibility in the way customers could shop at Dixons' clicks-and-bricks stores was underpinned by the systems necessary for maintenance of standard levels of service in terms of product availability and returns. Integration of product information and pricing across channels was also used to standardize and clarify the offer to customers, to build cross-channel synergy, and to reduce costs in marketing communications.

Source: www.dixons.com; MacDonald, 2002; Clare, 2000.

1   Show how Dixons exploited environmental challenges to extend its maturity phase of the life cycle.

References

Arnold, S.J., Kozinets, R.V. and Handelman, J.M. (2001) 'Hometown ideology and retailer legitimation: the institutional semiotics of Wal-Mart flyers', *Journal of Retailing*, 77(2) (Summer): 243–271.

Arnold, S., Shen, W., Bu, N. and Sun, Z. (2006) 'Retail food store patronage and Wal-Mart performance in China', Conference Paper, Globalising Retail Seminar, University of Surrey.

Berwin, L. (2007) 'ASOS eyes stores to raise brand profile', *Retail Week*, 23 November, www.retail-week.com/asos-eyes-stores-to-raise-brand-profile/295118.article (accessed 2007).

Bord Bia (2008) 'Overview of the French retail and food service market', Irish Food Board (Bord Bia), www.bordbia.ie/eventsnew/ConferencePresentations/FoodDrinksIndustryDayCountryOverviews/France%20Market%20Overview.pdf (accessed 2008).

Brockway, G., Gary, R. and Niffenegger, P. (1988) 'Retailing evolution in the 1980s: survival through adaptive behaviour', *Journal of Midwest Marketing*, 3(2).

Brown, S. (1995) 'Postmodernism, the wheel of retailing and will to power', *The International Review of Retail, Distribution and Consumer Research*, 5(3): 387–414.

Clare, J. (2000) 'Transcript of presentation on "Tomorrow's customer"', Royal Society of Edinburgh symposium, 22 February.

David, R. (2002) 'IKEA in £50m store expansion to offset planning frustration', *Retail Week*, 11 January.

Davies, K. (1998) 'Applying evolutionary models to the retail sector', *The International Review of Retail, Distribution and Consumer Research*, 8(2): 165–182.

Fernie, S. (1996) 'The future for factory outlet centres in the UK: the impact of changes in planning policy guidance on the growth of a new retail format', *International Journal of Retail and Distribution Management*, 24(6): 11–21.

Gilmour, D. (2007) 'Wal-Mart, the supply chain and the wheel of retailing', *Supply Chain Digest*, 11 October, www.scdigest.com/assets/FirstThoughts/07-10-11.php?cid=1292&ctype=contentober.

Hannan, M.T. and Freeman, J. (1989) *Organisational Ecology*. London: Harvard University Press.

Hart, C. (1999) 'The retail accordion and assortment strategies: an exploratory study', *The International Review of Retail, Distribution and Consumer Research*, 9(2): 111–126.

Hower, R. (1943) 'History of Macy's of New York 1858–1919', in *Retail Marketing* (Lush, R.F., Dunne, P. and Gebhardt, R., eds, revised 1993 edn). Cincinnati, OH: South Western Publishing, pp. 113–114.

Kent, T. (2007) 'Creative space: design and the retail environment', *International Journal of Retail & Distribution Management*, 35(9): 734–745.

MacDonald, G. (2002) 'Electric nation', *Retail Week*, 13 September.

Maronick, T.J. and Walker, B.J. (1974) 'The dialectic evolution of retailing', in *Proceedings: Southern Marketing Association* (Greenberg, B., ed.). Atalanta: Georgia State University, p. 147.

McNair, M.P. (1958) 'Significant trends and developments in the postwar period', in *Competitive Distribution in a Free High-Level Economy and its Implications for the University* (Smith, A.B., ed.). Pittsburgh, PA: University of Pittsburgh Press.

Parker, G. (2002) 'Travel firms seek to increase portfolios', *Retail Week*, 18 January, p. 3.

Retail Intelligence (1999) *Profile of Casino (Rallye)*.

Sampson, S.D. and Tigert, D.J. (1994) 'The impact of warehouse membership clubs: the wheel of retailing turns one more time', *International Review of Retail, Distribution and Consumer Research*, 4(1): 33–59.

USDA (2009) 'France retail food sector annual report', USDA Foreign Agricultural Service, gain.fas.usda.gov/recent%20gain%20publications/retail%20food%20sector_paris_france_7-17-2009.pdf (accessed 2009).

Verdict (2002) 'Verdict forecasts UK retailing to 2004', www.verdict.co.uk/fcpr.htm (accessed 11 January 2002).

Young, J. (2002) 'Playing to win at Casino', *Retail Week*, 18 January, p. 16.

3 Strategic retail marketing 1
The strategic planning process

Learning objectives

After studying this chapter, you should be able to:

- Outline the strategic planning process.
- Formulate corporate strategy and objectives.
- Use a variety of analyses for assessing strategic capability.
- Discuss generic strategies and expansion strategies.
- Critically evaluate strategic options.

3.1 Introduction

This chapter provides an overview of the strategic planning process to evaluate strategic choices available to retailers in order to implement marketing strategies and the retail marketing mix (Figure 3.1). Retail strategy is about corporate survival and prosperity in a changing retail environment. It is about environmental analysis; identification of those factors critical to success; recognition and building of corporate competences; developing, maintaining and communicating strategic direction – to staff, to customers, to competitors.

The organization's mission encapsulates its direction and its values in the changing marketplace, which are then developed into corporate objectives. Environmental audit and analysis will highlight the main opportunities and threats to the retailer, while a resource audit and analyses will develop understanding of its strategic capability. These two perspectives can be referred to as the 'outside in' environmental approach compared with the 'inside out' resource-based view. Such an assessment provides a platform for determining the strategic positioning of the company against the competition. The chapter will then consider the strategic choices and their evaluation in relation to organizational capability. Routes to growth and the methods of expansion are discussed; there is increasing overlap in the literature between business and marketing strategy, especially in the modifications of the Ansoff matrix in relation to products and markets.

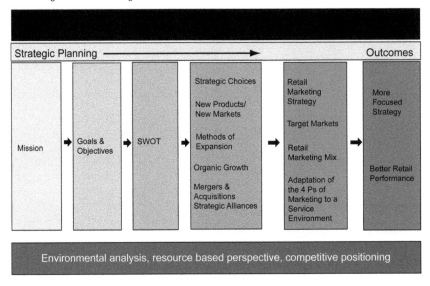

Figure 3.1 Retail strategic planning and marketing management model

3.2 The strategic planning process

The retail environment is always dynamic and sometimes volatile. The strategic planning process is cyclical, allowing the organization to maintain a successful strategic direction in a manner that is responsive to external, competitive and organizational pressures. The process encompasses three main steps. First, the external, competitive and organizational environment is audited and analysed. Second, strategic options are explored and evaluated, before a strategy or strategies are selected. Third, strategy is implemented through setting up action plans and allocating human, financial and material resources

3.3 Corporate strategy and objectives

Despite the changing environment, successful retail organizations tend to have a clear direction, or mission, which is really a rationale for the existence and progress of the company. Often organizations verbalize this in a mission statement, but even if they do not, the mission or direction creates the focus for corporate strategy, and for the setting of corporate objectives. The mission should encapsulate the core competences and critical success factors for the organization – that is, the company strengths and the areas in which the company has to succeed to thrive – as well as try to inform internal and external customers about what their role is in delivering success (Piercy, 2001). As the company reviews and adjusts its strategic direction over time, the mission, values and objectives will change.

Box 3.1 shows the mission and corporate values of Asda and the John Lewis Partnership. The mission and values of Asda changed considerably and were expressed much more simply in 2010. The mission in 2002 was more restrictive in its definition both in terms of the type of merchandise on which the organization is focused and in its target market. It is also very detailed in expressing its values – perhaps an indication of an expression of Walmart values soon after the takeover in 1999. The later, less prescriptive mission statement reflects several trends evident among the former UK 'grocery' retailers:

- a greater range of store formats;
- development of online portals; and
- increasing focus on non-food and clothing merchandise categories.

John Lewis Partnership operates department stores and a chain of over 300 food stores. The vision – for a retail organization with the staff at the heart of the business, co-owners sharing in its profits – was developed in the early twentieth century. This vision was expressed by the original founder, John Spedan Lewis, who created a written constitution so that his legacy of industrial democracy could be carried on by his successors. The constitution sets out the principles, governance system and rules. It is not surprising that the principles given in Box 3.1 are the same as in the earlier edition of this book. There are over 85,000 partners and the continuing success of John Lewis Partnership indicates that this approach to retailing works.

Box 3.1 Company mission statements and corporate values

Asda (2002)

Mission

To be Britain's best value fresh food and clothing superstore, by satisfying the weekly shopping needs of ordinary working people and their families who demand value.

Values

We are all colleagues; we are one team; we each need to improve the business every day in every way.

- Think about your work and put forward your ideas for improvement.
- Question or challenge if you don't agree.
- Learn from your mistakes and successes. Share your learning with your colleagues.
- Give people honest feedback so that they can improve.
- Ask yourself 'If this was my business, what would I do?'
- Praise good ideas and encourage others to put ideas forward.
- Give feedback to Colleague Circle members so that we can improve our working environment.

What we sell is better value.

- Be aware of current promotions and offers so that you can tell customers.
- Only offer quality products to the customer; remove any poor-quality products from display.
- Have a passion for product knowledge and keeping it up to date.
- Handle products with care.
- Help customers understand our Rollback policy and ensure all price communication is clear and accurate.
- Talk about our value message to customers.
- Feedback all customer comments to someone who can take action.

Selling is our universal responsibility.

- Love selling and actively get involved in company sales initiatives.
- Deal with availability issues as a priority.
- Know your products; explain features, give advice, offer alternatives or complementary products to customers where possible.
- Run a store and drive sales.
- Know your internal customers and how you can help them.
- Encourage customers to sample products being demonstrated.

Through selling we make our service legendary.

- Meet and greet customers with a smile.
- Always take customers to a product rather than pointing.
- Offer assistance to customers if you see them struggling.
- Recognise and help customers with special needs.
- Always strive to deliver what the customer wants. Remember that the customer is always right.
- Take ownership for a customer's problem and ensure it is resolved.
- Make a special effort to ensure children enjoy their shopping trip.

We hate waste of any kind.

- Shout out about things you notice that waste time, energy or money.
- Look after our resources.
- Car share where possible.
- Use stationery sparingly (e.g. if you have to photocopy always use double sided).
- Recycle where possible.
- Switch off lights, keep freezer/chiller doors shut and don't fill above the load lines.
- Keep phone calls short.
- Rotate stock correctly and follow all waste management procedures.
- Would you spend it? Think of Asda's money as your own.

Asda (2010)

Mission

To be Britain's best value retailer exceeding customer needs, every day.

Purpose

To save everyone money, every day.

Values

We put customers first, every day.
We care for our colleagues, every day.
We strive to be the best we can be, every day.

John Lewis Partnership (2001)

Mission and values

'We have a constitution – a framework of rules that defines how we run our business'.

Purpose: The Partnership's ultimate purpose is the happiness of all its members, through their worthwhile and satisfying employment in a successful business. Because the Partnership is owned in trust for its members, they share the responsibilities of ownership as well as its rewards – profit, knowledge and power.

Power: Power in the Partnership is shared between three governing authorities, the Central Council, the Central Board and the Chairman.

Profit: The Partnership aims to make sufficient profit from its trading operations to sustain its commercial vitality, to finance its continued development and to distribute a share of those profits each year to its members, and enable it to undertake other activities consistent with its ultimate purpose.

Members: The Partnership aims to employ people of ability and integrity who are committed to working together and to supporting its principles. Relationships are based on mutual respect and courtesy, with as much equality between its members as differences of responsibility permit. The Partnership aims to recognise their individual contributions and reward them fairly.

Customers: The Partnership aims to deal honestly with its customers and secure their loyalty and trust by providing outstanding choice, value and service.

Business Relationships: The Partnership aims to conduct all its business relationships with integrity and courtesy and scrupulously to honour every business agreement.

The Community: The Partnership aims to obey the spirit as well as the letter of the law and to contribute to the well being of the communities where it operates.

Sources: Adapted from www.asda.co.uk (9 August 2002), and www.youra sda.com (26 April 2010); www.john-lewis-partnership.co.uk (1 November 2001, and 16 December 2013); *Retail Week*, 2 May 2014.

The organization's mission and strategy are normally set out in a series of **corporate objectives**, which are explicit time-related goals against which to assess organizational progress and achievements. They often incorporate marketing objectives, for example setting a percentage of market share, or a level of sales as a corporate target. However, particularly in large organizations, the corporate objectives are sometimes more general targets. Box 3.2 shows Sainsbury's corporate objectives outlined in the organization's 2011 annual report. Clearly, Sainsbury's will remain focused on food retailing while non-food ranges and other services will comprise an increasing proportion of the business. Online retailing and other channels to market are important; however, the company plans to continue growth of its physical presence in the market and plans to manage its physical property assets in a way that generates more profitability. Corporate objectives form the basis for planning and setting objectives for other operational areas such as logistics, marketing and human resource management.

Box 3.2 J Sainsbury plc: objectives

- To provide great food at fair prices.
- To accelerate the growth of complementary non-food ranges and services.
- To reach more customers through additional channels.
- To grow supermarket space.
- Active property management.

Source: J Sainsbury plc, *Annual Report 2011*.

3.4 Environmental analysis

A detailed analysis of key retail environmental considerations is given in Chapter 1. Environmental scanning will highlight major external influences that create the climate of opportunity for the organization (many of which are considered in Chapter 1). Commonly known as the PEST, STEP or SPELT factors (political, economic, social, legal and technological), the main environmental factors affecting retailers are:

- **Demographic and socio-cultural developments**: examples include population structure and change; income distribution; lifestyle changes; communication methods; work and leisure trends; consumerism; environmentalism; attitudes to globalization.
- **Government policy, regulatory agencies, pressure groups** (at transnational, national, regional and local levels): examples include stability of home and market governments; policies on taxation; transport; environment; planning; construction;

agriculture, horticulture, fisheries and food; training and education; consumer associations and environmental groups.

- **Legal framework – European and UK laws and regulations**: examples include legislation on health and safety; packaging and waste; disability discrimination; data protection; e-commerce; equal opportunities; monopolies; environmental protection.
- **Economic environment, capital and labour markets**: examples include taxation and interest rates; pension values; spending and saving patterns; employment levels; stage of business cycle (recession, recovery, prosperity); gross national product (GNP) trends, inflation, disposable income.
- **Technological environment**: examples include government spending on research; focus of technological effort; speed of technology transfer; rates of obsolescence; biotechnology, robotics; information technology.

Although it is important to identify and focus on those elements of the external environment that most closely affect the workings and operational direction of the organization, a broad knowledge of PEST trends and developments is essential for retail organizations because they operate in fast-paced, highly competitive environments, and many problems and opportunities are created by trends in the wider environment. The key environmental influences on the organization should be listed in a simple PEST analysis. More extensive PEST analyses can be used to assess the variable potential impacts of the key influences, or to gauge the extent of the impact of the key influences on the main competing organizations in a sector (Johnson *et al.*, 2010). Some analysts would also consider the competitive market and the organizational environment at this stage; others would propose structural analysis of the competitive environment as a sequential stage to environmental analysis.

Much of the research undertaken on the competitive environment in retailing has its roots in the works of Michael Porter on competitive strategy (1980) and competitive advantage (1985). Porter posited that high-performance industries were those that had strong channel power attributes and high barriers to entry to the market. In the 1980s he used the pharmaceutical industry in the USA to illustrate high performers compared with the newly regulated airline industry which had low barriers to entry, a high degree of competition and weak channel power. This formed the basis of his 'five forces' model to analyse the structure of the competitive environment (see Figure 3.2). According to this approach, the five forces that form the theatre of competition are:

- threat of entrants;
- bargaining power of suppliers;
- bargaining power of buyers;
- threat of substitutes; and
- competitive rivalry.

Threat of entrants: this depends on the barriers to entry such as economies of scale, capital needed to enter the market, likely retaliation of existing competitors, and access to distribution channels. In retailing the barriers to entry are low. It is relatively cheap and easy to set up a retail store on a small scale. One of the reasons it can be difficult to get comprehensive data on the extent of retail activity on a regional basis is because so many

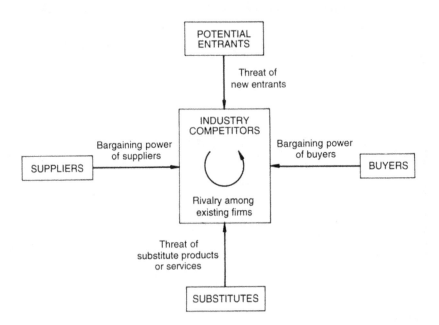

Figure 3.2 Porter's five forces model to analyse industry structure

small retailers start and fail on an annual basis. It is also relatively feasible for a major retailer to enter a local market and undercut local retailers through price competition enabled through cost advantages achievable through dominance in distribution channels. At transnational level, large-scale entry can be achieved through commercial, financial and political influence.

Bargaining power of suppliers: supplier power is likely to be high when there is a concentration of large suppliers with strong, established brands. A high cost of switching from one supplier to another increases power, as does technological 'tie-in'. Supplier power is also linked to the likelihood of forward integration in the marketing channel. The growth of retailer power over the last few decades has generally weakened the bargaining power of suppliers, as has the growth of globalization, where manufactured goods are sourced from cheap overseas suppliers. However, the growth of technological supplier–retailer links has increased bargaining power, as does the potential for larger-scale forward integration offered by factory warehouses, outlet centres and e-tailing.

Bargaining power of buyers: buyer power is clearly likely to be high when there is a concentration of buyers and volume of purchases is high, and this is especially the case where the goods being bought are difficult to differentiate in the eyes of the end customer. Bargaining power is also increased by the potential for buyers to integrate backwards in the distribution channel. Bargaining power is high among major retail organizations due to their large size and concentration in number; backwards integration is also a feature of large-scale retailing, and the growth of own-branding (and especially premium branding) also contributes to buyer power. In retailing it is also possible to conceive of 'the consumer' as buyer, and retailers who refer to the 'customer as dictator' are perhaps referring to the collective influence of customer bargaining power on the retail industry.

Threat of substitutes: this means substitution of organization, product or process. There have been a number of threats to the equilibrium of the retail market – the arrival of hard discounters threatened the grocery majors during the 1980s; the growth of retail parks threatened established town centre retailers; the dot.com boom and later strong growth in online retailing continues to undermine store-based retailing. Substitution also exists in the form of competition for customer spend. For retailers, the growing proportion of disposable income spent on leisure, travel and mortgages can pose substitution threat.

Competitive rivalry: this increases where barriers to entry are low, supplier or buyer power is high, and there is a high threat of substitutes. Other features of enhanced competitive rivalry that are evident in the retail market include:

- equality of size among the dominant organizations as each will push for market share;
- market in slow growth will further fuel rivalry;
- conditions in which weaker organizations will be absorbed (through merger, acquisition, alliance) by larger ones to increase market share; and
- high market exit costs through established property portfolios and long leases.

Five forces analysis can establish the balance of the competitive market and form a foundation for future strategy. Is it possible to reduce the threat of substitute by diversification, for example? Can barriers to entry be raised? What are the strengths and weaknesses of rival companies in relation to the key forces?

Retailing is a diverse sector and other aspects of Porter's work have relevance to our understanding of the competitive dynamics within the industry:

> A strategic group is the group of firms in an industry following the same or a similar strategy along the strategic dimensions … Usually, however, there are a small number of strategic groups which capture the essential strategic differences among firms in the industry.
>
> (Porter, 1980, p.129)

Porter draws on earlier work in his own university by industrial economists, notably Hunt (1972), who identified performance differences within an industry rather than between industries as discussed in the five forces model above. The term 'strategic groups' is therefore an attempt to identify clusters of companies within an industry that share similar strategic attributes. The number of attributes can vary from firm size to marketing channels, although most textbooks tend to use a two-dimensional framework, including our own example in Figure 4.4, which considers the relative positioning of UK grocery retailers on price and quality. Research on strategic groups has centred upon the grocery sector, with Lewis and Thomas (1990) assessing performance of strategic groups in UK grocery retailing, Flavian and Polo (1999) using cluster analysis to identify strategic groups in the UK and Spain to assess strategies in each market, and Cola (2003) segmenting 13 discount retailing brand names into three strategic groups.

3.5 Resource audit and analyses

Environmental audit and analysis will highlight potential external opportunities and threats to the organization. The exploitation of environmental opportunity requires:

- recognition that an opportunity exists; and
- assessment of whether the opportunity is viable.

The former requires management experience, creativity and acumen, in addition to organizational capability in environmental scanning and analysis, and organizational communication systems that facilitate the vertical flow of market and consumer information. The latter requires assessment of the opportunity against organizational capability.

A corporate audit is the objective assessment of the organization's financial, material and human resource capability, and should also take into consideration intangibles such as corporate image, goodwill, brand name, strength of supply network and contact network. Indeed, it can be argued, especially in a retail context, that intangible resources are the key to competitive advantage. De Wit and Meyer (2010) identify two forms of intangible resources: relational resources through the building up of relationships or reputation (branding), and competences through the creation of knowledge, capabilities and corporate culture. The financial resource audit may include:

- sources of capital and credit;
- control of debtors and creditors;
- cash management;
- relationship with key financial contacts; and
- investments.

The physical resource audit may include:

- property portfolio − size/age/location/state of repair;
- equipment − amount/capability/location/age/durability; and
- physical resources outsourced to organizations and relationships.

The human resource audit may include:

- organizational structure;
- numbers and deployment of staff;
- contracts/job descriptions/flexibility;
- staff skills and capabilities; and
- human resource function − recruitment agency and relationships.

A comprehensive, objective audit should highlight where the organization's core competences lie − that is, those strengths which give it a competitive edge. This allows a more rational judgement of its potential to exploit opportunities. Organizations do not operate in isolation, and there is a variety of supplementary theories and analyses which give further insight into resource capability in the retail context. Four of these are resource-based theory, value chain analysis, network theory and, most widely known, SWOT analysis.

Resource-based theory of the firm focuses on the various resources, capabilities and core competences within organizations that will allow it to compete effectively. This 'inside out' approach to competitive advantage was advocated by Prahalad and Hamel (1990), Barney (1991) and Peteraf (1993) in the early 1990s. Dynamic capabilities are created over time and may depend on the organization's past use of resources. Sustainable competitive advantage depends on the ability and creativity of the organization in the acquisition, combination and deployment of resources to yield productivity or value advantages. The resources that are a source of sustainable value are those which are difficult to copy because they lie within organizational activities and routines that represent core competences.

Competitive advantage is dependent upon the ownership or acquisition of superior rent earning, unique resources and relationships. The outsourcing of functions can be seen, therefore, as a means of accessing the resource base (and hence core competences) of other organizations to create sustainable value (Cox, 1996). For example, a company with specific core skills in logistics should contract internally for the use of these skills, but complementary skills such as information technology or human resource management might be better contracted out on a partnership basis, securing access to the resource base of partnership organizations. Unrelated skills such as car park maintenance could be outsourced on an 'arm's length' basis.

Value chain analysis (see Chapter 9 on retail logistics) focuses on achievement of competitive advantage through organizational competences, and helps to show where the organization can add value and create cost savings in business and supply chain processes. Porter's (1985) value chain is the horizontal axis in his five forces model whereby a firm performs a series of activities from designing a product to sourcing suppliers to produce it, then to brand and market the finished good to final consumers (see Figure 3.2). Many supply chain activities in retailing are not unique in that new processes and technologies can be copied and are easy to imitate. It is the intangible resources that are the key to adding value in the retail supply chain, especially in fashion, where design, branding and staffing skills give competitive advantage.

The **network theory** perspective assumes that organizations depend on resources controlled by other firms. Access to these resources is gained by interactions with these firms through the creation of value chain partnerships and networks. **Network theory** focuses on creating partnerships based on trust, cross-functional teamwork and inter-organizational cooperation (Ford *et al.*, 2011). Rather than one organization gaining competitive advantage over another, it is more a case of one network competing against another (Christopher and Peck, 1997). Again, non-core organizational activities are outsourced, but efficiencies and the effectiveness of the network are regarded as essential for organizational success (also see Chapter 9 and the Benetton case).

SWOT (strengths, weaknesses, opportunities and threats) analysis is a widely used means of rationalizing and prioritizing the outcomes of environmental analysis and the resource audit. First, the main strengths and weaknesses of the organization, highlighted through the resource audit, are listed. Then the main opportunities and threats for the organization, revealed by analysis of the external and competitive environment, are summarized. A SWOT analysis can be further refined by matching core competences to the key environmental trends and thereby provide weightings according to the potential level of effect – positive or negative – on the organization. This brings together the 'inside out' and 'outside in' perspectives so that retailers can plan investment in resources to meet challenges for the future. Even after refinement, SWOT analysis remains a subjective tool; nevertheless, it remains a well-used aid to strategy which is also used at a functional level. For example, a SWOT analysis is frequently carried out as part of the marketing planning process.

3.6 Strategic choice

3.6.1 Generic strategies

Traditionally, retailers have three main strategic choices using the framework derived from Porter's generic strategies (Porter, 1996). First, they can focus on **cost**, driving down organizational costs through streamlining their operations, logistics and other functions. This cost efficiency can be used either to create sufficient margin to provide quality products and services, or to drive down prices and create volume throughput. This cost focus has created success for a great many retailers, including Germany's Aldi and the USA's Walmart.

Second, retailers can differentiate their **offer**, creating value for their customers in the retailer brand itself. Here the organization's efforts are concentrated on achieving an offer that is different from those of other retailers, thereby attracting customers who are willing to pay a premium price for added value. Many retail organizations have benefited from this strategy, among them luxury fashion retailers such as Louis Vuitton and Versace, and department stores such as Harrods and Saks Fifth Avenue.

Third, retailers can focus on a highly targeted **market segment**, directing organizational efforts to filling the needs of a known and predetermined group of customers, using either a low cost base or differentiation depending on the segment. Smaller retailers such as Fortnum & Mason, with limited resources, can develop using this strategy, and since the 1990s larger retailers have used 'focus' as a means of developing successful targeted versions of their 'mother' retail format – for example, Tesco express and Tesco extra.

A fourth option, which is pursued by some large retail groups, is to pursue simultaneously all three strategies under the guise of differing retailer brands. This is facilitated by the growth in multi-channel retailing, in highly detailed customer and segment information, and in ways to shop – including by foot, online, mail order, TV and mobile phone. However, there is a risk that cost focus in one subsidiary of the business will compromise the differentiated quality brand of another subsidiary – for example, the move to diffusion brands by some luxury fashion companies.

Piercy (2001) claimed that **revolutionary** strategy is about **breaking free**. His views build upon Porter's (1996) seminal work on strategy, in which Porter criticized managers for confusing strategy with operational excellence. Strategy is about being different, not adopting the latest management fad. This is echoed by Piercy, who states that organizational strategists should free themselves from management tools and tactics such as TQM (total quality management), business re-engineering and efficient consumer response, because these focus on operations – no substitute for leadership and visionary strategic direction. It means that strategy is about breaking free of industry 'rules' and 'dogma', because customers do not know the 'rules' anyway. The term 'breaking free' really means that strategists:

- should embrace rather than fear change;
- should not be confined by current operational issues;
- should be careful not to be over-influenced by trendy management tools and theories;
- should not be over-reliant on performance indicators, which reflect only past performance; and
- need to understand the core competences of the organization, and think laterally to apply these core competences to add value to the business and build differentiation from the competition.

It is important here to distinguish between corporate strategy and marketing strategy. The former relates to the direction taken by the organization and the latter relates this to the market situation. However, in many market-orientated commercial organizations such as retailers, there is a strong correlation between the two, and then corporate strategy may incorporate strategic marketing elements such as format development, market entry, market penetration and diversification of market activities, as shown in the next section.

3.6.2 Expansion strategies

Marketing strategy entails a series of decisions about products (or product/service bundles) and markets which will exploit market opportunities. Although many market opportunities are spotted and exploited through market knowledge, networking and business instinct, there is a simple, though useful, aid to decision making called the product–market expansion grid (see Figure 3.3).

This grid categorizes opportunities under four headings:

Market penetration: this focuses on the products and services currently offered by the organization; opportunities are sought that will increase the organization's share of the market. There is a variety of ways in which this can be done, depending on the nature of the organization's business activities. It can be done by increasing the amount and scope of promotional activities – through advertising or sales promotions, for example. A change of pricing strategy can also increase penetration, as can making products more widely available within the current distribution network.

Product development: here the focus is on changing the products and services offered by the organization, through increasing the range or through product/service modification or extension. Marketers can build brand recognition and use the brand to launch new products/services, or to extend the product line through new additions. They can make current products more 'buyable' through the design of new or additional features.

Market development: this focuses the efforts of marketers on developing, profiling and meeting the needs of new segments of the market. This can be done by extending the range of the market into new areas, regions or countries, or by promoting products/services to a new category of users.

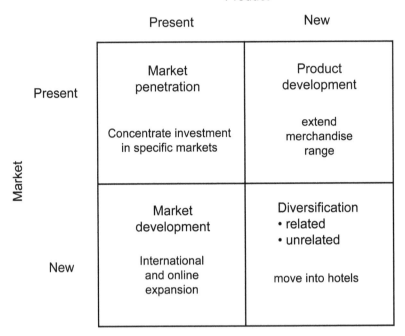

Figure 3.3 Alternative directions of growth for the luxury fashion brand
Source: After Ansoff 1988.

Diversification: opportunities can be sought that are very different from those traditionally exploited by the organization, through buying a new business, or using the strength of the organization's brand to launch new products or services that meet the needs of a new market area. Normally, opportunities for diversification exploit the core competences of the organization and will be confined by its resource capabilities. What kind of opportunities does the grid offer to retailers? They can use the grid to consider market opportunities for extending product and service range and markets, as explained above, or they can use the grid to consider corporate opportunities for the retail organization.

Fernie (2012) used the Ansoff grid to explain the evolution of luxury fashion brands (see Figure 3.3). Currently, most of the main Italian and French brands (and Burberry) are increasing their market penetration in China and moving into tier two and tier three cities as the main coastal tier one cities reach market saturation. The fact that China has become the market with most potential in the 2000s with growth rates of 20–35 per cent per annum shows how market development has evolved. The main European fashion houses targeted the USA in the 1960s and 1970s, Japan in the 1980s and 1990s, and now China. Other new market developments have occurred in the last decade, however, with the rise of online and off-price channels that account for around 8 per cent of sales in total. All major luxury brands have moved into new products and services, building upon their brand reputation for craftsmanship and heritage of their traditional core product: Louis Vuitton (handbags); Burberry (the trench coat). Armani has the most extensive product range of all the luxury brands and is one of five Italian fashion brands that have diversified into hotels. Even then it can be argued that Versace, Armani and Missoni have engaged in new product development in that their Casa collections are represented in their hotels. Nevertheless, nearly all of these fashion companies have entered into joint ventures or licensing agreements with international hotel chains or property development companies to develop this business. The locations of these hotels mirror Hollander's (1970) 'fashion capitals' of internationalization, adding Tokyo and Shanghai to the original fashion show sites (see Chapter 5 on internationalization). Some companies have a stronger focus on resort locations. Indeed, it is a Versace hotel to which stars of the British TV show *I'm a Celebrity …* *Get Me Out of Here* retire on the Gold Coast of Australia when exiting the jungle!

McGoldrick (2002) has also discussed expansion strategies through a series of growth vectors that overlap with many of the elements of the product/market matrix. They come under the following headings:

- existing proposition;
- new products/services;
- new segments;
- geographical development;
- new channels; and
- new formats.

Each direction of growth offers scope for expansion on a continuum from the existing operational platform through related activity to a new operational platform. Expansion of a nature related to the core retail offer (which houses the core competences of the organization) is less risky than expansion onto an operational platform that is new to the organization.

Expansion of the core operational platform is where the **existing proposition** grows market share through organic growth – that is, through investment in growing the current business, or by acquiring share through acquisition, merger or other methods of expansion, bringing the new business into line with the core business. Non-organic growth is likely to require adaptations to the core business, which interrelate with other growth vectors such as format modification and channel development, in order to integrate diverse operational platforms successfully.

New segment development involves developing, profiling and targeting new consumer and organizational segments. A fashion retailer could, for example, extend into childrenswear and menswear. A more radical strategy would entail moving into unrelated segments such as uniforms or workwear.

New products/services development has been the focus of much recent retail strategy, as new merchandise and an extended service offering exploits the potential of current markets. Simple examples include extended opening of grocery stores and addition of food or beverages in non-food retailers such as bookshops and travel agents.

Format modification and development is a further focus of retail strategy in which styles of retailing are tailored to the needs of customer segments. Examples include off-price stores and factory outlet units offering excess or experimental stock at value prices.

Channel strengths can be exploited in the development of new retail activity. Tesco, for example, made use of its national store network to roll out its e-tail format rapidly, then used its online platform to develop its range of producer–customer and wholesaler–customer distributed goods.

Geographical development involves growth of market share through movement into adjacent areas and regions and, more radically, into international or global expansion.

There are many links among the various growth vectors. Segment development will normally require development of new products and services; channel and segment development may be interrelated, as may format, segment and product/service development.

3.6.3 Methods of expansion

The three main methods of expansion are:

- organic growth;
- mergers/acquisitions; and
- strategic alliance.

Organic growth is investment channelled from the financial capability of the current organization into development of organizational capability – for example, to fund the development and roll-out of formats, horizontal or vertical integration and international growth. Growth tends to be slow or steady, and the organization retains autonomy, decision-making control, and benefits from development of new areas of competence, while avoiding the difficulties of integrating differing organizational cultures and management systems, experienced by organizations growing through acquisition or merger. However, rapid organic growth is possible where there is access to capital, by, for example, raising money through issuing extra shares rights to investors. With regard to international expansion, organic growth is the favoured option for many privately owned companies that wish to retain control over their development and are under less pressure than publicly listed companies for short-term returns. The German discounters Lidl and Aldi have tended to grow organically; indeed, Aldi's only international acquisition was Trader Joe's in the distant US market.

From a locational perspective, there are two major types of organic growth. Local and regional expansion from a single outlet, termed contagious diffusion, describes the early growth experience of long-established retailers that were geographically confined by transportation and distribution networks. It is the expansion method chosen by many small retail businesses, but has also been used by dominant retailers such as Walmart (Birkin *et al.*, 2002). The second type, **hierarchical diffusion**, is the growth route for many established retail organizations that open outlets in major cities and towns. We discussed this in the previous section with regard to luxury fashion retailers opening flagship stores in tier one cities in China, then moving to tier two and tier three cities, but this pattern is also evident in other markets, for example in the UK, targeting London before moving to provincial cities. On a more mundane level, Sainsbury's entry into Scotland is also an example. Stores were opened in rapid succession in Glasgow, Edinburgh, Aberdeen and Dundee – Scotland's four largest cities. Smaller stores were opened in regional town centres, and 'local' stores built to serve less populous communities as Sainsbury's progressed its expansion. Both strategies can be deployed simultaneously by rolling out operations in selected large urban centres and expanding outwards by contagious diffusion.

Merger and acquisition offers a route to growth in market share and market dominance in addition to rapid entry of new product and market areas. A merger is where two retail organizations come together to form a combined operation, whereas acquisition describes the action of one retailer buying more than a 50 per cent share of another. Both methods have been widely used by retailers competing in the international retail market, such as Tesco, Ahold and Casino, which benefit from the acquisition across diverse markets of sources of established expertise, knowledge, property portfolio, contact and supply networks in addition to the customer base.

Tesco's expansion into Scotland, in competition with Sainsbury's, was accelerated through acquisition of Wm Low & Co., a regionally dominant grocery multiple, and established the organization as a main player in the Scottish market both physically and in the minds of the Scottish consumer. Stricter planning policy came into force at about the same time, which also made organic growth through new-build operations more expensive and time consuming. Walmart used this method of international expansion when it acquired the chain of Asda superstores to secure entry to the UK market. While access to a wide geographical coverage in the UK 'fitted' Walmart's ambitions for global expansion, the property portfolio offered the potential for expansion of existing superstores to Asda-Walmart supercentres. The Asda mix of successful clothing and non-food merchandise categories with groceries also resembled that of the parent company. In addition, it could be argued that there was also a psychological 'fit', because Asda was one of the superstore pioneers in the UK, with a long-established and popular reputation among its customers for good value at low prices; indeed, its 'everyday low pricing' strategy also matched that of the parent company (see Chapter 5 on internationalization).

One of the main problems with acquisition is the merging of organizational cultures and styles of management, and this is exacerbated by the prospect of rationalization of activities and closure of outlets, which creates job uncertainty. Where organizations merge voluntarily, the potential for organizational conflict is reduced due to the focus on the synergistic benefits of the merger. However, rationalization is a common feature post-merger and acquisition, particularly where the organization is left with two or more competing stores within a comparatively small area, which affects potential profitability. Future merger or acquisition between grocery majors in the UK is likely to bring a level of monopoly that would force rationalization through the actions of the Competition Commission. For example, the 2008 inquiry into UK grocery retailing recommended a competition test that would restrict market development by dominant grocers (Competition Commission, 2008).

Strategic alliances, where two or more organizations come together to complete a project, to wield combined power or to gain synergy from the combination of diverse organizational competences and assets, are a growing feature of retailing, aided by implementation of principles of relationship marketing and facilitated by enhanced communication capability. There are three main types of strategic alliance:

- **Loose relationships**: collaborative networks and alliances to exploit a market opportunity or to combat a market threat. Examples include buying groups such as Agentrics (formerly WorldWide Retail Exchange (WWRE) and GlobalNetXchange (GNX) which were created to facilitate product procurement).
- **Contractual relationships**: subcontracting of licences and franchises. The former is where the right to produce or distribute a product is granted for a fee; the latter involves a contract to a franchisee to produce, distribute or sell merchandise or services, while the franchisor maintains and markets the brand. In-store franchising (or concessions) is where a retail or service organization leases floor space within an existing store format such as a superstore or department store. There are four main types of franchise:

  - Manufacturer–dealer. In this relationship the manufacturer is the franchisor and the dealer sells to the consumer. Cars and petrol manufacturers have traditionally used this method of distribution.
  - Manufacturer–wholesaler. The manufacturer is the franchisor while the wholesaler acts as franchisee, selling to retailers. Examples are cola and beer manufacturers.
  - Wholesaler–retailer. Voluntary chains such as Mace and Spar are examples. The parent organization offers marketing, distribution and merchandising support.
  - Business format. The parent company allows the franchisee to sell its products or services, and provides an established format together with help and support in setting up business.

  Franchising allows rapid expansion through the utilization of the financial and human resources of franchisees, although there is some loss of control, together with concomitant reduction in costs, of implementing standards and procedures.
- **Formalized ownership/relationships**: joint ventures and consortia where two or more organizations set up a jointly owned organization, to facilitate expansion or exploit a market opportunity. In many cases this may be the only feasible method of entering an international market, for example Walmart's initial entry into Mexico and Japan, and McArthurGlen's entry into the UK with factory outlet centres. In Walmart's case, the 1991 expansion in partnership with Mexican retailer Cifra was followed six years later by acquisition. The Cifra name was replaced by Wal-Mart de Mexico. Similarly, Tesco entered the Thai market in 1994 with a joint venture and gradually increased its shareholding until it fully owned Tesco Lotus in 2004. A joint venture also minimizes risk when diversifying into new product markets, for example when Sainsbury's moved into the DIY market with GB Inno and the clothing market with BHS, to develop Homebase and SavaCentre, respectively.

3.7 Summary

This chapter has reviewed the main strategic tools available to retailers to formulate and then implement a retail strategy. The two main approaches to strategy formulation were discussed; the 'outside in' macro-environmental approach which embraces a PESTLE analysis (political, economic, social, technological, legal and environmental factors), compared with the 'inside out' approach that assesses the unique resources that a company can marshal to gain competitive advantage. Many of the concepts explored here drew upon the works of Michael Porter, especially on assessing a company's competitive position in the marketplace. His generic strategies also provided a framework for determining strategic choices for companies prior to discussing growth strategies with the aid of growth vector matrices such as the commonly used Ansoff product/market matrix.

Review questions

1   Discuss the 'outside in' compared with the 'inside out' approach to formulating a retailer's strategy.
2   Evaluate the works of Michael Porter in assessing a retailer's competitive positioning.
3   Using strategic choice models, evaluate the growth strategies of luxury fashion brand retailers.
4   Critically evaluate the advantages and disadvantages of the three main methods of expansion adopted by retailers.

References

Ansoff, H.I. (1988) *New Corporate Strategy: An Analytical Approach in Business Policy for Growth and Expansion*. New York: John Wiley.
Barney, J. (1991) 'Firm resources and sustained competitive advantage', *Journal of Management*, 11: 99–120.
Birkin, M., Clarke, G. and Clarke, M. (2002) *Retail Geography and Intelligent Network Planning*. Chichester: John Wiley.
Christopher, M. and Peck, H. (1997) *Marketing Logistics*. Oxford: Butterworth-Heinemann.
Cola, E. (2003) 'International expansion and strategies of discount grocery retailers: the winning models', *International Journal of Retail & Distribution Management*, 31(1): 55–66.
Competition Commission (2008) *Groceries Market Investigation: Final Report* [online], www.competition-commission.org.uk/press_rel/2008/apr/pdf/14-08.pdf (accessed 27 July 2010).
Cox, A. (1996) 'Relationship competence and strategic procurement management. Towards an entrepreneurial and contractual theory of the firm', *European Journal of Purchasing and Supply Management*, 2(1): 57–70.
De Wit, B. and Meyer, R. (2010) *Strategy: Process, Content, Context – An International Perspective* (4th edn). London: Cengage.
Fernie, J. (2012) 'The evolution of the luxury fashion brand', Keynote address, The International Workshop on Luxury Retail, Operations and Supply Chain Management, Milan, December.
Flavian, C. and Polo, Y. (1999) 'Strategic groups analysis as a tool for strategic marketing', *European Journal of Marketing*, 33(5/6): 548–569.
Ford, D., Gadde, L.-E., Hakansson, H. and Snehota, I. (2011) *Managing Business Relationships* (3rd edn). Chichester: Wiley.
Hollander, S. (1970) *Multinational Retailing*. East Lansing: Michigan State University.
Hunt, M. (1972) *Competition in the major home appliance industry*. Doctoral dissertation, Harvard University, Boston, MA.

Johnson, G., Scholes, K. and Whittington, R. (2010) *Exploring Corporate Strategy*. Hemel Hempstead: Prentice Hall.

Lewis, P. and Thomas, H. (1990) 'The linkage between strategic groups and performance in the UK retail grocery industry', *Strategic Management Journal*, 11(5): 385–397.

McGoldrick, P. (2002) *Retail Marketing*. Maidenhead: McGraw-Hill Education.

Peteraf, M.A. (1993) 'The cornerstone of competitive advantage: a resource-based view', *Strategic Management Journal*, 14: 179–191.

Piercy, N. (2001) *Market-Led Strategic Change* (3rd edn). Oxford: Butterworth-Heinemann.

Porter, M. (1980) *Competitive Strategy: Techniques for Analyzing Industries and Competitors*. New York: Free Press.

Porter, M. (1985) *Competitive Advantage*. New York: Free Press.

Porter, M. (1996) 'What is strategy?' *Harvard Business Review* (November/December): 61–78.

Prahalad, C.K. and Hamel, G. (1990) 'The core competencies of the corporation', *Harvard Business Review*, 68(3): 79–91.

Reilly, W.J. (1931) *The Laws of Retail Gravitation*. New York: Knickerbocker Press.

Zentes, J., Morschett, D. and Schramm-Klein, H. (2011) 'Strategic retail management: Text and international cases', in *Customer Relationship Management* (2nd edn). Wiesbaden: Gabler.

4 Strategic retail marketing 2

Market segmentation and the service marketing mix

Learning objectives

After studying this chapter, you should be able to:

- Segment the retail market to position companies within their target market.
- Profile customers by various indices of consumer behaviour.
- Evaluate the role of retail branding in achieving competitive advantage.
- Critically assess the use of various elements of the service marketing mix in achieving market objectives.

4.1 Introduction

Chapter 3 mainly concentrated upon the main strategic retail marketing decisions – the nature of the macro environment, competition and routes to growth. This chapter focuses on how markets are segmented, the positioning of companies within markets, retail branding and the implementation of the marketing mix. Most retail textbooks incorporate elements of the service marketing literature into defining the retail marketing mix, for example, McGoldrick (2002) identifies nine elements from product design to customer relationships. Here discussion will focus upon the retail marketing mix within the context of the service marketing mix.

4.2 Market segmentation

A market is a set of actual and potential buyers of a product. Market segmentation involves:

- determining which segment or segments of the market the organization can serve profitably;
- profiling the customers – building an understanding of their values and buying habits, and finding out where they are;
- positioning the organization's offer against competitors in the marketplace;
- establishing the position in the mind of the target customers through building brand identity; and
- deciding on a coverage strategy.

Anyone can go into a store, and anyone with a computer and modem can go on a website, so why segment? Segmentation helps to build the retail offer around the needs of the key customer group or groups.

Traditionally, retailers served a geographic segment of the market, serving a village, town or city. The size of the segment was determined by the size of the population and hinterland. Traditional retail organizations tend to be organized around the regions served. Prices are often set according to regional or local levels of competitiveness, and products are often sold that appeal to regional tastes. Local media are used for promotions. With the growth of online retailing, even small retailers have the opportunity to operate nationally or internationally, and the importance of geographic segmentation will reduce in the future. In St Andrews, a number of retail businesses sell golf merchandise to visiting golfers and tourists. Now they can sell to golfers worldwide. These retailers have to decide whether to carry on using geographic segmentation or to segment by lifestyle – travellers, golfers, Internet users – and/or by demographic variables such as income, socio-economic group or age.

Fashion design retailers have made use of segmentation to develop their markets. In addition to entering and growing their presence in geographical markets, they developed their product markets by growing their 'diffusion brand' business targeted at different socio-economic groups (Moore *et al.*, 2000). Moore and Birtwistle (2004) used the case of Burberry to illustrate not only how the company segmented its market but how it repositioned a tired British brand as an iconic luxury heritage brand. Figure 4.1 shows how the couture brand (Burberry Prorsum) is targeted at exclusive customers, Burberry London is the ready-to-wear collection distributed through upscale department stores, and the diffusion brands (Burberry Brit, Burberry Blue and Burberry Black) have widespread distribution in stand-alone stores in the main fashion capitals of the world. Note that the Thomas Burberry line was discontinued in early 2010.

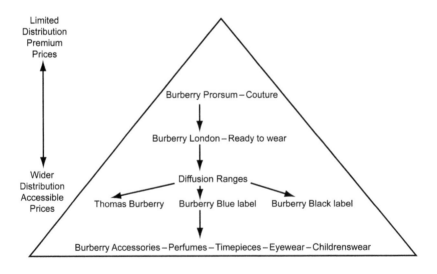

Figure 4.1 The Burberry model, 2004
Source: Moore and Birtwistle, 2004

Tesco is an example of a large retail organization that has successfully changed from using geographic segmentation to behaviour segmentation, building successful formats around the way people buy (convenience shop, work shop, one-stop shop, e-shop, etc.). Everyone shops for groceries, so that demographic segmentation would have been inadvisable. Behaviour segmentation in this case recognizes the growing trend for individuals to shop in different ways at different times. The same person on one occasion may want to grab a sandwich and a ready meal for dinner from a town centre shop, and on another occasion may want to enjoy a leisurely monthly superstore shop. This eventually, and logically, resulted in organizational change, with groups of stores managed not regionally, but by format.

4.2.1 Profiling: understanding customer values

Finding out about the size and make-up of the segment and building up a profile of customers within it is the key to successful positioning and branding. A variety of information on markets and customers can be found using secondary research, making use of reference materials, government and commercial statistical sources. The Mintel Group, Retail Knowledge Bank (part of EMAP), the IGD and the Oxford Institute of Retail Management all publish periodic market reports which retailers find useful. For example, the IGD publishes key account profiles of the leading grocery retailers in the UK and tracks consumer behaviour of grocery shoppers every month.

Widely used secondary reference materials include:

- *Social Trends.*
- *Economic Trends.*
- *Census of Population.*
- *Production Statistics.*
- *Business Monitor.*
- *Census of Distribution.*
- *Family Spending.*
- *Labour Market Trends.*

National Statistics Online now provides access to a wide range of information relevant for retailers operating in the UK, including economic, family spending, production, labour market and Census data, via www.ons.gov.uk.

With the advent of social media, retailers have access to even more data on which to target customers with a range of offers. Facebook has undertaken partnerships with data companies to combine records of customers' offline purchase histories with Facebook's customer audiences. The question here is do companies spend sufficient resources to personalize messages or do they adopt a traditional advertising 'scatter-gun' approach? Unless the company is a pure online player, such as Amazon, the answer is probably no.

The best commercial example of customer profiling through the use of loyalty card data is that of Tesco (see Box 4.1). This case shows how you can gain competitive advantage through investing in the IT infrastructure. This not only enabled the company to profile their customer base, but also allowed them to understand shifts in buying habits: most notably, the introduction of their 'Finest' range was prompted by defections of customers to

Marks & Spencer. None of their direct competitors at the time was willing to invest in loyalty cards – Sainsbury's, then the market leader, ridiculed the move as electronic Green Shield stamps, a reference to a trading stamps scheme common in the trade whereby books of stamps were redeemed for cash or gifts. Within a few years Tesco also launched their online service – another contributory factor that not only gave Tesco first mover advantage but market leadership that they have never looked like relinquishing since.

Box 4.1 Tesco's Clubcard and customer profiling

When the husband and wife team of Edwina Dunn and Clive Humby formed Dunnhumby in 1989 they probably did not realize that they would enable Tesco to become the international retailer it is today, and that their company would become a subsidiary of Tesco. In 1994 they trialled a preliminary loyalty card for Tesco. When discussing the venture, the chairman of the company at the time, Lord MacLaurin, was reported to have stated at a board meeting that they knew more about his company in three months than he knew after 30 years in the business. When Terry Leahy, the marketing director who was to become CEO, launched the Tesco Clubcard in February 1995, computer power was much slower than today so only a small proportion of all weekly data was analysed to build a profile of Tesco customers. These customers were 'rewarded' one loyalty point for every pound spent and could redeem these points by spending in store or through a range of organizations, for example to acquire air miles, hotel breaks and visit leisure attractions. By the 2010s, Tesco was issuing Clubcard statements to over 15 million British shoppers. Personal letters are sufficiently customized to offer 4 million variations to Clubcard members.

Tesco has been able to segment its customer base and build profiles of these segments through data derived from its Clubcard transactions and other feedback mechanisms, such as focus groups, consumer panels and complaints. Figure 4.2 shows the basic registration data collected from customers and how profiles are developed from transaction and other data sources. By using a range of increasingly sophisticated data-mining techniques, Tesco can form a profile of customers based on their loyalty/promiscuity, Finest/Value ranges, and type of format preferred. Over 25,000 products are rated against lifestyle segments such as those depicted in Figure 4.3. Here we can see how these products appeal to a range of consumers from the price conscious to the healthy eater.

Although the Clubcard has given Tesco greater insight into its grocery shoppers, it has also allowed the company to undertake market research on customers who are likely to seek Clubcard rewards in new markets that the company has developed as part of its corporate strategy. Tesco's move into personal banking, telecoms and the non-food sector, both in-store and online, has been facilitated by the first mover advantage of creating a strong IT infrastructure.

Source: Zentes *et al.*, 2011; Humby *et al.*, 2007.

Background: Tesco Clubcard

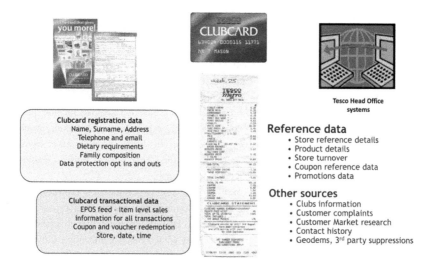

Tesco Head Office systems

Clubcard registration data
Name, Surname, Address
Telephone and email
Dietary requirements
Family composition
Data protection opt ins and outs

Clubcard transactional data
EPOS feed - item level sales
information for all transactions
Coupon and voucher redemption
Store, date, time

Reference data
• Store reference details
• Product details
• Store turnover
• Coupon reference data
• Promotions data

Other sources
• Clubs information
• Customer complaints
• Customer Market research
• Contact history
• Geodems, 3rd party suppressions

Figure 4.2 Background: Tesco Clubcard

Creating lifestyle segments

▪ Each product is categorised using a series of dimensions

▪Low Price
▪Tesco Own
▪Value range
▪Multipack

▪Fresh
▪Loose
▪Vegetarian
▪Adventurous
▪Healthy

▪Tesco Own
▪Pre-packed
▪Convenience

• 25,000 products are 'flagged' in this way, which accounts for about 95% sales

• Looking for the balance of key dimensions in each customers shopping basket

Figure 4.3 Creating lifestyle segments

4.2.2 Positioning

Positioning is about understanding and establishing the position of your brand in comparison to the relative positions of competing brands in the minds of your target customers, in terms of key dimensions such as price and quality. Figure 4.4 provides a basic positioning of UK grocery retailers on these dimensions. It should be noted that the German discounters are now perceived to be much further left on the quality axis (see Box 4.2 on Aldi's marketing communications strategy). Also note that Somerfield was taken over by The Co-operative Group, although the Co-op's positioning is similar to that depicted here. Taken further, what are the dimensions in which to establish a position? Examples include quality, value for money, value added, width of product range, reputation, convenience, level of service and level of credit. However, a comprehensive profile of the selected market segment (or segments) should include information on the criteria that govern target customers' choice of products within the proposed merchandise range.

In the first edition of this book we showed how French Connection repositioned its FCUK brand in the late 1990s. French Connection claimed that rather than repositioning, the intention was to reframe the FC brand to add 'attitude' to what French Connection already stood for. In fact, it is possible to argue that what French Connection did was to change the criteria in which they were positioning the brand from price/quality to price/

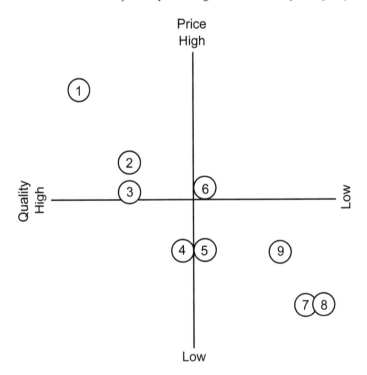

Figure 4.4 Possible relative positions of UK grocery retailers, 2010
Key: 1 Fortnum & Mason; 2 Marks & Spencer; 3 Sainsbury's; 4 Tesco; 5 Asda; 6 Morrisons; 7 Aldi; 8 Lidl; 9 Somerfield.

brand attitude. By doing so, this brand became clustered with more aggressive, design-led fashion brands in the minds of fashion shoppers, instead of being clustered with the more passive, mainstream fashion brands such as Gap, Next and Principles.

Understanding the relative positions of competing retailers helps a retail organization to decide its desired position, to establish it in the minds of its target customer group through branding and promotion, and to defend or redefine it as markets change. Positioning helps to establish the organization's unique selling proposition (USP) – that is, what it is that makes it different from other retailers, and what will bring in the customers. In the case of French Connection, the 'in-yer-face' slogan, which in the minds of customers was applied to the attitude of the merchandise, became the USP.

In the luxury brand sector, the repositioning of 'tired' brands has been a feature of the literature in the 2000s, with many companies hoping to 'do a Burberry' – a reference to the turnaround of the British fashion brand discussed in section 4.2. In addition to Burberry, the most celebrated case of repositioning was the turnaround of Gucci from near bankruptcy to the world's second most important luxury fashion brand. There are some parallels in the factors for success – a re-emphasis on design (Tom Ford/Christopher Bailey) and greater control over their supply chain through buying back licences and opening their own flagship stores. In addition, Moore and Birtwistle (2005) argue that a strong contributor to Gucci's success was the benefits of 'parenting advantage' – that is, having the benefit of capital infusion from being part of a larger group.

Positioning in a physical sense is also a useful tool for retailers. For comparison goods – merchandise for which customers visit several retailers to compare quality, prices and styles – location close to an established retail brand with a similar or complementary range of merchandise can attract customers of the right demographic or buying behaviour profiles. Thorntons established itself as a high street confectionery retailer by establishing small units close to Marks & Spencer outlets to attract volume ABC1 shoppers. Space NK locates close to Whistles to attract the high-spending fashion brand shoppers. In Edinburgh, French Connection opened on George Street, distancing itself physically from the high street fashion brands located on Princes Street, instead positioning itself with the design-led fashion brand retailers located on the street that ends at Harvey Nichols department store.

In the electronic shopping sphere, positioning via links quickly became a trend. For example, e-tailers of investment-related goods, such as art and photography (eyestorm.com), business travel (travelstore.com), fine wines (Virginwines.com) and upmarket foods (fortnumandmason.com), make offers to the moneyed investors on the interactive investors members' database.

4.3 Retail branding

If positioning is made easier through identifying target customers' perception of the retail offering relative to competing offerings on the desired dimensions, **branding** is the way to establish the position in the minds of customers. Successful branding, based on a consistent offering in the desired position within those dimensions, will build retail success.

The term 'brand' and the evolution of the brand concept has been the subject of much discussion over the last few decades. As the complexity of the concept has evolved, so has the complexity of branding definitions. Similarly, the evolution of the retail brand has led to a range of confusing terminologies. In essence, the brand has moved from being synonymous with physical identity (a name, logo, legal entity) to a range of emotional attributes through to an experience and a set of defining relationships (Rubinstein, 2002). Jevons (2007) provides a definition that covers all these elements of the brand:

> A brand is a tangible or intangible concept that uniquely identifies an offering, providing symbolic communication of functionality and differentiation, and in so doing sustainably influences the value offered.
>
> (Jevons, 2007, p. 7)

The problem with Rubinstein's and Jevons's definitions of branding is that they deal with product branding. As companies have internationalized their brands, they have used them as a vehicle to communicate their corporate values and image – they have become corporate brands:

> Product brands live in the present ... corporate brands live in the past and future; stimulate associations with heritage and articulate strategic vision of what is to come.
>
> (Hatch and Schultz, 2003, p. 1045)

This quote illustrates the importance of history and heritage in creating brand values; this is of paramount importance in the luxury fashion brand sector, discussed later. In their review of retail branding research, Burt and Davies (2010) discuss similar trends in retail branding to those in the general branding literature. In their review they show how early retail branding research focused upon product characteristics, and more recent research discusses retail internationalization and the corporate brand.

4.3.1 Growth and development of retail brands

Retail brands are those that have been developed by retailers rather than manufacturers. The rise of the retail brand is commensurate with the shift in balance of power between manufacturer and retailer over the last 20–30 years. Traditionally, retailers were the agents for manufacturer-branded products. The suppliers of fast-moving consumer goods (FMCGs) would market their product to the consumer, and consumers would buy from the retailer stocking it. As retailers moved from small family businesses to national or international companies, retailers began to move into new product development to meet the needs of an enlarged customer base, developing retail brands. As alluded to in the previous section, it should be noted that a range of typologies exist when referring to retail brands such as retail(er) brands, private brands/labels, own brands/labels and distributor brands (Burt and Davies, 2010; Fernie and Pierrel, 1996).

In terms of a classification of retail brands, Laaksonen's (1994) initial typology of generations of brands has been refined by later authors such as Huang and Huddleston (2009). As can be seen in Figure 4.5, the brands increase in both price and quality as we move from the bottom-left quadrant to the top-right, where the extended brands are premium-quality ranges of the finest, signature products of the main UK grocery retailers. It should be noted that these generations do not necessarily materialize in sequential order, especially in new markets where international entrants have introduced retail brands.

Initially, retail brands were 'generic' in nature, with a no-frills offering at cheaper prices than manufacturer-branded products. Not surprisingly, the launch of such brands, notably by Carrefour in France and defunct chains such as Victor Value and Shoppers' Paradise in the UK, were a response to increased price competition and the high-inflation environment of the 1970s. In the grocery sector, the market began to change by the early 1980s. There is a strong relationship between the extent of retail branding and the degree of centralization of distribution. Companies such as Marks & Spencer, J Sainsbury and Boots in the UK had established retail-controlled distribution centres from the late 1960s/early 1970s. They were the market leaders in their product categories and had established a brand identity with their customers. Other retailers, especially the major grocery retailers, were quick to follow, and by the late 1980s around 32 per cent of packaged grocery sales/toiletries were retail brands – an increase of 8 per cent in a decade. In fact, market penetration was much greater than this for some grocery categories. Chilled lines in particular were almost exclusively retail brands. Companies such as Northern Foods and Oscar Meyer grew in response to the buoyant demand for ready meals in Marks & Spencer and the supermarket chains – including Tesco, which had changed its positioning from a 'pile it high, sell it cheap' operator to one selling premium brands (manufacturer quality-level retail brands).

By the 1990s, these UK retailers were beginning to challenge some of the world's most prominent manufacturer brands for shelf space. The so-called 'cola wars' of the early 1990s was the most obvious example of this, when Sainsbury's followed by others, including Virgin, introduced their own cola brands to challenge Coca-Cola and Pepsi in the market. Procter & Gamble and Unilever were also facing retail brand competition to their detergents and health and beauty brands. Throughout the 1990s, retailers were spending more on promoting retail brands than was spent by their manufacturing counterparts.

The battle of the brands has continued, prompting much debate (and lawsuits) on the extent to which lookalike retail brands break trademark legislation. It has been argued

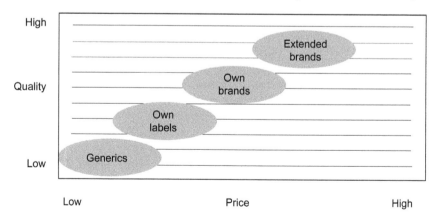

Figure 4.5 Four tiers of retail brands
Source: After Laaksonen, 1994; and Huang and Huddleston, 2009.

(Davies, 1998) that it is not only theft of the name, but also theft of identity. By looking at the values communicated by health and beauty products, Davies argues that retailers have copied the image that has been created by manufacturers in their research and development.

As consumers have become more 'brand literate' and retailers more precise in defining their market segments, a range of retail brands of specific product categories has been launched to appeal to different target groups. For example, from value lines to the 'finest', best-quality lines, in addition to organic and healthy eating categories. These brand values have led to corporate branding and the rise of the retailer brand. Hence the retailer brands are sufficiently strong for companies to diversify into other activities – for example, grocers into financial products, fashion retailers into perfume. Those companies, such as Tesco, with global aspirations and multi-channel strategies will undoubtedly use their brand loyalty to cross-sell a range of products and services (see Box 4.1).

It should be noted also that the retail brand share of UK supermarkets is fairly unique compared with other markets. Fernie and Pierrel (1996) showed that the French share of private label in the grocery markets was only half of that in the UK, despite the prominence of brands such as Carrefour, Auchan, LeClerc and Intermarché. The reasons for this disparity include the nature of the retail organization (LeClerc and Intermarché are trading groups with a fragmented buying structure), the initial inability of French retailers to promote their stores on TV (it was illegal until 2007) and the strong emphasis on price competition (for manufacturers' brands). In the USA, the level of retail branding is also low, but this is mainly due to the regional fragmentation of retail chains compared with the national coverage of manufacturers' brands. Walmart is the exception to this, but its 'everyday low pricing' strategy narrows the differential between retail and manufacturer-branded goods, thereby negating the need for consumers to trade up.

In the late 2000s and early 2010s private label market shares have increased in importance in most markets because of the financial crisis and subsequent recession. This has been particularly marked in some of the new emerging markets in Eastern Europe, with the advent of international entrants and continued high unemployment. For example, private label penetration in the Bulgarian grocery market increased from under 2 per cent in 2007 to 11 per cent in 2011 (Bozhinova, 2012). Furthermore, much of this growth has been in categories that have been relatively immune in markets such as the UK, for example, soft drinks, coffee and confectionery (Papalyugova, 2013).

The fashion brand in many cases is the retailer brand with a range of brand extensions – for example, Gap, GapKids. Too many extensions, however, can dilute the value of the brand, as Next found in the 1980s before returning to its core female fashion business in the 1990s. Such companies tie in suppliers to provide their retail brands without being involved in production, unlike Benetton and, to some extent, Zara, which are fully integrated companies. The luxury fashion brands also maintain a strong presence in producing high-quality crafted products from their country of origin. The evolution of the luxury brand and the repositioning of some of these brands have been discussed elsewhere in the chapter, but Figure 4.6 reinforces the key dimensions of these brands, showing how these brands express the essence of modern branding, stressing their heritage, culture and product integrity but ultimately providing a luxury experience to their upscale customers in iconic flagship stores (Moore et al., 2010).

In the mainstream fashion market, the relative positions of competing retail brands changed with new market entrants, so that maintaining the brand means reviewing the positioning in the market. The market for womenswear shifted fundamentally in the late 1990s/early 2000s with the growth of value fashion multiples such as Matalan and TK Maxx. The rise of fast fashion brands – H&M, New Look and Primark – at the discount end of the market meant that many of the traditional high street department stores were left in the middle market with relatively high-priced products for the quality on offer. C&A exited the UK market in 2000 and some traditional household names have struggled ever since, such as BHS and Marks & Spencer.

This market shift took place over a number of years, and could have been foreseen by market-aware retail managers, with steps taken to defend the positions of the brands affected. French Connection did this through repositioning and a successful marketing campaign in the 1990s. When similarly challenged by discounters a decade earlier, the grocery majors successfully diffused the initial danger to brand identity through establishing clearly identifiable value product lines within their stores. Therefore, brand identity was maintained at the same time as offering customers the alternative of cheaper, lower-quality merchandise under the same roof. In the case of Arcadia, it has many brands in addition to BHS in its portfolio and some, notably Topshop, have been extremely successful.

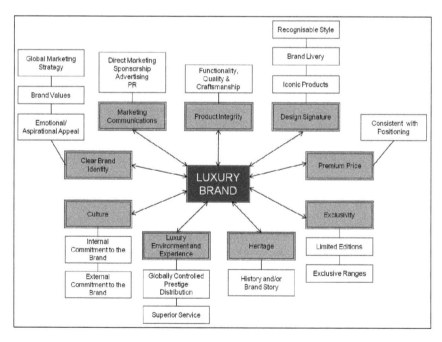

Figure 4.6 Dimensions of a luxury fashion brand

4.3.2 Brand extension

An established brand can be used to extend the retail and service offering to existing customers. Brand extensions facilitate choice for customers. The British master of brand extension is Richard Branson's Virgin group – a brand developed from a record store and applied to a variety of merchandise categories and services as diverse as investment, cola distribution and an airline. The brand has established quality levels in the minds of customers, and associations of bravado and buccaneering which the founder has fostered through carefully maintained publicity for stunts such as ballooning the Atlantic and posing in a bridal dress.

Figure 3.3 and section 3.6.2 in the previous chapter discussed how luxury brands have extended into new products and services. The Internet has also offered retailers an easy route to brand extension. Alongside their core offering they can apply their brand name to unrelated products and services. Tesco.com offers grocery shopping online with delivery in its own fleet of vans, and extended its online brand to clothing, gifts, entertainment and books through partnerships with established organizations such as Grattan and Bertrams, with merchandise delivered directly to customers via a range of parcel carriers.

Care has to be taken to maintain the 'expectational pact' with customers when extending the brand. Virgin's reputation was tainted by customers' perception of poor service and high prices offered by Virgin Trains. Customers' expectations were that the level of quality associated with Virgin's stores and airline would be extended to the train service. Similarly, some concern was expressed at fashion designers moving into diffusion brands in that it could dilute its traditional values and perhaps alienate its upscale customers by producing poorer-quality merchandise through a web of licensing agreements.

4.4 The service marketing mix

The service marketing mix is the combination of elements that retailers can use to bring their service to the target customer(s) for their mutual profit. There is a range of elements to consider (see Figure 4.7). The development of the traditional four Ps of the marketing mix to accommodate service organizations is discussed in more depth in Chapter 10.

4.4.1 Product

This service element can be considered on a number of levels, from the retailer brand or store brands that make up the retail organization, to the merchandise mix, the mix of retail and manufacturer brands that make up the retailer's merchandise. At any level, the product consistently has to meet or exceed the needs, wants and expectations of the target customer group, or groups.

Products (and brands) go through a life cycle (see Figure 4.8), and although it can be difficult to assess accurately when the progress from one stage to the next is made, recognizing life-cycle stages can help with market strategies and tactics. Investment has to be made in developing the product, incurring costs to the firm which can be offset against the profits from successful products. During the introduction phase, the cost of product launch, publicity and advertising can mean a continued loss to the organization. During the

Figure 4.7 The service marketing mix

growth phase, when sales and profits grow rapidly, marketers can concentrate on boosting sales and striving to gain a dominant share in the market sector through aggressive selling, sales promotions and continued advertising, while defending position against copycat products. When growth in sales starts to decline steadily the product has entered the maturity phase. The greatest profits are during maturity, when market share and sales peak. Marketers have to continue to defend share and to remind customers to buy through advertising and promotion, but at less intensity and less cost than during growth.

When sales and profits decline steadily, or suddenly, the product has entered the decline phase, and marketers have to make the decision whether to:

- allow the product to die slowly, reducing investment to a minimum;
- terminate the product; or
- redevelop and re-launch to attempt to boost it into a second growth phase.

Examples of retailer brands at various stages of the life cycle in 2014 were:

- **Superdry and ASOS**: still in the growth phase of the life cycle, as they internationalize their successful UK offering.

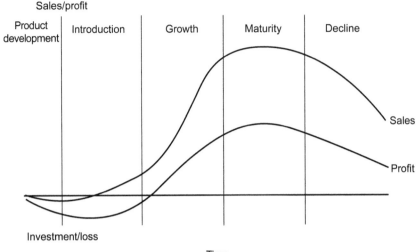

Sales/profit

Product development | Introduction | Growth | Maturity | Decline

Sales

Profit

Investment/loss

Time

Figure 4.8 Product life cycle

- **Next**: in the mature phase of the life cycle after strong growth in both store and online operations. A well-established high street fashion brand benefiting from problems with Marks & Spencer and closure of C&A stores.
- **Marks & Spencer**: the dominant high street brand for decades, senior managers have failed to arrest the decline in its market share this century.

The BCG growth-share matrix (see Figure 4.9) is another tool that can be used to aid management decision making on a number of different levels, from retail store brands to management of product/service ranges through their various life cycles. A retailer might map its various strategic business units (SBUs) or store brands on the grid to visualize their current relative positions, in order to decide potential future directions for each:

- **Stars**: high-growth, high-share brands – need investment to grow share within growing market. Growth will slow as they enter life-cycle maturity. Build share to transform into cash cows of the future.
- **Cash cow**: high-share brands in mature low-growth market – at maturity within life cycle, and profits can be used to support investment in new products/services/brands and to support star and question mark products/services/brands. Sufficient investment needed to hold share, or it may be appropriate to harvest profits.
- **Question mark**: low share of high-growth market – need investment to maintain share within growing market and to boost share. Where there are several 'question marks', decisions are needed about which to build in terms of share and which to let go or die.
- **Dog**: low share of low-growth market – in life-cycle decline stage, these may generate enough profit to maintain themselves, but will not yield sufficient to support more promising products/services/brands. Can be allowed to die, or be sold.

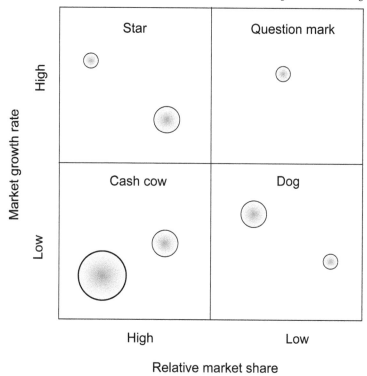

Figure 4.9 Growth-share matrix (adapted and simplified)

The buying and merchandising of a retailer's merchandise mix are two of the core activities in retailing. These topics, along with logistics, are discussed later in the book. The point to be made here is that techniques such as direct product profitability (DPP) and activity-based costing (ABC) have enabled managers to assess more accurately the profit contribution of products or categories, thereby product life cycle and the BCG growth-share matrix can be used to make strategic decisions in product/category management.

4.4.2 Price

Price is the most flexible element of the marketing mix: all other elements take time to change, but prices can be raised or reduced swiftly in response to changes in customer demand or market conditions. Price and quality are two of the most important dimensions in customer perception of the retail offer, and in customer buying decisions. Customers have an understanding of a 'just' price range for a level of quality, for a product, or for product ranges within a store brand. If the price falls below the just price, customers may suspect inferior quality. If the price rises above this range, customers will suspect they are being 'ripped off'.

Pricing strategy is therefore closely linked to product decisions, and to branding strategy. This is why price and quality are so frequently the main dimensions used for positioning in the market. Decisions on pricing strategy can be influenced by internal and external factors (Omar, 1999).

Internal factors include:

- marketing objectives;
- marketing mix strategy; and
- costs.

The marketing objectives of a retail organization will vary according to the competitiveness of the market sector and market conditions engendered by the stage in the economic life cycle. For example, in a concentrated market sector dominated by a few large and powerful organizations, competitive pricing is crucial for survival. Profit maximization can be achieved by a low-price/low-cost operation/volume sales strategy, or by a high-price/high-service/cost minimization strategy.

In addition to survival and maximization of profits, there are three further common marketing objectives:

- **Building market share**: this is seen by many retailers as the key to continued growth and success; it may require competitive pricing, or 'loss leading' in order to take share from competitors.
- **Achievement of excellent customer service**: investment in other elements of the service marketing mix will raise costs and at the same time customers value excellent service, so higher prices can be charged. However, it could be argued that low price itself is a service to the customer, and the savings created by streamlining logistical activities can be used to offer value for money. Walmart's failure in Germany could partly be attributed to a misconception of customer service. German perception of customer service is speedy, efficient checkouts, not more 'added services' such as bag packing, credit and personable, smiling staff.
- **Building quality leadership**: investment in quality – products, services, systems, customer service – means that higher prices can be charged. Investment in other elements of the marketing mix generally means that there is more flexibility in pricing strategy. For example, investment in product quality and store branding, in promotional activities, or in logistics management, can either allow a greater margin to be achieved or can be directed at increasing footfall at a lower margin. However, there does need to be integration of marketing mix decisions; for example, promoting the retail offer as 'cheap and cheerful' while retaining high prices, or vice versa, will lead to poor customer satisfaction and customer defection.

The costs incurred in maintaining the organization form the base level for pricing, and many small retailers use their costs as a basis for their pricing strategy. This is **cost plus pricing**, which means simply adding to costs a percentage margin for profit. Any organization has fixed costs and variable costs. Fixed costs are those that remain fixed no matter how much is sold – for example, rent and rates, salaries. Variable costs include all those that vary according to sales – for example, materials, flexible staffing.

External factors influencing pricing strategy include:

- macro-environmental factors; and
- nature of the market and competition.

Macro-environmental factors create the changing background, the framework within which retailers thrive or fail, and affect both the retailers' costs and customers' perception of price. For example, the stage of the economic cycle – prosperity, recession, depression, recovery – will affect the availability and cost of staff, as well as the propensity of customers to spend. In buoyant market conditions during a phase of economic prosperity, higher prices are more acceptable to customers where value for money is maintained by the retailer through merchandise quality and service provision. By contrast, during a recession, consumer willingness to spend is reduced, and discounting can be used to drive profits through volume sales. However, retailers have to be careful because their positioning and branding associates the organization with a perceived fair price range on the part of the customer. Since the economic downturn in 2007, grocery consumers in the UK have become more discriminatory in their spending. Whereas in strong economic conditions the prevailing shopping pattern was to one-stop shop with convenience store top-ups, now consumers are much more promiscuous and are behaving more like German consumers. Not surprisingly, German discounters have benefited from this change. Paradoxically, upscale food retailers have also benefited (Waitrose and Marks & Spencer food), at the expense of mainstream majors, especially Tesco and Morrisons.

Politics can affect reliability and cost of supplies as well as determining the cost of building and operating a retail unit. The high rate of fuel tax in the UK raises the costs of distribution of goods and is passed on in higher prices as well as affecting the customers' willingness to travel to buy. Investment in technology can streamline systems and increase efficiency, lowering costs over time, but many smaller retailers with less financial clout become less competitive, fail and change the nature of the market. Social trends also affect price. For example, as working parents became time poor and cash rich (relatively) in the UK, ready meals and takeaways became attractive to families. The high mark-up of these value-added items is acceptable because it reflects the worth families attach to the value of time and effort saved in the kitchen.

Price elasticity of demand is a concept that defines the consumer's reaction to price changes. If demand for a product changes more than 1 per cent with a 1 per cent change in price, demand is said to be elastic. If demand for a product changes less than 1 per cent with a 1 per cent change in price, demand is said to be inelastic.

Market conditions vary over time and according to the nature of the merchandise. Pure competition tends to exist where merchandise is cheap and plentiful, where the market is relatively easy and cheap to enter, and where there are numerous competitors. If one competitor raises the price of merchandise, customers can easily buy from another – demand is elastic and therefore prices tend to be stable. A modern example is a farmers' market. **Oligopolistic competition** exists in markets with very few, powerful competitors, with one example being petrol distribution, and another grocery distribution. In this type of market, price competition is tight – if one market competitor raises or reduces prices, the rest follow suit rapidly. The tight competitive situation means that there is a tendency for oligopolistic market competitors to reduce in number to a point where one organization dominates to the exclusion of others. This is called **monopoly**. In this situation there would be price inelasticity because consumers have nowhere else to shop. Because the power of the monopolizing organization would be to the detriment of both suppliers and consumers, any market situation tending towards monopoly will be investigated by the Competition and Markets Authority in the UK, and the monopolizing organization broken up if necessary.

Most retailers prefer a situation in which they successfully dominate one sector of the market – referred to as a situation of monopolistic competition – where a certain degree of price inelasticity is achieved. In this situation, not only is the customer preference for the retailer's products such that a rise in price will only minimally affect demand, but also the competitive situation is such that the price changes of a competitor will not affect demand substantially.

4.4.2.1 Pricing strategies

Product pricing decisions should be directed by a pricing strategy that is based on the company's market positioning and desired customer profile. Most writers classify a grocer's pricing strategy into either 'everyday low pricing' (**EDLP**) where stable low prices are made available across the assortment, 'high-low pricing' (or 'hi-lo') where deep and frequent promotions are made on a narrow range of goods, or a '**hybrid**' between the two (see Fassnacht and El Husseini, 2013 for a review). In an analysis of the US retail market, Gauri (2013) showed that EDLP and hybrid stores tended to outperform hi-lo stores on weekly sales.

In hi-lo strategies, higher prices are maintained generally with vigorous discounting of selected merchandise on a rotational basis to attract bargain hunters and achieve a low-price image among customers. The UK's Safeway (now Morrisons) successfully implemented this strategy after abandoning its loyalty card scheme. At the time the chief executive recognized that the savings from this and from reducing expenditure on customer service together could fund discounts which would drive volume sales. In doing so, however, they damaged the image of the Safeway brand among high-spending loyal customers, but countered this with aggressive petrol promotions for higher spenders. On its takeover by Morrisons, perhaps perceived to be more downmarket than Safeway, research in Scotland indicated a high degree of switching to other stores (Findlay and Sparks, 2008).

EDLP protagonists use the part of their budget that would go into promoting merchandise to maintain lower prices throughout the year. This is twinned with a refund policy for customers finding lower-price merchandise elsewhere. To implement EDLP successfully, costs have to be kept low through an efficient distribution system and low operating costs. A key element of Walmart's strategy is EDLP. Its UK subsidiary, Asda, has successfully adopted this strategy, which matched its image as a low-price retailer and was popular with customers. The argument for EDLP is that customers become suspicious of promotions, suspecting (rightly) that the higher price they pay for some items funds the savings they make on others.

Although there is a fair amount of literature on grocery price positioning strategy, there is little insight into how grocery practitioners set and manage prices on a regular basis. Watson (2013) has gone some way to redressing this problem with his research on regular pricing decision practices employed by a sample of 16 leading US and UK grocery pricing decision makers. These practitioners represent companies adopting both EDLP (six) and hi-lo (ten) pricing strategies. This research showed the high degree of inertia exhibited in practitioners' pricing behaviour and led the author to produce a model of passivity (see Figure 4.10).

This model utilizes Glaser's (1978) causes and consequences model of behaviour and illustrates the context within which pricing decisions are taken. The practitioners are risk averse and are unwilling to make major changes in price in fear of breaking trust with their customers. This in turn leads them to adopt a passive, coping role rather than a leading one. The causes in the model include decision uncertainty because practitioners possessed little disaggregated data on customers, compounded by the fact that these professionals were not formally trained for the role. The context and causes led to a range of consequences, including pricing inertia. This means that prices were only changed in relation to mandatory rules or minimum requirements rather than optimizing performance. The process is driven by the organization rather than the customer, leading to passivity pricing behaviours.

In addition to EDLP and hi-lo pricing strategies, we also have a **high price/quality service** strategy. Higher prices are maintained and matched with quality merchandise and merchandising, customer service and loyalty schemes to retain customers and drive profits. Customers can be attracted by branded products, prestige locations and superior, often personal, customer service associated with luxury products.

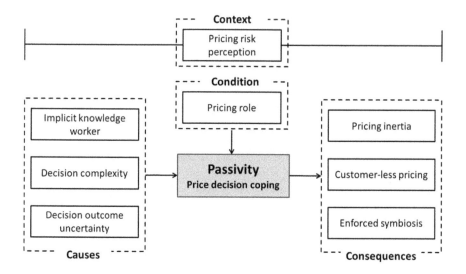

Figure 4.10 Passivity grocery pricing model
Source: Watson, 2013.

Price discrimination means that a company 'sells a product or service at two or more prices that do not reflect a proportional difference in costs' (Kotler *et al.*, 2009, p. 601). This allows retailers flexibility to vary price by customer group, by time, place of purchase or browsing behaviour. For example, retailers can offer goods at discount prices to loyalty card holders; they can offer regular sales of merchandise to make way for new stock; they can offer goods at different prices in different store locations or in different store formats; and in online retailing some retailers vary prices by browsing behaviour. Online retailing led to an increase in price discrimination as retailers exploit the visibility of customers' browsing patterns. Price comparison websites and discount websites offer customers pricing information and incentives to buy.

4.4.3 Place

In product and service marketing, the place element is about getting the goods/services to where the customer will buy. In retailing, the place element of the marketing mix is complex because of the large numbers of customers and the variety of goods and services involved. For this reason the place element is discussed in separate chapters. Not only do retail managers have to be concerned with logistics and physical distribution (see Chapter 9), but they need to understand the principles of merchandising and display (see Chapter 11). Here we will focus upon locational analysis techniques.

The study of retail location goes back to the 1930s and Reilly's (1931) law of retail gravitation whereby Reilly tried to determine the break-even point whereby customers would gravitate towards one town rather than a competing one on the basis of the size of the town and the distance to each destination. This was refined by Huff in 1964 by assigning probabilities to gravitating to a centre based on size of shopping centre, travelling time and the types of merchandise to be purchased. These types of crude models formed the basis of department store planning until the development of new formats and improvements in geo-demographic databases. For example, Marks & Spencer would open new stores on the basis of catchment area size. It is interesting to note that Walmart's locational positioning focused upon Mid-West rural towns – those that were neglected by JCPenney or Sears as being too small for their store offering.

The availability and refinement of complex data has led to the development of a wide range of methods currently used to find the best location for stores. **Checklists** are an easy way to compare store sites, and they are used by most retailers to supplement intuition. They are used to collect and compare data on population size and profile; to assess town/site accessibility issues such as car parking, site visibility and public transport; to weigh-up the amount of direct/indirect competition and cumulative attraction; and to assess unit or site issues such as size of selling area, Retail Saturation Index, potential for expansion and costs. **Analogue models** involve forecasting potential sales for a potential store through reference to trading data for an existing store in the retail organization's portfolio that is similar in terms of size, trading area and location (Birkin *et al.*, 2002). Alternatively, the retailer can define the key trading and locational criteria that underpin the performance of their leading store and attempt to replicate these in other areas. Birkin *et al.* (2002) are strong advocates of the use of the gravity model, in its simple, aggregate form:

$$Sij = Ai \times Oi \times Wj \times f(cij)$$

Where:

Sij = flow of people/money from residential area to shopping centre
Oi = measure of demand in area i
Wj = measure of attractiveness of centre
$f(cij)$= measure of cost of travel, or distance between i and j
Ai = balancing factor related to the competition, which ensures all demand is allocated to centres in the region, using the following formula:
Ai = 1 divided by the sum of $Wj \times f(cij)$

This assumes that flows of expenditure between origin and destination are proportional to the relative attractiveness of destination in comparison with all other destinations, and that the flows will be proportional to relative accessibility of destination in comparison with all competing destinations.

Due to the complexity of data sources, Birkin *et al.* (2002) prefer the term **spatial interaction model**. They feel that retail analysts could customize the spatial interaction models available in some geographical information systems packages to take account of the complexity of retail markets, and by doing so could forecast expenditure flows and revenue totals of a given location to a very accurate level.

In a study on the techniques employed by major retailers in the UK in 1998 (Hernandez and Bennison, 2000), it was found that most used experience, supported by one or more other techniques. Two thirds made use of checklists, and two fifths made use of the more complex analytical techniques – analogues, cluster and factor analysis, and gravity models. The most advanced, data-driven, knowledge-based techniques were used by a low percentage of retailers.

Further, it was found that the number of techniques used was related to the number of outlets operated by retailers, with most retailers operating fewer than 250 outlets reliant on three or fewer location techniques, while most retailers operating more than 750 outlets made use of up to six techniques. Usage of a variety of techniques was highest in the grocery, variety, public house and finance sectors of retailing.

In 2010 Reynolds and Wood did further work on location decision making, including building upon the earlier research by Hernandez and Bennison. In terms of techniques used, the authors show that increased use of analytical techniques has complemented their continued reliance on experience (see Figure 4.11). Furthermore, there was a greater degree of focus upon particular techniques, for example grocery retailers used analogue, multiple regression and gravity models extensively, with limited use of other techniques apart from experience. Indeed, all respondents noted the importance of the site visit to validate the modelling approach adopted. The authors comment that these techniques were most commonly used for new store developments/replacements rather than in cases of refurbishment or disposal where experience accounts for much of the decision support. They correctly point out that approaches to decision making in these areas would be necessary in the future. This has been borne out since the article was written in that the 'space

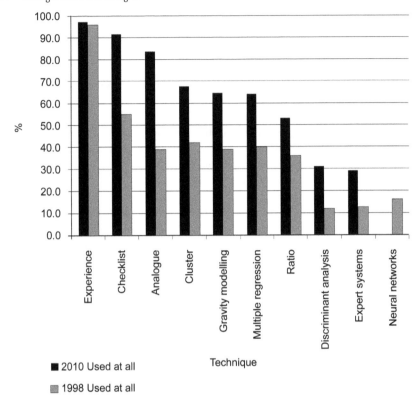

Figure 4.11 Decision-making techniques for retail location by usage (% respondents), 1998–2010
Source: Reynolds and Wood, 2010.

race' in grocery retailing has come to an end and the impact of recession and the Internet has witnessed a rationalization of non-food retailers' store portfolios (see Chapter 1).

4.5 Promotion

Promotion is about communicating with customers and is more correctly known as **marketing communication**. For communication to take place, the sender and receiver of information have to share understanding of the symbols, pictures and words used to transmit information, and have to make use of a mutually available medium through which the information is conveyed.

The process of communication is illustrated in Figure 4.12. The communication source, for example a group or individual that formulates an idea or concept for communication, has then to encode the idea into language, symbols, pictures or a combination of these, before selecting a medium or media for transmitting the message to their target audience (selected market segment or segments). In the decoding phase of communication, the symbols, words and pictures of the transmitted message are interpreted into ideas and concepts by the receiver of the information. Feedback completes the communication process because

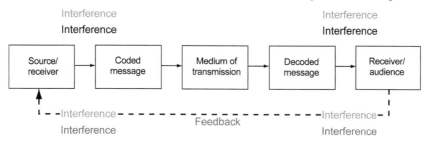

Figure 4.12 The communication process

it confirms whether the idea or concept formulated by the source has truly been received and interpreted correctly.

There is the potential for interference at every stage of the process in the form of physical or psychological barriers which prevent the desired communication from taking place.

Physical barriers include physical distance, distance in time, difference in educational levels, poor/non-access to media and sheer volume of competing information. Psychological barriers include preconceptions, emotions, perceptions and attitudes towards the sender, message or medium.

Promotion, as one element of the marketing mix, is reliant on the effective development and use of other elements – product/brand, price and place, people, process and physical evidence. Other elements of the marketing mix that have a particularly strong role in communicating with customers include people (staff and customers), product (in terms of quality, availability and packaging), and physical evidence (e.g. store logos, store design, visual merchandising).

The promotional mix is the range of promotional elements from which a retailer can select to communicate with existing and potential customers. Traditionally, it includes personal selling, advertising, sales promotion and publicity. However, additional elements, notably sponsorship and direct marketing, especially social media, which could be incorporated respectively into publicity and advertising, have grown in importance and complexity to the extent that they are considered separate promotional elements.

Promotional mix development in retailing is related to:

- strategic objectives;
- audience to be reached;
- size of the market;
- the message or product to be promoted; and
- relative cost of available media.

The promotional objectives of a retailer depend upon the organization's strategic objectives. For example, a retailer intent on expansion of a successful UK format into Europe will have the promotional objective of raising awareness of and interest in the retailer or store brand in the destination country, whereas an established retailer will focus promotional effort on defending or growing its successful position against major competitors. In

Box 4.2 the promotional strategy of Aldi in the UK is shown. The German discounter, which does not advertise in its home market, has launched a series of advertising campaigns to stress its price/quality credentials to consumers on a tight family budget. This is then complemented by mail drops and social media to reinforce the brand image.

Retailers utilizing cost-based strategies are liable to apply cost-based criteria to mix elements, focusing on those with greatest audience reach for money spent – hence the growth of publicity that generates audience coverage without payment for media space. A variety of sales promotions are generally used to encourage spend. Retailers engaged in differentiation-based strategies can focus on comparative advertising using visual media such as TV and print, which can help establish, fix or remind about retailer brand attributes in addition to promoting merchandise. Retailers targeting a restricted market segment are ideally positioned to use direct marketing. Fragmentation of audience has occurred with rapid development of technology and media, increasing the challenge of tracking and targeting the desired audience via a diverse range of media. This means it is essential to promote a coherent message across marketing and promotional elements. The effectiveness of marketing communication relies on integrating the desired message to customers (and staff and other stakeholders) regarding the retailer's offer in terms of brand value, quality, price and merchandise across all the elements of the mix.

Box 4.2 Aldi's marketing communications strategy in the UK

Aldi entered the UK in 1990 after successfully entering other neighbouring markets such as France. Initially Aldi made little impact in the UK market which was heavily dominated by the big four grocery retailers (Tesco, Sainsbury's, Asda and Safeway (now Morrisons)). Throughout the 1990s and early 2000s the major companies introduced value or basic lines as a response to the entry of hard discounters in the UK. Market share was small and dominated by the UK discounter, Kwik Save.

With the demise of Kwik Save and the takeover of the Danish discounter Netto UK by Asda, the German companies of Aldi and Lidl became the champions of hard discounting. After years of low growth, these companies have achieved spectacular growth since 2007. Aldi's annual report for 2012, published in September 2013, showed sales growth of 41 per cent to reach a figure of £3.9 billion. By late 2013, as their larger competitors continued to struggle, Aldi and Lidl accounted for a market share of 7 per cent of the UK market. Aldi had around 500 stores in 2013, with plans to open around 50 stores per year. Its success can be partly attributed to recession and shoppers looking to save money, but Aldi can achieve low prices because of its lean operation model. A no-frills operation where you shop in a basic environment and pack your own bags, Aldi sources from a small number of key suppliers and produces good-quality own-branded goods.

German consumers were well aware of Aldi's retail proposition – the company did not need to advertise the fact and therefore saved money. Aldi's consumer base is also across socio-economic groups.

In the UK, however, there has been a stigma attached to this downmarket image, and Aldi's communication strategy was geared to changing this. In the late 2000s it began a campaign with the strap line, 'Don't change your lifestyle, change your supermarket'. Aldi then undertook blind tests of a cross-section of shoppers to confirm that Aldi's brands were of equal quality to those of well-known manufacturers. This formed the basis of the 'Like Brands' TV campaign, which featured 20-second advertisements, each focusing on a specific product. Using humour, these advertisements showed a famous brand as a benchmark against an Aldi brand, to use the slogan 'Like Brands. Only Cheaper'. This TV campaign was reinforced through print media with mail drops to households in the vicinity of stores and newspaper advertisements/in-store posters communicating their 'Swap and Save' message on how much customers could save if they switched their weekly shop to Aldi. The company also uses more targeted communications through its website, Facebook page and Twitter account, to enable it to interact with customers and provide a vehicle to assess opinions of customers on their promotional campaigns and the product offering. Aldi has also been active in securing good PR and receiving endorsements such as being voted 'Supermarket of the Year' by the watchdog body Which?

4.5.1 The promotional mix elements

Personal selling is the most expensive element of the mix in relation to the audience reached, and is particularly used where merchandise is so complex or expensive that the customer needs one-to-one help in reaching the decision to buy. In self-service the sales role is more limited – to giving information and processing the customer's orders – but increasingly this role is being enhanced and staff encouraged to offer additional products and services for an additional sale. Personal selling is discussed in detail in Chapter 11.

Advertising is widely used by major retailers. Although expensive because payment for media space is required, major media such as TV and popular newspapers and magazines can reach the huge audience required at a comparatively small cost per person. The message and amount of information promoted can be varied over time, as in a 'teaser' campaign which releases more and more information to generate interest in new merchandise, or in a 'reminder' campaign in which a short clip of a previous advert is used periodically, using much less media space. Market segments can be targeted through associated media use. Internet adverts can be directed to potential online customers by tracking Internet activity. Advertising is particularly good for establishing awareness and interest in the retailer and merchandise.

Sales promotions include a variety of tools, including money-off coupons, competitions and two-for-one offers, which are primarily used to encourage customers to try or buy their merchandise, stimulating sales of promoted items. Retailers engaging in the hi-lo pricing strategy 'rotate' promotions, generating and maintaining the 'excitement' associated with a sale on a year-round basis.

Publicity generates media coverage through the reporting of significant events and information. Events such as openings, introduction of a new merchandise line or sponsorship of a community team can generate press coverage, as can positive publicity involving a high-profile chief executive. The message conveyed has more credibility with the audience and is often indistinguishable from news. However, media coverage is uncertain depending upon the competition for media space at the time of publication. Publicity is useful to raise awareness and interest in the organization rather than stimulate sales; however, it is sometimes linked with sales promotion in a combined retailer/media effort to raise sales.

Sponsorship is the funding of a non-related event, team or person, normally with the aim of reaching the audience through media coverage. Coverage is uncertain, however, depending on the success of the sponsored party. The two most important DIY companies in the UK, B&Q and Homebase, respectively, have sponsored Channel 4 TV programmes on property and food, with the intention of creating ideas for refurbishing their homes.

Direct marketing is increasingly used by retailers through mail order, website and direct mail. It allows customers to be targeted directly, at low cost, with information on which to make the buying decision or with promotional offers to generate purchase. Data-mining of loyalty card data (see Box 4.1, for example) can be used to generate a target database of individuals with needs/wants directly related to the merchandise being marketed, which improves the success rate. Social media have transformed elements of the promotional mix. For example, the rise in blogging, especially in the fashion industry, has resulted in fashion companies using blogs as a form of public relations. As some fashion bloggers – for example, Chiari Ferragni of Blonde Salad in Milan – have become so influential, companies have tended to collaborate with them in the viewing of new collections and for store openings.

4.6 People, process and physical evidence

People, process and physical evidence are three extra elements that particularly apply to service organizations. If marketing is about getting the right product at the right price in the right place at the right time and communicating this to the customer, in retailing, people, process and physical evidence are about the quality of the transaction experience.

4.6.1 People

Two sets of people affect the marketing effectiveness of a retail organization:

- service personnel; and
- customers.

Service personnel are those staff in the organization who operate at the customer interface. Increasingly, in a retail context, this means all staff. In a retail organization customer satisfaction is generated partially through the product bought, and partially through the service situation – including shop cleanliness, appearance, quality, display, stock levels and maintenance, additional services, after-sales service and the process of purchase.

In addition to their sales role, whether active or processing of orders, retail staff have a role to play in in-store promotions by giving customers verbal information about sales promotions, merchandise and stock levels, and about reinforcing external promotions by reminding customers about events, new merchandise and service initiatives.

Staff represent the service quality offered by the organization and have the key role in enabling customer satisfaction. Their appearance and behaviour can serve to reinforce and supplement, or inhibit, the success of the rest of the marketing. Standardization of procedures and staff training can reduce the potential for poor service encounters, but other considerations are motivation, retention and morale. The importance of retail staff is more fully addressed in Chapter 10.

Customers are the second set of people who can enhance or inhibit the marketing of retail organizations. Customers can be used in combination with other promotional elements. They can be utilized as referrals in advertising and sales promotional materials endorsing the retailer's own promotional statements. They can be used in publicity – for example, an event to celebrate a competition win. Sainsbury successfully incorporated customers into both roles by organizing a competition for schoolchildren to design a poster advertising the store opening, which resulted in an advert, free publicity and generation of community goodwill towards the new store. Customers can be used in a sales role, either through word-of-mouth advocacy of a store or its merchandise or service. For example, Aldi (Box 4.2) uses 'Aldi Advocates' on Facebook to spread the word about the company's value proposition, and promotes 'I love Aldi' campaigns with promotions for special events. Some companies use customers to recruit more selling agents in direct selling organizations such as Avon.

The marketing effort of the organization can, on the other hand, be inhibited through customers passing on dissatisfaction or disinformation to other people. Poor customer behaviour, overcrowding or lack of customers in a store can affect the quality of the shopping experience for other customers.

4.6.2 Process

Process deals with transforming resource input supplies such as bags, trolleys, baskets, merchandise and till rolls into outputs such as completed shopping and a satisfied customer. Process can include:

- **Planning and control of the process**: dealing with quality, quantity, delivery and cost of merchandise and services to meet customer requirements.
- **Planning operations**: detailing each operation required for consistent results, such as staffing levels for merchandising, customer service and sales.
- **Facilities design, layout and handling of materials**: to maximize speed and efficiency of service.
- **Scheduling**: detailed timing of operations such as shelf filling, serving, packing for customers.
- **Inventory planning and control**: making sure there is sufficient stock, staff, equipment.
- **Quality control**: checking and evaluating merchandise, operations and service.

In marketing a service, the process element can be used to attract and reassure customers in addition to being an important factor in ensuring their satisfaction. Most of a retail organization's operations are highly visible to customers, and can be affected by their presence.

As retailers increasingly compete not just against other retailers for customer spend, but also against other entertainment and leisure organizations, process has risen in significance. For most people the process of shopping is becoming as important as the merchandise bought, whether it be the excitement of a sale or the calm efficiency of a well-run department store. Process is becoming more complex too: for example, web booths in stores where customers can source merchandise unavailable on the shop floor, or male crèches with Internet access and electronic games facilities.

Process can be used as an active marketing tool in achieving customer satisfaction in a variety of ways. For example, special promotional displays of merchandise can clear shelves and allow restocking to take place, and a packing service can be scheduled at peak times to achieve volume sales. Customers can be persuaded to take on part of the process themselves, finding and scanning their own merchandise, or returning baskets and trolleys to base. IKEA, for example, advertised the use of its customers in keeping prices low through taking on the role of transport and assembly of merchandise.

4.6.3 Physical evidence

Services are essentially intangible. In retailing, while the merchandise is clearly tangible, the service offered to customers is not. Physical evidence is about how the service part of the shopping experience is made tangible (or physical) for customers and potential customers. There are two types of physical evidence: peripheral evidence, and essential evidence.

Peripheral evidence: this is evidence acquired by the customer as part of the service bought – the environment and atmosphere in which a service transaction takes place, but which has little or no intrinsic value in itself. Shoppers typically leave with at least a receipt of purchase, and normally with a bag or wrapping. Both of these are used as promotional tools bearing at least the name and/or logo of the retail unit. They can also be used to symbolize the quality of the service and merchandise. Designer shops normally provide carrier bags that promote both the store brand and its designer association through unusual colours, design or materials. These, in lending their customers fashionability by association with the store, can in themselves attract customers into the store to make a purchase. Receipts can be used in joint marketing offering customers discount offers on the back, or they can be used as a vehicle for offering coupons, points or other promotions.

Peripheral evidence allows retailers an opportunity to establish their brands in the minds of their customers after the purchase is made. In the form of loyalty cards, peripheral evidence additionally offers customers physical evidence of variable discounts offered for loyalty and the provision of extra products or services to regular customers.

Essential evidence: this is evidence that cannot be acquired by the customer, but which is important in the customer's selection of the service. Essential evidence includes external aspects of the store, such as location, parking, size, shape and quality of design of buildings, and fascia – all of which represent the quality of service to be expected and which can be used to attract customers into the store. It also includes internal aspects such as layout, quality of materials used in fixtures and fittings, lighting, signs and customer facilities.

Essential evidence physically portrays the quality of the service offered, and it can be actively used in the design of targeted store formats. However, it is important that essential evidence is integrated with the rest of the marketing offer. Where essential evidence contradicts the quality of service provision, customer confusion and dissatisfaction are the likely outcomes.

Sometimes retail organizations use peripheral evidence to support essential evidence – for example, free tea and coffee for waiting spouses, badges for children, collectible posters in the form of a mailshot. In the 1990s, St Andrews Woollen Mill gained widespread fame and custom through its 'Free Tooties for All' – a tiny nip of whisky offered to customers in the tearoom above the store. Apart from its popularity with customers, this fitted in with the tartan/sheepskin woollen mill image of the store, and gave them a memorable strap line for their advertisements.

4.7 Summary

This chapter focused upon marketing strategy, illustrating how markets were segmented and customers were profiled with Tesco's loyalty card data providing an illustration of how the company segments its customer base into lifestyle profiles. Store branding in the grocery sector has also become a means of positioning relatively standardized merchandise offerings in the minds of target consumers. The brand values created by major retailers through private-label branding and store branding have been strong enough for these organizations to diversify into other activities, such as financial products and fast food. The relative positions of competing retail brands change with new market entrants, so that in order to maintain the brand over time, periodic reviews of marketing positioning are required. The evolution of the luxury brand has been a major theme throughout this chapter, using the cases of Burberry and Gucci to illustrate how tired heritage brands have been repositioned to achieve success in this growth market.

The final part of the chapter was devoted to the service marketing mix, with particular emphasis on recent research into pricing and promotional strategies and tools of locational analysis. Some of this work relates to the impact of the recessionary environment on the marketing mix, for example Aldi's marketing campaign in the UK. However, it should be stressed that the people, process and physical environment elements of the service marketing mix are of particular importance to retailers because of the interaction between consumers, staff, systems and store/web environments. All of these elements add to (or detract from) the shopper's experience.

Review questions

1   Drawing upon examples from different retail sectors, discuss the various ways in which companies have segmented markets to profile and target consumers with their retail offer.

2   Discuss how retail branding has evolved from product-based marketing to corporate branding.

3   Outline the key elements of the services marketing mix and discuss the importance of process, physical evidence and people in retail marketing.

4   Discuss how the recessionary environment impacted upon specific elements of the service marketing mix.

References

Birkin, M., Clarke, G. and Clarke, M. (2002) *Retail Geography and Intelligent Network Planning.* Chichester: John Wiley.

Bozhinova, M. (2012) 'Own brands of commercial chains: a source of competitive advantage', *Central and Eastern European Library*, 3: 35–49.

Burt, S. and Davies, K. (2010) 'From the retail brand to the retailer as a brand: themes and issues in retail branding research', *The International Journal of Retail & Distribution Management*, 38(11/12): 865–878.

Competition Commission (2008) 'Groceries market investigation: final report', www.competi tion-commission.org.uk/press_rel/2008/apr/pdf/14-08.pdf (accessed 27 July 2010).

Davies, G. (1998) 'Retail brands and the theft of identity', *International Journal of Retail and Distribution Management*, 26(4): 140–146.

Fassnacht, M. and El Husseini, S. (2013) 'EDLP versus hi–lo pricing strategies in retailing – a state of the art article', *Journal of Business Economics*, 83(3): 259–289.

Fernie, J. and Pierrel, F.R.A. (1996) 'Own branding in UK and French grocery markets', *Journal of Product and Brand Management*, 5(7): 48–57.

Findlay, A. and Sparks, L. (2008) 'Switched: store switching behaviours', *International Journal of Retail & Distribution Management*, 36(5): 375–386.

Gauri, D.K. (2013) 'Benchmarking retail productivity considering retail pricing and format strategy', *Journal of Retailing*, 89(1): 1–14.

Glaser, B. (1978) *Theoretical Sensitivity: Advances in the Methodology of Grounded Theory.* Mill Valley, CA: Sociology Press.

Hatch, M.J. and Schultz, M. (2003) 'Bringing the corporation into corporate branding', *European Journal of Marketing*, 37(7/8): 1041–1064.

Hernandez, T. and Bennison, D. (2000) 'The art and science of retail location decisions', *International Journal of Retail Distribution Management*, 28(8): 357–367.

Huang, Y. and Huddleston, P. (2009) 'Retailer premium own-brands: creating customer loyalty through own-brand products advantage', *International Journal of Retail & Distribution Management*, 37 (11): 975–992.

Huff, D.L. (1964) 'Defining and estimating a trade area', *Journal of Marketing*, 28: 34–38.

Humby, C., Hunt, T. and Phillips, T. (2007) *Scoring Points: How Tesco is Winning Customer Loyalty.* London: Kogan Page.

Jevons, C. (2007) 'Towards an integrated definition of brand', in *Proceeding of the Thought Leaders International Conference on Brand Management* (De Chernatony, L., ed.). Birmingham: Birmingham Business School, University of Birmingham.

Kotler, P., Kelly, R.L., Brady, M., Goodman, M. and Hansen, T. (2009) *Marketing Management.* Harlow: Pearson Education.

Laaksonen, H. (1994) *Own Brands in Food Retailing across Europe.* Oxford: Oxford Institute of Retail Management.

McGoldrick, P. (2002) *Retail Marketing.* Maidenhead: McGraw-Hill Education.

Moore, C.M. and Birtwistle, G. (2004) 'The Burberry business model: creating an international luxury fashion brand', *International Journal of Retail & Distribution Management*, 32(8): 412–422.

Moore, C.M. and Birtwistle, G. (2005) 'The nature of parenting advantage in luxury fashion retailing: the case of Gucci Group NV', *International Journal of Retail & Distribution Management*, 33(4): 256–270.

Moore, C.M., Doherty, A.M. and Doyle, S.A. (2010) 'Flagship stores as a market entry method: the perspective of luxury fashion retailing', *European Journal of Marketing*, 44(1/2): 139–161.

Moore, C.M., Fernie, J. and Burt, S.L. (2000) 'Brands without boundaries: the internationalisation of the designer retailer's brand', *European Journal of Marketing*, 34(8): 919–937.

Omar, O. (1999) *Retail Marketing*. Harlow: Pearson Education.

Papalyugova, N. (2013) *An Exploratory Study of Retail Brands and their Impact on National Brands: A Cases Study of Bulgaria*, MLitt dissertation, The University of St Andrews, St Andrews.

Reilly, W.J. (1931) *The Laws of Retail Gravitation*. New York: Knickerbocker Press.

Reynolds, J. and Wood, S.M. (2010) 'Location decision making in retail firms: evolution and change', *International Journal of Retail & Distribution Management*, 38(11/12): 828–845.

Rubinstein, H. (2002) 'Branding on the internet: moving from a communications to relationship approach to branding', *Interactive Marketing*, 4(1): 33–40.

Watson, I. (2013) *Internal Reference Price Formulation in Support of UK and US Grocery Retail Price Decision Making*, DBA dissertation, Edinburgh Business School, Heriot-Watt University.

Zentes, J., Morschett, D. and Schramm-Klein, H. (2011) 'Strategic retail management: text and international cases', in *Customer Relationship Management* (2nd edn). Wiesbaden: Gabler.

5   The internationalization of retailing

Learning objectives

After studying this chapter, you should be able to:

- Discuss the internationalization of retail concepts and formats.
- Critically discuss four main themes of retail internationalization:

  - motives for internationalization;
  - directions of growth;
  - methods of market entry; and
  - degree of adaptation to new markets.

- Analyse the internationalization strategy of retail organizations using a variety of conceptual models.
- Evaluate the changing nature of the global retail market.

5.1 Introduction

Many of the world's largest retailers are US in origin, and several operate solely in their domestic market (Albertson, Kroger and Target). Consolidation in the retail industry is low compared with other sectors, and the share of foreign to total assets is correspondingly low. This is indeed the case, but there has been considerable change in retail markets during the last 15 years which will lead to further restructuring of global markets in the future. The catalyst for much of this change has been the rise of Walmart as the world's dominant retailer. Its sales of US$473 billion for the fiscal year 2014 not only make it larger than the combined sales of its next four major competitors, but also make it one of the world's largest companies. Yet in the late 1990s, Walmart's sales in international markets were around 9 per cent of total sales. By 2014, this figure had risen to 29 per cent, which equates to more than Tesco's total sales in 2014. This chapter will focus upon international operations of companies such as Walmart; however, it is necessary to discuss other forms of internationalization and the conceptual framework within which retail internationalization (RI) research takes place.

5.2 Internationalization of concepts

The internationalization of 'know-how', concepts and formats was highlighted by Kacker (1998), who detailed the range of 'technologies' that could be transferred from one market to another. Early examples of copying operational practices and applying them to their domestic market are 'fact-finding' missions undertaken by Simon Marks in the 1920s to the USA for Marks & Spencer and the early post-war forays by Alan Sainsbury that led to the introduction of US-style self-service supermarkets into J Sainsbury in the early 1950s. Such 'tours' continue to the present day, aided and abetted by the advances in modern technology, which allow managers to scour the globe for ideas to incorporate into their retail offer. This alerts us to one of the key differences between the internationalization of manufacturing and retailing innovations. Whilst you can patent a new product, you cannot patent a retail format or operational procedure. First-mover advantage is important in retailing, but new ideas will be copied and perfected, so constant innovation is imperative to maintain competitive advantage.

This has become more evident with the internationalization of retail businesses. As the large retailers open more subsidiaries in new markets, best practice principles can be applied across the world. The transfer of people, merchandise and operational procedures can greatly benefit different parts of the chain. This dissemination of ideas also takes place in an informal way through meetings of trade associations hosting conferences on themes that affect 'national' retailers. The efficient consumer response (ECR) annual events discussed in Chapter 9 provide further examples where case studies of the application of ECR principles can equip retailers with the wherewithal to capitalize upon efficiency savings.

Most academic attention on the internationalization of concepts has focused upon the 'export' of retail formats into new markets, thereby linking this form of internationalization with retail operations strategy. Much of the transfer of such formats relates to US companies seeking expansion opportunities because of saturation at home – for example, Costco's move into Latin America and Europe with its warehouse clubs and US developers' attempts to enter the European market with the factory outlet concept (McArthurGlen, Value Retail). Conversely, the hypermarket concept developed in France and championed by Carrefour was successful in Latin America and Asia but failed in the USA, where the format was not innovative enough to take trade away from the existing competition (Dupuis and Prime, 1996). From the 1980s, however, Walmart experimented with a super-hypermarket concept which was eventually rolled out as Supercenters in the 1990s. This enabled Walmart to bolt-on a food offering to their traditional discount department stores. The company's expansion into Europe and Asia is enhanced by this move in that acquisition targets tend to be hypermarket operators rather than discount department stores, such as Woolco in Canada.

5.3 Sourcing of products and services

The first step to internationalization for many retailers is often through their buying decisions. Large clothing firms have been sourcing products 'offshore' for some time, securing the benefits of low-cost manufacturing in countries of the Pacific Rim, Eastern Europe and North Africa. Marks & Spencer, renowned for its 'Buy British' sources, succumbed to the pressure of high costs and increased competition by switching to lower-cost markets in the late 1990s. It will be shown in Chapter 9 how The Limited, which has its store operations entirely within the USA, revolutionized the US apparel market by flying stock from its Hong Kong supply base to its warehouse in Columbus for onward distribution to its stores. This reduction in time to market through coordinated supply chain management enables buyers to source ideas, designs and products from around the globe.

This is not confined to fashion markets. Food retailers, especially the 'big box' companies that are forming a super league of global players, are introducing new 'ethnic' products in the continents throughout the world. The global consumer is acquiring global tastes as travel and media exposure place increasing demands on the retailer to provide a cosmopolitan retail offer.

In order to enhance their buying power, companies have joined buying alliances and web exchanges to foster coordination in international sourcing. In the grocery sector, initial alliances were dominated in Europe by voluntary trading groups and consumer cooperatives, but by the late 1980s multiple retail groups became affiliated to particular alliances to coordinate marketing and logistics activities.

The retail industry has followed in the footsteps of other sectors in utilizing a range of 'international' services. As companies play on the international stage, they draw upon an international labour pool, the world's financial markets, and the services of professional service providers (logistics, IT, accountancy and legal, for example).

5.4 Internationalization of store development

The academic literature on RI tends to focus on retail operations as evidenced by the key themes promulgated in textbooks by Alexander and Doherty (2009) and Sternquist (1998). See also the *International Marketing Review* (2000, nos 4/5) and Alexander and Doherty (2010). The starting point for research in this area was Stan Hollander's seminal work, *Multinational Retailing*, published in 1970. Hollander charted the international flows of retail investment up until this time, indicating that Sears Roebuck, F.W. Woolworth and other famous names of their time did have international aspirations going back to early in the twentieth century. Hollander's work therefore provided a benchmark for later research into RI when the scale of investment increased in the last decades of the century.

Much of the research into RI focuses upon four main themes:

- motives for internationalization;
- direction of growth;
- method of market entry; and
- degree of adaptation to new markets.

5.4.1 Motives for internationalization

McGoldrick (1995) provides a framework within which decisions to internationalize are taken. The classic push–pull factors are at either end of the spectrum, with inhibitors and facilitators influencing the nature of the strategic decision (see Figure 5.1). In the earlier section on the internationalization of retail concepts, the spread of warehouse clubs and

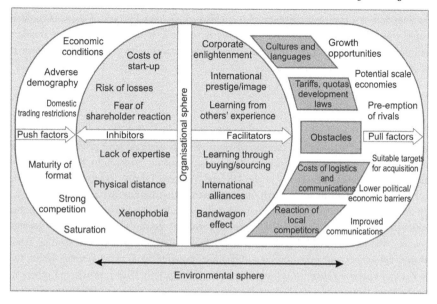

Figure 5.1 Driving forces of internationalization
Source: McGoldrick, 1995.

factory outlet centres to new markets could be attributed to saturation (a push factor) in the domestic US market and the attraction of the UK for political and cultural reasons (pull factor). The history of early internationalization in the post-Hollander era is marked by push factors and is often a reactive approach to internationalization. It is not surprising that European retailers dominate the literature on RI in that their small domestic markets (Ahold, Delhaize) or tight regulations constraining format development (Carrefour) have forced them to seek growth opportunities in international markets.

The so-called proactive retailers who have embraced internationalization and have been 'pulled' towards new markets were invariably the subjects of case histories. These companies had a differentiated retail offer, and a strong brand image, and were either category killers (Toys 'R' Us, IKEA) or specialist clothing retailers (Gap, Benetton, high-fashion houses such as Armani and Donna Karan). Despite all of the time and effort deployed by academics in studying these companies, the impact of specialist retailers in terms of international sales is minimal. Until recently, supermarket chains and department store operators were viewed as reactive to RI; food products, in particular, were deemed 'culturally' grounded.

These arguments are now beginning to look rather hollow. The facilitators listed in Figure 5.1 are encouraging consolidation in the food/mass-merchandise sector. The creation of major political trading blocs in America, Europe and Asia has opened new markets and removed prohibitive regulation in the movement of goods and people across national boundaries. Consumers, whilst retaining local tastes, are becoming more geocentric in experimenting with 'international' products, especially from the country of origin of the foreign retailer. Europe provides a potential battleground for international development.

The adoption of a common currency and an enlarged 'Greater Europe' of over 500 million people offer market attractions for international retailers. It is the 'powerhouse' retailers with their large-scale formats – hypermarkets, discount warehouses – which have dominated the international scene in recent times.

5.4.2 Direction of growth

With the motivations for RI clear, retailers then have to decide which markets to enter and the entry strategy to deploy. Commercial research organizations have tended to monitor the flow of international activity, superseding earlier academic research by Burt (1993) and Robinson and Clarke-Hill (1990) in the UK and Western Europe, respectively. Most evidence suggests that firms in the early stages of internationalization prefer a low-risk strategy and favour markets that are geographically or culturally proximate to their home market. The latter idea of cultural or business proximity relates to the concept of psychic distance, whereby 'a firm's degree of uncertainty about a foreign market resulting from cultural differences and other business difficulties presents barriers to learning about the market and operating there' (O'Grady and Lane, 1996, p.330). This research and others in retailing (see Evans *et al.*, 2000) draw heavily upon the stages theory of internationalization of the firm. Better known as the Uppsala model, Swedish researchers developed a four-stage model to show how manufacturing firms incrementally moved to new markets based on increased market knowledge and therefore reduced psychic distance (Johanson and Vahine, 1974, 1977).

This explains why US retailers target the UK as a bridgehead to the European market, in that a common language and similar business practices are deemed 'culturally proximate' in terms of country selection. Indeed, in the 1990s, 31 per cent of all foreign retailers entering the UK originated from the USA (Davies and Finney, 1998).

The pattern of international investment shows that early internationalization is to near neighbours in order that the venture can be more easily managed and controlled. Hence, retailers from:

- the UK favour Ireland and, to a lesser extent, the Netherlands and France;
- France target Spain;
- Germany target Austria;
- Japan target Hong Kong and Singapore;
- Australia target New Zealand; and
- the USA target Canada and Mexico.

As retailers gain experience (sometimes negative experience), they reshape their international strategies. With the development of the North American Free Trade Agreement (NAFTA), the European Union (EU) and Association of Southeast Asian Nations (ASEAN) markets, the main players are represented in two or more of these major trading blocs, thereby seeking opportunities for growth as and when they arise.

5.4.3 Method of market entry

The literature on entry strategies in retailing mirrors that of the research undertaken on manufacturing concerns. The main difference is one of scale and investment required for international expansion. The step-by-step approach in manufacturing goes from the low-cost, low-risk exporting of goods through licensing, to foreign direct investment (FDI). International management gurus such as Ohmae and Porter have then discussed the type of management structure that evolves beyond the FDI stage to create a support function in key world markets.

Retailers also evaluate low-risk to high-risk stages in their entry strategies. Initial low-investment strategies to glean better knowledge of the market can occur through minority shareholdings or franchise agreements. In the case of **minority shareholdings**, several of the buying alliances in Europe involve cross-shareholdings of 'partners', which open the door for greater collaboration or even merger activity in the future. When Sainsbury's first ventured into the USA in 1987, it took a 40 per cent share of Shaws, and only took full control of it a decade later. Tesco's foray into the USA in 2001, with its shareholding in the Safeway (US) Internet project, also gave the company experience of the American market to assess its options for further investment. In both cases, however, pressure from share-holders after poor performances at home led both companies to exit from the USA. In March 2002, Walmart secured a 5.1 per cent stake in Seiju, the fourth largest supermarket group in Japan, with an option to raise the stake to 65.7 per cent. By 2008 Seiju had become a wholly owned subsidiary.

Franchising has been a popular method of market entry for companies in domestic as well as international markets. Akin to licensing in manufacturing, the advantages of fran-chising are the speed of market entry, the availability of local management knowledge and expertise, and the low costs of entry, as costs are borne by the franchisee. The problem with franchising is the policing of the franchise network. It is important that franchisees conform to the strict rules laid down by the franchiser in terms of merchandising, brand image and store design. Franchising is particularly popular with niche retailers with a strong brand image. Body Shop, for example, has over 1,500 franchise outlets in 65 coun-tries. Benetton, with 6,500 shops in 120 countries, sells and distributes its products through agents who develop a given market area. These agents then set up a franchise agreement with the owners of stores who sell Benetton products. However, Benetton did build and manage in-house 100 megastores throughout the world accommodating the full Benetton range.

Box 5.1 and Figure 5.2 illustrate the market development and entry strategies of fashion design houses. In the context of this discussion on franchising, fashion design houses can use this method of market entry in stage four in their market expansion (see Figure 5.2). These design houses, such as Versace, Donna Karan, Calvin Klein and Christian Lacroix, have developed chains of diffusion stores within the major cities of Europe, America and Asia. While the flagship stores highlight their ready-to-wear collections and generally are owned and controlled by the design house, the diffusion stores can be operated under a franchise agreement to avoid the high start-up costs and risks associated with managing a national chain of stores. Moore *et al.* (2000, p.932) quote a foreign operations director for an American diffusion brand who states that:

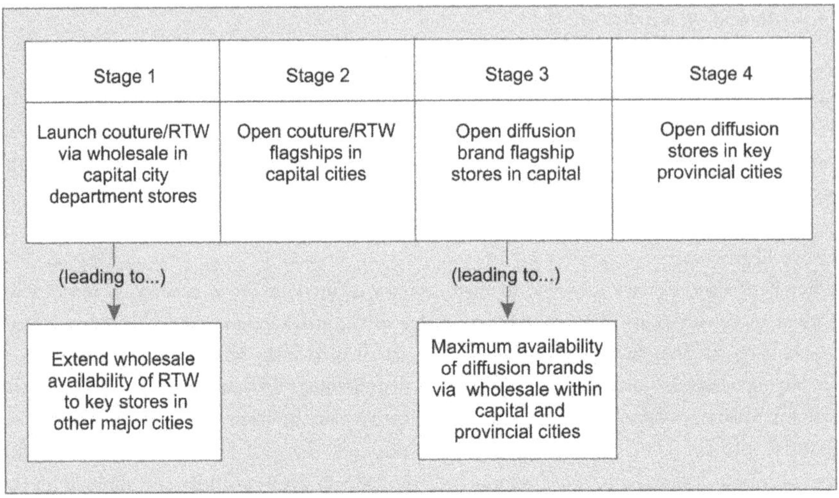

Stage 1	Stage 2	Stage 3	Stage 4
Launch couture/RTW via wholesale in capital city department stores	Open couture/RTW flagships in capital cities	Open diffusion brand flagship stores in capital	Open diffusion stores in key provincial cities

(leading to...)   (leading to...)

| Extend wholesale availability of RTW to key stores in other major cities | Maximum availability of diffusion brands via wholesale within capital and provincial cities |

Figure 5.2 The four stages of fashion designer foreign market development
Source: Moore *et al.*, 2000.

We, like most fashion designers, are relatively small and our resources are finite, so it is a division of labour. Our partners run the diffusion chains and we supply the product and, most important of all, create the brand image through our advertising which has a high cost in terms of time and money.

The example of fashion design retailing shows a complex web of relationships in entering new markets from wholesaling through franchising to operating company-owned stores. The FDI decision poses a further set of options for the international retailer. Do you grow organically or do you acquire a going concern? Do you operate a wholly owned subsidiary or do you partner with a host company in the target market and form a joint venture? In many markets there is no option. In India and China, for example, it used to be the case that a joint venture was the only route to entering their markets: however, regulations have been relaxed in the 2000s. This has meant that companies have bought out their initial partners once they have gained experience of the market, for example Burberry bought out its franchisees in China in 2010.

Box 5.1 Market entry strategies of fashion design retailers

Figure 5.2 shows the four stages of international market development adopted by fashion design houses. In stage one, wholesaling plays a key role in establishing the brand at low cost. Limited couture and ready-to-wear collections were distributed to elite department stores (Harrods, Saks Fifth Avenue) and, once established, made available to other provincial department stores and bespoke independent fashion retailers. Stage two involves the opening of flagship stores within capital cities, typically in premium shopping streets (Bond Street, London; Fifth Avenue, New York; Rue Saint

Honoré, Paris). These stores, because of the high rental and operating costs, tend to be 'loss leaders' that promote the brand for stage three, which is the promotion of diffusion lines. The diffusion brand is aimed at the middle market and has been the catalyst for designer retailers' growth in international markets. This is why so many of these famous family companies achieved stock market listings in the 1990s – they needed the capital to fund wholesaling and franchising agreements and to open new company-owned stores in international markets. The fourth and final stage of expansion is the development of diffusion stores throughout countries, spreading out from the capital cities to provincial cities. Agreements are often made to allow a franchisee to operate a chain of fashion designer stores on behalf of the brand owner: for example, Calvin Klein has allowed CK diffusion stores to be opened under a franchise agreement.

Much of the evidence from the international marketing/management literature indicates that approaches to FDI differ according to 'country culture'. US and UK companies, for example, prefer an acquisition strategy that gives them speed of entry to a new market, the purchasing of a going concern, albeit the possible problems of integrating the management culture of the target company with the predator. This strategy is underpinned by a corporate culture that demands quick results to appease institutional investors who are short term in their stock market perspective. Japanese and German companies, in contrast, prefer the organic growth strategy and are willing to build up market penetration in new markets over a long time period through developing their own sites. This again is related to country culture, with Japanese institutions looking for long-term returns even at the expense of short-term losses.

In retailing there is some evidence to support this hypothesis, in particular in mass-merchandise or big box retailing. In order to achieve market growth, Walmart and Tesco have adopted an acquisition strategy to move into new markets during the last 10–15 years. In the case of niche retailers, however, an organic growth strategy is more prevalent for companies such as Gap, The Body Shop and the category killer companies such as IKEA and Toys 'R' Us. An organic growth strategy is also pursued when companies 'boundary hop' to near neighbours – the route adopted in early internationalization for many European companies. Several German companies, especially discounters such as Aldi, which are private corporations, have built up a presence in Europe through the gradual development of new sites, acknowledging that losses will be made in the short run.

It should be noted, however, that such strategies are not necessarily country specific, as company cultures can also vary markedly. In the UK, the two leading grocery retailers, Tesco and Sainsbury's, have adopted different approaches to internationalization. Although Sainsbury's was first to internationalize in the USA in the late 1980s, its minority shareholding typified its cautious approach. In order to increase its market penetration in Scotland, Tesco bought the Wm Low chain in 1994 and then moved to Ireland with the purchase of Power Supermarkets in 1997. Sainsbury's has preferred an organic growth strategy, building its presence in Scotland and Northern Ireland with the incremental development of new sites. Now, a large part of Tesco's capital investment programme (over

40 per cent) is in overseas markets, especially in Eastern Europe and Asia. At the same time institutional investors questioned Sainsbury's continued presence in overseas markets when it had been losing market share to Tesco in the UK. Its withdrawal from the Egyptian market in 2001 and the USA in 2004 reinforced its renewed focus on the domestic market. While most academic research has investigated the motivations and entry strategies of international retailers, Alexander and Quinn (2002) have explored the divestment and strategic withdrawal strategies of retailers from international markets, using Marks & Spencer (M&S) and Arcadia as case studies. M&S illustrates the 'hype' associated with some of the research into retail internationalization. In 1998, Davies and Finney based a chapter on internationalization, in a contribution edited by one of the authors of this textbook, strongly on M&S, which was championed as a retail leader within the UK on internationalization. The company was in 33 countries and 'no other company anywhere has this diversity of international expression' (p.138) – a reference to the numerous entry strategies deployed by the company. The strong performance in the UK had in many ways concealed the poor trading performance of the international division. When M&S began to experience serious problems in the late 1990s with strong competition in its home market, it was no surprise that a planned withdrawal from international markets ensued, with the closure of its stores in North America and Europe leaving a rump of mainly franchised operations from the M&S empire (see Box 5.2).

Box 5.2 The rise and fall of Marks & Spencer's international aspirations

Marks & Spencer's initial foray into international markets was the exporting of its unique private label brand, St Michael. The expatriate and military (Navy, Army and Air Force Institutes – NAAFI) markets were the main focus of this business, and its success in exporting to around 50 countries earned it the Queen's Award for Export on five occasions. This business was eventually to lead to franchise agreements which were to become a key element of M&S's international strategy.

Its first store-based international entry was in Canada in 1972, with a 50 per cent shareholding in three clothing chains. Although it took full ownership of these chains in the late 1970s, the Canadian operation never made a profit, and M&S cut back store numbers in the 1990s, finally closing the business in 1999. The successful UK format of clothing and food was not popular in Canada, and adjustments to the merchandising mix could not save the operation.

M&S also entered the Continental Europe market in the 1970s with its first store in Paris in 1975, and then developed company-owned stores in Belgium and Ireland with a further wave of activity in the 1990s in Spain, the Netherlands and Germany. It was in the late 1980s and early 1990s that M&S undertook expansion into the USA and South-East Asia, with the acquisition of the Brooks Brothers menswear chain and King Supermarkets in the USA, and the opening of company-owned stores in Hong Kong from 1988.

Franchising was a key element of the company's strategy, utilizing master franchises throughout the world. With the exception of Hong Kong, this was a favoured strategy for 'peripheral' markets in Europe so that in 1999, M&S had 54 franchise stores across 12 European countries. This method of marketing was also used in the East Asian market, and was to produce greater profit than the Brooks Brothers chain of company-owned stores.

In 1997, the company announced an ambitious expansion plan which included further growth in its international operations to make M&S a global retailer. However, its plans were poorly received in the City, and market factors began to work against the company. The Asian crisis led to problems with the Hong Kong business and other Far East franchises. The German market was proving problematic with the higher price points of M&S products and the difficulties of accepting the M&S brand (a feature also evident in Spain). With increased competition at home in both its core clothing and food markets, M&S began to scale back its operations in the Far East and Europe. By 2000, international activities represented 25 per cent of the company's retail floor space, 17.2 per cent of its retail turnover, but less than 1.25 per cent of its pre-tax profits. It is interesting to note that in its most profitable year (1997) pre-tax profits were only 8.3 per cent of the total.

The announcement in March 2001 that the company was selling its USA businesses and closing most of its European stores (except Ireland) came as no surprise in the light of its plummeting share price and falling profits from 1997 to 2000. It was also turning its Hong Kong stores into a franchise operation, thereby turning the clock back 30 years to where M&S's international operations had begun.

The obituaries were written, including a journalistic contribution (Bevan, 2001). It is clear that management wanted M&S to be a global player but the strategy was ad hoc, with little synergy between acquired businesses and a mistaken belief that the St Michael brand could be transferred to international markets with similar success to that in the UK.

M&S later successfully internationalized abroad, largely via franchise stores and, from 2010, the internationalization strategy hardened with the advent of a new CEO, Marc Bolland. The intention was to consolidate a presence in markets where internationalization had already taken place and to enter new markets via a flagship store, later supported by other stores and Internet presence. The main method of internationalization was to remain franchising.

Source: After Alexander and Quinn, 2002; Burt *et al.*, 2002; Felstead, 2010.

5.4.4 Degree of adaptation to new markets

The general international management literature has used Levitt's ideas on globalization of markets, published in the *Harvard Business Review* in 1983, as the benchmark for the standardization versus customization debate when companies take their products into international markets. Levitt argued that consumers have the same needs and aspirations around the world, and companies should recognize this in their product and service offerings. This view is supported by specific sectors of service businesses – hotel chains, credit card companies and car rental operators – in addition to well-known global brands such as Coca-Cola and McDonald's. Nevertheless, these companies have had to adapt their product to specific markets, and the communications message has to be conveyed in different ways in new markets. In fast-moving consumer goods (FMCG) markets, adaptation for specific country markets has been deemed necessary because of the 'culturally grounded' nature of tastes, but is this necessarily the case? In Japan, Carrefour entered the market as a low-cost operator trying to appeal to Japanese tastes when the consumer wanted to buy French goods and enjoy a French shopping experience. In retailing, the degree of adaptation to specific markets is driven largely by the image of the store brand and whether values associated with the brand can be transferred across international boundaries. In our earlier example of fashion design houses, the spreading of these brands to a global market has been highly successful. To reinforce the Levitt approach to global markets, communication strategies ensure global advertising campaigns promote a standard brand image across markets.

While fashion houses may be unique in their approach, category specialists and brand-differentiated niche players also exhibit a high degree of standardization in their retail offer. The brand image, store name and well-tried format is much the same for IKEA, Toys 'R' Us, The Body Shop, Gap and Benetton in the markets in which they are represented. Some degree of adaptation is necessary in the range, but this could be due to physical constraints on site acquisition or the need to adapt colours/sizes for different markets. Benetton, for example, offers the same range of products in all markets, but allows a significant percentage of its ranges to be customized to meet the needs of specific country markets (smaller sizes for Far East countries, different colour ranges for the Middle East). In order to communicate one image throughout the world, Benetton streamlined its brands so that all garments are sold under the United Colors of Benetton and Sisley brands, and customization was reduced to between 5 and 10 per cent for different markets.

For the mass merchandisers and hypermarket operators, approaches differ according to the scale of operation and management style of companies. The larger big box operators that focus on fewer, large-scale formats – hypermarkets and warehouse clubs – have tried to create a global brand identity. Walmart has four large-scale formats, three of which have an international dimension. These are the Walmart Discount Department Stores, Supercenters and Sam's Clubs. Carrefour and Tesco also adopted large-scale formats and a global brand approach to internationalization. Conversely, Ahold and Sainsbury's, which operated smaller retail formats, tended to retain local brand names of companies that they acquired. In the USA, both companies dominated grocery retailing in the north-east for a time, with Giant, Stop & Shop, BI-LO, Tops, Finast and Edwards owned by Ahold, and Shaws and Star Markets by Sainsbury's. (Later structural changes, divestment and merger activity removed some of the above store brands from the Ahold portfolio, while Sainsbury's Shaws and Star Markets eventually were merged and sold to Albertsons.)

5.5 Towards a conceptual framework

As RI gathered pace in the 1980s and 1990s, academics provided conceptual frameworks within which to base their empirical research. Much of the early work drew upon research from the manufacturing sector, such as the Uppsala model discussed above, in section 5.4.2, and Dunning's (1988) eclectic paradigm. This model shows that the nature of international expansion is a function of a series of advantages: **ownership specific**, where the product (retail offer) gives competitive advantage; **location specific**, where the host country can yield cost or market opportunities (Eastern Europe, Asia); or **internalization**, where management innovation or other corporate advantages can lead to success. This borrowing of concepts has led to criticisms that the internationalization of retailing differs fundamentally from that of manufacturing. This is true in terms of the scale of capital flows and the degree of complexity in an FMCG environment compared with the industrial sector; however, methods of entry and values associated with an international brand are comparable. Early models discussed stages of international expansion, which mirrors much of the literature in international marketing textbooks on entry strategies. Furthermore, authors such as Treadgold (1989, 1990) and Salmon and Tordjman (1989) provided taxonomies of retail international development strategies which 'borrow' from the initial work of Levitt on globalization of markets.

The problem with most of these models is that they were derived at a time when RI was small scale in terms of global impact. The retail internationalists of the time were niche players, mainly clothing chains with strong franchise agreements. The 1990s and the early part of the twenty-first century have witnessed true internationalization, so many of these initial works, although valuable then, tend to discuss early internationalization. In the late 1990s, two US works made a more relevant contribution to our knowledge of this complex subject. Sternquist (1997) produced her strategic international retail expansion (SIRE) model to explain the international expansion of US retailers (see Figure 5.3). Her model integrates the eclectic paradigm (left side of the diagram), stages theory and the global versus multinational strategy literature. She observed that multinational retailers' expansion is slower than global retailers, that they adapt rather than standardize, and that they concentrate their expansion within a geographical area before moving to a new country or region. The other model is by Vida and Fairhurst (1998), and it draws on behavioural work in international marketing. They acknowledge that RI is a complex issue, but the internal driving forces behind internationalization are the firm's ownership advantages and management perceptions of specific markets, i.e. knowledge, experience and attitudes towards markets. Clearly, as managers move up the learning curve through experience of international markets, they become more ambitious and less cautious than their first move into a new market. Their model considered antecedents, which encapsulate the environment within which a decision is taken, the process whereby expansion or withdrawal is decided and the outcomes, which considered the strategic options on entry method and selection of market.

Alexander and Myers (2000) have integrated previous research into a framework that encapsulates the internationalization process from the corporate perspective. In Figure 5.4, they illustrate the drivers of change in the market of origin. Here the retailer has asset-based advantages (Dunning, 1988) through innovation of format and retail brand. Its ability

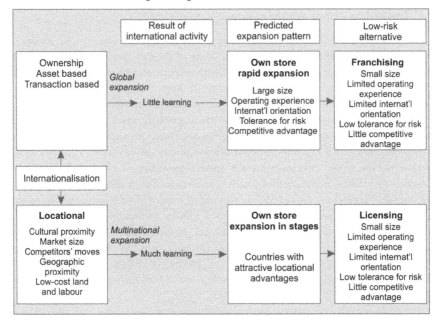

Figure 5.3 Model of strategic international retail expansion (SIRE)
Source: Sternquist, 1997.

to internationalize these assets will largely be determined by the internal facilitating competences within the retail organization (Vida and Fairhurst, 1998). On the basis of the internal competences, strategic decisions will be taken on market selection, entry method and the approach to be adopted in an international retailing strategy. As the retailer gains experience within the international environment, the internal facilitating competences are upgraded to accommodate the lessons learnt from its operations in new geographical markets.

In Figure 5.5, Alexander and Myers (2000) have produced a 2×2 matrix in an attempt to explain international retail strategies. They use the extension of the retail concept along the x-axis and the firm's perspective on internationalization on the y-axis. They measure the latter in terms of a company's ethnocentricity or geocentricity. An ethnocentric approach is one whereby the retailer adapts a domestic orientation to its international strategy. The geocentric approach is to adopt a one-market view of the world where like-minded consumers will demand the retail offer with limited adaptation in specific markets. In Figure 5.5, they classify the proximal retailer as one that provides a similar retail offer to customers in adjacent countries – the boundary hopping which typified much of the early internationalization strategies of retailers. This would equate with the domestic market extension concept applied to manufacturing companies.

The other quadrants in the matrix are much more controversial in terms of a typology of strategies. They argue that the multinational retailer has considerable global reach but remains psychologically rooted within the competitive market of the domestic market, whereas the global retailer may embrace change rather than replicate an existing formula.

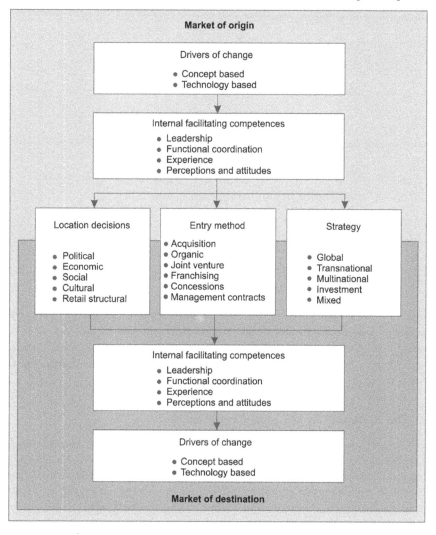

Figure 5.4 Operational organization
Source: Alexander and Myers, 2000.

The difference between a transnational and a global retailer is the scale of operations, in that a transnational operates only in a limited number of markets. On the basis of this taxonomy, they classify Ahold as a global retailer, Walmart and Gap as multinationals, and Zara as a transnational. Burt (2002) acknowledges problems with taxonomies of this nature; however, he classifies global retailers as high fashion retailers and specialist chains, and multinational retailers as grocery chains such as Ahold, which adapt their strategy to individual country markets. Much of the confusion about these taxonomies is due to their relative simplicity. In the matrix in Figure 5.5, a 2×2 grid is shown. In the marketing

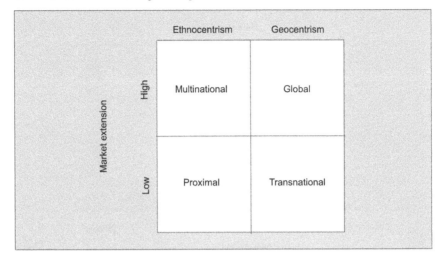

Figure 5.5 Market and operational internationalization
Source: Alexander and Myers, 2000.

literature a broader definition of a firm's view on internationalization would be given. For example, a polycentric approach would equate with a multinational approach. Here, a company recognizes that country markets are very different and that market success requires a more 'hands-off' approach by the corporate parent to allow local management to develop the retail offer accordingly.

5.6 The reshaping of the global retail market

Retail internationalization is a relatively recent topic of interest for researchers, and much of the work presented here, including the development of conceptual models, has tended to discuss the international strategies of companies of modest size. IKEA, Toys 'R' Us and Benetton are truly global companies, but they are not going to have any significant impact on the retail structure of large national markets. During the 1990s and the early part of the twenty-first century, retail markets throughout the world were transformed by the emergence of an elite super league of retail multinational groups. The growth of these companies through merger and acquisition has transformed the global retail landscape, and at the turn of the millennium many of the world's largest retailers in the food and general merchandise sector believed that further consolidation would take place, leading to a small number of mega-groupings (see Aggarwal *et al.*, 2000). In 1990, the majority of US and European retailers were predominantly national retailers. Of the European retailers, only Tengelmann, Ahold and Delhaize, all with US interests, had a significant proportion of their turnover in international markets.

Table 5.1 shows the top ten retailers in the world by group revenue in 2012. Most of these companies are food and general merchandise retailers, and with the exception of Kroger and Target are committed to international growth. It can be argued that the rise of Walmart to be the world's largest company, and its international aspirations, has been

Table 5.1 Top ten world retailers ranked by group sales, 2012

Rank	Firm	Sales ($ billion)
1	Walmart	469
2	Tesco	103
3	Carrefour	101
4	Costco	99
5	Kroger	97
6	Schwarz	87
7	Metro	86
8	Home Depot	75
9	Aldi	73
10	Target	72

Source: After Deloitte, 2014.

the key driver for consolidation in the markets of the USA, Latin America, Europe and Asia. It is therefore necessary to glean an overview of Walmart's international aspirations in order to assess the response from competitors such as Carrefour and Tesco.

When Sam Walton opened his first Wal-Mart Discount City store in 1962, he did not realize that his company would become the largest in the world 40 years later. The rise has been meteoric (see Figure 5.6). Yet most of this growth was achieved in its large domestic market as it rolled out key formats: Discount Department Stores, Sam's Clubs, Super-centers, Markets (previously named Neighborhood Markets) and Express. Its initial moves into the international market were to its near neighbours (confirming the proximate principle), Mexico in 1991 and Canada in 1994, before entering the higher-risk, more distant markets in Asia and Latin America. Even though it entered Europe through two small acquisitions in Germany in 1997/98 and the UK through the purchase of Asda, international sales accounted for only 9 per cent of the group's total turnover in 1999. Table 5.2 shows the spread of Walmart stores until 2014, although these figures conceal slower growth in the 2000s than originally anticipated.

As can be seen in Figure 5.7, Walmart's forecast sales for 2010 were estimated to approach $700 billion, and international expansion was to account for 25 per cent of these sales and was therefore a major element of this growth strategy. Retail sales were $405 billion in 2010 and while international sales did account for 25 per cent of sales, this was from a lower sales base. Former CEO of Wal-Mart Stores Randy Mott spoke of the large number of countries on Walmart's shopping list in 2000. These included Poland, France, South Africa, Turkey, Thailand, Chile, Venezuela, Malaysia, Hungary, the Czech Republic, Spain, Italy, Australia and Japan. To date, only Japan, Chile and South Africa have been entered from this list since 2000, while they have withdrawn from South Korea and Germany and entered India and a number of small Central American markets.

The strength of Walmart is based largely on its strong retail proposition. It is a discount operation with wide assortments and good customer service and community support. It is a huge operation with a small-town focus that goes back to its roots in small-town

Table 5.2 The geographic spread of Walmart stores by country

Country	Number of Walmart stores
Argentina	105
Brazil	557
Canada	391
Chile	390
China	401
Costa Rica	216
El Salvador	87
Guatemala	214
Honduras	81
India	20
Japan	431
Mexico	2,235
Nicaragua	85
South Africa (and 11 African countries)	391 (35)
United Kingdom	589
USA (incl. Sam's Club)	5,009
Total Walmart stores	11,202

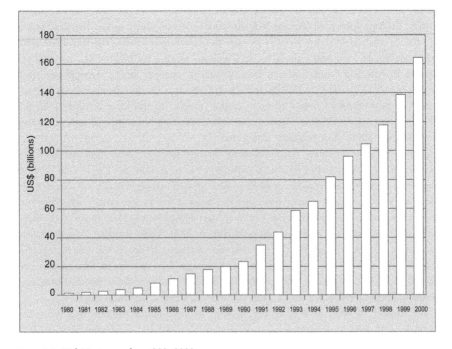

Figure 5.6 Wal-Mart net sales, 1980–2000
Source: Wal-Mart, *2000 Annual Report.*

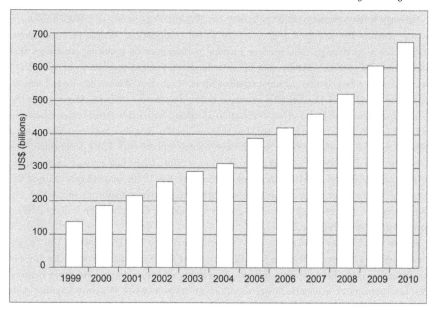

Figure 5.7 Future Walmart sales
(Lehman Bros. and *Discount Store News* estimates)

America. Its everyday low pricing (EDLP) strategy can be achieved through the economies of scale in its buying, its innovative Retail Link information system and its high inventory turnover because of efficient logistics.

Moreover, Walmart has a unique organizational culture embodied in the spirit of its founder, Sam Walton. Employees are known as 'associates', who are empowered to be innovative and to try out their own ideas. Team spirit is engendered amongst associates with the 'morning cheer' and the motivation to win in the marketplace. To maintain community spirit and good customer relations, Walmart contributes to local causes, has a 'greeter' to welcome customers to the store, and operates an aggressive hospitality '3 metre' rule, i.e. if a customer comes within 3 metres an associate is obligated to help.

Walmart's successful formula propelled it to become the leading retailer in the USA, and its acquisition of Woolco in Canada also led the company to achieve market share gains with the demise of once-famous names, such as Eatons. Steve Arnold and colleagues have written extensively about the impact of Walmart when it enters new markets in North America. He has argued that Walmart has a 'market spoiler' effect upon the markets that it enters – that is, it changes store choice attributes towards its own positioning and low price emphasis. The evidence from empirical research suggests that it is difficult, if not impossible, to compete with Walmart on price, head to head, so differentiation and adaptation to the new entrant is necessary. For details of such research studies, see Steve Arnold's special issue on this theme in the *International Journal of Retail and Distribution Management* in 2000, nos 4/5.

Although it has internationalized relatively late, Walmart's presence or intended presence in new markets has reshaped the nature of global competition. Walmart's international strategy has been strongly influenced by forming partnerships or acquiring companies that can be moulded to the 'Walmart way' of doing business. For example, its move into Brazil was built upon a long-lasting personal relationship between Sam Walton and Jorge Lemann, one of the founders of the Garantia group, a major shareholder of Lojas Americanas. The relationship allowed for the cross-fertilization of ideas, and Lojas Americanas executives visited the USA to acquire ideas on how to develop the Brazilian business. Thus, when Walmart entered Brazil in 1993 it was through a joint venture with Lojas Americanas. The development of Supercenters and the introduction of Sam's Clubs had a major impact upon the structure of the retail market in Brazil. Throughout the 1990s, acquisitions changed the nature of the industry, as small and medium-sized chains were acquired, and Ahold and Casino acquired shareholdings of leading groups to challenge Carrefour, the well-established market leader, and Walmart Brazil.

Similar parallels can be drawn with Walmart's entry into the UK market. The enlightened leadership of Archie Norman and Allan Leighton in turning around Asda's fortunes in the 1990s has often been attributed to the borrowing of management ideas from Bentonville, headquarters of Walmart. It was therefore no surprise when Walmart acquired Asda in June 1999 because of its large store portfolio, a similar retail offer and its Waltonian style of management. Walmart has implemented changes that caused a shake-up of the British retail market. EDLP is a major focus of the strategy by using price as a 'market spoiler' in changing consumers' store choice variables away from convenience, quality and assortment. The rolling out of Supercentres and the utilization of superior Walmart IT systems is allowing greater space utilization and the introduction of more non-food lines.

Although Walmart has achieved success in the UK, it has not made any impact on Tesco's domination of the UK retail market (Sparks, 2011), and the situation in the rest of Europe is problematic. Analysts have commented that to be a truly global retailer, a company needs to have credible scale in Europe, which means a leading position in at least two of the three largest markets: Germany, France and the UK. Yet none of the main supergroups has a major presence in these key markets; indeed, the linkages that do exist involve a presence in the more peripheral, but growing, markets of Southern and Eastern Europe (see Figure 5.8). This position has been reinforced over the last decade, with little prospect of Tesco or Carrefour making a major acquisition in Europe; indeed, all of the major companies have tended to focus upon Central and Eastern European markets, most notably the Czech Republic, Slovenia and Poland. Walmart's withdrawal from Germany illustrates the problem of trying to achieve market penetration in Europe (Fernie *et al.*, 2006). Walmart had plans to enter France and Germany but the Carrefour-Promodes merger in 1999 limited the acquisition options in France because of the large number of family-owned or franchised operations in the country. Similarly, in Germany Walmart bought two disparate chains, had difficulty integrating them to the Walmart banner and then could not achieve sufficient scale either through organic growth or available acquisition targets to achieve profitable growth.

It had been suggested that Walmart might have to acquire another UK company if it were to challenge Tesco for market leadership, but although it made a bid to take over the

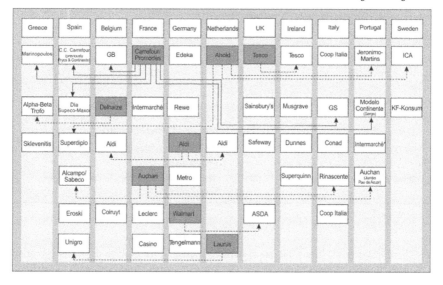

Figure 5.8 The structure of the EU food retail market, and the interlinks between firms in that market in mid-2001
Note: + excludes the markets of Austria, Denmark, Finland, Luxembourg. * Exact nature of Inter-marché holding in Portugal unclear.
Source: Wrigley, 2002.

UK's Safeway, Wm Morrison acquired Safeway in the wake of a Competition Commission investigation.

Along with Walmart, all of the major supermarket groups have consolidated and restructured their international operations throughout the 2000s. In 2002 Wrigley maintained that the spectacular growth of Ahold in the late 1990s/early 2000s would see it overtake Carrefour in the global league table. By 2012, Ahold had fallen to 26th in the Deloitte league table with sales of $42 billion, mainly because of accounting irregularities in its US Foodservice division in 2003. The net result of a restructuring exercise was the disposal of its Latin American and Asian subsidiaries to focus upon the European and US retail markets. Although Ahold's divestment activities were a result of financial pressures, other groups have reappraised their international operations to reallocate resources to areas with best investment potential (see Palmer, 2005; Palmer and Quinn, 2007). Thus Carrefour, the most international of all the groups, has been concerned at losing its market share in France and has withdrawn from some markets in Europe and in Asia, for example Slovenia and Thailand. Similarly, although Tesco has increased its group profits from international sales from 1.8 per cent in 1997 to 25 per cent in 2011, it has focused upon markets where it is market leader or has a large market share. In 2005, therefore, Tesco did an asset swap with Carrefour whereby it came out of Taiwan to buy Carrefour's stores in Slovenia and the Czech Republic. In 2011 it exited from Japan, followed by withdrawal from the USA in 2013.

In terms of the operational approach to global expansion, Wrigley (2002) outlines two corporate models (Table 5.3). The 'intelligently federal' model is the one adopted by Ahold.

Table 5.3 Alternative corporate models of globalized retail operation

'Aggressively industrial'	'Intelligently federal'
Low format adaptation	Multiple/flexible formats
Lack of partnerships/alliances in emerging markets	Partnerships/alliances in emerging markets
Focus on economies of scale in purchasing, marketing, logistics	Focus on back-end integration, accessing economies of skills as much as scale, and best practice knowledge transfer
Centralized bureaucracy, export of key management and corporate culture from core	Absorb, utilize/transfer, best local management acquired
The global 'category killer' model	The umbrella organization/*corporate parent* model

Source: Wrigley, 2002.

Here there is more of a 'hands-off' approach to acquisition, with a high degree of retention of the local brand and management skills. The umbrella organization model is flexible, with a focus on local partnerships, format adaptation and best practice knowledge transfer. The 'aggressively industrial' model, by contrast, is a more centralized organizational culture which has low format adoption and a category killer approach to internationalization. This is the Walmart approach to international expansion, with Tesco also adopting such an approach with its internationalization based on the hypermarket format. Carrefour lies somewhere between the two models, with a more decentralized management structure but a multiformat international strategy.

5.7 Summary

This chapter has devoted much time to the new evolving landscape of international retailing. Largely ignored in the literature until very recently, the aspirations of Walmart, Carrefour, Ahold and Tesco can be applied to the conceptual context sketched out in the early part of the chapter. Here we discussed internationalization of concepts, including the transfer of know-how, ideas and best practice as identified in the 'intelligently federal' model discussed above. The chapter focused upon store development and the four key areas of research into retail internationalization were discussed – motives for internationalization, direction of growth, method of market entry, and the degree of adaptation to new markets. Early internationalization invariably leads to a cautious, near-neighbour approach as retailers take their format to new markets. Then, with experience, they become more ambitious in higher-risk, more distant markets where the joint venture is sometimes the only method of market entry. The degree of adaptation is tied up with the nature of the retail offer. In differentiated, high brand image formats such as category killers or niche fashion brands, the format is replicated throughout global markets. This was illustrated in Box 5.1 with the case of fashion design retailers, which promote their image with the development of diffusion lines and franchising of stores in provincial areas.

The next section discussed the conceptual framework within which retail internationalization research was framed. Much of the early work drew heavily on models derived from the international management literature, which focused upon the manufacturing sector with taxonomies of international strategies being produced in the late 1980s. Although these have been revisited over the last decade or so, the 1990s witnessed a new global retail landscape. The so-called internationalists of the 1980s are either niche players on the global scene or they have re-orientated their strategies to focus upon their domestic market (see Box 5.2 and the case of Marks & Spencer).

This is why we focused upon the reshaping of the global retail market in the final section. The meteoric rise of Walmart with its grandiose international expansion plans has created change in the markets that it has entered, and has redefined the nature of global competition. Throughout the first decade of the new millennium, however, a restructuring of global operations has occurred with companies divesting from markets to focus upon countries offering the best investment potential.

Review questions

1   Comment upon the main motives for internationalization by retailers and discuss the role of psychic distance in determining the markets that they enter.
2   What are the key factors that determine the entry strategy of international retailers?
3   Critically review the main theoretical models that have been developed to explain retail internationalization.
4   To what extent is divestment and reallocation of capital investment reshaping the global retail marketplace in the 2010s?

References

Aggarwal, R., Brodier, A., Spillard, L. and Webb, S. (2000) *Global Retailing: The Future*. Letchmore Heath: IGD.

Alexander, N. (1997) *International Retailing*. Oxford: Blackwell.

Alexander, N. and Doherty, A.M. (2009) *International Retailing*. Oxford: Oxford University Press.

Alexander, N. and Doherty, A.M. (2010) 'International retail research: focus, methodology and conceptual development', *International Journal of Retail & Distribution Management*, 38(11/12): 928–942.

Alexander, N. and Myers, H. (2000) 'The retail internationalisation process', *International Marketing Review*, 17(4/5): 334–353.

Alexander, N. and Quinn, B. (2002) 'International retail divestment', *International Journal of Retail and Distribution Management*, 30(2): 112–125.

Arnold, S.J. and Fernie, J. (2000) 'Wal-Mart in Europe: prospects for the UK', *International Marketing Review*, 17(4/5): 416–432.

Bevan, J. (2001) *The Rise and Fall of Marks & Spencer*. London: Profile Books.

Burt, S.L. (1993) 'Temporal trends in the internationalisation of British retailing', *International Review of Retail, Distribution and Consumer Research*, 3(4): 391–410.

Burt, S.L. (2002) 'International retailing', in *Retail Marketing* (McGoldrick, P.J., ed.). Maidenhead: McGraw-Hill.

Burt, S.L., Mellahi, K., Jackson, T.P. and Sparks, L. (2002) 'Retail internationalisation and retail failure: issues from the case of Marks & Spencer', *The International Review of Retail Distribution and Consumer Research*, 12(2): 191–219.

Colla, E. and Dupuis, M. (2002) 'Research and managerial issues on global retail competition: Carrefour/Wal-Mart', *International Journal of Retail and Distribution Management*, 30: 103–111.

Da Rocha, A. and Dib, L.A. (2002) 'The entry of Wal-Mart in Brazil and the competitive responses of multinational and domestic firms', *International Journal of Retail and Distribution Management*, 30(1): 61–73.

Davies, R. and Finney, M. (1998) 'Internationalisation', in *The Future for UK Retailing* (Fernie, J., ed.). London: Financial Times Retail and Consumer, pp. 134–145.

Deloitte (2014) *Global Powers of Retailing, 2014*. London: Deloitte.

Dunning, J. (1988) 'The eclectic paradigm of international production: a restatement and some possible extensions', *Journal of International Business Studies*, 19(1): 1–31.

Dupuis, M. and Prime, N. (1996) 'Business distance and global retailing: a model for analysis of key success/failure factors', *International Journal of Retail and Distribution Management*, 24(11): 30–38.

Evans, J., Treadgold, A. and Mavondo, F. (2000) 'Psychic distance and the performance of international retailers: a suggested theoretical framework', *International Marketing Review*, 17(4/5): 373–391.

Felstead, A. (2010) 'M&S set for further forays', *Financial Times*, www.ft.com/cms/s/0/d787433e-ec3d-11df-9e11-00144feab49a.html#axzz1oFiRXQCj (accessed 5 March 2012).

Fernie, J. and Arnold, S.J. (2002) 'Wal-Mart in Europe: prospects for Germany, the UK and France', *International Journal of Retail and Distribution Management*, 30(2): 92–102.

Fernie, J., Hahn, B., Gerhard, U., Pioch, E. and Arnold, S.J. (2006) 'The impact of Wal-Mart's entry into the German and UK grocery markets', *Agribusiness*, 22(2): 247–266.

Hollander, S. (1970) *Multinational Retailing*. East Lansing: Michigan State University Press.

Hollinger, R. and Hayes, R. (1992) *1992 National Retail Security Survey: Final Report (with Executive Summary)*. Gainesville: University of Florida.

Johanson, J. and Vahine, J.E. (1974) *The International Process of the Firm*. Working paper, Department of Administration, University of Uppsala.

Johanson, J. and Vahine, J.E. (1977) 'The internationalization process of the firm: a model of development and increasing market commitment', *Journal of International Business Studies*, 8: 23–32.

Kacker, M. (1998) 'International flows of retailing know-how: bridging the technology gap in distribution', *Journal of Retailing*, 64(1): 41–67.

Levitt, T. (1983) 'The globalisation of markets', *Harvard Business Review*, 61 (May–June): 92–102.

McGoldrick, P.J. (1995) 'Introduction to international retailing', in *International Retailing: Trends and Strategies* (McGoldrick, P.J. and Davies, G., eds). London: Pitman, pp. 1–14.

Moore, C.M., Fernie, J. and Burt, S.L. (2000) 'Brands without boundaries: the internationalisation of the designer retailer's brand', *European Journal of Marketing*, 34(8): 919–937.

O'Grady, S. and Lane, H. (1996) 'The psychic distance paradox', *Journal of International Business Studies*, 27(2): 309–333.

Palmer, M. (2005) 'Retail multinational learning: a case study of Tesco', *International Journal of Retail & Distribution Management*, 33(1): 23–48.

Palmer, M. and Quinn, B. (2007) 'The nature of international retail divestment: insights from Ahold', *International Marketing Review*, 24(1): 24–45.

Robinson, T. and Clarke-Hill, C. (1990) 'Directional growth by European retailers', *International Journal of Retail and Distribution Management*, 18(5): 3–14.

Salmon, W.J. and Tordjman, A. (1989) 'The internationalisation of retailing', *International Journal of Retailing*, 4(2): 3–15.

Sparks, L. (2011) 'Settling for second best? Reflections after the tenth anniversary of Wal-Mart's entry to the United Kingdom', *International Journal of Retail & Distribution Management*, 39(2): 114–129.

Sternquist, B. (1997) 'International expansion of US retailers', *International Journal of Retail and Distribution Management*, 25(8): 262–268.

Sternquist, B. (1998) *International Retailing*. New York: Fairchild.

Treadgold, A. (1989) 'Retailing without frontiers', *Retail and Distribution Management* (November/December): 8–12.

Treadgold, A. (1990) 'The developing internationalisation of retailing', *International Journal of Retail and Distribution Management*, 18(2): 4–11.

Vida, I. and Fairhurst, A. (1998) 'International expansion of retail firms: a theoretical approach for further investigation', *Journal of Retailing and Consumer Services*, 5(3): 143–151.

Wrigley, N. (2002) 'The landscape of pan-European food retail consolidation', *International Journal of Retail and Distribution Management*, 30(2): 81–91.

6 Electronic commerce and retailing

Learning objectives

After studying this chapter, you should be able to:

- Discuss the growth of the e-commerce market.
- Identify the changing nature of the e-consumer.
- Understand the essential attributes of successful online retailers.
- Evaluate key issues of e-fulfilment.

6.1 Introduction

e-commerce, or 'e-tail', the sale and distribution of goods and services via electronic means, has developed rapidly over the last couple of decades. There is a variety of e-commerce sectors, including business-to-business (B2B), business-to-consumer (B2C), business-to-government (B2G), consumer-to-consumer (C2C), and government-to-business (G2B). This chapter is concerned primarily with B2C and C2C e-commerce. m-commerce, or 'm-tail', the use of mobile technology for the selling of goods and services, is developing even more rapidly. Although many retailers use m-tail as a new and popular route to selling goods and services to consumers, its development is in its infancy at the time of writing and many consumers use mobile technology as an additional interface with the e-tail platform and distribution network.

Non-store shopping is not new. Traditional mail order goes back well over a century. The 'big book' catalogues of the mid-twentieth century, which were used to sell to family and friends, experienced slow decline with the advent of more upmarket and more precisely targeted 'specialogues'. Some large UK retailers like Argos and Next use catalogues as an additional channel to market as well as to support their store and e-tail formats. Nevertheless, the tradition of selling to friends and family continues with party plans, most notably through Ann Summers, and with door-to-door selling through Avon and Betterware catalogues. These 'low-tech' forms of selling had accounted for around 4–5 per cent of all retail sales in the UK and the USA for many years, but this is changing as 'higher-tech' options dominate the marketplace. After many false dawns and dot.com collapses, Amazon.com reported a quarterly profit for the first time in 2001. A considerable shakeout of the industry occurred after 2000 and a stable pattern of development has occurred during the last 10–15 years.

It should be noted that the body of research that has grown up around this topic refers to online retailing, electronic retailing, virtual retailing and e-tailing, which can be considered interchangeable terms. Within e-tailing, those retail companies that developed using the Internet as a means of exchange are termed 'pure players'; retailers that have added online retail formats to their physical store portfolios are often referred to as 'clicks-and-bricks' retailers, while those retailers that operate traditional physical retail outlets are called 'bricks-and-mortar' retailers.

This chapter will discuss the growth of e-commerce and the evolving e-tail market. The e-commerce consumer will be considered prior to an introduction to e-tail store developments, including those made by pure-play and clicks-and-bricks retailers. Online store attributes will also be outlined, as will proposed critical success factors in e-tailing. Developments in the grocery sector are discussed before the final section considers the costly issue of e-fulfilment delivery and returns.

6.2 The growth and development of the e-commerce market

While it is generally accepted that e-commerce grew considerably in the 1990s and the early part of this century, accurate, reliable figures were difficult to ascertain because of the need to agree upon a widely accepted definition. Now statistics on Internet use, e-commerce and e-tailing are widely available. For example, in the UK, www.ons.gov.uk provides a monthly index of retail sales including non-store retail sales, while leading online trade body IMRG provides global and country e-commerce statistics plus in-depth e-commerce data.

The growth of e-commerce was closely linked to the development of Internet usage. In 2000 there were just over 350 million Internet users in the world, a figure that grew to more than 2 billion in the next ten years and is forecast to grow to 5 billion by 2015 (IMRG, 2011). Asian Internet users form the highest proportion, followed by European and North American users. However, Internet access itself was not initially sufficient to deliver large-scale online retailing. Early download speeds were too slow to support creative online visual merchandising and the interactivity with customers that retailers enjoy today. The growth of broadband allowed faster download speeds and facilitated the growth of successful e-tail websites. This, together with a strong focus on improving the security of transactions, encouraged growth in online spend by consumers. The rapid growth of mobile broadband added a further channel for e-commerce, bringing with it consumers who had never shopped via 'traditional' e-tail websites.

Early research focused upon B2C transactions, although few companies in this sector made a profit in the early years of e-commerce. At this stage, it was the B2B and C2C sectors that produced real benefits to customers and increased profitability for the partners involved. In C2C markets, intermediaries such as eBay acted as online auctioneers brokering deals between bidders and sellers. Similarly, B2B exchanges promoted online auctions and collaborations between partners to reduce costs. Businesses involved in exploiting these e-commerce markets are called **infomediaries**, in that they are trading information and are facilitators in reducing transaction costs between buyer and seller.

The problem with the B2C model compared with the C2C and B2B models was the requirement to trade goods that were tangible and needed to be stored and transported to the final consumer. (Later, some of these goods, such as music and books, were converted to electronic formats that were downloadable directly to consumers' computers, mobiles, MP3 players and e-readers.) Additionally, a market presence and brand identity were necessary ingredients to wean customers away from their traditional methods of buying behaviour. Yet, despite these apparent drawbacks, the 'hype' associated with this new form of trading led many analysts to discuss the notion of **disintermediation** in B2C markets. This meant that the role of intermediaries – agents, wholesalers and even retailers – would be reduced as manufacturers were enabled to interact with and sell directly to consumers. Traditional retail channels were to be disrupted as new players entered the market with online offers. Not surprisingly, many conventional retailers reacted passively to the new threat due to concern that they would cannibalize their existing customer base and jeopardize their investment in capital assets (e.g. stores). Many early pure-play e-tailers, such as European fashion entrant Boo.com, sustained losses, and there were numerous bankruptcies. Others, such as grocery retailer Peapod, were taken over by major retail groups (Ahold in this case).

With hindsight, a multichannel strategy was the obvious route to success, especially for companies with a mail order presence. Some early multichannel retailers, such as Eddie Bauer and Dixons, indicated that customers shopping at all channel alternatives (stores, catalogues and online sites) spent more than single- or dual-channel customers. This clicks-and-bricks approach gave a customer greater flexibility, including, in the case of clothing products, the opportunity to return goods to their nearest stores. This customer flexibility was to be a focus for e-tail differentiation as the platforms for selling diverged – first with the growth of mobile retailing and retailing via social networks; second as customers drew strength from their ability to review products and retailers, and their influence over sales grew through 'e-word-of-mouth' on networking sites like Twitter and Facebook; and third as customers began to demand diverse delivery options for the goods they bought online.

In some countries with well-established e-commerce sectors, the early years of the twenty-first century produced enormous growth in sales for successful e-tailers. Growth levels began to steady after a decade or so. According to retail commentators, this was not due to an unstable economic environment but a sign of a maturing B2C e-commerce market. Within this market some multichannel retailers (retailers operating multiple shopping channels including but not confined to physical stores, catalogue and Internet shopping) were producing growth levels far in excess of market norms, and consolidation was apparent among smaller and weaker pure players. Increasingly, in maturing online markets, large-scale multichannel retailers were becoming dominant.

According to Williams (2009), there has been a four-stage process in the evolution of e-tailing. The first stage included the hype and experimentation that led to the dot.com boom and bust at the turn of the millennium. This was followed by a stage of retrenchment and sobriety as funding sources for innovators dried up at the same time as the potential of the e-tail market developed and became more apparent for many established retailers. The third stage, sustainability, featured stability in the market and consolidation among e-tailers. A fourth stage of focus and fragmentation is evident as retailers provide shopping opportunities in multiple and mobile platforms, tailor their marketing mixes more precisely to the needs of individual consumers and develop multiple delivery options (see Figure 6.1).

Maturing e-tailers in economies where the strong rate of growth of the online market is slowing increasingly view international e-tail activity as the way to continued prosperity, with the Asia–Pacific and South American markets offering the most potential. The UK is one of the strongest e-tail markets, with high penetration of broadband and experienced consumers, who, in 2011, had the highest per capita online spend in the world. It is also the base of a range of e-tailers with up to 20 years' experience in online activity. As in all countries, there is considerable year-on-year change in the e-commerce market and its main players. A snapshot of the state of the market in 2011 based on IMRG statistics appears in Table 6.1. (Students can obtain similar snapshots for selected countries in the world at www.imrg.org.) At this time, online spend was estimated to be 18 per cent of total retail sales and forecast to grow 11–16 per cent in the next year.

In the UK there has been considerable change year on year in terms of e-tailer rankings, although pioneer pure player Amazon and mature clicks-and-bricks retailers Argos and Tesco have featured prominently for a long time. A snapshot of the leading e-tail players in 2012 appears in Table 6.2. In terms of the emerging m-commerce market, it can be argued that Amazon, electronics retailer and manufacturer Apple, and infomediaries Google and Facebook are key competitors.

6.2.1 Web 2.0

Web 2.0 is a term encapsulating a number of software developments that allowed the web to be used for information sharing and collaboration, and for fostering creativity, user-centred design and interoperability. Web 2.0 encouraged collaboration among professionals and academics and underpinned the development of wikis, blogging and social-networking sites.

Hype & Experimentation	Retrenchment & Sobriety	Sustainability	Focus and Fragmentation
Rapid and erratic change	Slower and more predictable change	Stability emerges with predictable cyclical patterns of differentiation	Continued cycle of differentiation by low prices or specialisation
Entrepreneurial pioneers with ambitious expansion plans, high start-up and failure rate	E-pioneers forced to adapt or die, physical retailers enter market through various modes of entry	Consolidation, focus strategy through cost leadership or differentiation	Increased business efficiencies → lower prices, integrated multi-channel systems

Figure 6.1 The evolution of e-tailing
Source: Williams, 2009.

Table 6.1 A snapshot of the UK e-commerce market in 2011

Population (UN)	61 million
Internet users	51 million
Internet shoppers	37 million
Internet household penetration (2010)	73%
Broadband household penetration (2010)	70%
Mobile subscriptions (2010)	80 million
e-commerce spend per capita (2010)	£963
Online sales (2010)	€70 billion / £58.8 billion
Online sales growth rate	18%
Average e-tail basket value	£136
Average e-tail basket value: multichannel retailers	£189
Average e-tail basket value: online-only/catalogue retailers	£101
Online spend per shopper/annum (2010)	£1,870
Online vs high street comparison	17% / 83%
Top three sectors (2010)	clothing beer, wine and spirits health and beauty
Top male purchases	films and music
Top female purchases	clothes and sporting goods
e-tail parcel deliveries/annum (2010)	£1.2 billion

Table 6.2 Top ten UK e-tailers in 2013

Amazon UK
Apple
Argos
Amazon.com
Next
Tesco
ASOS
Your M&S
John Lewis
Debenhams

Source: After IMRG, 2013.

The power of information sharing was understood comparatively early in the history of e-tailing by Amazon. The company exploited this by facilitating customer reviews of books purchased and by making the reviews easily available to online shoppers, together with professional reviews and author information. Later, potential customers were given information on book alternatives and on the final buying decisions of other viewers of the same product.

Web 2.0 allowed for the application of pure marketing principles to the e-tail market. There was a move from straightforward brochure-like visual content on e-tail web pages to the placing of the user/customer at the heart of the service, certainly in terms of service participation and personalization of content. This was further refined and exploited by mobile phone apps that gathered customer-customized data from a range of sources. Many academics and retail professionals noted that the digital revolution shifted power in the marketplace to consumers. The increase in power came from more information and transparency of information, which enabled group power, allowing consumers to influence products and prices. This affects not only how retailers market products but also how they communicate with their customers (Kucuk and Krishnamurthy, 2007).

The level of disintermediation that was expected in a virtual market did not take place to the extent predicted early in the development of the e-tail market, partly because large multichannel retailers exploited the strong brand presence gained in traditional markets to pursue a share of the online market. However, the existence of Web 2.0 enhanced the role infomediaries played in the online market, and some, such as Google, eBay and Facebook, became household names. Consider the phases of the consumer buying process, for example: infomediaries can provide much of the information consumers need to proceed through each of the phases from problem recognition to post-purchase evaluation. Infomediaries also provide much of the basic marketing information needed for both buyers and sellers, from providing search facilities to the collection and evaluation of data. Web 2.0 technology, in facilitating interaction and information sharing, for example, has contributed not only to the power of 'traditional' infomediaries but also to the growing adoption of an infomediary role among high-profile e-tailers like Amazon and Apple.

6.2.2 Exploiting the 'long tail'

When e-commerce was in its infancy, a transformation of marketing was predicted, including the facilitation of one-to-one marketing, which is one of the features of e-tail today. The web allowed for the accumulation and refinement of an enormous amount of customer data. This was made possible through the integration of customer-facing retail websites with customer relationship management (CRM) software. The relatively easy accessibility of a wealth of individualized customer data, including browsing and shopping habits, allows e-tailers to market effectively and profitably on an individual basis (Doherty and Ellis-Chadwick, 2010; Frow and Payne, 2009).

The 'long tail' was a term coined in the early 2000s to describe an emerging feature of the online marketplace in which niche demands could be profitably exploited. In some e-commerce market sectors, supply is not limited by shelf space and how much it costs to manufacture, store and distribute a product. The product becomes virtually abundant at such low costs that it can be provided at low levels of demand, whereas the costs of providing it through traditional channels outweigh potential revenues. Two examples are downloadable books and downloadable music.

Amazon developed its retail website, just-in-time delivery and huge capacity for storage to offer an almost limitless range of book titles, so that niche demand could be profitably exploited for physical books. It then successfully launched an early e-reader so that niche demand for reading materials could be exploited even more seamlessly and cheaply. Facilitation of the publishing process was a logical development so that reading materials could be supplied more efficiently for niche consumption. Apple used its innovative design capability to launch a stream of interactive hardware devices that attempted to 'tie-in' customers to products such as music and software that could be purchased or downloaded only via Apple stores.

The conventional Pareto Principle (or 80:20 rule) assumes that 80 per cent of sales can be attributed to 20 per cent of products – most sales are linked to bestselling items. The evidence of the long tail indicates that this is not applicable for online distribution and that collectively niche products can rival bestsellers in terms of sales volume. One study investigating the long tail concept found that for the same multichannel retailer, the Internet channel showed less-concentrated sales distribution than the conventional channel. Product availability and pricing were the same in both channels, so the long tail effect was not caused by differences in distribution but by the use of Internet search and discovery tools that lowered search costs for customers (Brynjolfsson *et al.*, 2011).

If Web 2.0 has enabled, simplified and reduced consumer costs for making buying decisions and underpins the long tail of the online market, it seems clear that there will be similar influences on the marketing of goods and services – a case of 'the tail wagging the dog', perhaps. Eric von Hippel (1986) has long noted the importance of user innovators sharing ideas with manufacturers to enable development of the products they want. More recently, Hippel (2005) concluded that innovation has become more user centred. Web 2.0, having made the sharing of information easier, faster and more commonplace, means that businesses that want to compete for the sizeable long tail market can implement long tail marketing (Andrei and Dumea, 2010). This includes reaching niche customers in innovative and cheap ways that will change over time. Some current examples include:

- exploiting the potential interactions through social networks and online networks;
- communicating via blogs, RSS feeds, webcasts;
- stimulating 'e-word-of-mouth' through buzz and viral marketing; and
- pay per click (PPC) and search engine optimization (SEO) that focus on less competitive long tail keywords which offer a higher return on investment than generic keywords.

Clearly, the development of Web 2.0 implies future fluidity in online markets and in the methods and means of reaching and interacting with online customers in the future.

Marketing-orientated retailers, being customer-facing organizations, have been at the forefront of user-centred innovation for many years. Many major retailers have been involved in product manufacturing through the development of their own brands, with some vertically integrating the supply chain to the level where they influence the raw materials from which the products sold in their stores are made. So it is not surprising that maturing e-tailers are in a position to exploit long tail marketing, not only in the development of their retail goods and services but also in the development and maintenance of their organizational brands, using 'Internet technologies to enable an organized cooperation with their users, giving them a voice and relying on their contribution to the process of innovation and brand value creation' (Andrei and Dumea, 2010, p.214).

The interactivity, transparency and fluidity among online social groups and customers that were fostered via Web 2.0 and which contributed to the emergence of the long tail have been exploited by large pure players like Amazon, eBay and ASOS.com as well as by multi-channel retailers like Tesco and Apple, and by Internet brands such as Google and Facebook. For example, Amazon allows customers to choose to buy books from them or from partners, with transparent pricing, and eBay lets buyers and sellers of niche collectible products agree their own price for trade. ASOS.com encourages customers to post pictures of themselves wearing ASOS merchandise. Tesco allows customers to shop for brands with partner retailers via its website. Apple hosts apps for the Amazon Kindle so that Apple customers can download books from its competitor. Google launched its own social network in 2011 and runs YouTube and Android, which offer music, TV and book apps. Facebook launched new music TV and news apps, and launched co-branded mobile phones in 2011.

6.2.3 Online shopping formats

The e-commerce market allowed for a great deal of creativity in the design of e-tail stores. As the B2C market developed, a number of distinct online retail formats could be distinguished (Zentes *et al.*, 2011).

First, **price formats** such as Overstock.com, ASOS Outlet and Tesco Outlet which sell overstocks or products from previous seasons, and auction sites such as eBay, where buyers and sellers mutually agree the selling price. Customers are attracted to e-tail portal sites that offer points or cashback for accessing other e-tailers via their websites. Examples at the time of writing were Quidco and Topcashback.

Second, **experiential formats** apply the potential of technology in creating an interesting and enjoyable online shopping experience, leading the way in exploiting social networking and discussion forums. Examples include fashion e-tailers such as ASOS and Net-A-Porter, which have developed editorial content and two-way/multi-way channels of communication between the customer and e-tailer, and among customers. Another example is that of pop-up, linear 'shops' advertising products that can be downloaded for view or purchased via mobile phone for delivery, which exploited an increasing desire for mobile shopping and explored the potential for selling via the 'm-channel' as mobile Internet access moved towards overtaking desktop Internet access in 2013–14.

Third, **community-based formats** began to emerge, which placed a virtual social community at the heart of the shopping experience. Amazon's customer reviews and customer purchase trends positively affected sales of popular products (as discussed in section 6.2.2), and the popularity of Facebook led many e-tailers to establish Facebook formats.

Fourth, **mass-customization formats** emerged which exploited the interactivity of the online environment to provide merchandise precisely tailored to the individual desires of customers. For example, customers can customize fashion items like shoes, selecting from a range of heel heights, fabrics, leathers and decorations on Shoesofprey.com, or trainers with Vans or Nike online, while Apple customers can choose various features for the hardware they buy and add engravings and accessories to their personalized mix.

Finally, merchandise-orientated formats focus on achieving a product mix that attracts customers. Types of merchandise-orientated e-tailer include **online department stores** like Debenhams.com or Johnlewis.com, which replicate or adapt the 'high street' store online, while **niche e-tailers** are online speciality stores specializing in a limited product range. Examples include the bicycle e-tailer Wiggle.com, and Net-A-Porter specializing in upmarket fashion clothing. **Online market places** like Tesco Direct and Amazon Marketplace allow customers to access a wide variety of products from partner organizations and/or from other customers. **Online category killers** achieve depth of range of a limited product category such as toys (Toys 'R' Us) or electronics (Pixmania), aiming to compete on price.

6.2.4 Multichannel retailing and growth of brand importance

The potential for exploiting brand synergy achievable through providing multiple routes for customers to shop was recognized by some large retailers early in the development of the online retail market. **Brand equity** is a term used to denote the non-financial, market-based intangible assets that build long-term marketing success and create future profits. Brand equity is an important source of competitive advantage, particularly where benefits of products or services are intangible and customers perceive high risk. The intangibility of the Internet shopping experience, the necessity of mediation technology to complete online purchases and the deferred benefit that is a result of the time gap between purchase and receipt of goods all mean that customers shopping in online stores need to trust the e-tailers providing the shopping experience. The importance of brand equity for online shoppers was confirmed by early international studies of online consumers. In 2006 the main dimensions associated with brand equity for online retailers were identified as emotional connection, online experience, responsive service nature, trust and fulfilment, and a 12-point scale was developed that could be used to measure brand equity for online retailers (Christodoulides *et al.*, 2006). The scale could be used to monitor the effect of marketing mix decisions on brand equity down to the individual consumer level.

The CEO of Dixons in the UK in the 1990s referred to the 'Martini Principle', in which customers would be able to shop anywhere, anyhow and at any time – at the time Dixons was adding online retailing to its catalogue and portfolio of in-town and out-of-town store formats, but mobile retail formats became a logical, technologically enabled extension of his vision. He also forecast the importance of customer focus, customer service and a centralized logistical function operating across channels, and believed that it was essential to portray a single corporate image across multiple channels. By 2010, six out of the top ten online retailers operated multiple channels and some pure players such as ASOS had experimented with (or had considered opening) physical retail stores.

As the online market developed in the UK, established retailers like Tesco, Marks & Spencer and Next could use their brand name to communicate their new online formats and use their online presence to reinforce the attraction of their store portfolios. These new e-tailers did not need to spend money to establish their brands (and distribution centres) from scratch, unlike Boo.com, ASOS or Amazon. Similarly, Apple exploited its brand name and innovative reputation in establishing both physical stores and an e-tail store. The brand equity built by multichannel retailers, based on their existing consumer trust in their store-based formats, could be transferred to the online stores, their logistical frameworks, returns systems and established customer service centres facilitating fulfilment, gaining trust and building customer satisfaction. There were also important opportunities for multichannel retailers to harness the geography of their store and logistics networks to minimize the exposure of e-tailing revenues to taxation and other regulatory mechanisms (Wrigley, 2010).

6.2.5 International e-tailing

The growth of the Internet audience across countries and continents referred to in section 6.2 means that experienced and mature e-tailers like ASOS.com are following Amazon's early lead into taking advantage of cross-border opportunities. In 2010 ASOS, which already distributed to more than 100 countries from its UK distribution centre, launched American, German and French websites, and in 2011 Spanish, Italian and Australian sites (in addition to launching mobile and Facebook shops in the same period). The Australian website took advantage of one of the fastest growing online retail markets, offering localized content, free shipping and local returns, with pricing in Australian dollars. The launch of Russian- and Chinese-language sites in 2013 was to be followed in 2015/16 with a second wave of development with Japan, South Korea, Brazil and India as prospective targets. This pace of investment has come at the expense of short-term profitability, with a 22 per cent decline in six months' profits up until 2014. The Chinese venture has also incurred higher than expected start up costs, mainly in meeting regulations in the clothing sector.

Colton *et al.* (2010), in a study of organizational drivers of international e-tail performance, noted the importance of brands and relationships with suppliers. While brand strength attracts customers and is related to customer satisfaction and loyalty, efficient and effective order fulfilment is essential in creating successful transactions, so good supplier relationships are an essential element in e-tail performance.

The study highlighted how important it is that e-tailers understand both their customers and the markets in which they operate. More specifically, it was found that the organizational culture of an e-tailer, exhibited in its market orientation, put it in a stronger position to achieve performance internationally. The study recommended relatively basic fundamentals of market orientation. First, an e-tailer without foreign market knowledge or expertise needed to invest in acquiring this; and second, the development of customer-centric processes including understanding customers' needs, communicating with them and sharing information about customers across business functions. To perform in international markets e-tailers need to consider market differences rather than attempt a global approach. They should deploy their understanding of international customers and markets not only in developing an internal market orientation but also in building and strengthening both brand and supplier relationships.

Founder of Amazon Jeff Bezos would agree. His annual letter to shareholders normally incorporates his 1997 letter that laid out Amazon's fundamental management and decision-making approach. The approach was clearly and firmly customer obsessed, stating: 'We will continue to focus relentlessly on our customers' (Bezos, 2010).

Table 6.3 Organizations supporting cross-border logistics in Europe

	Type of organization	Examples
1	Postal networks	UK: Royal Mail, Parcelforce; France: La Poste; Germany: Deutsche Post/DHL; Netherlands: Post NL/TNT
2	International carriers	UK: UPS, FedEx, DPD; France: UPS, GLS, DHL; Germany: UPS, GLS, DPD; Netherlands: GLS
3	Local delivery solutions	UK: Yodel, City Link, Shutl; France: Mondial Relay, Kiala; Germany: Hermes Logistik, GLS; Netherlands: Selektvracht/DHL, Kiala

Source: After IMRG, 2011.

Customer satisfaction depends not only on a successful shopping experience but also on efficient delivery and returns. Profitability is related to cost-effective logistics. According to IMRG (2011), three types of organization support cross-border logistics: postal networks, international carriers and local delivery solutions, some of which provide store-based collection points. Some organizations (for example TNT) are also developing Europe-wide reverse logistics solutions for e-tailers. Examples of organizations supporting cross-border logistics in Europe appear in Table 6.3.

6.3 The e-commerce consumer

In only a decade or so, Internet connectivity changed from an English-speaking, developed-country phenomenon to become a global one. This concealed the different stages of development for different country markets and the geo-demographic profile of Internet consumers. Most European countries lagged behind the USA, which had more than 80 per cent of households connected to the Internet as early as 2001. As the market matured, the profile of the consumer began to become more representative of the population it served. In the early stages of development the profile of the e-commerce shopper was a young male professional living in a middle-class neighbourhood. As the technology became more accepted, the gender and socio-economic mix also changed. In 2000 the market research group CACI conducted an analysis of online behaviour and buying activity of adults (over 18 years of age) in the UK. Box 6.1 provides a classification of e-types, combining CACI's core database of 30 million lifestyle records with Forrester Research's UK Internet Monitor. This shows an online lifecycle from infrequent online purchases (virtual virgins, chatters and gamers, and dot.com dabblers) to frequent online purchases (surfing suits and wired living).

Box 6.1 Segmentation of online consumers in the UK

Group 1: Virtual virgins

Of those online, this group is least likely to have bought online. Their time online is half that of the national average, and they are likely to have started using the Internet more recently than other people.

With the exception of chatting, this group do Internet activities less frequently than average. Because of their relative inexperience, they are more likely to worry about security and delivery problems with online purchases and to consider the process difficult.

Group 2: Chatters and gamers

This group might spend as much time online as the most avid type of Internet user; however, they tend not to be buyers. They may consider shopping online to be difficult, and their fear of delivery and security problems is above average.

These people are keen chatters and gamers who use newsgroups and download as frequently as the most active and experienced surfers.

Group 3: Dot.com dabblers

As average Internet users, these people have mixed feelings regarding the pros and cons of online shopping.

They may see benefits of the Internet in convenience and speed of delivery. Alternatively, a specialist product not available elsewhere may have introduced them to buying online. In any event, their enthusiasm for e-commerce is not yet complete.

Group 4: Surfing suits

Although they spend less time on the Internet than average, these people can be quite enthusiastic online purchasers.

Shopping online is seen to offer benefits such as range of product information, speed of ordering, price advantages and an element of fun. They are less likely to fear e-commerce.

They control their time on the Internet, and surfing, searching, e-mail and newsgroups tend to be preferred to chat, games or magazines.

Group 5: Wired living

These are cosmopolitan people and the most extensive Internet users. They are more experienced than most online, and the majority will have purchased over the Internet, covering between them the full range of products available for purchase. At the time of the survey, most of these people were educated to degree level.

These people use the web as part of their lifestyle. Preferred interests tend to be newsgroups, news and magazines, with only an average interest in games or chat.

Source: CACI, 2000.

This classification of online shopping categories was applied to 3,000 retail catchment areas, giving a more detailed picture of online geo-demographics in a growing e-commerce market. As would be expected, London and south-east England led the way in terms of online shopping. Nevertheless, there were 'hot spots' across the UK, with Edinburgh, Aberdeen and Bristol scoring highly despite poor overall representation in Scotland and the south-west. Areas with a poor score were cities in the north of England with a mixed income profile, and rural towns.

In a growing e-commerce market, the technology necessary for confident online shopping and the profile of those able and willing to exploit it to shop were evident first in prime urban areas. In terms of online grocery provision, shopping and delivery services all tended to become available in urban areas first.

A lot of research has taken place recently into profiling the Internet shopper. In terms of demographic variables, key influences on online behaviour include income, education, race, age and gender, with lifestyle, culture and social factors also of importance. However, research has found that as the online market has matured, the general demographic profile of the online shopper has become more similar to that of the traditional shopper. Psycho-graphic/behavioural variables include the perceptions, attitude and beliefs that can influence online shopping intentions and behaviour. Internet shoppers, according to a major international study, value convenience, are heavier users of Internet and e-mail, and tend to be wealthier and more impulsive. They also have favourable attitudes to advertising and direct marketing (Doherty and Ellis-Chadwick, 2010).

The profile of an online shopper is not just linked to demographic and psychographic/ behaviour variables that favour online shopping, or to geography, technology and confidence in the online market, but also to the merchandise being bought. For example, the age profile for online grocery shoppers tends to be younger, in the 18–40 age range. There tend to be children in the household. A study by the Institute of Grocery Distribution (IGD) found that online shopping for groceries was linked to the birth of children, and to times such as school holidays, when children are around the house more. Grocery shoppers also tend to be in the higher social categories. Older shoppers (65 plus) were less likely to shop online for groceries (IGD, 2011).

As in physical stores, the online shopping experience is now carefully designed to retain shopper interest and influence purchases, so the various store attributes (to be discussed in section 6.5) influence in-store and between-store shopping behaviour and Internet purchases.

Much of this discussion on the e-shopper has focused upon a PC or laptop connected to the Internet as the medium of choice. For much of the 1990s, however, the development of TV shopping was often mooted as the likely channel to dominate the e-commerce market. Television shopping channels were already common in the USA, and by the early 1990s had entered the UK market. Penetration of cable and satellite TV was low in Europe compared with North America, but the arrival of digital TV (DTV) was seen as the catalyst for the growth of interactive TV. Much of this optimism failed to materialize. Evidence from the USA had already suggested that the motivations for watching TV were very different from those for PC usage. The latter is individualistic compared with the companionship associated with the TV. The convergence of television and Internet technology was slower than expected, and to a large extent the rapid development and growth of mobile devices such as tablets and Internet-enabled mobile phones became the focus for shoppers and retailers.

Early research into m-commerce customers indicates some similarities to customers in the early years of the uptake of e-commerce, for example most shoppers (62 per cent in 2005) were young (14–24-year-old) males. They tended to be confident Internet users and experienced Internet shoppers (Bigne *et al.*, 2005). The demographic and gender profile is likely to rebalance as the technology becomes widely familiar and the market develops. Internet use was not found to influence mobile shopping, but previous experience of Internet purchase meant consumers were more predisposed to buy on mobile devices.

6.4 e-tail store development

6.4.1 The role of the web in retailing

Internet retailing is not just about providing 24/7 online shopping opportunities. Online retailing offers retailers sales via potentially limitless shelf space, unconfined by store size, shape and location (although there are virtual equivalents of all three), and the large online retailers have exploited this potential to increase share of consumer online spend.

The web plays a variety of roles for retailers, depending upon their size, maturity and objectives. According to Berman and Evans (2010), the web plays a much wider role in terms of communication with customers. It is used to communicate a retail or brand presence to a wider, more geographically dispersed audience and to enhance retailer image. Many retailers provide extensive product information online so that customers can shortlist products to look at in store, and some provide video material to demonstrate the features and benefits of complex products. It is used to promote new products and offers and for selling excess stock via 'in-store' outlet web pages, through online discount outlets or through auction outlets like eBay.

The web also has a role in providing customer service. Retailers can provide simple and easy routes for customers to secure advice, give feedback, make complaints or gain information about products. It is used for personalized contact with customers via e-mail and to provide a more targeted shopping experience. Many retailers use the web to provide information for shareholders and potential investors, as an aid for recruiting employees or franchisees, and as a resource for media and education. Large retailers will present their corporate, marketing and corporate responsibility strategies, for example, and often provide a 'potted history' or key facts section as a further means to promote the desired corporate image.

6.4.2 e-tail store development

Although there were online malls and transactional retail websites from the mid-1990s, they were small and crude by today's standards. Broadband was not widely available, and download speeds were too slow to attract large numbers of shoppers. Nevertheless, there was great excitement about the potential of online shopping, and some companies invested huge sums of money. Boo.com, an early example of an over-ambitious fashion e-store, launched in Europe in the early days of e-commerce in 1998 and foundered after investing

US$135 million in 18 months on developing, launching and advertising a retail offer that was flawed in the face of a market that was not yet technologically or socially ready for it. Creating awareness of a new online store required spending an enormous amount on advertising through traditional media. The advertised launch was delayed, impacting on potential sales. Accessing Boo.com web pages was a very slow process, as was viewing merchandise. Packaging was unnecessarily elaborate. The company soon found out about the high rate of returns experienced by most online retailers, which were not charged for but incurred costs. Boo.com was an early, and deserved, victim of the dot.com crash of 2000 as funds for driving its aggressive growth plan dried up.

Meanwhile, other retailers established an early web presence with a limited range of stock before launching full-scale e-tail stores. One example is Tesco.com, which was selling from an online store in 1996, offering merchandise such as alcohol and flowers. At the time, many people did not even have computers, and levels of Internet access were low in the UK, so potential customers tended to be young, male, well educated and technically literate – a limited market. Technological and market developments were so fast that by 2000 Tesco had launched an ambitious UK-wide online grocery service. By contrast with Boo.com, Tesco, with experience of e-commerce on a small scale, planned for early losses; put in place a picking and distribution model using its existing store portfolio; planned for returns; and had in place an outstanding customer service centre to handle the inevitable problems that would emerge as both customers and company developed their online expertise. As a known and trusted business brand before launching its full grocery e-store, Tesco did not have to spend advertising money establishing brand awareness.

Berman and Evans (2010) identify five phases in developing a web presence. In the early years of e-commerce most established retailers did not progress past phase one: establishing a brochure website with limited company, store location and product information. Phase two comprises establishing an e-commerce transactional retail website. Phase three involves integrating the transactional retail website with buying, inventory and accounting, so that, for example, high-selling items are replenished or out of stock products automatically removed from the website. Phase four is the 'webified store'. This is about integrating information among physical stores and transactional retail website. For example, customers or staff can access web browsers in store to get real-time information on stock. They can buy items that are not available in store, find the location of a store carrying the items wanted or arrange delivery to a suitable location. Phase five is where suppliers can automatically replenish stock or ship stock directly to the customer.

6.5 Online store attributes

As online usage increased, more research was conducted into the shopping service attributes of e-tailing compared with conventional store attributes. Most products and services can be obtained through alternative channels, so the e-tail offer has to provide additional benefits to the consumer that they cannot receive from traditional channels. The majority of studies indicated that such benefits are convenience, the saving of time and lower prices associated with some Internet retailers. Companies such as Priceline.com hoped to change the nature of the retail and service market through its 'name your price' auctions for airline seats, hotel rooms, petrol and grocery products.

Broadly, online store attributes fall into the following categories:

- navigation and convenience;
- merchandise mix;
- pricing;
- customer service; and
- security.

Navigation and convenience relate to a consumer's ability to reduce transaction costs through visiting a website rather than a retail outlet. Navigating easy-to-use, unfettered sites will minimize the time and effort to search and buy products and services. Conversely, a time-constrained consumer will be inconvenienced by a site that is slow to navigate and difficult to use.

Merchandise mix relates to the merchandise on offer with regard to the overall assortment, variety and product information. One of the advantages that pure-play e-tailers had over their bricks-and-mortar counterparts was that they developed their websites around their position in the market and the product assortment on offer. Many conventional retailers with a large number of stock-keeping units (SKUs) and a variety of product categories found it difficult to make available the same product range on their online stores.

Conceptually, **pricing** should be a key online shopping attribute in that consumers should have a reduction in search costs, more product information and a greater opportunity to compare prices. In practice, the importance of price as a choice attribute is not unlike the situation with conventional store choice. Price is only one of a multitude of factors that influence patronage behaviour. Reynolds (2002) reported that much of the research into online pricing was inconclusive and at times contradictory. Nevertheless, price is clearly an important variable for specific online product categories where consumers know what they want and are prepared to buy at the cheapest price. This explains the relative success of early online retailers selling books, CDs and computer equipment.

Customer service or the overall service quality experience embraces some of the other attributes discussed in this section: convenience, navigation and security. Here we will focus more upon the service process. Customers surfing a website invariably need help with product selection and services available. Having traded off the inconvenience of going to the store, customers need to know how/when to pay, when the goods will be delivered, and what after-sales service is available for returning goods or complaining about elements of poor service.

Security was a major negative factor in deterring consumers from buying online in the early years of e-commerce development. Consumers were initially concerned about credit card and other forms of payment fraud. More recently, issues about the disclosure of personal as well as financial information, and possible theft of goods in transit to the customer's address are also of concern to customers. Americans led the way in experiencing the deluge of junk e-mail to parallel that of the junk mail revolution of earlier decades.

Longitudinal surveys undertaken by various authors in the late 1990s illustrated how the e-tailing market developed in terms of both the customer base and the range of online offerings. In the USA, the peak period of demand for Internet retailing is between Thanksgiving and Christmas. Lavin (2002) drew upon consumer surveys undertaken by consultancy companies during Christmas 1998 and 1999 and her own primary research of retailers' websites during the same period. She commented that the profile of the web shopper was changing, that e-tailers had to work to meet rising consumer expectations, and that the 'first-to-market' advantage of early adopters had been eroded. The customer of 1998 was predominantly male, technologically proficient and relatively affluent. More significantly, they were not mainstream shoppers and had low expectations for their online purchase experience. Lavin equated this with the innovator and early adopter stages of the adoption lifecycle. A year later, with a rapidly growing market, the profile of the online customer had changed to a more balanced gender and age, with overall lower average incomes. These were more likely to be mainstream shoppers with higher expectations from their purchase experiences. This early majority segment raised the stakes for online providers. Considerable investment was made to upgrade sites, to advertise on traditional media to attract customers, and in logistical infrastructure to ship products to customers' homes. Despite this, the Christmas period has remained notorious for failure of online retailers to meet the Christmas deadline, partly due to consumers delaying purchase to the last minute but also to sheer volume of business in the network or weather problems hampering delivery.

In the UK, Ellis-Chadwick *et al.* (2002) completed a longitudinal study of Internet adoption by UK multiple retailers from 1997 to 2000. Again, as in Lavin's study, the primary research was largely based on reviewing retail websites over this four-year period to ascertain how Internet business models were being developed. They reported a six-fold increase in the number of retailers offering online shopping to their customers. Companies moved from offering purely informational services to a fully serviced transactional e-shop. More well-established retailers started to become more creative in linking their sites to other companies with complementary products – for example, Birthday.co.uk to Thorntons, suppliers of chocolates, and Wax Lyrical, a specialist candle retailer.

These studies, and other more sector-specific research investigations, indicated that retailers were responding to the choice attributes identified earlier. However, as the market matured, consumers tended to behave in a similar fashion to when dealing with traditional retail outlets. The basics of convenience, product range, customer service and price will always feature in a consumer's 'evoked set' of attributes. Above all, retailers became established brands and customer loyalty was established through continually high levels of service. It is not surprising, therefore, that traditional retailers with strong brand equity could gain even more leverage through a sound web strategy. They had the trust of the consumer to begin with and the capital to invest in the necessary infrastructure. Many pure players needed to build a brand and tackle the formidable challenge of delivering to customers' homes. This is why it took Amazon.com so long to register a profit. Nevertheless, even in 2000 Amazon.com had strong brand presence, and research by Brynjolfsson and Smith (2000) indicated that the company could charge higher prices because of this brand equity, or what they termed **heterogeneity of trust**. In their survey of online pricing in specific markets, they showed that Amazon.com had a market share of around 80 per cent in books, yet charged a 10 per cent premium over the least expensive book retailer in their research. Internet pricing has, of course, come a long way since the relatively simplistic early millennium models.

6.5.1 Factors affecting online shopping

Despite the strong growth in online shopping, B2C e-commerce remains a relatively small sector of the retail market. So what factors prevent people from shopping online? Lack of broadband access remains a problem for an increasing minority of people, and the inconvenience of shopping online also inhibits uptake of shopping opportunities. However, as online shopping opportunities move away from the home computer and as uptake of mobile broadband increases, the inconvenience of shopping online reduces.

Lack of trust and fear are further inhibitors of online shopping. The growth of e-commerce has underpinned similar growth in fraudulent activity and websites. One of the reasons for the success of 'high street' retailers in achieving online sales is the trust associated with their business brand. For example, if a person shops with John Lewis online, they have the confidence of knowing it is a long-established brand, that there is associated trust that the systems and policies will work in the customer's favour, and that the company is financially sound. Buying from an unknown or unfamiliar e-tailer brings with it a fear that money may be lost, goods undelivered and customer service unavailable. Information can be gained on unfamiliar e-tailers through e-word-of-mouth, via review or social-networking sites, but this is time consuming. Lack of privacy is also a growing concern for online shoppers. With registration required to shop, personal data are available to retailers, and browsing and shopping activity tracked. While this allows personalization of the shopping experience that may favour the customer, there remains the fear that privacy can be violated and data misused.

Some people prefer the personal interaction and entertainment provided through shopping in bricks-and-mortar stores. They like to compare goods, touch and try out products or try on merchandise. Others are put off by the cost of delivery; even though there is an increasing choice of price and method of delivery in some stores, free delivery is rare. This can also contribute to high returns as people order in more merchandise than they need to make the final choice at home, returning the rest.

6.5.2 Critical success factors in e-tailing

A study by Sahney (2008) found that critical success factors for online retailers include:

- simple and unambiguous purchase transactions;
- clear transaction policies;
- online interactivity between buyer and seller;
- transaction safety;
- transaction privacy;
- quick loading times;
- ease of navigation and search; and
- an accurate product and service delivery system.

The study found that e-tailers needed to focus most on the final three factors because they drive the success of the whole system. In terms of online store attributes, focus is needed on making merchandise easy to find and quick to load. Merchandise has to be accurately represented visually and in terms of availability. This study highlights that trans-action privacy is of key importance in addition to safety. Interactivity is also important, and it is interesting to note that it is online interactivity that is required, which indicates the maturity of technological capability among online shoppers (as well as disillusionment with retailers that provide automated, slow and difficult-to-access telephone help). Another study (Pentina *et al.*, 2011) also referred to the importance of interactivity, finding that enriching relational and interactive experiences on a website increase satisfaction of shop-pers. However, that satisfaction does not necessarily result in immediate purchase decisions, but can create positive e-word-of-mouth that leads to an increase in website traffic and repeat visits, and hence potentially increased sales.

6.6 The online grocery market

Despite the fact that online grocery sales account for a small percentage of retail sales in most country markets, this sector has attracted most attention from researchers and gov-ernment bodies, including the UK Department of Trade and Industry (DTI, 2001). Gro-cery shopping impacts all consumers. We all have to eat! However, our populations are getting older, so shopping is more of a chore; conversely, the younger, time-poor, affluent consumers may hate to waste time buying groceries. The relatively slow uptake of online grocery shopping in the USA could be attributed to the lack of online shopping availability, in that only about one third of supermarket operators offer some type of home shopping service.

Morganosky and Cude (2002) undertook one of the first studies into the behaviour of online grocery shoppers. Their research was based on a longitudinal study of consumers of Schnucks Markets, a St Louis-based chain of supermarkets operating in Illinois, Missouri and Indiana. The first two surveys, in 1998 and 1999, asked Schnucks' online shoppers to complete a questionnaire online on the completion of heir order. The final survey re-contacted respondents from the 1999 survey to track their shopping behaviours in 2001. The results here did have some parallels with other surveys of non-food online shopping, most notably more sophisticated consumers who had moved on from being 'new' users to experienced online shoppers. This was further reflected in their willingness to buy most or all their groceries online and to improve their efficiency at completing the shopping tasks. The main difference noted from this research compared with other work was the profile of the consumer, which remained relatively stable over the time period. Online grocery shoppers bought for the family. They were younger, female and better educated, with higher incomes. The final survey showed that customer retention rates were good. The main reason for defections was relocation to another part of the USA where the same online service was not available.

Although similar empirical research has not been carried out in the UK, trade sources indicate that the online consumer has become more experienced and is buying more online. Two of the main e-grocers in the UK, Tesco and Sainsbury's, claim that their online cus-tomers spend more than their conventional customers. Tesco also explodes the myth that online customers would not buy fresh products because of the so-called 'touch and feel' factor. Indeed, the opposite is true – as early as 2001, seven of the top ten selling lines were fresh, with skinless chicken breasts at number one (Jones, 2001). Tesco, however, is one of the few success stories in e-grocery. The company has come a long way since its pilot trials in December 1996. It now dominates the UK online grocery market and is the world leader, mainly through the development of online operations in most of its international subsidiaries. The company experienced double-digit growth in online sales throughout the late 2000s/early 2010s, although profitability has been affected with costly innovations in reducing time windows for delivery and the introduction of the 'click and collect' scheme, whereby customers can order online and pick up in store. It should be noted that it is difficult to disaggregate performance of grocery from non-food operations, as Tesco.com sales are aggregated in the annual reports. The success of Tesco can be attributed to, inter alia, its strong brand presence, its first-mover advantage and its choice of the most suitable e-fulfilment model, the latter of which is discussed later in this chapter (Hackney *et al.*, 2006).

In Europe, grocery retailers are powerful bricks-and-mortar companies, and the approach to Internet retailing there has been reactive rather than proactive. Most Internet operations have been small, and few pure players have entered the market to challenge the conventional supermarket chains.

The situation is different in the USA, where a more fragmented, regionally orientated grocery retail structure has encouraged new entrants into the market. In the late 1980s, this came in the form of warehouse clubs and Walmart Supercenters; by the 1990s, dot. com players began to challenge the traditional supermarket operators (Table 6.4 identifies the key players, along with Tesco for comparison, at that time). Unfortunately, these pure players have either gone into liquidation, scaled down their operations or been taken over by conventional grocery businesses. Lim *et al.* (2009), in their study of web content of

Table 6.4 The major existing and former e-grocers

	Tesco UK	Webvan USA	Streamline USA	Peapod USA
Background	The biggest supermarket chain in the UK	Started as a pure e-grocer in 1999	Started as a pure e-grocer in 1992	Started home delivery service before the Internet in 1989
Initial Investments in e-grocer development	$58 million	Approx. $1,200 million	Approx. $80 million	Approx. $150 million
Main operational mode	Industrialized picking from the supermarket	Highly automated picking in distribution centre (DC)	Picking from the DC, reception boxes, value-adding services	Picking from both DC and from stores
Current status	The biggest e-grocer in the world. Expanding its operations outside the UK through international subsidiaries	Operations ceased July 2001	Part of operations was sold to Peapod in September 2000. The rest of operations ceased in November 2000	Bought by global grocery retailer Royal Ahold. Second biggest e-grocer in the world

Source: After Tanskanen et al., 2002.

e-grocers in the USA, indicate the volatility of the market, in that during the data-collection period of their survey numerous companies both entered and exited the market; the authors noted that this relatively low adoption rate is because e-grocery is considered a service innovation to US consumers. Most of the literature at the turn of the millennium focused on how this innovation did not give consumers a perceived competitive advantage over entrenched traditional grocery retailers.

Commenting on why pure players have failed, Laseter *et al.* (2000) identify four key challenges:

- limited online potential;
- high cost of delivery;
- selection variety trade-offs; and
- existing entrenched competition.

Ring and Tigert (2001) came to similar conclusions when comparing the Internet offering with the conventional bricks-and-mortar experience. They looked at what consumers would trade away from a store in terms of the place, product, service and value for money by shopping online. They also detailed the 'killer costs' of the pure-play Internet grocers, notably the picking and delivery costs. The gist of the argument presented by these critics is that the basic Internet model is flawed.

Even if the potential is there, the consumer has to be lured away from existing behaviour with regard to store shopping. Convenience is invariably ranked as the key choice variable in both store patronage and Internet usage surveys. For store shoppers, convenience is about location, interaction with staff and the store experience. Internet users tend to be trading off the time it takes to shop. However, as Wilson-Jeanselme (2001) has shown, the 58 per cent net gain in convenience benefit is often eroded by 'leakages' in the process of ordering to ultimate delivery. Furthermore, the next two key store choice variables in the USA tend to be price and assortment. With the exception of Webvan, pure players offered a limited number of SKUs compared with conventional supermarkets. Price may have been competitive with stores, but delivery charges push prices up for the customer. In the highly competitive US grocery market, customers will switch stores for only a 3–4 per cent differential in prices across leading competitors. Ring and Tigert therefore pose the question:

> What percentage of households will pay substantially more for an inferior assortment (and perhaps quality) of groceries just for the convenience of having them delivered to their home?
>
> (Ring and Tigert, 2001, p. 270)

Tanskanen *et al.* (2002) argue that e-grocery companies failed because an electronic copy of a supermarket does not work. They claim that e-grocery should be a complementary channel rather than a substitute, and that companies should be investing in service innovations to give value to the customer. Building upon their research in Finland, they maintain that the clicks-and-bricks model will lead to success for e-grocery. Most of the difficulties for pure players relate to building a business with its associated infrastructure. Conventional retailers have built trust with their suppliers and customers. The customer needs a credible alternative to self-service, and the Finnish researchers suggest that this has to be achieved at a local level, where routine purchases can be shifted effectively to e-grocery. To facilitate product selection, web-based information technology can tailor the retail offer to the customer's needs. The virtual store can be more creative than the restrictions placed on the physical stocking of goods on shelves; however, manufacturers will need to provide 'pre-packaged' electronic product information for ordering on the web.

6.7 e-fulfilment

Regardless of the nature of the 'accepted' e-grocery model of the future, the 'last mile' problem continues to pose difficulties for e-grocers. In many ways, the initial pure players in the USA have pioneered the various fulfilment models (see Table 6.4). Webvan raised $360 million of share capital in October 1999 partly to fund the construction of 26 giant warehouses, each greater than 300,000 sq. ft, in 26 cities. The model is a hub-and-spokes logistics system in each of these regions. The highly automated warehouses stocked around 50,000 SKUs, and orders were picked and moved by conveyor belt to loading trucks, which transported products to 10–12 substations in the region. Here, loads were broken down into customers' orders for onward delivery by company trucks. Webvan could not generate sufficient volume to cover the fixed costs of the investment in its warehouse infrastructure and ceased operations in July 2001. Streamline, the other innovative US pure player, did offer value-added services. It was the pioneer of unattended reception whereby the Stream Box was accessed by keypad entry systems in the garage. The company also offered to replenish automatically inventory of key value items for customers, in addition to other services such as dry cleaning, video rental and shoe repairs. This fragmentation of offering did not build up a customer base quickly enough before the company ran out of cash in 2000.

In the UK, much of the early experimentation with online grocery focused upon the London region because of the high density of drops that could be achieved. Tesco opted for the store fulfilment model while its main competitors, Sainsbury's and Asda, developed picking centres. Waitrose, a major south-east England chain, developed its Waitrose@Work service, delivering to the workplace of key businesses along the corridor of the M4 motorway. It is interesting to note that in 2014 Waitrose and other major grocery retailers were trialling lockers at transport nodes to target working commuters as part of their 'click and collect' initiatives.

Discussions on the main fulfilment models can be found in Chapter 9. It is necessary to note here, however, that the store-based fulfilment model, as advocated by Tesco, offers the best short-term solution to meeting growing market demand for online grocery retailing. Once an optimal level of demand is reached, picking centres become a viable option, and Tesco now operates six centres in the south-east of England, the first opening in Croydon in 2006. Even then, the so-called 'killer costs' of order processing, picking and delivery for groceries in the UK were estimated to be between £8 and £20 per order, depending on the system operated and utilization of vehicle fleets (DTI, 2001). As delivery to the customer was estimated to be around £5 per order, it is clear that unless the order value is high, retailers will make a loss on every delivery that they make.

The potential solution to this 'last mile' problem is to have some form of unattended reception facility at home/collection, or to persuade customers to accept more flexible time windows for attended deliveries. Indeed, Tesco initially trialled differential cost structures for attended delivery in 2002 so that customers would have a reduced delivery charge: £3.99 for deliveries determined by Tesco, and more expensive charges, £6.99, for time slots fixed by the customer. As indicated in the previous section, Tesco has offered one-hour delivery slots in the London region to improve customer service, albeit at the expense of profitability.

Initially, to achieve the cost savings required, it will be necessary to change customer attitudes to existing forms of home delivery. However, unattended delivery options provide another series of challenges, such as potential crime threats in the e-tailing channel. For example, what security measures will be necessary to protect reception boxes from burglary, and how will attended deliveries be accounted for when the recipient is not at home and the goods are stolen? Many retailers, including non-food retailers, have been investing in the 'click and collect' option as a more cost-effective solution, in that it is the consumer who is bearing the transport costs.

6.8 Summary

This chapter has charted the major changes that have occurred in e-commerce in recent years and the impact that these changes have had on the retail sector. The growth and size of the market were illustrated and the development of e-commerce introduced. The e-commerce consumer has changed in a relatively short period of time from the initial adopter, who tended to be a young male professional living in a middle-class neighbourhood. As the technology became more widely available and access to online retailing more flexible, the gender and age biases were removed and the socio-economic mix changed.

e-tailers had to respond to a more discerning consumer as sales volumes began to grow. To lure customers away from traditional shopping patterns, these retailers have had to embrace many of the same attributes evident in store choice models: convenience, product range, customer service and price. The best pure players, such as Amazon.com, have built up a reputation for their high levels of customer service and have therefore achieved a high degree of brand loyalty.

However, the strong, established multichannel retailers capitalized on the failure of many dot.com companies. An Internet presence allowed them to capitalize on their existing brand equity in addition to having the required investment to develop the necessary infrastructure. A clicks-and-bricks approach has proven the most successful model to date, in that synergies can be achieved through a multichannel strategy.

The one retail sector that has attracted most interest, despite the fact that its percentage of online sales is low or even non-existent in most country markets, is the grocery sector. The potential market is large, but success remains elusive to all but a few companies. In the USA, in particular, the demise of Webvan and Streamline shows that you can have the 'ideal' online model but that without sufficient market demand, losses are inevitable. Tesco is one of the few success stories here, primarily because it grew the business incrementally and used a store-based delivery model until demand was sufficient to build picking centres. Even for Tesco, the 'last mile' problem still requires a solution. Order processing, picking and delivering groceries are the 'killer costs' of online grocery retailing. A range of solutions has been proposed to solve this problem, and 'click and collect' schemes appear to be the favoured, cost-effective option in the mid-2010s.

Review questions

1   Discuss Williams's four-stage model of e-commerce evolution.
2   To what extent has Web 2.0 reshaped the e-commerce market, especially in exploiting the 'long tail'?
3   Discuss the changing profile of the e-commerce and, more recently, the m-commerce consumer over time.
4   Discuss the key choice attributes for shopping online and compare these with conventional store choice attributes.
5   Evaluate the problems of e-fulfilment in online grocery retailing and comment upon the types of fulfilment model and solutions to the 'last mile' problem.

References

Andrei, A.G. and Dumea, A. (2010) 'Economics of long tail: a challenge for branding', *The Annals of the Stefan cel Mare University of Suceava, the Faculty of Economics and Public Administration*, 10: 210–216.

Berman, B. and Evans, J.R. (2010) *Retail Management: A Strategic Approach* (11th edn). Upper Saddle River, NJ: Prentice Hall.

Bezos, J. (2010) '2010 Letter to shareholders', Amazon.com Investor Relations: Annual Reports and Proxies, phx.corporate-ir.net/phoenix.zhtml?c=97664&p=irol-reportsannual (accessed 30 November 2011).

Bigne, E., Ruiz, C. and Sanz, S. (2005) 'The impact of Internet user shopping patterns and demographics on consumer mobile buying behaviour', *Journal of Electronic Commerce Research*, 6(3): 193–207.

Brynjolfsson, E., Hu, Y.J. and Simester, D. (2011) 'Goodbye Pareto Principle, hello long tail: the effect of search costs on the concentration of product sales', *Management Science*, 57(8): 1373–1386.

Brynjolfsson, E. and Smith, M. (2000) 'Frictionless commerce? A comparison of Internet and conventional retailers', *Management Science*, 46(4): 563–585.

CACI (2000) *Who's Buying Online?* London: CACI Information Solutions.

Christodoulides, G., De Chernatony, D., Furrer, O., Shiu, E. and Abimbola, T. (2006) 'Conceptualising and measuring the equity of online brands', *Journal of Marketing Management*, 22: 799–825.

Colton, D.A., Roth, M.S. and Bearden, W.O. (2010) 'Drivers of international e-tail performance: the complexities of orientations and resources', *Journal of International Marketing*, 18(1) (March): 1–22.

Department of Trade and Industry (DTI) (2001) *@ Your Home, New Markets for Customer Service and Delivery*. London: Retail Logistics Task Force, Foresight.

Doherty, N.F. and Ellis-Chadwick, F. (2010) 'Internet retailing: the past, the present and the future', *International Journal of Retail and Distribution Management*, 38(11/12): 943–965.

Ellis-Chadwick, F., Doherty, N.F. and Hast, C. (2002) 'Signs of change? A longitudinal study of Internet adoption in the UK retail sector', *Journal of Retailing and Consumer Services*, 9(2): 71–80.

Frow, P. and Payne, A. (2009) 'Customer relationship management: a strategic perspective', *Journal of Business Marketing Management*, 3(1): 7–27.

Hackney, R., Grant, K. and Birtwistle, G. (2006) 'The UK grocery business: towards a sustainable model for virtual markets', *International Journal of Retail and Distribution Management*, 34(4/5): 354–368.

Hippel, E. von (1986) 'Lead users: a source of novel product concepts', *Management Science*, 32(7): 791–805.

Hippel, E. von (2005) *Democratizing Innovation*. Cambridge, MA: MIT Press.

IMRG (2011) 'United Kingdom e-business information', www.imrg.org (accessed 25 October 2011).

IMRG (2013) 'Top 100 online retailers in the UK, 2013', www.imrg.org (accessed 13 June 2014).

Institute of Grocery Distribution (IGD) (2011) 'Online grocery retailing: building capacity for a digital future', www.igd.com/index.asp?id=1&fid=2&sid=2&cid=1845 (accessed February 2012).

Jones, D. (2001) 'Tesco.com: delivering home shopping', *ECR Journal*, 1(1): 37–43.

Kucuk, S.U. and Krishnamurthy, S. (2007) 'An analysis of consumer power on the Internet', *Technovation*, 27(1–2): 47–56.

Laseter, T., Houston, P., Ching, A., Byrne, S., Turner, M. and Devendran, A. (2000) 'The last mile to nowhere', *Strategy and Business*, 20 (September).

Lavin, M. (2002) 'Christmas on the web: 1998 v 1999', *Journal of Retailing and Consumer Services*, 9(2): 87–96.

Lim, H., Widdows, R. and Hooker, N.H. (2009) 'Web content analysis of e-grocery retailers: a longitudinal study', *International Journal of Retail and Distribution Management*, 37(10): 839–851.

Manjoo, F. (2011) 'The great tech war of 2012', Fast Company, www.fastcompany.com/1788728/the-great-tech-war-of-2012-ongoing-skirmishes (accessed 25 October 2011).

Morganosky, M.A. and Cude, B. (2002) 'Consumer demand for online food retailing: is it really a supply side issue?' *International Journal of Retail and Distribution Management*, 30(10): 451–458.

Pentina, I., Amialchuk, A. and Taylor, D.G. (2011) 'Exploring effects of online shopping experiences on browser satisfaction and e-tail performance', *International Journal of Retail and Distribution Management*, 39(10): 742–758.

Reynolds, J. (2002) 'E-tail marketing', in *Retail Marketing* (McGoldrick, P.J., ed., 2nd edn). London: McGraw-Hill.

Ring, L.J. and Tigert, D.J. (2001) 'Viewpoint: the decline and fall of Internet grocery retailers', *International Journal of Retail and Distribution Management*, 29(6): 266–273.

Sahney, S. (2008) 'Critical success factors in online retail: an application of quality function deployment and interpretive structural modelling', *International Journal of Business and Information*, 3(1): 144–163.

Tanskanen, K., Yroyla, M. and Holmstron, J. (2002) 'The way to profitable Internet grocery retailing – 6 lessons learned', *International Journal of Retail and Distribution Management*, 30(4): 169–178.

Williams, D.E. (2009) 'The evolution of e-tailing', *The International Review of Retail, Distribution and Consumer Research*, 19(3): 219–249.

Wilson-Jeanselme, M. (2001) 'Grocery retailing on the Internet: the leaking bucket theory', *European Retail Digest*, 30: 9–12.

Wrigley, N. (2010) 'Globalising retail and B2C e-commerce: a report commissioned by the OECD Trade Policy Linkages and Services Division for the OECD Experts Meeting on Distribution Services, Paris', *European Retail Digest*, 30 (17 November 2011), 9–12.

Zentes, J., Morschett, D. and Schramm-Klein, H. (2011) *Strategic Retail Management: Text and International Cases* (2nd edn). Wiesbaden: Gabler Verlag/Springer Fachmedien.

7 Product management

Learning objectives

After studying this chapter, you should be able to:

- Understand the impact of online developments upon product management in retailing.
- Evaluate the nature and value of a product management approach within retailing.
- Understand the five main roles that contribute to an effective product management team.
- Analyse the central importance of trend analysis, supplier selection and the open to buy budget as part of the retail product management process.

7.1 The new age of product management

> The Internet has transformed every aspect of how retailers manage their products. But perhaps the fundamental change is that everything that was once unknown and unobtainable is now known and obtainable all because of the Internet. Every product that the customer sees online becomes a purchase possibility. Every site where they can buy becomes a rival. We live in a completely new age for buying and merchandising.
>
> (Buying director, UK department store group)

The way in which consumer goods and services are accessed and consumed has been fundamentally transformed in the past decade as a result and consequence of the Internet. The Internet has shrunk distances between buyers and sellers, and consumers now have perpetual access to a global shop front. The Internet has had a profound impact upon retail product management in three important ways.

The first relates to the nature and variety of information that is now readily available to consumers. Ever since formal retailing structures were established, and distribution systems became formalized and stable, information about consumer goods and services was controlled, in the main, by retailers. Consumers really only knew about certain products and services by the will of their local retailers and what they chose to stock. Consumers' product intelligence was therefore narrow, their sources of information were few and their engagement with new products was localized to the retail stores where they shopped. Product information was highly concentrated to that of the retailer.

The advent of mass advertising did result in something of a shift in power. As manufacturers sought to subvert the product information power of the retailer by using television and print advertising to promote their new products to consumers, they were able to inform customers directly about their new products and their brands. The rise of manufacturer brand communications displaced some of the retailers' power, but not all of it. While consumers may well have been more aware of new and alternative manufacturers' products, they still relied upon their retailers to stock these products in order for them to be able to buy, and while the development of catalogue retailing did provide alternative access channels for consumers, these never reached the market penetration levels enjoyed by store-based retailers.

So, prior to the 'Internet Age' consumer access to intelligence about alternative products and services was limited, controlled and restricted. The Internet changed the information dynamic and made product information access readily available to consumers.

Second, and inextricably linked to an improved access to product intelligence, the advent of the Internet also provided unprecedented access to purchase new products for consumers. With the advancement of transactional websites, improved security reliability and developments in financial transaction infrastructures (such as the emergence of payment intermediaries like PayPal), consumers were now able to access products and buy them safely and easily not only from sellers within their own country, but also internationally.

The emergence of international e-commerce companies, such as Amazon.com, further facilitated and enhanced product access by bringing together disparate product categories conveniently and attractively. Now, consumers can access products from the other side of the world, confidently and easily. They no longer need to rely solely upon their local retailer to provide the international product assortment of their choice.

Third, the Internet has created important and highly influential consumption-sharing communities. Through the development of myriad social media platforms, consumers have seized the opportunity to exchange information about their brand, product and service experiences. They are able to express views and opinions freely and openly. As direct users of brands, products and services, their opinions are potent in terms of integrity and, as a result, the views expressed have influence and impact.

In the past, consumers could rely only upon the experiences and advice of a narrow field of user experts. These influencers were usually friends, colleagues or family members, and while the views and opinions that these personal communities exerted were often very powerful, their reach did not necessarily extend to cover all brand or product areas. As such, consumers had to rely also upon the views and opinions expressed in the media for guidance, such as that expressed in editorials and newspaper articles. While some of these media-based opinions were certainly independent, the majority was the result of a paid influence. Consequently, consumers become increasingly sceptical about the truth and integrity of the advertisements that they saw and the articles that they read about products and services. It is within this context of 'product scepticism' that people grasped the communications possibilities that the Internet provided and so consumer-managed online discussion communities emerged. Initially through the establishment of informal chat rooms, blogs and discussion forums, and then through social-networking sites, these have emerged as the most potent form of consumer influence on contemporary consumption behaviour.

In order to replicate the perceived authority, honesty and integrity of unadulterated consumer comment and exchange, many leading retailers have provided opportunities for customers to comment directly and openly about their experience of specific products and services. While many retailers have sought to maintain these as neutral spaces, consumers could be forgiven for disbelieving that these customer comment areas are not policed and vetted by the retailers in some way.

Regardless of whether these retailer comment areas are expressed freely and independently, what is clear is that the Internet has provided an important vehicle of expression about products and services that asserts and affirms consumers' power and influence.

Bringing together the various strands of impact that the Internet has had upon contemporary consumption, access to information, direct access to sources of product supply, and freedom of expression about brands, products and services, it is clear that the fundamental change has been, at least in broad terms, to democratize the process of consumption.

These changes have and will continue to reshape what, how and where consumers buy brands, products and services. However, for the purposes of this chapter, it is important now to identify how these Internet-led changes have had a significant and far-reaching impact upon the role, function and scope of retail buying and merchandising activities.

7.2 The impact of online upon product management

The influence and impact of the Internet upon buying and merchandising is an ongoing process; it is far from complete. As the reach of online business extends, in terms of both penetration and capability, then so too will the impact and consequences for how retailers manage their products.

In some respects, it is impossible to delineate comprehensively all aspects in which buying and merchandising have been affected by the growth of online selling. However, it is possible to isolate four significant areas where the Internet has had a profound impact upon buying and merchandising activities.

As was identified in the previous section, an important change brought about by the rise of online selling is the impact that it has had upon consumers' access to information. This includes information about the latest market trends, the newest product innovations, the launch of new brands and product concepts, the list goes on. Previously, buyers and merchandisers were the custodians of this information. They had exclusive access to information that they could filter on their own terms. Now, though, customers very often are equally as informed and perhaps even better informed. A significant dimension in all of this is that the Internet globalizes information. Previously, consumers would only have been familiar with regional and perhaps, at best, national trends, products or innovations. Now, the Internet shares possibilities, informs of developments and encourages consumer interest on a global scale. This puts significant pressure upon buyers to make sure that they are globally informed and they must be as expert in their knowledge of products as their prospective customers.

A second area of Internet influence relates to how trend information is generated and dispersed. Previously the exchange of trend information was piecemeal and sporadic. It was developed far in advance of seasons – particularly in the fashion sector – and was

communicated through presentations, trend books and trade shows. The costs of accessing this information were high and because they were developed far in advance of the launch of a season, the predictions were unable to absorb and integrate the latest developments in a market.

The Internet has radically altered the way in which predictions, trends and other forecasts are formed, constructed and communicated to buyers. Digital photography has facilitated the capture of street trends as they happen and the immediacy with which these can be communicated online is unprecedented. For example, within the fashion and beauty sector, the web-based trend forecaster WGSN provides analysis of trends as they happen using their legion of on-the-ground trend spotters. Then, through the use of a sequence of live feeds, WGSN communicates its interpretation of these trends to designers, buyers and merchandisers in real time.

The Internet has not only transformed the way in which established trend and forecasting agencies gather information and communicate it to retailers, but it has also provided a new and powerful visual route for designers and buyers to understand market trends and developments as they emerge. Social-networking and micro-blogging sites, such as Tumblr, Pinterest, Facebook and Instagram, allow retailers to access directly these informal repositories of trend information. Further, by participating directly in each of the main blogging channels, by establishing their own corporate sites, retailers are able both to test customer reaction to their ideas and products in development, and gain insight into other areas of customer interest and engagement. As such, these informal channels serve both as a means of obtaining fresh and relevant insight into market trends, and as a means of testing customer reaction to proposed new developments and ideas.

The third area of Internet impact relates to the identification, selection and formation of relationships with product and brand suppliers and manufacturers. Previously, retailers identified appropriate suppliers through previous experience, word-of-mouth recommendation, the use of agents, trade searches, exposure at trade events and, sometimes, through accidental meetings. Internationally, the larger retailers delegated the responsibility for finding new foreign-based suppliers to their international buying offices or to third-party intermediaries. Most retailers continue to use this method of non-domestic supplier identification and relationship management. However, just as the Internet has brought an awareness of new products to consumers, so too has it provided opportunities for international manufacturers and suppliers to connect directly with retailers.

As a result of the opportunities derived from an online presence, small-scale, specialist and remotely located suppliers can now promote their capabilities and capacities, and go on to form strong partnerships with previously inaccessible retailers. While these suppliers are motivated by the scale opportunities associated with supplying large retailers, retailers, likewise, are also interested in forming links with new and unknown suppliers. There are three main reasons for this. The first is that these suppliers may have the potential to provide new and exclusive products to the retailer's product assortment. Second, these relationships can be short term and so provide the retailer with the flexibility to turn supply on and off quickly. Finally, the identification of new suppliers online is an inexpensive and fast search method. Importantly, it also avoids the add-on costs that the use of an intermediary would incur.

The fourth significant area of Internet impact relates directly to the remit of merchandisers – specifically the placing of order quantities and the allocation of stock to specific stores, areas and territories. As a result of their development of online distribution channels, retailers are able efficiently and effectively to trial new products and immediately gauge the level of customer interest based upon sales, views and customer comment. In so doing, they can estimate sales for trial products and so mitigate against the risk of underestimating (or overestimating) demand.

Online channels are by their nature immediate. Customer reaction and interest in a product can be instant and the speed of reaction through this channel far outpaces that which would be available through retail outlets. In addition, online selling affords the opportunity to identify in which areas and territories demand for a product is likely to be strongest. Using online sales data, a retailer can then allocate products within retail stores within a region with greater confidence and certainty.

The Internet has therefore significantly changed the landscape of retail product management, particularly since the beginning of the twenty-first century. The remainder of this chapter will delineate the dimensions of retail product management, and will consider further how online channels have influenced and will continue to affect buying and merchandising strategy.

7.3   What does retail product management mean?

Retail product management is best described as the plans, systems and actions that retail companies utilize in order to assemble a range of products and services that will best satisfy the aspirations, wants and needs of potential customers. We say aspirations first because, in the majority of cases, consumers make buying decisions not just on their assessment of the functional performance of a product; it is as likely that they will select a particular product because they perceive that it will benefit them emotionally, as well as functionally.

Following on from the work of Pine and Gilmore (1999), where we adhere to the view that all retailers and their consumers 'live and operate' within an experience economy, it is important that we also recognize that the 'centre of gravity' for that experience economy is the product that is to be consumed. Products and, more specifically, the selling of products lie at the very heart and essence of retailing. Retailer success depends on having the products that customers want in the first place. That is non-negotiable.

Within this context, the process of creating a retailer's product assortment cannot be left to chance. It requires a structured and controlled approach that is based upon clear thinking and good planning. The buying plans and merchandising activities vary significantly between and among retailers. Many of the differences in approach arise as a result of variations in corporate scale, culture and trading markets. However, it is still possible to identify common dimensions or characteristics of effective product management in retailing.

7.3.1   A clear understanding of customer product value

Customer product value relates to those features of a product that matter most to a customer. These dimensions are the factors that customers most want and it is upon these that they make their purchase decisions. Customer product value should not be confused with price. Customer product value may include considerations of value for money but it includes a variety of other aspects. For example, in a food retailer, the principal customer product values relevant to their ready-made range may be preparation convenience, nutritional balance and ingredient traceability. In fact, economic value (price) may not figure so highly, especially if the company has a premium market positioning.

Having established the principal customer product values, the product management team will then use this insight to shape and inform their buying decisions.

7.3.2 Product range coverage

Consumers' product demands are often complex and extensive. The influences on their product choice may be economic, cultural or gender based. Furthermore, individual customers' needs may vary depending on the context for using a product. For example, if a customer has dinner guests, they may choose to purchase more expensive wines in order to impress. Alternatively, if they are buying for private consumption, they may elect to buy wine from an unknown producer which is less expensive. In order to cover as many eventualities as possible and so maximize the potential to secure sales, it is vital that the retailer develops/assembles a comprehensive range of products. However, in so doing, the retailer must also ensure that each product in the range is viable in terms of profit contribution and business success.

A comprehensive range will have breadth – i.e. offer as many different products as possible. It will also have depth of offer, which means there will be a sufficient number of product variants. So, using a wine example again, a comprehensive range of red wines would offer a wide breadth of choice, such as by country of origin (French, Australian, Italian), as well as a depth of choice (as demonstrated by a wide selection of grape varieties, price points and perhaps even variations in bottle volume). The development of an 'efficient' product range is critical for many retailers – not least for the fact that consumers now regard product choice as an important measure of customer service.

Having determined what customers most want from the products they buy, as well as the range of products that must be included in the product assortment, the third and fourth features of effective retail product management relate to the sourcing of products and managing their flow within the retailer's supply chain.

7.3.3 Utilization of a critical path platform

The assembly of a range of products that is very likely to be supplied by a diverse global supply base requires considerable coordination and careful control. For all retailers, a significant proportion of their product ranges is seasonal. This means that customer demand is concentrated into a specific time period. Consequently, it is critically important for retailers to plan and manage carefully the flow of goods into and out of their businesses in order to meet customer demand at exactly the right moment. This is where the establishment of a critical path becomes so important.

A critical path breaks down the various stages necessary for the production and delivery of a product assortment into a specific and specified timeframe. The intention is to ensure that each stage deadline is met and that products eventually arrive into the retailer's supply chain in a timely and ordered manner. The management of critical paths is resource intensive but necessary from both a cost management and also a customer service perspective. Typically, a retailer will have a standardized critical path platform that is web-based and developed for shared use by all involved in the selection and supply of products.

7.3.4 Established supplier strategy

Suppliers – either of branded goods or those that manufacture or source a retailer's own-branded goods – provide an important source of competitive advantage for retailers. The issues surrounding supplier selection and evaluation will be discussed later, but it is important to note here that attitudes and approaches to suppliers are typically formed and established as part of an overarching business philosophy. This business philosophy may be connected to retailers' pricing and quality requirements, or their selection may be dependent upon the suppliers' or manufacturers' ability to integrate with retailers' own information management systems.

7.3.5 Coherent brand strategy

The role of the brand in retailing has been discussed in Chapter 4 but it is important to note that the retailer's corporate and product-level branding strategy has a huge bearing upon the decision making of buyers. The retailer's brand sets out a positioning of what the company wants to be known for in the market. The brand is a statement of the retailer's identity and it expresses its core values. Furthermore, the retailer's brand serves as an expression of its personality. Given all of these elements, the retailer's brand serves as an important device for the delivery of competitive differentiation.

Within this context, buyers are compelled to source and select products and deliver services that are compatible with the positioning of their corporate brand. So as an example, as a brand, Selfridges, the UK-based department store retailer, is known internationally as having an upscale brand positioning, which targets the most affluent and fashion-conscious customers. The company has achieved that upscale brand positioning through the development of luxurious store environments, and the adoption of stylish and highly creative advertising campaigns and PR events. Perhaps, most crucially, the company has secured a premium/luxury brand positioning by stocking the world's most luxurious and desirable products and brands. The Selfridges' product management approach has been only to stock those brands that match and support the Selfridges' brand position.

The need for product managers to align their product selection clearly with the branding of their business is especially important for those retailers with own-brand merchandise. Own-brand ranges are exclusive to the retailer and, as such, serve as a powerful means of securing differentiation and customer loyalty. Own-brand products typically are more profitable than manufacturer-branded goods. These goods also give the retailer power over their design and creation and total control over their distribution. However, with these benefits come certain risks and responsibilities.

Own-branded goods must reflect and support the values that are associated with the retailer's reputation and brand image. Any inconsistencies are detrimental and potentially damaging to the retailer's positioning. In those instances where the retailer operates a variety of own brands, it is important that each range clearly supports and is consistent with the values that each own brand represents. For example, Marks & Spencer's womenswear department has eight sub-brands. Each is named separately and has its own distinctive identity and target customer segment. It is vital, therefore, that Marks & Spencer's product management team for womenswear ensures that the product ranges for each of the eight own brands clearly and consistently represent the values and personality of each brand. It is also important that each collection is sufficiently distinct so as to support and emphasize the difference and distance that exists between and among each brand.

It would be inaccurate to state that product management in retailing is the responsibility of buyers alone. There is a wider community of professionals involved in the process and each makes a distinct and significant contribution to the achievement of an effective product management strategy. The designation and number of professionals involved in product management can and does vary according to the scale and type of retailer. Despite these variations, it is possible confidently to identify four principal players in the product management process. The role of each contributor will be delineated below: the product designers (in section 7.4), buyers (section 7.7), merchandisers (section 7.8), and brand marketers/visual presentation managers (section 7.9).

7.4 The product designer

Most retailers have at least some direct involvement in the design and development of the products that they sell. This is especially true for those retailers that sell products that are marketed using their own brand name. For these retailers, the decision to sell own-brand merchandise is driven by the desire to influence directly, to their advantage, the nature and characteristics of products. While this is a potentially high-risk strategy, the rewards for successful own-development are significant. When retailers design and market their own goods, the profit margins are typically much better than when compared with the buying of manufacturer-branded goods and because such products are exclusive to the retailer, own-branded goods also encourage and support deeper levels of customer loyalty.

Of course, not all retailers sell products under their own-brand name, but they may nevertheless still have an influence on some, if not many, of the features of the manufacturer-branded products that they sell. The scope of their influence may include stipulating package size, product colour or the materials used. Alternatively, the scope of influence can be more extensive and can lead to the retailer directing the design of a manufacturer's product, which has a significant influence on both form and function.

This latter form of influence is more likely to exist for those retailers that have considerable power and status in the market, as demonstrated by an established reputation in a territory, high levels of market share and the achievement of good levels of business profitability.

Product designers have two important areas of responsibility. The first relates to their management of corporate intelligence with respect to trends and developments in the market. While some of this market reconnaissance activity is certainly shared with the retailer buyer, the gathering of information relevant to the latest product, competitor and consumer trends is something that all product developers must undertake. Their second key responsibility is then to assimilate all of the market data identified and use them as the basis to develop and create ideas, concepts, specifications and plans for new or upgraded products for the retailer. Below we shall examine the product designer's central responsibilities.

7.5 Trend management strategies

Before considering the ways in which designers and others in the product management team undertake the gathering and disseminating of trend information, it is important to note that the process has changed radically. The Internet has been the principal vehicle for radically disrupting the mechanics of trend intelligence gathering within retailing. Through the development of excellent and expert trend-reporting websites, designers and product management teams can have access to the latest global trends immediately and easily at the touch of a button. These sites not only provide immediate access to information about trends as they emerge, but they also give useful commentary and analysis. This allows designers to interpret and act upon trends quickly and efficiently. However, a negative dimension of the Internet as a common trend resource is that it can lead to market homogeneity because many retailers draw from the same information pool.

However, while the advent of online trend information may have improved the speed and range of access, the process of trend gathering and interpretation has been made more complex as a result of three important factors. The first relates to the speed of innovation in the sector. Most product categories are driven by a constant flow of new product launches, incessant product refinements, extensions and re-launches. This means that an under-standing of the status of products in a market is complex and something of a 'moving target'.

Second, the race for product innovation and development is as much fuelled by con-sumer interest as it is by the energy of retailers themselves. As consumers utilize the Internet for information about new product developments and innovations, a driving desire among consumers to access and consume new products has become a defining feature of many product markets.

Third, the globalization of consumer goods and services has resulted in unprecedented levels of consumer awareness and access to goods and services from across the world. This demands that product designers must be globally minded and, by necessity, they must connect deeply into the trends and developments as they emerge across international markets.

Consequently, it is imperative that product designers commit to deep and extensive trend research and this typically requires them to consider three core dimensions: product, consumers and competitor developments. Each of these will be considered below.

7.5.1 Product trend analysis

Product designers are usually experts in their product area or field. They will perhaps have studied design and will be highly engaged with recent developments in their product area. They will retain an ongoing interest in these trends through their engagement with Internet sites, magazines, social media and their own personal consumption.

However, product development is too important a process to be based solely and only upon informal insight. Product trend analysis needs formal interventions in order to provide designers and product management teams with robust insight and relevant information to serve as the basis for credible decision making. The extent of the investigation undertaken by the product design team will vary according to both the product market within which the retailer operates, and the size and scale of the business itself. Taking into account these variations, most product designers will undertake at least some (if not all) of the four main methods of product research gathering detailed below.

7.5.1.1 The product trend agency

Within each product category, there is a legion of trend agencies that specialize in monitoring and recording product developments. These firms undertake product trend spotting, and then predict and report which trends are likely to be the most important in the market. These specialist trend companies may work on a one-to-one basis with a large retailer in order to provide the product design teams with detailed information and advice on the best areas for development.

Alternatively (and in addition to the above), agencies may provide regular seminars/ workshops for the retailer where they will outline the trends that they believe should influence and shape the retailer's new product development thinking. These workshops typically lead to an idea-generation exercise that sustains a steady flow of business-enhancing products.

7.5.1.2 Product trade fairs

A second route is for the product designers and other members of the product management team to attend one of the major national/global product trade fairs relevant to their product category. While the Internet may serve as a powerful route to obtaining up-to-date information about product trends and developments, the age of the annual product fair has not yet passed. Trade fairs serve as a showcase for new product developments and inventions, and these have remained relevant within the Internet age because they afford the possibility for the designers and buyers to see up close the latest product ideas in reality. Further, these events allow the opportunity for designers to meet face to face with suppliers and manufacturers in order to exchanges ideas and form relationships.

Product trade fairs exist for all product categories, from fashion to jewellery, home furnishings to toys. Most occur in an established location, such as Baselworld, the premier trade event for the watches and jewellery sector that happens each year in Basel, Switzerland.

Within the retail fashion sector, Premiere Vision (PV), which is held twice yearly in Paris, showcases the latest developments in textiles, production, technology and marketing which serve to shape and inform the product development activities of fashion retailers.

7.5.1.3 Inspiration trips

In recognition that the retail sector is affected and influenced by global trends and developments, retailers acknowledge that their intelligence gathering for insights about new products and services cannot be restricted to their development in the domestic market. Instead, product designers will visit the most influential and 'happening' locations in order to obtain an 'up-close' insight into the latest innovations as they occur.

As trends come and go, so too do the cities and places that are selected as a source of inspiration. Among the most important centres for inspiration trips by food retailers will be cities such as New York, Mumbai, Tokyo and Sydney. In contrast, home furnishing designers have been more likely to visit Copenhagen, Berlin, Shanghai and Kuala Lumpur for design ideas. As well as visiting manufacturers and suppliers for design ideas, product designers also visit other retailers to assess their offerings and consider the transferability of their product ranges into the designers' own businesses. Furthermore, many designers also keep a close eye on consumers and their consumption patterns within these important cities – again, in order to derive ideas and inspiration. Further detail of what product designers consider with respect to competitors and consumers will be discussed later in this chapter.

7.5.1.4 New product forecast reports

A fourth but important means for product designers to obtain information about the latest product trends is to subscribe to the trend reports of one of the major forecasting companies in their sector. Typically technical and specialist in nature, these publications give product designers insight, direction and guidance with respect to the nature and form of new products in the prototype and pre-release stages.

Having delineated the mechanisms by which designers gain information about the latest advances, the next section will consider the specific dimensions that designers and the product management team must consider when developing new products for a retail company.

It is important at this stage to note that all forms of market trend analysis will involve, and be of significance to, members of the product management team, and not just those involved in product design directly. However, bearing in mind that these trends shape and inform the product ideas that the designers propose and then develop, it is appropriate to consider trend analysis as a primary responsibility of a retailer's product design team.

7.5.2 Product trend analysis

Product trend analysis usually includes consideration of three specific product trend dimensions: these are forecast/pipeline developments, imminent and recent product launches, and upgrading/extension of current product range activities. The key issues of each will be considered below.

7.5.2.1 Forecast/pipeline development

The last thing that a retailer wants to happen is to find that a major competitor has launched a new product unexpectedly and without their knowledge. A surprise launch of a good product or service could provide a competitor with significant advantage and make rivals seem out of touch and inferior in consumers' eyes.

To avoid this, retailers will carefully scrutinize the pattern of new developments that a rival is following in the hope of securing some clue as to where they may progress in future. This is in recognition of that fact that most new product developments are incremental in nature and are based upon what has been previously established. In addition, retailers will also use other information sources, such as via suppliers, media and other contacts, in order to gain intelligence about forecast developments.

Trade publications provide the most accessible and the least expensive access to information about pipeline developments, and while this is an important information source, specifically in relation to the technical characteristics and market feasibility of proposed developments, often the information is generated from press releases provided by manufactures and/or retailers. As such, the information that is included can be biased in terms of over-playing positive attributes and the potential for success.

In certain circumstances, and particularly when products are complex and technologically based, product design teams will employ the specialist research skills of consultants, who will undertake deep and extensive research on a global basis in order to identify new ideas, innovations and prototypes with a view to assessing their commercial potential.

Perhaps the most important means of identifying emerging and pipeline developments is derived from the development of strong collaborative relationships with suppliers. In those cases where a retailer is important to a supplier, perhaps because of their reputation and/or the size and stability of their business, a manufacturer may choose to share their new products and innovation plans. In doing this, a supplier can benefit from early-stage, pre-launch feedback from the retailer on such issues as commercial viability, likely consumer interest and areas where refinement of the product idea would be helpful.

From the retailers' perspective, ideas that are generated and developed by trusted suppliers are a significant and valuable way to obtain ideas quickly and at low cost. If the essence of a new product concept appears commercially viable, the retailer and supplier may then collaborate to advance and refine the idea and, where possible, bring it to market at an appropriate point in time. At any rate, supplier relationships that involve the sharing of ideas and innovations early in the development process provide buyers with an important first-hand account of developments before these actually reach the market.

7.5.2.2 Imminent and recent product launches

Social media have emerged as a significant and effective mechanism for retailers to locate imminent and actual product launches, from competitors and other retailers on both a domestic and global basis. In order to galvanize and encourage consumer interest and engagement, retailers will release advanced product launch 'teasers'. These teasers may take the form of simple announcements on their various social media platforms or they may be cryptic and unclear so as to arouse customer curiosity. When H&M announced its collaboration with Maison Martin Margiela in November 2012, three weeks before the launch of the new range, the company released a 37-second video of the process of illustrating a dress which, at the same time, incorporated abstract references to the Margiela brand. The video was meant to 'whet customers' appetite' and encourage curiosity about the collaborative collection. While there was little that rival competitors could do to mitigate against the impact of this collaboration by H&M, many used the ideas contained in the preview of the collections to shape and inform their own fast fashion ranges.

Some manufacturers will use a range of marketing communications techniques in order to inform retailers of their imminent product launches. From hosted events that showcase the new products, to brochures that provide details of product specifications, manufacturers seek to find new and innovative ways to capture the interest and business of retailers. Increasingly, manufacturers are electing to work with retailers directly and at an early stage of the product development process so as to obtain the retailer's views and input. In many cases, this has resulted in retailers and manufacturers working in close collaboration in order to produce new products that exploit the power of two brands working together in product development.

Within this context, many product designers keep a particularly close eye on collaborative developments undertaken by rival companies. For example, the British department store retailer John Lewis has engaged in a number of collaborations with successful fashion brands in order to revive its menswear business. John Lewis has collaborated with brands such as Barbour, John Smedley and Joe Casely-Hayford to produce exclusive ranges that improve John Lewis's fashion credentials. In response to these developments, a number of other high street chains, including Marks & Spencer, have replicated this model in order to revise and advance the credibility of their menswear ranges, such as in the form of the David Gandy for Autograph underwear collection.

7.5.2.3 *Upgrading/spin-offs*

It is reasonably rare for a retailer to offer a product that is completely new to the market. Most newly launched products are an upgrade or an extension of one that is already available. Designers therefore closely monitor upgrade and extension activity very closely. Upgrades typically incorporate incremental changes that are modifications which appeal to customers' needs and interests. An analysis of competitors' upgrades therefore provides a useful indication of how rivals anticipate market changes, trends and developments.

As important as a source of new product information and inspiration is the analysis of the undertaking of product extensions by retailers. The entry of a retailer into a new product category is perhaps the clearest indicator of whether that company anticipates new and future growth to emerge. It indicates whether they believe the best opportunities for profit advancement exist for the company, as well as where they believe their customers would like to see the company develop and extend.

With the advent of the Internet, retailers are increasingly investigating ways in which they can utilize their Internet resources and distribution competences in order to develop new income streams for their businesses. Taking the lead from online retailers such as Amazon, many have developed partnerships with other brands in order to extend the range and reach of their product offer. Again, product designers keep a very close eye on these new ventures, since these provide a useful indicator of where competitors think that new market opportunities exist and these provide guidance on the sorts of goods and services that competitors predict may be appealing to their customers. Box 7.1 illustrates this point through the example of Next's one-off e-commerce business, The Label.

Box 7.1 The launch of Next's spin-off, The Label

The Next Directory has been an important part of Next's success story since it was launched in the late 1980s. Through its use of engaging photography produced in a high-quality 'coffee-table book' format, the directory has provided the Next brand with an attractive identity and brand positioning. Having extended the Next brand widely across most complementary product categories, the company recognized that there was an opportunity to make the Next Directory the basis for building a powerful and successful online business. By not withdrawing the directory, but instead making sure that it connected and integrated with their online offering, Next was able, perhaps uniquely, both to protect its mail order arm and use it to build a strong e-commerce business.

Having developed an integrated (and highly successful) digital and mail order business, which was achieved due in no small part to development of a world-class distribution system, Next also recognized its need to protect and develop their business strategically. With an aggressive store opening strategy, based upon large-format stores located in out-of-town and edge-of-town locations, the company recognized that demand for the Next brand would inevitably reach a maturing and saturation point. Therefore, from the mid-2000s, the company began to stock other fashion, home and electronics brands in their Next Directory and on their website. Through this extension, Next achieved three things. First, it extended consumer choice, which was now no longer restricted to the Next brand. Second, it allowed Next to utilize and exploit capacity in its supply chain, by handling the distribution of additional brands. Third, it provided Next with an additional external revenue source.

Incrementally, sales of these external brands grew through Next's digital and directory platforms and, by early 2014, Next had overtaken Marks & Spencer to be the UK's most profitable fashion and home retailer. In an attempt to extend and diversify the Next business model away from an over-reliance upon the single Next brand platform, the company launched a new website and directory in March 2014. Called The Label, the new business included many of the external brands already stocked on their website and in the directory, but with a clean, fresh, editorial style. Through this diversification, Next as a business could expect to gain three major advantages. First, by separating the external brands from the Next brand, the business would be better able to attract new customer segments that perhaps would otherwise avoid the safe and predictable positioning of the core Next brand. Second, the new business provides Next with access to market intelligence and insight about the buying preferences and shopping behaviours of customers who shop with these other brands and who are not known to the business. Because Next can closely monitor actual sales, buyers obtain credible and useful information. Third, the new independent website provides Next with an opportunity to experiment with new business ideas and initiatives and to do so without risking the reputation and success of their current business.

Source: Goldfingle, 2014.

7.5.3 Competitor trend tracking

It would be wrong to suggest that the tracking of competitor behaviour is only the designer's responsibility: all members of the product management team must be engaged in that process. However, the outcome of the competitor analysis has a direct bearing upon the product development initiatives that the design team leads. Therefore, given this critical connection, the process of competitor tracking will be considered through their 'business lens'.

Knowledge of competitor activity – particularly in terms of how they entice customers to shop with them, affords retailers (and therefore designers) an opportunity to develop adequate defensive strategies that can secure customer loyalty. In addition, a sound understanding of the competition may enable the buyer to exploit their weaknesses, gain inspiration and ideas from their strengths, and be prepared for any new initiatives that the competition may adopt.

Like consumer trend tracking, the analysis of the competition is an ongoing activity and is undertaken on an informal, as well as formal, basis. The development of e-commerce has made the activity of competitor analysis both easier and more complex. It has made it easier, because retailers can quickly and cost-effectively identify the developments and activities undertaken by their rivals through a simple analysis of their websites. It has also made it more complex since it has increased the number of competitors that customers can consider. Furthermore, many retailers have developed online product assortments that are distinctly different from their retail stores. This therefore means online has added a further complexity to the competitor analysis process. There are five dimensions of competitor activity that are closely examined by rivals, each of which is delineated below.

7.5.3.1 Product range and assortment

When analysing the products offered by competitors, product designers typically consider three important dimensions. The first relates to the structure of rivals' ranges. This considers the balance of product breadth (the number of different product types) and product depth (the number of different options of a particular product). The brand mix is examined, in terms of the range of manufacturer brands stocked, as well as those sold under the retailer's own brand name.

Second, and specifically in relation to own-branded products, careful reviews of the design features, quality standards and any areas of technological and/or performance innovation are undertaken. Those product attributes felt to be particularly distinctive and which offer some form of competitive advantage will be noted for future consideration and adoption.

Third, and perhaps most importantly, product design teams will review competitors' products to identify any interesting and engaging collaborations between the rival retailer and external parties. This is a strategy that the American clothing retailer J. Crew has developed as part of a strategy that has served to differentiate its offering. Box 7.2 provides further detail of their collaborative activity.

Box 7.2 The 'In Good Company' strategy at J. Crew

J. Crew was founded initially as a catalogue-based fashion business in 1983. It specialized in classic apparel, with a utilitarian emphasis. It was not particularly fashion-led and did not include children's clothing. It opened its first store in New York in 1989 at South Street Seaport. The turning point for the company came in 2003 when it appointed Mickey Drexler as chairman and CEO. Drexler had previously masterminded the transformation of Gap from being a domestic apparel retailer to an internationally successful fashion chain. When he joined J. Crew, Drexler set out to achieve a similar transformation.

As well as creating better retail stores, Drexler saw the importance of good design for fashion success. He made Jenna Lyons creative director, and encouraged her to create an engaging design aesthetic for J. Crew that mixed the latest fashion trends with wearable design. In the development of a new J. Crew aesthetic that would integrate across all channels and every customer touch point, Lyons also recognized that the J. Crew brand would benefit from connecting with other trusted and respected brands. In marketing terms, this is called the 'halo effect', whereby one brand, through an association with another, well-established and respected brand, benefits from that brand's positive market positioning.

Recognizing that J. Crew, particularly in the menswear market, would benefit from association with other strong brands, J. Crew launched the 'J. Crew in Good Company' strategy. This brought together a diverse and extensive range of more than 70 brands, including Alden, Barbour, Birkenstock, Converse, Filson, Mackintosh, New Balance, Sperry Top-Sider, United Arrows and Vans.

These brands, sold by J. Crew on their website and in selected J. Crew stores, also include products exclusive to J. Crew or which have been developed in collaboration to match the J. Crew design aesthetic.

The 'J. Crew in Good Company' strategy does three important things for the J. Crew brand. First, it helps to enhance the status and standing of the J. Crew brand. Second, it provides J. Crew with access to a different customer segment who perhaps would not consider J. Crew as a proposition, but who 'find' J. Crew in their search for these other established brands. Third, it provides the company with an additional revenue source, as well as a useful customer intelligence insight into their behaviour with respect to products and brands external to the company.

Source: Sacks, 2013.

As well as reviewing collaborative activity, product designers will also consider any limited edition products or Internet-only products (i.e. sold only online and not in stores) that are offered by their rivals. Analysis of these products provides invaluable early intelligence on the 'direction of travel' of their product development initiatives. Limited edition and online-only products are typically of a higher price, design and quality positioning compared with their regular products. Consequently, these serve often as a trial that measures the level of customer engagement, interest and take-up. Based upon the sales performance of these lines, rivals will then use the insight gained from these products to generate mainstream products that will be attractive to a wider consumer market. By identifying and evaluating the performance of limited edition and Internet-only lines, product designers can also begin to predict how rivals may advance their product ranges in the near future.

7.5.3.2 Pricing strategy

While buyers and merchandisers must have a clear grasp of competitor pricing, it is vital too for product designers to understand the pricing activities of rivals. This is because they must develop products that are commensurate with current market price levels.

There are three aspects of competitor pricing that must be considered. The first relates to the price entry point in each product range or category. The entry point is the cheapest product. Entry price defines the market positioning of a company. For example, for a luxury retailer such as Hermès, the entry point for a ladies' handbag in 2014 was around £2,100. That entry point immediately indicates where Hermès sits in the market. So an analysis of the entry price is critical to understanding a retailer's market position. It is common for retailers within a particular market to set common entry point prices so as to minimize the impact of that form of inter-retailer rivalry.

The second is price lining. Price lining refers to the various price points that a retailer sets within a particular product range. So, for example, a wines and spirits retailer may offer champagne at five price points, for example £20, £25, £30, £35 and £50. These various price points would serve to indicate a differential to customers with respect to perhaps the quality, quantity or reputation of each of the champagne marques on sale. Consideration of the price-lining policies of the competition is useful since it provides some insight into the competition's assessment of the target market's price tolerances, in terms of how little and how much they are prepared to pay. Furthermore, it also indicates the level of price choice that customers may expect within a product range or category.

The third aspect of pricing that is typically considered relates to the extent to which competitors' prices have changed in a given period. In order to undertake this sort of analysis, it is necessary for the retailer to record, at regular intervals, their competitors' prices for specific products. The products that are usually monitored include those in high demand, those that are common among competitors and those to which customers are price sensitive. Within the food sector, price monitoring is a priority and for many retailers this is a central plank of their competitive strategy. Price matching is achieved through the frequent monitoring of competitors' listed prices online as well as in stores, and the information is often used in real time to adjust the retailers' own price points.

Of particular interest to merchandisers and buyers are the range and number of price markdowns undertaken by the competition. This is especially important since it provides some indication of the success of the competition's product selection and pricing strategies, and gives some insight into consumer demand for specific products and categories.

7.5.3.3 *Promotional strategy*

Most product management teams will create and agree upon a seasonal promotions calendar for their business. The calendar plans out the flow of promotions over a year and is used as a framework that ensures that there is a sufficiency of available product in order to meet customer demand and maximize business opportunities. Promotions help generate demand and provide for immediate cash flow into a business. Likewise, promotions can help stimulate demand for slow-selling products and so can help reduce product over-stock.

In general, an analysis of competitors' promotions will review the ranges of products included in the promotion, as well as the conditions of the promotion itself. Wherever possible, product management teams will seek to evaluate the success, or otherwise, of competitors' promotions by estimating the level of consumer demand for the promoted lines, the length of time in which a promotion operates, and the volume of products left unsold.

Many retailers operate off-price retail channels. In the early days of their establishment, these channels were used to liquidate slow-selling lines in order to make space for newly arriving stock. With the rise in consumer interest and engagement with off-price retailing, many companies have seen these to be important revenue channels in their own right. Consequently, in order to maximize the opportunities afforded by these channels, many companies also develop products to be sold especially within these stores. The monitoring of competitors will also therefore include consideration of those items that have been specifically designed for in-store promotion events or for off-price retail sites. This may then provide inspiration with respect to which product areas the design team should develop.

7.5.3.4 *Store environment*

In situations where there is often little to differentiate one retailer's product and brand assortment from another, what then becomes important is the context and environment within which products and services are sold. Retailers' environments are now carefully designed to generate a sense and feeling of differentiation and uniqueness. Environments serve to support and emphasize the retailers' identity, and often the retail spaces will significantly augment the brand positioning.

To that end, store environments can play a critical role in 'selling' products to consumers by generating interest, stimulating and enticing customers to spend. Because of the strong relationship between environment and product, product designers must consider carefully the characteristics of the environments within which goods are sold and then use these to shape their product design decisions. Two examples from the clothing retail sector make this point clearly.

Uniqlo is a Japanese-owned fashion retailer that has developed a highly successful business selling good-quality clothing essentials at highly competitive prices. Part of the secret of Uniqlo's success has been its development of high-impact, bright and colourful retail stores. Merchandise ranges are displayed product by product, and the presentation of merchandise is made impactful by a careful management of colour and the logical structuring of product by type, design and size. The careful management of presentation is not accidental. At the earliest stages of development of its seasonal collections, those responsible for product management at Uniqlo immediately consider how the products in each collection will be presented in stores. This imposes a discipline with respect to the product design decisions within the company. It ensures that all products in a collection are connected and it mitigates against the inclusion of products that mis-connect with others in the collection, perhaps as a result of poor colour, shape or texture matching. Through the careful integration of product design with considerations of product presentation, Uniqlo has been able to create a store environment experience that is authoritative and is, for many customers, the world over, convenient and easy to shop.

Likewise, the Spanish fashion retailer Zara, owned by the Inditex Group, provides an excellent example of how through the careful integration and co-management of product and store environment design, a brand's market status can be enhanced and differentiated. With more than 2,000 stores worldwide, it is critical that Zara develops a consistent and coherent store experience that can be easily rolled out globally at a reasonable cost. Like Uniqlo, Zara has developed a clear brand aesthetic, which is precise, refined and carefully controlled. When product designers create collections for Zara, a critical consideration is how the ranges and brand collections will be presented in Zara stores. The company has a clear environment template that emphasizes the connection between products that allow for attractive and wearable outfits to be constructed easily by customers. The company does not design with the intention of just selling one product. Instead, it presents merchandise to encourage customers to buy complementary products that create outfits. This is clearly in the mind, then, of Zara's design teams, and it shapes how they approach the design, construction and presentation of their collection and ranges.

7.5.3.5 Service

From a product management perspective, a particular area of interest is how competitors use technology to engage and support customers. Among the brands that have pioneered the use of technology in this way has been the British luxury brand Burberry. Through their development of an e-commerce business that integrates music, ideography and stylish photography to create an aspirational and engaging online experience, the company has also developed a strong sense of an online community through their 'Art of the Trench' website. This micro-site encourages the public and street photographers to post photographs of cool, fashionable people wearing the Burberry trench coat. The site has a global reach, with thousands of posts and millions of followers. It has created a community of Burberry wearers, and in so doing, it provides customers with an opportunity to 'belong and connect' to a wider community and gives them the opportunity to take direction and guidance from fellow users on how to style and wear Burberry products. In addition to this informal interaction of support and direction, the company also offers direct forms of guidance to their e-commerce customers. Appointments can be made to meet with a stylist in Burberry stores who can assist customers in the selection of Burberry product and the creation of a Burberry outfit. The company also has a 'Live Chat' facility where a consultant will provide guidance and styling support to customers online to help them select product and mix and match outfits.

7.5.4 Competitor customer profile

The product management team, and specifically product designers and buyers, will have a strong interest in understanding the profile of customers who shop with their rivals. This information is invaluable, not least for the fact that it helps to identify who they could capture as customers and what they would need to offer in order to achieve that.

Therefore, as well as considering the various interventions that rivals adopt in order to influence consumer behaviour, it is also worthwhile for a competitor review to consider who is actually shopping with the competition at any given time. As such, through personal observation methods, a record may be made of the number of customers, their age and any other distinguishing characteristics. Of the latter, some buyers will record, where possible, the bags that competitors' customers are carrying, the types of cars that are in the car park, and the sorts of products that they are buying. It is not uncommon for determined buyers and product designers to strike up conversations with a rival's customers in order to obtain some insight as to why they chose to shop with that retailer in the first place.

7.6 Customer trend analysis

There is no doubting the fact that e-commerce has radically transformed the nature and pattern of consumer behaviour. As Shaw and Koumbis (2013) note, the Internet has radically transformed retail product markets and enabled consumers to access information easily, cheaply and efficiently. It has provided the opportunity for people to purchase what they want, where they want and at any time they want it. Perhaps, most importantly, the Internet has given the majority of customers greater choice and, as a result, it has heightened their expectations of service, choice and availability.

However, looking more broadly at customer trends, a product management team will certainly want to focus upon macro and micro consumer trends and, perhaps as importantly, they will want to understand the attitudes, values and behaviour of opinion leaders within their respective markets.

7.6.1 Macro consumer trends

Macro consumer trends are concerned with changes in the demographic, economic, technological and social dimensions of the market in its widest sense. While product management teams are especially interested in these dimensions as they affect their specific target customer group, their interest must extend to other social groups. There are two reasons for this. The first is that experienced buyers recognize the convergence in behaviour between and among customer segments, and that developments within one market segment often have an influence and bearing upon changes within other customer groups. Second, through having such awareness, buyers can then develop new products that capitalize upon trends just as they emerge within their target market.

The analysis of market-level consumer trends is not driven by the desire to generate a one-dimensional overview of the current and likely future status of consumers. Rather, the more expert product management teams will utilize general information pertaining to consumers' demography, economic status and social situation in order to provide a holistic understanding of those factors that determine the nature and characteristics of their consumption. In addition to these 'hard' facts, teams typically overlay these with extensive, qualitative information, which provides details of trends in consumers' attitudes and behaviour patterns. By drawing together qualitative and quantitative data, it is possible to construct a more rounded lifestyle profile of their specific customers.

This lifestyle profile may take a variety of forms. A common approach is to construct a **lifestyle portrait** of various customer segments. Typically presented in narrative form, the lifestyle portrait presents a summation of relevant qualitative and quantitative data with the intention of identifying how these trends may explain the attitudes and behaviour of their target customer segments. Starting with an outline of their demographic characteristics, the lifestyle portrait will seek to describe who delineates the attitudes, behaviours, wants and aspirations of customers. It will consider the current dimensions of the consumer's lifestyle, and will also seek to predict how that lifestyle may alter in the future. The benefit of developing a lifestyle portrait resides not solely in focusing the product management team's attention upon the factors that define, restrict and determine the way people consume, but it also helps teams predict which products soon, and in the future, will best match the customer's lifestyle requirements.

7.6.2 Micro consumer trends

While macro-level consumer analysis is broad in its scope, micro analysis is concerned with more specific intelligence about the retailer's customers. Arguably, access to this insight is critical for the success of any retailer. They must clearly understand what, where, when, why and how their target customer group consumes products and services. Retailers typically only have access to information about how customers interact within their business. They rarely understand how consumers interact with rival companies. In order to do this, they need to engage with consumers through primary research, led either by their own research teams, or through the use of external market research companies.

As well as using external consumer data, the product management team will interrogate internal data as a means of identifying their existing customers' patterns of buying behaviour. These internal data are used to provide information across a number of dimensions. Among those areas typically considered are sales trend analysis for specific products, brands and product variants (such as size, colour or material). This analysis of sales may be even broader and include a comparison of buying trends across product categories. This sort of analysis will examine a number of other factors in order to generate an intimate profile of their customers' purchasing habits and will incorporate detail on the average amounts they spend in each transaction, the price levels that they will tolerate, where, when and how they pay for merchandise, as well as information about the products they buy in combination.

In addition to the intelligence generated through sales history analysis, product management teams also utilize the insights that online data provide. In particular, they will consider:

- frequency of views for products;
- dwell time spent looking at an item;
- the journey from one product view to the next;
- inter-product comparisons;
- failed sales (i.e. placed in a basket but not purchased) and
- the volume, value and combination of successful sales.

This intelligence is obtained quickly and it tends to be accurate. It provides important information with respect to customer interest and buying activities in real time.

In addition to the information obtained from the macro- and micro-level research surveys identified above, many retailers augment these findings with qualitative studies that track the consumption behaviour of opinion-forming consumers. Before the rise of the Internet, information concerning the attitudes, values and behaviour of opinion formers was really only accessible from a distance. Market researchers or product management teams would visit places and venues, and observe, interview and tacitly engage with those who appeared to be at the cutting edge of ideas and whose opinions influenced and directed the market.

However, with the emergence of the 'online blogger', product managers can more readily access and understand the views and perspectives of individuals who influence consumer tastes and behaviours through their blogs and their other involvement in the marketing of brands and products. Based upon the assumption that the consumption characteristics of these influential bloggers will 'trickle down' into a wider range of social groups, it is vital that product designers, in particular, are familiar with the views that bloggers express so that they can adjust their buying decisions accordingly.

Drawing together these information strands, the product management team will then seek to construct a profile of the consumer that will identify, predict and understand their consumption needs and wants. For all retailers this is an ongoing activity, but for large retailers with complex product management functions, this is also a process that is formalized on a regular basis.

All of the intelligence obtained from the analysis of consumer, product and competitor trends is analysed and digested, and is then structured to form a comprehensive basis for product design, development and range construction decisions.

For those retailers that restrict their product ranges to the selling of manufacturer goods and services, the trend analysis should provide them with clear guidance on:

- which manufacturer brands to stock, as well as the specific products that should be selected from the manufacturer's assortment;
- the price bands that the range should cover, from entry, exit and intermediate (where the majority of the offer typically lies);

- the ratio mix of brands to own brands and the percentage of the offer delivered by each brand;
- the balance of new product launches versus established products; and
- promotion and service support levels required for each brand/product category.

Perhaps the most important and valuable aspect of the undertaking of the trend analysis is that it should identify opportunities for the product management team to enhance and grow the profitability of their business from manufacturer brands, the retailer's own brands or from a combination of the two. There is a variety of reasons that explain why retailers develop their own-branded ranges and collections. These include the assumption that own brands secure higher margins and gain from cost-related benefits because they exclude the participation of some third-party players in their development. The own brand also gives the retailer exclusivity over distribution. If the own-brand range is distinctive and attractive to customers, then the exclusivity in distribution can also then secure customer loyalty (Elliott and Rider, 2007).

The first stage in the own-brand development process requires a review of the external environment, in much the same way as has been discussed in detail above. The principal outcome of this review has to be the identification of opportunities for the own brand, which arise as a result of the insights gained from the trend review. The identification of opportunities has no significant value if these do not translate into clear product propositions for the retailer's own brand. Therefore, the value of the trend review and the main contribution of the product design team to the product management process is the identification of new product propositions that clearly respond to identified market opportunities.

The next stage is a concept development phase, which must be led by product designers. A first stage is the creation of mood boards that serve as a visual representation of their interpretation of the trend analysis findings. Most importantly, their mood boards incorporate their prediction and forecasts of the future of their sector. Following from the presentation of the mood boards, the product design team will then offer their interpretation of these trends in the form of a range of product design options which can be adopted by the own brand for development for their own brand range.

Within the fashion retailing sector, the designers will generate a range of illustrations that will visually illustrate the products that they propose. They will also suggest colour schemes, fabrics and trims to be used, and in some cases they may also suggest how the collection of products would be best presented in store. They may also suggest how the range could be marketed to prospective customers.

Within the food sector, the process of developing product concepts is broadly similar. Product developers will create recipes and their test kitchens will test, refine and further develop the product concepts before they are presented for consideration in tasting sessions. As the process suggests, tasting sessions are when members of the retailer's product selection team come together in order to taste, assess and discuss the product concepts that the product development team has proposed. If recipes are felt to be suitable for further consideration, these then progress to the next stage where taste tests are undertaken and reviewed.

The decision as to whether ideas and initiatives can be progressed beyond the concept phase is led, in the main, by the retail buyer. Therefore, it is appropriate to consider the role and remit of the buyer within the retail product management team at this point.

7.7 The retail buyer

There can be no mistaking the fact that buyers play a critical role in the product management processes of all retail companies. It is their responsibility to make the retailers' brand identity a reality through the product assortments they develop, create and buy. To undertake the role of a buyer, various skills and competences are required, but arguably the most important is the ability to understand and predict the needs and wants of consumers, then to assemble a product range that responds to consumers' requirements.

This task is complex. Within every market, the process of forecasting trends and predicting consumer demand requires a mix of creative and analytical skills. It requires that buyers have a close affinity with and understanding of market trends, the developments in consumers' taste preferences, as well as a firm grasp of the activities of competitors. However, the most challenging task of all is for the buyer to interpret all of that information and develop a brief for product designers to create a range of products that will accurately reflect the market trends, meet customers' expectations and match (and preferably exceed) the offer of competitors.

While it is certainly the case that the retailer buyer's role is both comprehensive and extensive, it is possible to identify three significant responsibilities that encapsulate the buyer's contribution to the product management team. The first relates to the assembly of the product range to be bought.

7.7.1 Product range assembly

A product range must do three things. First, it must satisfy the needs of customers while at the same time offering them choice in the form of variations in product, brand, price, product quality and performance characteristics. Within the context of a specific customer segment and a precise product category, the buyer seeks to meet every eventuality by assembling a product range that will provide sufficient choice for customers.

Second, a product range is constructed to provide maximum profit opportunities for the retailer. The achievement of profitability targets can be a complex undertaking. Typically, the buyer will work closely with their merchandiser partner, who is specifically tasked with monitoring, controlling and securing the financial performance of a product range. In collaboration, the buyer and merchandiser will establish margin targets that determine both the maximum price that the retailer can pay a supplier and the price/volume of goods that the retailer must sell to customers. Margin management is a crucial undertaking and is used as an important method of assessing buyer and merchandiser performance.

On the basis of the margin targets that the merchandiser/finance team require, the buyer must then construct a product range that satisfies the following considerations:

- On price: an entry and exit price that meets customers' expectations and budgets; as well as sufficient choice variation between the two price extremes.

- On brand: where applicable, a coherent mix of supplier and own-brand options that will satisfy both consumer expectations and demand, but also deliver sufficient profit contribution levels.
- On promotion and mark-down: most retailers offer some form of promotional discount or end-of-season price reduction. These price reductions serve to satisfy customers' desire to obtain a 'bargain' and a 'good deal'. Promotions and mark-downs can have a detrimental impact on margin targets if these are not managed carefully. It is therefore very important for buyers to plan, as much as possible, for mark-downs at the beginning of the buying cycle so that these can be built into the financial forecast.
- On availability: there is no point in developing an excellent product that is impossible to produce in sufficient quantities to meet consumer demand. Product non-availability is the enemy of product profitability. Therefore, a buyer must consider not only the likely level of demand for a product (and thereby make an assessment of its likely levels of profitability), but also whether their suppliers can fully meet the availability targets that the product must meet in order to deliver required profit levels.

Third, a product range must give the retailer some form of good competitive advantage. There is no benefit in a buyer assembling a product range that merely replicates that which is already available from other retailers. Instead, they must ensure that the product range offers adequate levels of differentiation, distinction and benefit to the company. There are two main ways in which a buyer can secure a compelling differential advantage for their company. The first is to provide something that is exclusive and unique within the market. One way of doing that is through the provision of exclusive products, such as through the development of a collaboration with a leading manufacturer brand. The fact that a manufacturer's unique product is only available through a specific retailer is a powerful means of securing loyalty for that retailer. A second way of achieving differentiation, and at the same time delivering a superior profit margin, is through the development of limited edition products. Limited edition products – as the name implies – are available in limited quantities and for limited time periods. Their short 'shelf life' serves to maintain customer engagement and so secures a level of loyalty.

Bringing together these considerations of customer requirements, profitability and differential advantage, the buyer will then develop a buying plan which combines clear guidance on the types of products and brands that are to be bought with information about the level of margin that must be achieved. These factors then serve to direct and inform supplier selection decisions.

7.7.2 Selection of the supply base

It is principally the responsibility of the buyer to lead on the identification, selection and formation of relationships with a supply base. The selection of a supply base is a complex undertaking. Only a very few retail companies own their supply base. Those that do tend to be manufacturers that have forward integrated to include retailing and distribution as part of their core business model.

The integration of production and retailing is most commonly found in the luxury retailing sector, with luxury companies such as Louis Vuitton and Hermès initially manufacturers of luxury goods which then forward integrated in order to take direct control of the retailing of their brands. Other luxury brands such as Giorgio Armani started off as a design company and used third-party suppliers and third-party stockists to make and sell its goods. However, the company soon developed a global network of retail stores and thereafter began to acquire ownership of important suppliers. This was done for three reasons. The first was to gain control over product quality standards and to stabilize availability. Second, direct ownership provided an opportunity to maintain exclusivity and prevent competitor access. Third, it improved flexibility in responding to market opportunity which would then lead to improved margins.

Retailer ownership of suppliers is not common in the retailing mainstream. The notable exception to this is the Inditex Group. While now the world's leading fashion retail business, Inditex began as a traditional clothing manufacturer which then forward integrated in order to take control of its global distribution through stores that are, in the main, company owned. While the majority of the group's products are made in Inditex-owned factories, some ranges are made by external manufacturing companies. These external suppliers tend to focus upon the making of core products and most of them are located near to the group's main headquarters in La Coruña in the north of Spain.

The Inditex Group owns a subsidiary manufacturing company called Tempe. This is a shoe design and manufacturing business that supplies footwear to all of the Inditex Group brands. This ownership provides two important benefits. First, it provides an opportunity for the shoe collection to integrate with the trends that are incorporated into each of Inditex Group's fashion brands. Second, and most importantly, it allows the company to be flexible in responding to consumer trends and purchase patterns as quickly and efficiently as possible (Inditex Group, 2013).

7.7.3 *Off-shore sourcing*

The past two generations have witnessed a significant restructuring of the geography of supply for retailers from the advanced economies. Increases in labour costs, changes in production capability (both technical and human), as well as the change in aspirations of workers, has resulted in a situation whereby most advanced economies – such as in Western Europe, North America and Japan – rely on other economies for the production and supply of the goods sold in their retail stores (Pyndt and Pedersen, 2005).

When developing their sourcing strategies, retailers must think about a range of dimensions. These include where they will source from (the geography of the supply base), whether the supply channels will be from in-house or outsourced, and from an organizational perspective, decisions need to be made as to whether relationships with suppliers will be strategic and long term or opportunistic and short term.

Important, too, is the tactical decision of whether to use a single supplier, a double supplier (one main supplier and a smaller back-up provider), or a hybrid of multiple suppliers for a product range. Figure 7.1 also identifies that decisions need to be made with respect to whether suppliers are going to be concentrated in specific international locations or whether the supply base is global in terms of the breadth and diversity of the countries from which products are sourced.

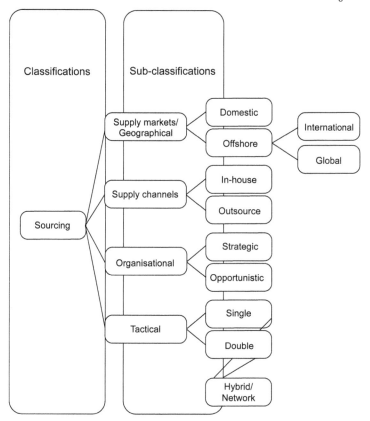

Figure 7.1 The international hubs of fashion retailers
Source: Fernie *et al.*, 2009.

Trent and Monczka (2005) identified a stages approach to understanding the shift from domestic to global sourcing within the sector. They propose that stage one is where small retailers purchase from within the domestic market. Stages two and three identify a gradual progression towards international sourcing that is driven mainly by a lack of suitable suppliers in the domestic market. In many ways, their assessment of buying approach is naive. It fails to recognize that at the first stage there is no guarantee that a small retailer is buying from a domestic manufacturer. Instead, they are likely to be buying from an agent or distributor which wholesales to small retailers goods that have been made in international markets. Nor does the stages approach take into account the power of international brands to appear to be locally developed, when in reality they can be sourced from a diverse range of international locations. Perhaps the significance of their work is best found at stages four and five, which consider how retailers move towards a global sourcing strategy. At this point, the decision is made to release the organization and control of the supply base away from the domestic market and instead to delegate that responsibility to a network of buying hubs.

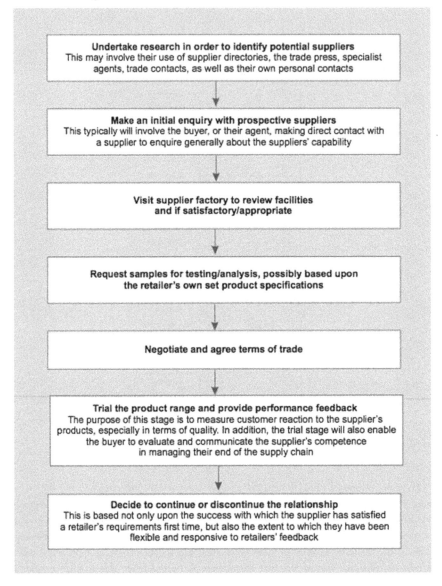

Figure 7.2 Procedures for new supplier selection

Fernie *et al.* (2009) provide an important analysis of international buying hubs and the critical role that hubs play within the buying strategies of major retail companies. In its simplest form, an international buying hub is a management and administration centre that is placed within or close to important sourcing territories. The function of the international buying hub is four-fold.

First, it identifies potential suppliers and manufacturers for a retailer within its geographic region (which can cover more than one country), in order then to make recommendations to the retailer's product management team. Its second function is then to evaluate, on the team's behalf, the capability, expertise and suitability of the prospective supplier. Its third function – once a supplier has been approved as a formal supplier for the retailer – is to establish the terms of supply, such as in relation to quality standards, productivity and service-level agreements. Finally, it will be the responsibility of the local buying hub to monitor the ongoing performance of suppliers in a region, as well as to identify prospective suppliers for future relationships.

7.7.4 Procedures for developing new supplier relationships

Figure 7.2 illustrates the stages that buyers may go through as part of the selection of a new supplier. After their initial investigation to identify possible suppliers, obtained from secondary sources, market recommendations and previous experience, buyers will make initial approaches, directly or via their international hubs, to prospective suppliers, with a view to looking at factory facilities and obtaining sample products.

Retailers typically develop standard procedures for the evaluation of prospective suppliers. In the past, these criteria would have focused solely upon business-related matters and little consideration would have been given to the manner and means by which suppliers operated their business. In recent years, driven initially by the corporate social responsibility (CSR) agenda, retailers now more carefully consider the ethical and environmental behaviours of their suppliers as part of their supplier selection decision making. Consideration of the ethics of supplier choice came even more to the forefront as a result of the Rana Plaza disaster in 2013, when more than 1,000 garment workers in Bangladesh lost their lives when the clothing factory in which they were working collapsed. The atrocity caused global outrage and many fashion businesses declared that they would look even more carefully at the ethical standards of their suppliers.

The shift towards retailers becoming more socially responsible has been dramatic in the past decade. Among the leaders in adopting a sustainable business strategy is the Swedish global fashion retailer H&M. See Box 7.3 for details of their sustainability strategy.

Box 7.3 Sustainable business activities at H&M

In 2002, H&M began to report formally on the sustainability actions that the company was adopting in order to address many key concerns that the company, investors and consumers had about the impact of business actions upon the environment and people. Under the title 'H&M Conscious', the company has sought to find ways of making fashion sustainable and also sustainability fashionable.

In order to achieve this aim, the retailer has adopted seven commitments that seek to be advantageous for society, the environment and their business:

Our commitments

1   Provide fashion for conscious customers
2   Choose and reward responsible partners
3   Be ethical
4   Be climate smart
5   Reduce, reuse, recycle
6   Use natural resources responsibly
7   Strengthen communities

As a result of these commitments, H&M has identified a number of key requirements that shape and determine how the company selects and retains suppliers, as well as how the company influences the behaviour of their supply base. As part of the new supplier selection process, H&M ensures that all new factories must be fully audited to ensure that they meet H&M's standards with respect to workers' pay and working conditions, health and safety regulations, skill development and trade union representation.

Source: H&M, 2013.

7.7.5 New supplier selection criteria

In addition to factors relevant to a prospective supplier's sustainability performance, the buyer will also assess the supplier in relation to five key areas.

7.7.5.1 Supplier reputation

The reputation of a supplier is a crucial consideration for all buyers. Reviews will include consideration of the reputation of the supplier's senior management and staff, for quality, delivery and margin target record, as well as in areas such as safety and ethical standards. The reputation of a prospective supplier is perhaps best evidenced by a review of the supplier's current customer portfolio. The number and reputation of their customers, and the extent to which these customers may be significant rivals, will certainly have a powerful impact upon any evaluation of the supplier's reputation and status in the market.

7.7.5.2 Product portfolio

Most buyers do not want to purchase just a single product from a supplier. Greater scale economies and better margins can be secured if the supplier is able to provide a wider base of products. Therefore, and while perhaps not to buy initially, a buyer will be interested to know the types of product a new supplier could provide, both now and in the future. Buyers are also interested in the product development capability of a supplier (since this reduces some of the burden of new idea development if a supplier is able to develop good products well). An evaluation of the quality standards of the supplier will also be essential, while considerations of the extent to which a supplier can provide exclusive ranges is also of interest to retailers who require differentiated product offerings.

7.7.5.3 Terms of trade

The core requirement of any buyer selection process is a consideration of the pricing structure that the supplier operates. If the buyer represents a large and powerful retailer, then there is every likelihood that the financial assessment of a prospective supplier will extend beyond considerations of their ability to deliver a competitive cost price. These buyers will assess the extent to which one supplier compared with another can provide financial support for marketing campaigns, promotions, mark-downs and discounts for the meeting of volume sales targets.

7.7.5.4 Technology and supply chain competence

Buyers will also carefully assess any new supplier's technological capability, not only in terms of machinery, product design, production scale and quality control, but also in relation to information and effective supply chain coordination. A buyer will also want to be satisfied that the supplier has an efficient and effective stock management system so as to ensure that the supplier will be able to provide excellent levels of customer service with respect to stock availability, quality control and payment transfer systems.

7.7.5.5 Marketing support

In highly competitive markets, the need to ensure maximum product and brand exposure is critical. In the food retailing sector, which across all developed markets has become highly competitive, the major retailers now expect their suppliers to provide substantial support for the marketing and promotion of their goods and services. Suppliers, particularly those that sell branded goods, will also be expected to provide rebates to retailers in exchange for meeting agreed sales targets. Within the grocery sector, in particular, suppliers of major brands bid against each other in order to get the best locations within a supermarket's stores. Suppliers may be required to pay a listing fee in order to ensure that their product is carried by a retailer, and these payments will be in addition to payments made to fund and support promotional activities. The purpose of these initiatives is to encourage volume sales of the suppliers' products. The benefit to the supplier is that the more of their products sold, the more efficiently their factories will operate.

7.7.5.6 Supplier performance evaluation

Buyers continually monitor the efficiency and effectiveness of suppliers. Various dimensions are considered as part of that evaluation, including careful consideration of the quality and service standards that a supplier can provide. If performance by a supplier is erratic or late and results in a loss of business income, then it is unlikely that the relationship will be allowed to continue. If a manufacturer fails to honour agreed contract terms (such as in relation to meeting product specification requirements or the provision of sufficient marketing support), such failures are likely to result in sanctions, such as in the form of fines/penalties, and may even result in the termination of the relationship.

7.8 The role of the merchandiser

The role of the merchandiser is critical to the product management process. Merchandisers have four core areas of responsibility, relating to managing the financial performance of the buying budget and merchandise plan; controlling the flow of goods by managing the critical path; ensuring the availability of products to meet demand through the 'open to buy'; and by effectively allocating products to match customer demand across the retailer's distribution channels. Each of these important responsibilities will be considered in turn below.

7.8.1 Controlling the buying budget and merchandise plan

While it is principally the buyer who decides what is bought and included in a product range, it is the merchandiser who decides how much of a product is actually bought. While it may seem that it would be the buyer who would be responsible for managing the buying budget, this is rarely the case. The financial management of the buying activity is typically the responsibility of the merchandiser.

At the beginning of every buying season, forecasts are made which predict the sales for specific products, groups of products, product categories and for the buying function in its totality. Sales forecasts are based upon previous sales histories and performances, as well as predictions of future market demand. Every retailer must cover all of its costs and ensure that a sufficient income surplus is achieved in order to be profitable. Precision in sales and profit forecasting is especially important if the retailer is a publically listed company, as the profitability levels will directly affect the level of dividend that shareholders receive at the end of the financial year.

Within this context, retailers are motivated, incentivized and censored on the basis of the levels of sales and profitability they achieve, especially against the forecast plans. No publically listed retailer wants to have to inform the stock market that their predictions of success were wrong and that the levels of sales and profitability initially predicted cannot be achieved. In order to reach the required levels of income and profitability, merchandisers, in collaboration with the financial management within the company, will establish the buying budget for the whole buying function, which is then disaggregated to cover each of the main buying areas. Box 7.4 provides details of the core dimensions included in the merchandiser's plan.

Box 7.4 Merchandising plan: core dimensions

- Total buying budget: the amount that a retailer has available to spend on products, based upon current predictions of income and profitability.
- The gross buying margin: the difference between the cost of goods and their retail price. The gross margin is calculated as the selling price of goods minus the cost price of goods divided by the selling price.
- Input margin: a term used to indicate the difference between the cost of goods and their retail selling price.
- Mark-downs: the price reductions that buyers plan in order to move excess stock at the end of a designated sales period.
- Sell-through rates: the percentage of stock of a particular item that will be sold at full price.
- Output margin: final profit contribution for a buying category after all costs and markdowns have been calculated.
- Sales against budget: the sales achieved against the planned sales levels.
- Year-on-year comparison: actual sales performance for a stock item against sales performance the same time the year before.
- Sales against plan: compares actual sales performance against the forecast sales plan.
- Weeks cover: the availability of stock relative to the current levels of weekly sales.

7.8.1.1 *Managing the profitability of the buy*

Essentially, it is the merchandisers' responsibility to advise and cooperate with the buyer on how the buying budget should be allocated and to make clear the margin that must be achieved for each item/product category. They must also stipulate the amount of stock required in order to meet customer demand and secure sufficient levels of profitability. Ultimately, it is the responsibility of the merchandiser to ensure that once a product range has been designed, made and bought, that it meets its financial performance targets. The achievement of full-price product sell-through targets, alongside the controlling of mark-down levels and overseeing of stock availability, all contribute directly to the achievement of profit targets.

Each of these activities is concerned with measuring the performance of the buying process. However, measurement ought never to be an end in itself, but instead should also serve to provide a direction for taking prompt and decisive action if the target performance, and particularly underperformance, requires it. If the range bought is underperforming against plan, then the merchandiser may advise the following:

- Reconfiguration of the product mix: this may require the product team to focus upon the reasons for poor performance and this may result in their altering the balance of the buy. For example, when price competition is fierce, the merchandiser may recommend a reduction in the number of slow-selling, high-priced lines, compared with high-volume, cheaper products that can compensate for the margin loss.

- Reviewing the product pricing and margin mix: in certain circumstances it may be necessary to reduce the retail price of underperforming lines or for those lines for which there are high levels of competition among retailers, in order to improve sales, cash flow and profitability.
- Sales and profit forecast adjustments: if it appears that a product category is unable to achieve its forecasts, then a merchandiser may decide to revise down the forecasts for the line or category and will instead look to identify other products in the portfolio that could compensate for the loss in margin. Through a direct change in the merchandise mix, whereby high-demand products, with higher gross margins, assume a proportionately greater profile within the assortment, the initial gross margin estimate may still be achieved.
- Alternatively, the merchandiser, particularly from a large and powerful retailer, may decide to compensate for gross margin decline by renegotiating (or imposing) a decrease in the original cost price with their suppliers. Or they may decide to increase the selling price. In difficult situations, it may be necessary for the merchandiser to countenance both forms of action.

7.8.2 Managing the critical path

The merchandiser will also establish a direct relationship with suppliers. They will monitor supplier performance in two main areas. The first relates to the scheduling of production and deliveries. Using the buying critical path, the merchandiser is responsible for ensuring that the flow of goods from supplier to retailer is consistent with the calendar of critical stages that was established and agreed with the supplier. An example of a critical path for a jeans buyer is provided in Box 7.5.

Box 7.5 Critical path for ladies' jeans buy for autumn/winter season

2nd February	All product specifications on design, fit, colour, fabric and trim to be sent to suppliers.
12th February	First sample of product specification to be couriered to buyer.
16th February	Review of first sample to be completed and change instructions sent.
28th February	Modified sample to be sent to buyer.
4th March	Final sample agreed by buyer.
15th March	Gold seal sample sent to buyer (this is the sample that is the standard for all quality control and contract agreements).
22nd March	Bulk sample sent to buyer for checking by quality manager for approval.
25th March	Full production commences of 15,000 units.

28th April	15,000 units available for shipping.
30th June	Arrival at port for customs and excise review.
15th July	Arrival at warehouse.
15th August	Distribution to stores commences.
25th August	Launch of A/W: selling and marketing activity.

7.8.3 Managing the open to buy

For most retailers, the buying year is divided into two distinct periods. For fashion companies, homewares, and shoes and accessory retailers the buying year division is spring/summer and autumn/winter. For food retailers the divide is broadly similar, and for nearly all retailers, the three months leading up to Christmas are their most important in terms of customer demand. However, it would be wrong to assume that at the start of each buying season the product management team will have spent all of the buying budget upfront.

Instead, they will retain a proportion of their budget to buy within the season rather than spending all the budget before the period has commenced. The sums that are left unspent are called the 'open to buy'. There are two main reasons for operating an open to buy. The first is that it allows flexibility to respond immediately to up-to-the-moment trends in consumer behaviour. For example, if in the women's fashion market a particular dress shape suddenly and unexpectedly becomes very popular (perhaps as the result of the influence of a celebrity), a retailer can then use the buying budget reserve to buy into the latest fashion trend within the season, and so not miss the opportunity. Second, an open to buy budget affords the opportunity for the product team to delay committing their total spend on perhaps a new and untested brand or product range until initial sales trends indicate the nature of market reaction. If the sales are strong, the open to buy budget allows for additional quantities to be bought.

Regardless of the reasons for operating an open to buy budget, certain conditions have to be met before this can be regarded as a feasible option. First, because the open to buy is done within a season, and the product that would be bought would be needed quickly in order to be sold quickly, it is necessary that suppliers are able to manufacture and deliver with great speed. This usually means that the manufacturers that gain from open to buy orders are geographically close to the retailers' principal markets. For example, the British women's fashion retailer Dorothy Perkins operates an open to buy policy. This allows the brand to respond quickly to in-season trends and so maximize the associated opportunities. However, in order to operate an open to buy policy, the Dorothy Perkins product team cannot use their open to buy budget to purchase from their existing suppliers, which made the majority of a current season's range, because these suppliers are based in Bangladesh or China. It would take too long for these suppliers to make and then ship the required products to the UK on time. Instead, the company spends its open to buy budget on buying from in-stock wholesale companies, based in London. These suppliers make smaller batches of product, typically in the UK, and have product ready and available for product teams to purchase immediately, to be delivered to stores within days.

The consequence of the immediate availability of these products is that the input margin is less when compared with the margin that would have been available had these goods been bought in the forward buy and from far distant suppliers. However, because these are in-trend products, the company can be more certain that demand will be strong. So while the input margin may be less, the level of product sell-through at full price is higher, the level of mark-down is lower and so the final output margin should compensate for the higher cost price.

7.8.4 Managing the allocation of stock

Not all retail stores are equal. Those in large city locations may generate the greatest volume of sales, while a store in a very affluent town may contribute a higher level of profitability to a retailer. It is therefore important that a merchandiser ensures that stock is made available in locations that will generate both high levels of sales and also the required levels of profitability.

When it comes to the allocation of stock, a hierarchy exists in terms of store importance. Ten years ago, the most important store for any retailer would have been its main flagship store. This store would have received every product and would have been the priority, not only for the initial allocation of stock, but also for the replenishment of stock. Now, a retailer's most important store is likely to be their online store, and it is this store that now commands the 'first rights' to the full allocation of stock, as well as subsequent replenishment allocations.

The reason why online stores get priority is clear. First, online stores often attract the largest number of customers and therefore a priority allocation to an online store makes good commercial sense. This is where the products are most likely to be sold. Second, stock availability is not only critical for the success of an online site, but it is also the most visible place for external agents, notably customers, to see whether products are available or not. Frequent non-availability of product on a website indicates poor customer service levels and is therefore damaging to a retailer's reputation. For this reason, online stock availability should be a priority.

There is a variety of allocation processes that can be used for stock assignment and distribution throughout a store network. The most common stock allocation method is a store grading system. Store grading requires that the store network is divided into subsets or clusters. The number of clusters is dependent upon the number of stores in the network and the differences that exist between and among these stores. For retailers that operate more than 50 or so stores, it is common for them to grade their stores into three or more cluster groupings. Stores with similar characteristics, normally in terms of their sales turnover, store size and location (such as city centre, out-of-town and local neighbourhoods), will share the same cluster group. The grading that a store receives directly determines the breadth and the depth of products that are subsequently allocated to it. Many retailers recognize their need to include greater degrees of flexibility in their allocation and grading procedures so as to maximize the sales and profit potential within their markets. As such, the most successful retailers, while broadly adopting the rigidity needed for a grading system, will also allow merchandisers the freedom to allocate, albeit on a restricted basis, product lines to outlets regardless of their classification status. Decisions of this kind are very much motivated by the desire to exploit market potential where this arises, and are a recognition that in certain cases the application of rigid allocation classifications does not fully acknowledge the variety that exists with respect to differences in consumer demand between similar types of outlet.

It is also important to note that store grading can change. It is not uncommon for a retailer, especially within the food sector, to re-grade a store (usually upwards if the store becomes more commercially important to the company) in response to a new market entrant or as the result of a refurbishment of a branch or in response to a competitor's redevelopment. Table 7.1 illustrates the store-grading scheme that is used by a British fashion retailer.

7.9 The role of the brand visual presentation manager

In most retail markets, some common conditions prevail. The first is that many consumers have more choice than they actually need, or in fact want. Second, their product choice decisions are as likely to be based upon emotional dimensions, as rational considerations. Third, and connected to the second condition, it is clear that the consumption decisions that they make in store and online are significantly influenced and guided by the environment within which their consumption takes place.

Therefore, mindful of the significant level of choice that consumers have and in recognition that their choices are influenced by the shopping environment experience and the emotions that these environments can provoke, it becomes necessary for the product management team to take serious account of how their products are presented to consumers, in store and online. It is their responsibility to make sure that the retailer's products, brands and collections stand out in a crowded marketplace. Furthermore, they must ensure that the shopping environment that they create fully enhances and supports the positioning, attractiveness and credibility of the range.

To this end, brand visual presentation managers now seek to create experiences that aim to allow the customer to engage with the brand in a more emotional and imaginative way. Consumers therefore do not just buy products, but encounter experiences that should, if developed well, serve to extend the value, distinctiveness and benefits provided by the product range that they purchase.

There are three crucial ways in which brand visual presentation managers serve to enhance and advance the status of the product selection, and these are outlined below.

Table 7.1 Store grading scheme of a British fashion retailer

Store type/grade	Product allocation
Digital flagship store	Full range + online exclusives, limited edition/trial lines
Flagship store	Full range + exclusives
Triple A stores	Full range
Double A stores	85 per cent of range
A stores	75 per cent of range
B stores	50–70 per cent of range, depending on store size

7.9.1 Brand environment schemes

Given the influence of the store environment and experience upon customers' assessment of the viability and attractiveness of a product range, it is vital that the retailer develops a memorable brand experience that both supports and also extends the attractiveness of the product assortment that is offered for sale.

Brand visual presentation managers are responsible for the creation, development and implementation of selling environments that will achieve three key goals. First, the scheme must provide a personality for the brand in a way that is distinctive, credible and memorable. This is achieved through the careful and consistent use of a common colour scheme, graphics, fixtures and fittings, and furniture. Second, as well as being distinctive, the scheme must also clearly represent the positioning and values of the brand; so, for example, if the brand has a premium positioning, then the environment dimensions must clearly represent a premium identity. Third, the scheme must be replicable across all relevant stores, concessions and boutiques. It must be flexible in order to adapt to the different locations and cultures, as well as variations in scale, architecture and space characteristics. Box 7.6 explains the scheme that Marks & Spencer developed to support their Indigo womenswear brand.

Box 7.6 The Indigo store experience at Marks & Spencer

Targeted at female customers in their thirties or forties, the Indigo brand at Marks & Spencer is positioned to serve as the company's main casual fashion brand for women. Denim is the anchor product for the brand which is focused upon the delivery of a comfortable, stylish and informal product offer. In addition, the brand emphasizes product layering and its essence is that of femininity and casual chic. The identity of the brand is allied to the mood and fashion tastes of California. The vibe is relaxed, informal and allied to a casual lifestyle. Because of the connection to California, the brand reference points are drawn for the beach, road trips and from a sense of vintage Americana.

With these brand attributes in mind, the company's brand visual managers created an in-store scheme that was distinctly different from the other brand spaces within Marks & Spencer stores. This was achieved in four main ways. The space was imagined to be like a Californian beach hut. Perimeter walls sought to signal a natural, outside feeling with whitewashed wood and exposed beams. The flooring incorporated beach rugs with zigzag print designs. The rugs were made of natural, heavy-duty materials. Lighting had marine references and a vintage look, while all Indigo signage used the Strangelove typography in order to provide an informal, accessible and handwritten feel. The mood of the brand was best expressed through the use of large-format photography used on walls and mid-floor. The photography is a central way in which Indigo creates a personality experience for the brand. Usually taken on location in California, the images incorporate scenes and settings that clearly communicate the origin and identity of the brand.

Source: Marks & Spencer, 2014.

7.9.2 Product presentation policies

All retail space is a cost, and therefore it is imperative that companies utilize the space as effectively and efficiently as possible. Within the food sector, retailers are acutely aware of the importance of effective space utilization. They understand – through careful research and sales analysis – which parts of their stores, which aisles, which shelves and which places on those shelves are the most lucrative. With that insight and intelligence in mind, food retailers negotiate with food suppliers over which space and how much space their products will get within the retailers' stores.

Likewise, in the department store sector, retailers have known for many years that their most profitable floor is the ground floor, principally because this is the one where customers flow into the store. Products and brands on this floor secure the greatest level of customer exposure and for this reason department stores always locate their beauty/ cosmetics departments there, as these are the high-margin and high-volume product categories. For their part, the world's leading cosmetics and perfume companies vie to secure the bestselling space within the world's leading stores. By securing the premier ground floor selling space, the cosmetic brands secure an enhanced profile among target customer groups and obtain superior sales income, despite the high rental costs to secure the best ground floor space.

Whether it is a decision relevant to the placement of a Ralph Lauren concession in a clothes store, the placement of a Tom Ford counter in a department store or the positioning of Heinz tomato soup in a supermarket, it is important that retailers develop standard presentation policies that can be applied across their retail estate. This is to ensure two things. First, that the terms of the contract with suppliers that stipulate the exact placing and presentation requirements of their products are fully met. Second, that the customer enjoys a coherent and consistent experience when shopping for goods and services.

7.9.3 Visual support

Being faced with an array of products in store can make shopping a complex and even daunting prospect for consumers. Customers need help and support to understand what is on offer and to make their purchase decisions in confidence. It is therefore the role of the brand visual presentation manager to achieve three goals (deliver three messages) in terms of the visual support that they provide for products.

First, it is important to engage customers' interest. The most effective way of securing customer engagement is to provide a visual clue that captures their attention. This is typically achieved through point-of-sale signage. Two messages are especially important here. One that indicates to customers that a product is *new* can create high levels of curiosity and interest. Or it could be a message that indicates that a product is now of a *lower price.* In all markets, price sensitivity is a common characteristic and many retailers know that a price message is a powerful means of securing customers' interest.

The second goal is to inform customers about the characteristics of a product. This can be achieved through signage, video messages and demonstrations of the product in use. Within the food sector, activities such as food tasting and pop-up demonstration cooking sessions provide customers with information about the features and positive attributes of products that are used in the tasting and which are then available for sale. Furthermore, they can be used to encourage link sales with other products in the offer.

Third, it is important to recognize that the role of brand visual presentation manager is also to elicit an emotional response to a product from the customer. Through the use of photography, props and furnishings, images, music and smells, the visual landscape in store can create an emotional response in consumers and increase their engagement with the brand by entertaining and seducing their senses. Two brands that very successfully entertain and seduce their customers through an engaging brand environment are Urban Outfitters and Anthropologie (see Box 7.7).

Box 7.7 The branded store environments of Urban Outfitters and Anthropologie

Founded in 1970, and now with more than 130 stores in the USA, Canada and Europe, Urban Outfitters is a lifestyle brand aimed at consumers aged under 30. The brand's identity is founded and inspired by urban living, humour and eclecticism. Urban Outfitters is positioned to be 'cool' and in order to communicate that identity, the brand's visual team draw upon their interests in contemporary art, music and fashion to create a distinctive shopping environment and experience. Consequently, the stores feel raw and unadorned; spaces appear spontaneous, and natural. While the environments are carefully considered, they are not designed. There is a warehouse feel in store and a sense that items are presented in a non-planned way and so the discovery of a product in Urban Outfitters feels more like a special find than a premeditated purchase.

Anthropologie is the sister brand of Urban Outfitters. Founded in 1992, the company operates stores in the USA, Canada and the UK. Anthropologie is a female lifestyle brand that has an emphasis upon beauty, design and craft. The brand has an artisan vibe and confidently offers consumers a strong appreciation of design. The stores reflect this positioning. The colours, textures and lighting of the stores represent a sense of vintage, femininity and a global design sensibility. Merchandise is presented as if it were a beautiful market stall. While there is a sense of randomness about the presentation, there is also a clear sense of confidence and intelligence which helps to underpin the brand's more premium status within shopping malls and on premier shopping streets in cities such as New York, Chicago and London.

Through the development of carefully designed experiences, both brands have sought to create destination stores, rather than just clothing. This means stores that customers would be motivated to visit as much to enjoy the experience of the stores, as just using the stores to shop for products.

Source: Rupp, 2013.

7.10 Summary

The landscape of product management has changed markedly over the past ten years in particular. The arrival of the digital age has provided consumers with unprecedented access to market, product and trend information. It has also provided customers with immediate access to a global market of choice. The consequences for those responsible for retail product management have been profound. As a result, these professionals must be quicker, better, sharper than their rivals; they must be more engaging, creative and innovative than ever before in order to secure the business of customers. It is no overstatement to say that the success of any retailer is ultimately dependent upon the ability, experience and skill of their product management teams.

Review questions

1   Outline why and how the emergence of online retailing has transformed the role of the retail product management team.
2   Evaluate the scope, purpose and advantage of adopting a product management approach within retailing.
3   Identify the key considerations to be taken into account when selecting a new supplier for a retail company.
4   How does the role of the merchandiser differ from that of the buyer within a retail product management team?
5   Outline why and how the retail product management team contributes so significantly to the achievement of competitive advantage within retailing.

References

Elliott, R. and Rider, J. (2007) *Retail Buying Techniques*. London: BSSA.
Fernie, J., Maniatakis, P.A. and Moore, C.M. (2009) 'The role of international hubs in fashion retailers' sourcing strategy', *International Review of Retail, Distribution and Consumer Research*, 19(4): 421–436.
Goldfingle, E. (2014) 'Next to launch branded fashion spin-off website label', *Retail Week*, 10 March.
H&M (2013) *H&M: Conscious Actions Sustainability Report, 2013*.
Inditex Group (2013) *Inditex Group: Annual Report, 2013*.
Marks & Spencer (2014) *Marks & Spencer Annual Report, 2014*.
Pine, J. and Gilmore, J.H. (1999) *Work is Theatre and Every Business a Stage*. Boston, MA: Harvard Business School Press.
Pyndt, J. and Pedersen, T. (2005) *Managing Global Offshoring Strategies: A Case Approach*. Copenhagen: Copenhagen School Press.
Rupp, L. (2013) 'Urban Outfitters to supersize Anthropologie stores', www.bloomberg.com/news Sept26.

Sacks, D. (2013) 'How Jenna Lyons transformed J Crew into a cult brand', *Fast Company*, 13 April.

Shaw, D. and Koumbis, D. (2013) *Fashion Buying: From Trend Forecasting to Shop Floor*. London: Fairchild Books, .

Trent, R.J. and Monczka, R.M. (2005) 'Achieving excellence in global sourcing', *MIT Sloan Management Review*, 47(1): 23–32.

8 Offshore sourcing and corporate social responsibility (CSR)

Learning objectives

After studying this chapter, you should be able to:

- Evaluate the various sourcing strategies available to retailers – offshore sourcing, outsourcing, use of intermediaries or direct sourcing.
- Apply conceptual models of sourcing to the international fashion retail sector.
- Discuss the supply chain issues that have arisen from an increase in global sourcing – namely, balancing cost, lead time and flexibility considerations.
- Analyse the CSR consequences of offshore sourcing and how to reconcile commercial and ethical pressures using Sri Lanka as a case study.

8.1 Introduction

The purpose of this chapter is to explore the sourcing of retail products offshore with particular reference to issues pertaining to CSR. The collapse of a garment factory building in Dhaka, Bangladesh in 2013 killing 1,100 people implicated a number of Western retailers in this tragedy and cast into the public eye the ethical issues pertaining to cost and lead-time pressures in sourcing products. This chapter therefore provides a bridge between discussions on the buying process in the previous chapter and the challenges for logistics managers in the next chapter.

Western retailers source most non-food products offshore and they have established international offshore hubs around the world to coordinate and consolidate products sourced from factories in particular regions, especially the Asia–Pacific region. Tesco, for example, in 2008 had nine hubs supporting 40 countries throughout the world to supply food and non-food ranges. The focus of most activity centres around the division Tesco International Sourcing (TIS), based in Hong Kong. TIS is responsible for designing, sourcing, overseeing production, quality control and customs procedures for 50,000 Tesco product lines. More recently, Tesco has been sourcing more products from Central Europe, with 2,000 food lines coming from the region and a growing presence in the clothing market. This example shows the scale and importance of international sourcing to a retailer's business. Most of the chapter will focus upon the international fashion retail supply chain and the intricate network of relationships between retail buyers and a global network of independent contractors. First of all it is necessary to provide a background to the sourcing strategies and types of model adopted by retailers.

8.2 Sourcing strategies

Sourcing can be defined as the process of determining the way, the place and the time of the procurement of finished goods (Lee *et al.*, 2004). Zenz (1994, p. 120) provides a more comprehensive definition that is beyond the traditional view. According to him, sourcing is 'the strategic philosophy of selecting vendors in a manner that makes them an integral part of the buying firm for a particular component or part they are to supply'. In other words, sourcing is not considered to be just a business function of getting products at desired prices, but an integral part of an organization's strategy (Zeng, 2000). Traditionally there were two main dimensions to sourcing strategy: supply markets (the geography of sourcing), and supply channels (whether or not to outsource the task of supplying products). Figure 8.1, however, shows two further dimensions, classified as 'organizational' and 'tactical'. The organizational dimension includes strategic or opportunistic sourcing. For example, sourcing from a large supplier using integrated technology enabling sustained retailer–supplier relations enhances reliability of supply or facilitates category management as opposed to opportunistic sourcing of 'good deals' in the market. The tactical dimension includes single, double or hybrid/network sourcing (sourcing from a single supplier; sourcing mainly from a single supplier with backup supply from a second supplier; or sourcing from multiple suppliers – the last option can be used where there are multiple suppliers of products that are low in price and where market conditions enable the buyer to switch suppliers easily and cheaply).

The literature on global sourcing emerged during the early 1970s, when the benefits of purchasing offshore started to be realized (Matthyssens *et al.*, 2006). Cost is the earliest determinant factor to be recognized in the literature; Leontiades (1971) and Leff (1974) argued that the shift of production to foreign (less developed) countries was due to low-cost production (after Matthyssens *et al.*, 2006).

More contemporary models were developed by Swamidass (1993) and Monczka and Trent (1991; Trent and Monczka, 2003, 2005). Initially Monczka and Trent (1991) suggested a four-phase development process that progressed from domestic purchasing to global sourcing but in their later work added a fifth phase (Trent and Monczka, 2003, 2005) (see Figure 8.2). Smaller retailers will source domestically at level one. Level two is the use of international sourcing only when needed, i.e. the products cannot be sourced in the domestic market (reactive sourcing). Level three involves proactive international purchasing as part of an overall sourcing strategy. Level four is the first of two global sourcing strategies integrated across worldwide locations. Operating at this level requires executive leadership that endorses the global perspective. It requires highly skilled personnel, advanced information systems and an organizational structure that enables coordination of global operations. At level five, global sourcing strategies are integrated not only across worldwide locations but also across functional groups such as product development or marketing. There is a horizontal link between sourcing and other functional areas, in particular engineering, operations and marketing. Activities such as design, product

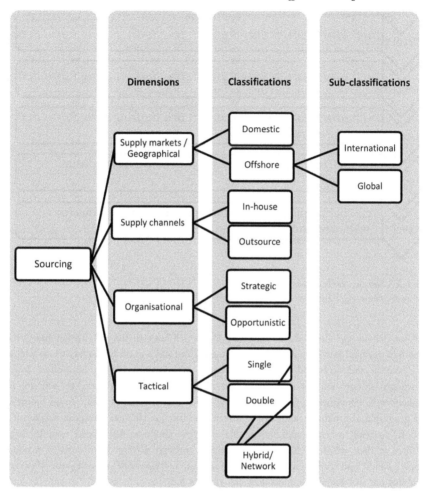

Figure 8.1 The four dimensions of sourcing and their classifications
Source: Fernie *et al.*, 2009.

development and sourcing are assigned to the most competent units across the world. Worldwide capabilities in design, product development and sourcing are necessary to operate at this level.

There are a number of key countries and country groups that retailers use to source the majority of their products. China supplies the great majority of many non-food products sold in UK stores – about 80 per cent of luggage and toys, and more than 70 per cent of digital cameras were sourced there at the beginning of the second decade of the twenty-first century. The Indian subcontinent is the second-largest sourcing location in the world – dominated by India but also comprising Bangladesh, Pakistan and Sri Lanka. South-East Asia is growing in importance as an area of manufacturing and sourcing, with Vietnam

Figure 8.2 The five levels of sourcing
Source: Fernie *et al.*, 2009, after Trent and Monczka, 2005.

well established and Cambodia an emerging location. Closer to the UK, Turkey has developed as a regional hub for neighbouring countries and has a good infrastructure as well as good ethical and ecological credentials. Central and Eastern Europe also offers lower transportation costs and faster response times. Latin America is well placed for sourcing by retailers in North America, due to time zone similarities (making it easier to do business) and geographical proximity, although it is less appealing for UK and European retailers.

Both sourcing overseas and outsourcing non-core functions have been used by large retailers in their quest for achieving profitability through driving down costs of product supply. Pyndt and Pedersen (2005) put forward a framework showing the different combinations of outsourcing and offshoring (Figure 8.3).

8.3 Managing offshore sourcing activities

There are two main ways retailers manage offshore sourcing activities. First, they can use direct sourcing from a centralized headquarters established in the home country or establish international hubs. Sourcing hubs allow direct sourcing from suppliers, thereby retaining control without incurring costs associated with 'full-package' outsourced intermediaries. The role of international hubs includes identification and evaluation of suppliers, obtaining product samples, making site visits, dealing with operational issues and coordinating suppliers. Second, they can source via third-party specialists (outsourcing the sourcing to import or export intermediaries such as trading agents, export management companies, foreign trade companies, export merchants and sourcing organizations).

With regard to sourcing from third-party specialists, the primary distinction of these intermediaries is whether they are based in the country of their customers (import intermediaries) or their suppliers (export intermediaries). Additionally, there are multinational

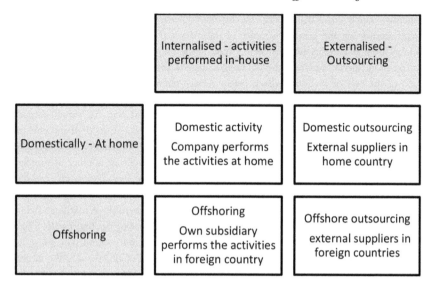

Figure 8.3 Framework that addresses the different combinations of offshoring and outsourcing
Source: Fernie *et al.*, 2009, after Pyndt and Pedersen, 2005.

trading companies that have offices in their customers' or more often suppliers' countries (or both). A typical example of a multinational trade intermediary is the Hong Kong-based Li & Fung, with 12,000 suppliers in 40 economies and offices in developed (customer-based) and developing (supplier-based) countries (Magretta and Fung, 1998; Fung, 2010). Their role is changing in order to meet the contemporary challenges of the market. For example, in the contemporary fashion environment, the need for supply chain efficiency and satisfaction of quick response strategies has led to the rapid development of 'full-package' intermediaries (Hines, 2007). These sourcing specialists can cover all operational pre-retail activities and deal with the problem of suppliers' coordination. The term 'full-package' identifies the range of their offered service, from the raw material selection to the labelling and packaging of the end product.

Some of the most common functions performed by intermediaries are the following (Fung *et al.*, 2007; Ha-Brookshire and Dyer, 2008):

- product development and design;
- sourcing activities;
- identification and evaluation of new suppliers;
- supplier quality control for both products and processes through site visits etc; and
- shipping management and distribution.

Additionally, they simultaneously negotiate with suppliers and customers, in order to finalize orders, reduce inventories and spread risks. Ha and Dyer (2005) add a number of other functions, traditionally related to the retailers' activities: market research, assortment planning, and often customer service. Their overall scope is the development of a competitive supply chain that meets end customers' needs. This scope is achieved by their in-depth knowledge and great experience of the market (Fung *et al.*, 2007). Arguably, it is this knowledge and experience that drives their single existence.

In terms of direct sourcing, the advantages include price reduction through the elimination of the cost of an intermediary, better service obtained from suppliers, better control over manufacturing and delivery time (Palpacuer, 2006). The simplest way of performing direct sourcing is through the headquarters. In that way, the parent company has direct contact with its suppliers. However, the fragmented nature of the textile and clothing manufacturing sector, with numerous production stages in addition to an extensive product range, requires the parent company to deal with a significant number of suppliers. In addition, dispersed production across different countries, or even continents, creates a complex network that is difficult to manage by the headquarters of a single company. Sourcing hubs can provide a solution to the aforementioned labyrinth of textile and clothing suppliers. There is a trend towards direct sourcing. According to Braithwaite (2007, p.334), 'the surge in growth of global trade is the result of more companies going into markets to deal direct – cutting out the middleman'. The effect of this trend is the increase of both margins and risk. In other words, it is preferable to source directly from manufacturers in financial terms, but the complexity of dealing with them increases the risk of supply chain disruption.

Sourcing hubs might propose a solution to the above problem. Their operation allows direct sourcing from suppliers without sacrificing the direct cooperation between two domestic organizations. Fundamentally, they represent the insourcing mechanism of the critical functions of sourcing and can fully substitute export intermediaries. Trent and Monczka's research identified the operation of international sourcing hubs as a potential critical success factor of global sourcing: 'organisations that are committed to global sourcing should seriously consider making international purchasing offices part of their structure' (Trent and Monczka, 2005, p.31).

8.4 Offshore sourcing and the international fashion supply chain

The evolution of the textile supply chain can be related to Figures 8.2 and 8.3 in that until the 1970s and early 1980s much sourcing was still at the early stages of the Trent and Monczka (2005) model and was domestic in nature. However, some companies such as Zara, Benetton and Burton (in the UK) were vertically integrated companies that supplied their own stores; by contrast, Marks & Spencer was always known as a manufacturer without factories as it sourced from UK suppliers and stressed its 'Buy British' credentials in its marketing campaigns. In the last 20 to 30 years, however, the position has changed dramatically, with most fashion retailers (and belatedly Marks & Spencer) acknowledging that offshore sourcing from external suppliers was the preferred model. The exceptions to this rule are Benetton and Zara, with their unique business models (see the next chapter) and the luxury fashion houses.

Historically, the luxury segment of the market was structured in a vertically integrated manner to allow those luxury brands to retain control over merchandise quality and exclusivity, and thereby to demand premium prices for their products (Brun *et al.*, 2008). French couture houses such as Chanel and Hermès therefore tend to internalize the production function in order to retain control over quality and to protect the artisan skills that underpin the production of bespoke luxury goods, which is paramount for protecting brand values. In 2012, Chanel bought its long-term cashmere supplier in Scotland (BBC, 2012), while in recent years luxury groups, including Kering (formerly PPR) and LVMH have acquired a number of exotic skin suppliers and elite tanneries as part of a strategic move to secure a sustainable supply of high-quality raw materials (Socha, 2013). However, the luxury fashion sector is certainly not homogenous (Caniato *et al.*, 2011) and there is some movement towards a networked structure. For example, in 2011, up to 20 per cent of Italian couture house Prada's collections across clothing, shoes and handbags were reported to have been made in China, with some manufacturing also taking place in Turkey and Romania (Sanderson, 2013), with a similar tendency towards using full-package over-seas suppliers discussed in the case of Burberry (Tokatli, 2012). Globalization, heightened competition, advances in IT and the changing nature of the luxury consumer have resulted in a greater level of complexity and turbulence in the market; hence, flexible modular organizations are viewed as sometimes more effective than vertical integration (Djelic and Ainamo, 1999).

In the mid-market segment, the vertical integration model is rare, with a predominant global shift of production to newly emerging markets, as retailers respond to and, in doing so, create further downward price pressure. Mass outsourcing was facilitated by a combi-nation of geopolitical reasons (end of quotas), market needs (increased competition) and technological advancements (information technology and transport improvements) (Azuma and Fernie, 2004; Djelic and Ainamo, 1999). For example, in 2014, fast-fashion chain H&M used 872 suppliers from 1,964 factories worldwide (H&M, 2014). Walmart, the world's largest retailer, has over 100,000 suppliers (Walmart, 2009). Zara is no longer an exception to the globalization of production. While traditionally sourcing from Spain and Portugal, Zara has expanded its supplier base to include lower-cost countries such as Morocco, Turkey and India, finding that suppliers are able to respond quickly and to the standard required (Tokatli, 2008).

Thus, retailers and brands increasingly move towards a design/source/distribute model by focusing on their core competences of design, branding and retailing, with the production function outsourced to global networks of independent suppliers, as shown in Figure 8.4.

Many international clothing retailers have either developed strong partnerships with key suppliers or allowed 'intermediaries' to carry out the sourcing, coordination and logistics to their stores from overseas markets. In the mass 'supermarket' clothing sector, Walmart has been able to build upon the relationships fostered by George at Asda in Turkey (GATT – George and Atila Turkmen), to Latin American markets (*Retail Week*, 8 December 2006). This illustrates how a Turkish company developed its business by working in partnership with George Davies, then of Asda, to develop the business through sharing ideas on design, production and service. The Turkmen business has now grown to the extent that he not only produces for George but other clothing retailers, and coordinates production from 75 factories in Turkey, Romania, Egypt and China.

In their paper on global fashion supply chains, Masson *et al.* (2007) discuss how UK clothing retailers manage offshore production and distribution to the UK from two mar-kets, China and Romania. In their research they 'found that the common norm, and of

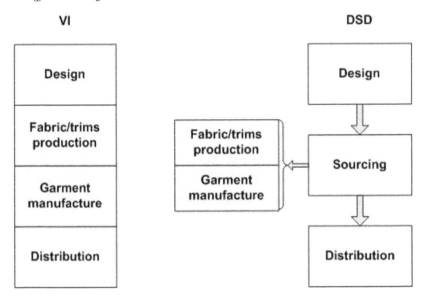

Figure 8.4 Supply chain models in the fashion industry: vertical integration (VI) and design/source/
distribute (DSD)

course, a practice that could eliminate complexities at a stroke, was simply for the retailers
to make use of third party indirect sourcing import/expert agencies or what many choose
to call intermediaries' (Masson *et al.*, 2007, pp. 244–245). These intermediaries act as
agents through coordinating a network of suppliers to produce to retailer demand from
around the globe. Masson *et al.* (2007) also classify some of these companies as integrated
service providers in that they provide in-house services from product design through
manufacture to logistics provision to their customers' (the retailers) distribution centres.

Many companies wish to retain control over the sourcing function so while they offshore
source, they continue to have a presence in these foreign markets, often through the use of
international hubs. Many fashion retailers have key strategic hubs to coordinate both the
buying and distribution function in order that better service can be obtained from suppliers
and that goods can be distributed through key strategic locations. Fernie *et al.* (2009)
analysed the role of international hubs in a UK fashion company's sourcing strategy in
relation to the Pyndt and Pederson, and Trent and Monczka taxonomies discussed in Figures 8.2 and 8.3, respectively. The case study company was committed to offshore sourcing
but wished to retain control through a buying office and international hubs. In terms of
Trent and Monczka's model, the first two stages are not relevant and stage four is equivalent to that of the company's integrated international hub structure. Each hub also had a
strategic role: its Italian hub focused upon design and innovation for high-value items such
as tailored jackets, the Turkish hub provided cost and agility advantages to react to trends,
whilst the Hong Kong hub represented the lean supply model of low-cost production of
basic items such as T-shirts and vest tops.

This confirms earlier research on sourcing by UK fashion firms where Birtwistle *et al.* (2003) commented that basic lines from the Far East can be ordered three months in advance, seasonal lines are augmented by Eastern European and North African suppliers in three weeks, and shorter runs of re-makes are manufactured by British companies. Through a series of case studies, Bruce *et al.* (2004) also show how a combination of lean, agile and 'leagile' approaches have been taken by UK companies to reduce production costs from offshore sourcing whilst at the same time retaining capacity closer to home in order to be able to respond flexibly to an increasingly volatile fashion market.

The main driver for the global shift of production to developing countries is cost, given the labour-intensive nature of apparel production and the large differential in labour rates. Garment manufacturing is not suited to extensive automation due to the flexible properties of fabric. Meanwhile, the low-tech nature of much garment manufacturing means that labour-intensive sewing operations can be located where there is a readily available labour source, and potentially be moved from one low-cost country to another according to business requirements (Sethi, 2003). As countries progressively industrialize and economic development grows, labour rates increase and competitive advantage on the basis of cost moves successively to the next newly industrializing country, where labour rates are even cheaper (Singleton, 1997). For example, Hong Kong, South Korea and Taiwan were popular sources of low-cost manufacturing labour, but by the beginning of the 1990s, rising domestic labour costs meant they were no longer competitive on a purely cost basis. More recently, as labour rates in China's coastal areas have increased, garment manufacturing operations for longer lead-time products have relocated to cheaper inland regions (Zhu and Pickles, 2013). Likewise, as costs in Turkey have increased, some garment manufacturers have shifted production for shorter lead-time merchandise to nearby Egypt (Tokatli and Kizilgün, 2010). One response to this 'race to the bottom' has been for some individual supplier firms or wider economies to 'move to more profitable and/or technologically sophisticated capital- and skill-intensive economic niches' – something referred to in the research literature as 'industrial upgrading' (Gereffi, 1999, p. 52; Neidik and Gereffi, 2006).

In certain cases, garment sourcing decisions may be influenced by historic regional specializations. These are not easily replicated and result in certain countries becoming manufacturing centres for particular types of garment, based on the quality of the basic fabric (e.g. southern India for silks), proximity to fabric source (e.g. China for cotton), specialization in design and production (e.g. Italy for leatherwear and tailoring), and particular highly skilled sewing details (e.g. India for hand embroidery and embellishment) (Dunford, 2006; Fernie and Perry, 2011). Sometimes, a specialized labour skill-base combines with cost advantages – for example, the existence of skilled workers in the East-Central European apparel industry enabled the region to develop a reputation for relatively high-value tailored garments, which complemented its cost and proximity advantages (Begg *et al.*, 2003; see also Kalantaridis *et al.*, 2008; Smith *et al.*, 2008). However, despite the existence of regional pockets of specialization, suppliers continue to face price pressure from low-cost developing countries.

In addition to cost and lead-time pressure, a further challenge in recent times has been the management of ethical issues in complex and fragmented global sourcing networks (Hughes *et al.*, 2007) – something made more challenging in the economic downturn in the early 2010s (Hughes, 2012). Although worker exploitation may be found in a range of industry sectors, the fashion industry is particularly at risk as it is a high-profile consumer segment which attracts the scrutiny of the global media and the general public (Jones, 1999). For example, in 2010, following a media investigation into Indian garment suppliers, fashion retailers Gap, Next and Marks & Spencer faced strong media scrutiny of alleged inhumane working practices, such as long hours, wage violations and forced labour (Chamberlain, 2010). More recently, the tragedy of the garment factory building collapse in Dhaka, Bangladesh, referred to in the introduction, highlights how retail buyers and suppliers have to reconcile ethical issues alongside the commercial pressures of cost and lead time. We now consider the importance of corporate social responsibility (CSR) in international fashion supply networks.

8.5 Corporate social responsibility (CSR) in international fashion supply networks

According to the World Business Council for Sustainable Development, CSR refers to a firm's obligations to the society in which it exists. Namely:

> ... the continuing commitment by business to behave ethically and contribute to economic development while improving the quality of life of the workforce and their families as well as of the local community and society at large.
>
> (WBCSD, 1999, p.3)

The application of CSR to the fashion supply chain requires retailers to consider the social and environmental impacts of their business operations on stakeholders, such as workers and local communities. Environmental issues of pollution and the use of natural resources mainly relate to the textile pipeline, while social issues concern worker welfare and relate to the garment manufacturing function, due to its labour-intensive nature. The social issues of CSR can be further broken down into three main areas of wages, working hours and working conditions (Sethi, 2003). Because of the lack of universal laws or regulations concerning the social aspects of CSR, these issues may be managed by means of private standards which are set at an individual company level, such as retailers' own ethical codes of conduct, or via multi-stakeholder initiatives such as the Ethical Trading Initiative (ETI) (Christopherson and Lillie, 2005; Tallontire, 2007).

Despite growing awareness of ethical issues in fashion supply chains, CSR implementation remains challenged by the context of the global fashion supply chain, in terms of commercial cost and lead-time pressures, as well as the poor working conditions, weak regulatory compliance and corruption often encountered in the production contexts of less developed countries (Schwartz and Tilling, 2009). Globalization has led to a situation whereby multinational corporations based in developed countries are able to apply local standards to their operations in less developed nations in order to maximize profits (Werther and Chandler, 2005). Invariably, host country regulatory standards on issues such as pollution, discrimination and wages appear inferior to accepted home country standards. Consequently, there is arguably an inherent conflict between the commercial pressures of cost and lead time, and the calls for improvements in worker welfare (Ruwanpura and Wrigley, 2011).

Three areas, in particular, have a negative effect on the ability of the supplier to uphold ethical requirements: lead time, flexibility and cost (Acona, 2004). With unpredictable demand and shortening product lifecycles, retail buyers reduce their risk of under- or over-buying by placing orders as close to the season as possible; however, short lead times and unrealistic delivery schedules increase the likelihood that suppliers may have to work over-time to complete orders in a timely fashion. Lack of advance commitment to orders and a requirement for supplier flexibility affect the supplier's ability to plan the demands on business resources and recruit the necessary permanent employees, instead necessitating the use of temporary workers who may also belong to vulnerable social groups such as eco-nomic migrants. Pressure to reduce garment cost could also force the supplier to lower wages and fail to pay overtime. Extended payment terms, which vary widely from 30 to 160 days, put added pressure on CMT (cut, make and trim) suppliers that need to pay wages on time, and particularly on full-package suppliers that must also pay for fabric and trims in advance. For example, in 2013, UK fashion retailer Monsoon Accessorize requested a 4 per cent retrospective discount from all suppliers, as well as an increase in payment terms from 60 to 90 days (Hurley, 2013). Similarly, Laura Ashley requested a 10 per cent discount on cost price from suppliers with immediate effect, including on orders already placed (Cookson, 2013). Given these competing demands, Pickles *et al.* (2006) note that as order volumes and contract manufacturing prices declined in western Slovakia, compliance with codes of conduct became more tenuous for suppliers. Such conflict between managing commercial requirements and ethical demands was neatly summarized by a factory manager of an Indian Walmart supplier in Hearson's (2009, p.7) study:

> Of course Walmart has many compliance standards. If we try to implement all of them, we can sit at home. No production will happen ... To ask us to complete production with a code of conduct is one thing and to implement it is another thing.

Furthermore, national laws and regulations may be purposely relaxed to increase and attract foreign buyers, as evidenced by relaxed labour regulations in export processing zones (Miller, 2004; Arnold and Han Shih, 2010; Hancock *et al.*, 2010) which conflict with the International Labour Organization (ILO) Core Convention for respecting workers' rights to freedom of association and collective bargaining. It becomes apparent that the implementation of CSR initiatives at factory level becomes highly problematic, given the backdrop of industry commercial pressures, labyrinthine global production networks, and inconsistency in labour standards between codes of conduct and governmental foreign direct investment (FDI) incentives.

The rise of complex global subcontracting relationships results in reduced visibility and control of ethical issues in the fashion supply chain. Despite the development of ethical codes of conduct and audit procedures to guide socially responsible practices, these have questionable effectiveness, given the complexity of global fashion supply chains (Welford and Frost, 2006; Mares, 2010). As the competitive challenges of the sector give rise to retailer buying practices designed to minimize buying risk, reduce cost and increase fre-quency of shipments, there is a need to reconcile CSR implementation and concern for ethical issues with the competitive challenges of the fashion sector.

Research suggests that certain supply chain management initiatives may reconcile these conflicting objectives (see Perry and Towers, 2013). Frenkel and Scott's (2002) empirical study of Asian athletic shoe manufacturers found that collaborative trading relationships were dynamic and promoted joint learning and innovation, whereas with compliance-type relationships the setting of functional targets merely resulted in their achievement and maintenance, rather than a push for further improvement. Industrial upgrading from CMT to full-package manufacture may lead to some degree of empowerment for the supplier, which may offer potential for improved employment opportunities and working conditions (Palpacuer and Parisotto, 2003), though the evidence for this assertion remains mixed (see Bernhardt, 2013). This is echoed by Perry's (2011) study of CSR implementation in garment production in Sri Lanka. She shows how suppliers, especially full-package manufacturers, to Western retailers, have developed long-term trusting relationships that have fostered strong CSR compliance. Sri Lanka is quite unique in establishing a 'Garments Without Guilt' initiative to assure buyers of the country's ethical credentials (see Box 8.1). In 2006, the Sri Lankan textiles and garments industry body launched a campaign to brand the nation as the world's number one ethical garment sourcing destination in order to capitalize on its growing ethical reputation and garner more business from global fashion retailers.

Because Sri Lanka does not produce fast fashion but rather fashion basic products, retail buyers can forecast more accurately and mitigate the problems of over- or under-buying. By offering fashion retailers a full-package garment supply solution as well as low-risk sourcing due to its strengths in ethical and eco-manufacturing of garments, Sri Lanka has achieved a sustainable point of differentiation in a competitive marketplace.

Box 8.1 CSR in garment production in Sri Lanka

Sri Lanka has a reputation for high levels of social responsibility and compliance with norms of ethical sourcing (Ruwanpura and Wrigley, 2011; Loker, 2011) and produces garments for many Western brands and retail groups, including Victoria's Secret, Liz Claiborne, Polo Ralph Lauren, Nike, Next, Gap and Marks & Spencer. It has gained a reputation among retail buyers for high-quality, on-time deliveries and good customer service in key product categories of casualwear, sportswear and lingerie (Tait, 2008). For retail buyers, Sri Lanka's competitive advantage is based on relatively low-cost labour, a literate labour force, high labour standards, investment-friendly government policies and strategic shipping. Continuous reinvestment in backward integration has resulted in the development of a sophisticated apparel industry that has moved from contract manufacturing to higher value-added total supply chain solutions (Knutsen, 2004). The importance of speed, responsiveness and flexibility in the aftermath of quota removal explains the tendency for the vertical integration of Sri Lanka's larger suppliers: as orders are placed closer to the season, raw materials needed for production are close at hand to enable suppliers to coordinate upstream functions of fabric and accessory production.

Although Sri Lanka is unable to compete purely on cost with other Asian garment manufacturing nations, such as Bangladesh, Pakistan, Cambodia and Vietnam, it is able to provide a high-quality full-package service for mid- to upper-market retailers who put a premium on ethical compliance (Montlake, 2011; Loker, 2011; Ruwanpura, 2012). In 2006, the Sri Lankan textiles and garments industry body launched a campaign to brand the nation as the world's number one ethical garment sourcing destination in order to capitalize on its growing ethical reputation and garner more business from global fashion retailers. The 'Garments Without Guilt' initiative assured buyers that garments produced in Sri Lanka were made under ethical conditions. Under the scheme, factories are independently certified and monitored to confirm that they do not use child or forced labour, and provide good working conditions for employees. Despite downward price pressure and the shift of garment production to lower labour-cost countries, Sri Lanka has managed to carve out a unique position in the highly competitive global garment industry through industrial upgrading and a reputation for low-risk ethical garment manufacturing.

Empirical data from Perry's (2011) study of seven case study suppliers providing both full-package supply and contract manufacture to mid- to upper-market casualwear retailers provides evidence of long-term, mutually beneficial retailer–supplier partnerships, characterized by commitment, trust and continual improvement. Sri Lankan garment suppliers have developed strong relationships with US and European Union (EU) retailers over long time periods: trading relationships of 10–20 years were common. Although there was little evidence of formal commitments for future orders, there was an unwritten assumption of continuity based on the duration of the relationship and satisfactory past performance. Many of the case study companies were key suppliers to their retail buyers and thus formed part of a rationalized supply base. There was no evidence of traditional adversarial relationships characterized by short duration, an arm's length approach, competitive bidding, multiple sourcing or decisions based on short-term cost. Despite facing customer pressure for lower costs because of adverse market conditions in the late 2000s/early 2010s, the larger full-package suppliers experienced less downward price pressure than contract manufacturers. The main negative issue detected was an increase in buyer payment terms as a result of recent adverse market conditions – in some cases up to 90 days, subsequently affecting suppliers' cash flow. However, the size and increasing sophistication (industrial upgrading) of many of the suppliers resulted in some redistribution of the power imbalance, and enabled suppliers to negotiate retailers' terms to some extent rather than merely accepting them. For example, one full-package supplier was able to refuse to supply Zara once the retailer insisted on 90-day payment terms, as there was sufficient demand from other retail buyers due to its specialism in working with high-tech fabrics.

Increased collaboration and coordination between retail buyers and suppliers helped to reduce cost, as well as improve agility by developing fashion product closer to demand: most large full-package suppliers had dedicated product development centres, where buyers could come and work alongside the production team to speed up the product development process and reduce lead times, without having a detrimental impact on worker welfare. By collaborating with retail buyers during product development or by integrating design and product development into the sourcing task, suppliers could reduce uncertainty as well as lead times, thereby reducing the likelihood of order changes or cancellations further down the line. Sourcing from full-package, vertically integrated suppliers reduced complexity in the supply chain and thus improved visibility and control of social compliance issues. The size and sophistication of the larger suppliers, coupled with the fact that their competitive positioning in the marketplace was based on their ethical credentials, protected them to some extent (but not absolutely) from continued chronic downward price pressure.

8.6 Summary

This chapter sought to address one of the most controversial aspects of a retailer's operation, namely that of their sourcing strategies for procuring much of their non-food ranges. The early part of the chapter discussed the sourcing strategies available to retailers within the conceptual framework developed by Trent and Monczka, and Pyndt and Pederson. These authors stressed the different stages in the sourcing process with most emphasis on the global procurement of goods and the management of offshore locations. One of the key decisions facing retailers is whether to retain control directly through the headquarters and international hubs, or to outsource this function to full-package intermediaries.

These concepts were applied to the international fashion supply chain to show how fashion retailers have established a vast network of suppliers and factories across countries and continents. Although most attention has tended to focus upon fast-fashion retailers and their quest for ever-cheaper sourcing locations, it was shown that luxury-branded retailers have also sourced increasingly offshore. Indeed, the traditional vertically integrated model developed by manufacturer-retailers and fostered by Zara and luxury retailers is giving way to the design/source/distribute model promulgated by fast-fashion retailers.

Such complex and fragmented global sourcing networks have led to significant management challenges as retailers balance issues of cost, lead times, flexibility and ethical standards, especially during a period of economic austerity in the late 2000s/early 2010s. The fashion sector is constantly in the glare of media publicity as exposés of poor working conditions, underage employees and excessive overtime portray the downside of cheaper prices and exciting new ranges on the high street. As retailers minimize over- or under-buying, they order as close to the season as possible, thereby putting suppliers under pressure to subcontract work and force workers to do excessive overtime.

This inherent conflict between these commercial pressures and the calls for improvements in worker welfare has led to concerns about the effectiveness of ethical codes of conduct, audit procedures and CSR implementation. The final part of the chapter focused on initiatives to reconcile these conflicting objectives. Research has shown that companies go beyond the basic terms of compliance when there is a trusting relationship between partners, and joint initiatives are carried out in planning and design through to the final delivery of product. This is particularly the case with full-package manufacturers which have a degree of empowerment to negotiate rather than just accept retailers' terms. This theme was brought out in the case study of Sri Lanka, which has positioned itself as the country of choice for ethical sourcing. This can be attributed to strong government commitment to uphold ethical standards coupled with a focus on high-quality 'slow' fashion products such as lingerie, casual and sportswear lines. This means that suppliers are under less pressure than their fast-fashion counterparts to reduce costs and change orders at short notice.

Review questions

1   Applying the conceptual models presented in the chapter, discuss how retailers' sourcing strategies have evolved over the last 30 years.
2   To what extent has the shift to offshore sourcing led to the decline of the vertically integrated model of supply at the expense of the design/source/distribute model?
3   Evaluate the key drivers for choosing particular locations for offshore sourcing.
4   The term 'race to the bottom' is often used to explain the changing geography of garment production. Discuss the evolution of garment production networks.
5   Comment upon the key CSR issues pertaining to offshore sourcing.
6   Discuss the conflicting pressures facing managers to be competitively priced in slow-growth consumer markets yet to maintain strong ethical credentials in supplier markets.
7   To what extent has Sri Lanka managed to reconcile the pressures identified in question 6, above?

References

Acona (2004) *Buying Your Way into Trouble? The Challenge of Responsible Supply Chain Management.* London: Acona.

Arnold, D. and Han Shih, T. (2010) 'A fair model of globalisation? Labour and global production in Cambodia', *Journal of Contemporary Asia*, 40(3): 401–424.

Azuma, N. and Fernie, J. (2004) 'The changing nature of Japanese fashion: can Quick Response improve supply chain efficiency?' *European Journal of Marketing*, 38(7): 790–808.

BBC (2012) 'Chanel buys Hawick cashmere mill Barrie', www.bbc.co.uk/news/uk-scotland-scotland-business-19968231 (accessed 16 July 2013).

Begg, R., Pickles, J. and Smith, A. (2003) 'Cutting it: European integration, trade regimes and the reconfiguration of East-Central European apparel production', *Environment and Planning A*, 35(12): 2191–2207.

Bernhardt, T. (2013) 'Developing countries in the global apparel value chain: a tale of upgrading and downgrading experiences', Capturing the Gains Working Paper 2013/22, Manchester: University of Manchester.

Birtwistle, G., Siddiqui, N. and Fiorito, S.S. (2003) 'Quick response: perceptions of UK fashion retailers', *International Journal of Retail & Distribution Management*, 31(2): 118–128.

Braithwaite, A. (2007) 'Global sourcing and supply', in *Global Logistics – New Directions in Supply Chain Management* (Waters, D., ed., 5th edn). London: Kogan Page.

Bruce, M., Daly, L. and Towers, N. (2004) 'Lean or agile – A solution for supply chain management in the textiles and clothing industry?' *International Journal of Operations and Production Management*, 24(2): 151–170.

Brun, A., Caniato, F., Caridi, M., Castelli, C., Miragliotta, G., Ronchi, S., Sianesi, A. and Spina, G. (2008) 'Logistics and supply chain management in luxury fashion retail: empirical investigation of Italian firms', *International Journal of Production Economics*, 114(2): 554–570.

Caniato, F., Caridi, M., Castelli, C. and Golini, R. (2011) 'Supply chain management in the luxury industry: a first classification of companies and their strategies', *International Journal of Production Economics*, 133(2): 622–633.

Chamberlain, G. (2010) 'Gap, Next and M&S in new sweatshop scandal', *The Observer*, 8 August.

Christopherson, S. and Lillie, N. (2005) 'Neither global nor standard: corporate strategies in the new era of labor standards', *Environment and Planning A*, 37(11): 1919–1938.

Cookson, R. (2013) 'Laura Ashley seeks 10% supplier discount', *Financial Times*, 25 March, p. 22.

Djelic, M.L. and Ainamo, A. (1999) 'The coevolution of new organizational forms in the fashion industry: a historical and comparative study of France, Italy, and the United States', *Organization Science*, 10(5): 622–637.

Dunford, M. (2006) 'Industrial districts, magic circles, and the restructuring of the Italian textiles and clothing chain', *Economic Geography*, 82(1): 27–59.

Dyer, B. and Ha-Brookshire, J.E. (2006) 'Apparel import intermediaries' secrets to success – redefining success in a hyper-dynamic environment', *Journal of Fashion Marketing and Management*, 12(1): 51–67.

Fernie, J., Maniatakis, P.A. and Moore, C.M. (2009) 'The role of international hubs in a fashion retailers' sourcing strategy', *International Review of Retail, Distribution and Consumer Research*, 19(4): 421–436.

Fernie, J. and Perry, P. (2011) 'The international fashion retail supply chain', in *Fallstudien zum internationalen management* (Zentes, J., Swoboda, B. and Morschett, D., eds). Wiesbaden; Gabler Verlag, pp. 271–290.

Frenkel, S. and Scott, D. (2002) 'Compliance, collaboration, and codes of labor practice: the Adidas connection', *California Management Review*, 45(1): 29–49.

Fung, P.K.O., Chen, I.S.N. and Yip, L.S.C. (2007) 'Relationships and performance of trade intermediaries: an exploratory study', *European Journal of Marketing*, 41(1/2): 159–180.

Fung, S. (2010) 'An assessment of the changing world of manufacturing', Drapers Fashion Summit, London, 16–17 November.

Gereffi, G. (1999) 'International trade and industrial upgrading in the apparel commodity chain', *Journal of International Economics*, 48(1): 37–70.

Gereffi, G. and Memedovic, O. (2003) *The Global Apparel Value Chain: What Prospects for Upgrading by Developing Countries?* Vienna: United Nations Industrial Development Organization (UNIDO).

Ha, J.E. and Dyer, B. (2005) 'New dynamics in the US apparel import trade; exploring the role of import intermediaries', *International Textile and Apparel Association Proceedings*, www.itaaonline.org/template.asp?intPageId=95.

Ha-Brookshire, J.E. and Dyer, B. (2008) 'Apparel import intermediaries – the impact of a hyperdynamic environment on US apparel firms', *Clothing & Textiles Research Journal*, 26(1): 66–90.

Hancock, P., Middleton, S. and Moore, J. (2010) 'Export Processing Zones (EPZs), globalisation, feminised labour markets and working conditions: A study of Sri Lankan EPZ workers', *Labour and Management in Development*, 10: 1–22.

Hearson, M. (2009) *Cashing In: Giant Retailers, Purchasing Practices, and Working Conditions in the Garment Industry*. Amsterdam: Clean Clothes Campaign.

Hines, T. (2007) 'Supply chain strategies, structures and relationships', in *Fashion Marketing: Contemporary Issues* (Hines, T. and Bruce, M., 2nd edn). Oxford: Butterworth-Heinemann, pp. 27–53.

H&M (2014) 'Our supply chain', www.hm.com/supplychain (accessed 8 July 2014).

Hughes, A. (2012) 'Corporate ethical trading in an economic downturn: recessionary pressures and refracted responsibilities', *Journal of Economic Geography*, 12(1): 33–54.

Hughes, A., Buttle, M. and Wrigley, N. (2007) 'Organisational geographies of corporate responsibility: A UK–US comparison of retailers' ethical trading initiatives', *Journal of Economic Geography*, 7(4): 491–513.

Hurley, J. (2013) 'Dressing down Monsoon in discounting', *The Daily Telegraph*, 24 February, p. 2.

Jones, M.T. (1999) 'The institutional determinants of social responsibility', *Journal of Business Ethics*, 20 (2): 163–179.

Kalantaridis, C., Slava, S. and Vassilev, I. (2008) 'Globalisation and industrial change in the clothing industry of Transcarpathia, Western Ukraine: a microlevel view', *Environment and Planning A*, 40(1): 235–253.

Knutsen, H.M. (2004) 'Industrial development in buyer-driven networks: the garment industry in Vietnam and Sri Lanka', *Journal of Economic Geography*, 4(5): 545–564.

Lee, E.J., Lee, K.B. and Moore, M. (2004) 'Global sourcing and textile and apparel import values: a four-country study as an application of global commodity chains theory', *Journal of Textile and Apparel, Technology and Management*, 3(4): 1–10.

Leff, N.H. (1974) 'International sourcing strategy', *Columbia Journal of World Business*, 6(3): 71–79.

Leontiades, J. (1971) 'International sourcing in the LDCs', *Columbia Journal of World Business*, 6(6): 19–26.

Loker, S. (2011) 'The (r)evolution of sustainable apparel business: from codes of conduct to partnership in Sri Lanka', jaafsl.com/news/500-the-revolution-of-sustainable-apparelbusiness-from-codes-of-conduct-to-partnership-in-sri-lanka.

Magretta, J. and Fung, V. (1998) 'Fast, global, and entrepreneurial: supply chain management, Hong Kong style', *Harvard Business Review*, September–October.

Mares, R. (2010) 'The limits of supply chain responsibility: a critical analysis of corporate responsibility instruments', *Nordic Journal of International Law*, 79(2): 193–244.

Masson, R., Iosif, L., MacKerron, G. and Fernie, J. (2007) 'Managing complexity in agile global fashion industry supply chains', *The International Journal of Logistics Management*, 18(2): 238–254.

Matthyssens, P., Pauwels, P. and Quintens, L. (2006) 'Guest editorial', *Journal of Purchasing & Supply Management*, 12(4): 167–169.

Miller, D. (2004) 'Preparing for the long haul: negotiating international framework agreements in the global textile, garment and footwear sector', *Global Social Policy*, 4(2): 215–239.

Monczka, R.M. and Trent, R.J. (1991) 'Evolving sourcing strategies for the 1990s', *International Journal of Physical Distribution & Logistics Management*, 21(5): 4–12.

Montlake, S. (2011) 'Brandix adapts to Sri Lanka's post-civil war world', www.forbes.com/global/2011/1205/companies-people-ashroff-omar-brandix-apparel-sri-lankan-montlake.html.

Neidik, B. and Gereffi, G. (2006) 'Explaining Turkey's emergence and sustained competitiveness as a full-package supplier of apparel', *Environment and Planning A*, 38(12): 2285–2303.

Palpacuer, F. (2006) 'The global sourcing patterns of French clothing retailers: determinants and implications for suppliers' industrial upgrading', *Environment and Planning A*, 38(12): 2271–2283.

Palpacuer, F. and Parisotto, A. (2003) 'Global production and local jobs: can global enterprise networks be used as levers for local development?' *Global Networks*, 3(2): 97–120.

Perry, P. (2011) *Garments without guilt? An exploration of Corporate Social Responsibility within the context of the fashion supply chain: case study of Sri Lanka*, unpublished PhD thesis, Heriot-Watt University.

Perry, P. and Towers, N. (2013) 'Conceptual framework development: CSR implementation in fashion supply chains', *International Journal of Physical Distribution & Logistics Management*, 43(5/6): 478–501.

Pickles, J., Smith, A., Bucek, M., Roukova, P. and Begg, R. (2006) 'Upgrading, changing competitive pressures, and diverse practices in the East and Central European apparel industry', *Environment and Planning A*, 38(12): 2305–2324.

Pyndt, J. and Pedersen, T. (2005) *Managing Global Offshoring Strategies: A Case Approach*. Copenhagen: Copenhagen Business School Press.

Ruwanpura, K. (2012) 'Ethical codes: reality and rhetoric – a study of Sri Lanka's apparel sector', Working Paper, Hampshire: School of Geography, University of Southampton.

Ruwanpura, K.N. and Wrigley, N. (2011) 'The costs of compliance? Views of Sri Lankan apparel manufacturers in times of global economic crisis', *Journal of Economic Geography*, 11(6): 1031–1049.

Sanderson, R. (2013) 'Manufacturing: consumers push big luxury names to account for supply chains', *Financial Times*, 3 June, p. 4.

Schwartz, B. and Tilling, K. (2009) '"ISO-lating" corporate social responsibility in the organizational context: a dissenting interpretation of ISO 26000', *Corporate Social Responsibility and Environmental Management*, 16: 289–299.

Sethi, S.P. (2003) *Setting Global Standards: Guidelines for Creating Codes of Conduct in Multinational Corporations*. Hoboken, NJ: Wiley.

Singleton, J. (1997) *The World Textile Industry*. London: Routledge.

Smith, A. (2003) 'Power relations, industrial clusters, and regional transformations: pan-European integration and outward processing in the Slovak clothing industry', *Economic Geography*, 79(1): 17–40.

Smith, A., Pickles, J., Buček, M., Begg, R. and Roukova, P. (2008) 'Reconfiguring "post-socialist" regions: cross-border networks and regional competition in the Slovak and Ukrainian clothing industry', *Global Networks*, 8(3): 281–307.

Socha, M. (2013) 'Kering acquires tannery France Croco', *Women's Wear Daily*, 205(60) (25 March): 2.

Swamidass, P.M. (1993) 'Import sourcing dynamics: an integrated perspective', *Journal of International Business Studies*, 24(4): 671–691.

Tait, N. (2008) 'Textiles and clothing in Sri Lanka: profiles of five companies', *Textile Outlook International*, 133: 59–81.

Tallontire, A. (2007) 'CSR and regulation: towards a framework for understanding private standards initiatives in the agri-food chain', *Third World Quarterly*, 28(4): 775–791.

Tokatli, N. (2008) 'Global sourcing: insights from the global clothing industry – the case of Zara, a fast fashion retailer', *Journal of Economic Geography*, 8(1): 21–38.

Tokatli, N. (2012) 'Old firms, new tricks and the quest for profits: Burberry's journey from success to failure and back to success again', *Journal of Economic Geography*, 12(1): 55–77.

Tokatli, N. and Kizilgün, Ö. (2009) 'From manufacturing garments for ready-to-wear to designing collections for fast fashion: evidence from Turkey', *Environment and Planning A*, 41(1): 146–162.

Tokatli, N. and Kizilgün, Ö. (2010) 'Coping with the changing rules of the game in the global textiles and apparel industries: evidence from Turkey and Morocco', *Journal of Economic Geography*, 10(2): 209–229.

Trent, R.J. and Monczka, R.M. (2003) 'Understanding integrated global sourcing', *International Journal of Physical Distribution & Logistics Management*, 33(7): 607–629.

Trent, R.J. and Monczka, R.M. (2005) 'Achieving excellence in global sourcing', *MIT Sloan Management Review*, 47(1): 23–32.

Walmart (2009) 'Walmart announces sustainable product index', walmartstores.com/pressroom/news/9277.aspx (accessed 20 January 2012).

Welford, R. and Frost, S. (2006) 'Corporate social responsibility in Asian supply chains', *Corporate Social Responsibility and Environmental Management*, 13(3): 166–176.

Werther Jr, W.B. and Chandler, D. (2005) 'Strategic corporate social responsibility as global brand insurance', *Business Horizons*, 48(4): 317–324.

WBCSD (World Business Council for Sustainable Development) (1999) 'Corporate social responsibility', Geneva: WBCSD Publications.

Zeng, A.Z. (2000) 'A synthetic study of sourcing strategies', *Industrial Management & Data Systems*, 100 (5): 219–226.

Zenz, G.J. (1994) *Purchasing and the Management of Materials* (7th edn). New York: John Wiley & Sons Inc..

Zhu, S. and Pickles, J. (2013) 'Bring in, go up, go west, go out: upgrading, regionalisation and delocalisation in China's apparel production networks', *Journal of Contemporary Asia*, in press.

9 Retail logistics

Learning objectives

After studying this chapter, you should be able to:

- Understand the changing nature of supply chain management from a variety of theoretical perspectives.
- Discuss efficient consumer response (ECR) and management of supply chain relationships.
- Analyse the application of supply chain concepts in international markets.
- Discuss future challenges for retail logistics.

9.1 Introduction

The principles behind logistics and supply chain management are not new. Managing elements of the supply chain has been encapsulated within organizations for centuries. Decisions such as where to hold stock, in what quantities and how it is distributed have been part of the 'trade-off' analysis that is at the heart of logistics management. It is only in the last few decades, however, that logistics has achieved prominence in companies' boardrooms, primarily because of the impact that the application of supply chain techniques can have on a company's competitive position and profitability. Retailers have been in the forefront of applying best practice principles to their businesses, with UK grocery retailers being acknowledged as innovators in logistics management. This chapter discusses:

- the theoretical framework that underpins logistics and supply chain management (SCM) concepts;
- quick response (QR)/efficient consumer response (ECR) and managing supply chain relationships;
- the application of supply chain concepts in different international markets; and
- future trends, most notably the impact of e-commerce upon logistics networks.

9.2 Supply chain management: theoretical perspectives

The roots of SCM as a discipline are often attributed to the management guru Peter Drucker, and his seminal article in *Fortune* magazine in 1962. At this time he was discussing distribution as one of the key areas of business, where major efficiency gains could be achieved and costs saved. Then, and through the next two decades, the supply chain was still viewed as a series of disparate functions. Thus logistics management was depicted as two separate schools of thought, one dealing with materials management (industrial markets), the other with physical distribution management (consumer goods markets) (see Figure 9.1). In terms of the marketing function, research has focused upon buyer–seller relationships and the shift away from adversarial relationships to those built upon trust (see the work of the IMP group, for example, Ford *et al.*, 2011). At the same time a body of literature was developing, mainly in the UK, on the transformation of retail logistics from a manufacturer-driven to a retail-controlled system (McKinnon, 1989; Fernie, 1990; Fernie and Sparks, 1998; see also Fernie *et al.*, 2010 for a review of the development of retail logistics in the UK).

In both industrial and consumer markets, several key themes began to emerge:

- the shift from a push to a pull, i.e. a demand-driven supply chain;
- the customer gaining more power in the marketing channel;
- the role of information systems to gain better control of the supply chain;
- the elimination of unnecessary inventory in the supply chain; and
- the focusing upon core capabilities and increasing the likelihood of outsourcing non-core activities to specialists.

To achieve maximum effectiveness of supply chains, it is imperative that integration takes place by 'the linking together of previously separated activities within a single system' (Slack *et al.*, 1998, p.303). This means that companies have had to review their internal organization to eliminate duplication and ensure that total costs can be reduced rather than

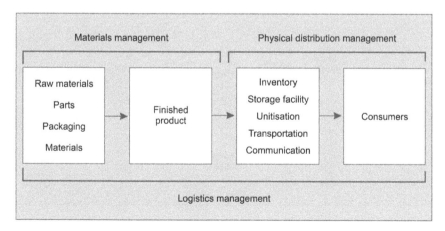

Figure 9.1 Logistics management

allow separate functions (including marketing) to control their costs in a suboptimal manner. Similarly, supply chain integration can be achieved by establishing ongoing relationships with trading partners along the supply chain.

Throughout the 1970s and 1980s, attention in industrial marketing focused upon the changes promulgated by the processes involved in improving efficiencies in manufacturing. Total quality management, business process re-engineering and continuous improvement brought Japanese business thinking to Western manufacturing operations. The implementation of these practices was popularized by Womack *et al*'s (1990) book on *The Machine that Changed the World*. Not surprisingly, much of the literature on buyer-seller relationships focused upon the car manufacturing sector.

During the 1990s, this focus on lean production was challenged in the USA and UK because of an over-reliance on efficiency measures rather than innovative responses. Harrison *et al.* (1999) have therefore developed an agile supply chain model (see Figure 9.2) that is highly responsive to market demand. Agility as a concept was developed in the USA in response to the Japanese success in lean production. Agility plays to US strengths of entrepreneurship and information systems technology. Harrison *et al.* (1999) argue that the improvements in the use of information technology to capture 'real-time' data mean less reliance on forecasts and create a virtual supply chain between trading partners. By sharing information, process integration will take place between partners who focus upon their core competences. The final link in the agile supply chain is the network where a confederation of partners structure, coordinate and manage relationships to meet customer needs.

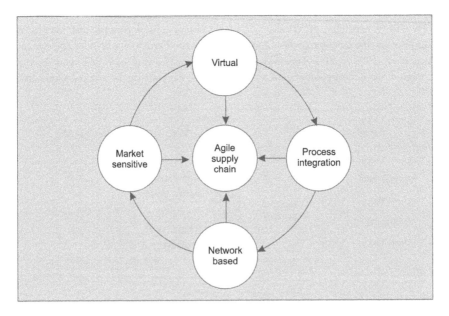

Figure 9.2 The agile supply chain
Source: Harrison *et al.*, 1999.

Both approaches, of course, have their proponents. There is, however, no reason why supply systems may not be a combination of both lean and agile approaches, with each used when most appropriate (the so-called 'leagile' approach; Mason-Jones *et al.*, 2000; Naylor *et al.*, 1999; Towill and Christopher, 2002). Table 9.1 provides a summary comparison of lean, agile and leagile supply chains (Agarawal *et al.*, 2006). It can be seen that they have value in particular circumstances.

From this background to the evolution of supply chain management, it is clear that SCM draws upon a range of disciplines with regard to theoretical development. Initially, much of the research was geared towards the development of algorithms and spatial allocation models for the determination of the least-cost locations for warehouses and optimal delivery routes to distribute to final customers. The disciplines of geography, economics, operational research and mathematics provided solutions to management problems.

As SCM has developed into an integrated concept seeking functional integration within and between organizations, the theories to explain empirical research have been increasingly

Table 9.1 Comparison of lean, agile and leagile supply chains

Distinguishing attributes	*Lean supply chain*	*Agile supply chain*	*Leagile supply chain*
Market demand	Predictable	Volatile	Volatile and unpredictable
Product variety	Low	High	Medium
Product lifecycle	Long	Short	Short
Customer drivers	Cost	Lead time and availability	Service level
Profit margin	Low	High	Moderate
Dominant costs	Physical costs	Marketability costs	Both
Stock out penalties	Long-term contractual	Immediate and volatile	No place for stock out
Purchasing policy	Buy goods	Assign capacity	Vendor-managed inventory
Information enrichment	Highly desirable	Obligatory	Essential
Forecast mechanism	Algorithmic	Consultative	Both/either
Typical products	Commodities	Fashion goods	Product as per customer demand
Lead-time compression	Essential	Essential	Desirable
Eliminate muda [waste]	Essential	Desirable	Arbitrary
Rapid reconfiguration	Desirable	Essential	Essential
Robustness	Arbitrary	Essential	Desirable
Quality	Market qualifier	Market qualifier	Market qualifier
Cost	Market winner	Market qualifier	Market winner
Lead time	Market qualifier	Market qualifier	Market qualifier
Service level	Market qualifier	Marker winner	Market winner

Source: Agarawal et al., 2006, p.212.

drawn from the strategic management or economics literature. The key concepts and theories in SCM are:

- the value chain concept;
- the resource-based theory (RBT) of the firm;
- transaction cost economics; and
- network theory.

The thrust of all these theories is how to gain competitive advantage by managing the supply chain more effectively. The concept of the value chain was originally mooted by Michael Porter (1985), and his ideas have been further developed by logisticians, especially Martin Christopher (see Christopher and Peck, 2003). In Figure 9.3, a supply chain model is illustrated which shows how value is added to the product through manufacturing, branding, packaging, display at the store and so on. At the same time, at each stage cost is added in terms of production costs, branding costs and overall logistics costs. The trick for companies is to manage this chain to create value for the customer at an acceptable cost. The managing of this so-called 'pipeline' has been a key challenge for logistics professionals, especially with the realization that the reduction of time not only reduces costs, but also gives competitive advantage.

According to Christopher and Peck, there are three dimensions to time-based competition that must be managed effectively if an organization is going to be responsive to market changes. These are:

- **Time to market**: the speed at bringing a business opportunity to market.
- **Time to serve**: the speed at meeting a customer's order.
- **Time to react**: the speed at adjusting output to volatile responses in demand.

They use these principles to develop strategies for strategic lead-time management. By understanding the lead times of the integrated web of suppliers necessary to manufacture a product, they argue that a **pipeline map** can be drawn to represent each stage in the supply chain process, from raw materials to customer. In these maps it is useful to differentiate between 'horizontal' and 'vertical' time:

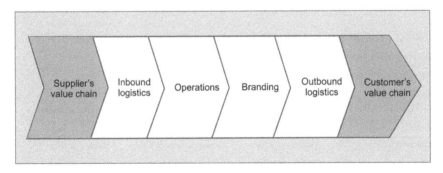

Figure 9.3 The extended value chain
Source: Christopher, 1997.

- **Horizontal time** is time spent on processes such as manufacture, assembly, transit or order processing.
- **Vertical time** is the time when nothing is happening, no value is added, but only cost and products/materials are standing as inventory.

It was in fashion markets that the notion of time-based competition had most significance in view of the short time window for changing styles. In addition, the prominent trend in the last 20 years has been to source products offshore, usually in low-cost Pacific Rim nations, which lengthened the physical supply chain pipeline. These factors combined to illustrate the trade-offs that have to be made in supply chain management and on how to develop closer working relationships with supply chain partners. Christopher and Peck have used the example of The Limited in the USA to illustrate the accelerating 'time to market'. The company revolutionized the apparel supply chain philosophy in the USA by designing, ordering and receiving products from South-East Asia to stores in a matter of weeks rather than the months of its competitors. New lines were test marketed in trial stores and orders communicated by electronic data interchange (EDI) to suppliers, which also benefited from computer-aided design/computer-aided manufacturing (CAD/CAM) technology in modifying designs. The products, already labelled and priced, were consolidated in Hong Kong, where chartered 747s air-freighted the goods to Columbus, Ohio, for onward despatch to stores. The higher freight costs were easily compensated for by lower mark-downs and higher inventory turns per annum.

Along with The Limited, another catalyst for many of the initiatives in lead-time reduction came from work undertaken by Kurt Salmon Associates (KSA) in the USA in the mid-1980s. KSA was commissioned by US garment suppliers to investigate how they could compete with Far East suppliers. The results were revealing, in that the supply chains were long (one and a quarter years from loom to store), badly coordinated and inefficient (Christopher and Peck, 1998). The concept of quick response was therefore initiated to reduce lead times and improve coordination across the apparel supply chain. In Europe, quick response principles have been applied across the clothing retail sector. Supply base rationalization has been a feature of the last decade as companies have dramatically reduced the number of suppliers and have worked much closer with the remaining suppliers to ensure more responsiveness to the marketplace.

The **resource-based perspective** builds upon Porter's models by focusing upon the various resources within the firm that will allow it to compete effectively. Resources, capabilities and core competences are key concepts in this theory. As a supply chain perspective to competitive advantage increases the resource base within which decisions are taken, this theory links to transaction cost analysis and network theory. Thus, firms have to make choices on the degree of vertical integration in their business, to 'make or buy' in production and the extent of outsourcing required in logistical support services. Building upon Williamson's (1979) seminal work, Cox (1996) has developed a contractual theory of the firm by revising his ideas on high-asset specificity and 'sunk costs' to the notion of core competences within the firm. Therefore, a company with core skills in either logistics or production would have internal contracts within the firm. Complementary skills of medium-asset specificity would be outsourced on a partnership basis, and low-asset specificity skills would be outsourced on an 'arm's-length' contract basis.

The nature of the multiplicity of relationships has created the so-called **network organization**. In order to be responsive to market changes and to have an agile supply chain, flexibility is essential. Extending the resource-based theory, the network perspective assumes that firms depend on resources controlled by other firms and can gain access to these resources only by interacting with these firms, forming value chain partnerships and subsequently networks. Network theory focuses on creating partnerships based on trust, cross-functional teamwork and inter-organizational cooperation.

In industrial markets, especially the automobile and high-technology sectors, a complex web of relationships has been formed. This has led Christopher and Peck (1997, p.22) to claim 'that there is a strong case for arguing that individual companies no longer compete with other stand-alone companies, but rather, that supply chain now competes against supply chain'. Tiers of suppliers have been created to manufacture specific component parts, and other supplier associations have been formed to coordinate supply chain activities. In these businesses the trend has been to buy rather than make, and to outsource non-core activities.

Benetton, which has been hailed as the archetypal example of a network organization, is bucking the trend by increasing vertical integration and ownership of assets in the supply chain (Camuffo *et al.*, 2001). While it is retaining its network structure, it is refining the network from product design through to distribution to its stores (see Box 9.1). Benetton and Zara are the most quoted examples of companies embracing time-based competition but their business models are relatively unique (Tokatli, 2008; Lopez and Fan, 2009; Fernie and Perry, 2011; Bhardwaj and Fairhurst, 2010). They have a high degree of vertical integration compared with their fast-fashion competitors (H&M, Topshop, Primark, New Look) which do not own factories but deal with hundreds of suppliers around the globe.

Zara broke the traditional four seasons collections and 'slow' fashion that dominated the high street. By the 1990s it had invested heavily in an information and logistics infrastructure that allowed it to respond quickly to the latest fashion trends (Ferdows *et al.*, 2004). New ideas and fashion trends were evaluated so that around 11,000 items were selected from 30,000 designs. These were then produced in house with the labour-intensive finishing stages being contracted to nearby Spanish and Portuguese suppliers. Lead times were three to six weeks, and stores received product twice a week from its 500,000-sq. metre distribution centre based at its headquarters in La Coruña. More importantly, store managers monitored sales through hand-held monitors so that the correct quantities of stock could be allocated across the store portfolio. This meant that Zara offered a wider range yet a lower inventory than its competitors. It played upon the notion of freshness and originality, thereby creating a feeling of exclusivity. It is not surprising, therefore, that customers visited Zara's stores more frequently than the competition.

The success of Zara and its business model built up expectations that the drift to off-shore sourcing could be reversed and create a revival of production in industrialized economies. Tokatli (2008) claims that these hopes were overestimated in that by the early 2000s Zara had already produced more than half its products away from its traditional Iberian base, and that this has intensified with the globalization of its store network. Furthermore, she questions the moral stance of domestic production in that seamstresses in Galicia and Portugal were earning less than the average industrial wage.

Box 9.1 The Benetton Group

The Benetton Group has around 6,500 shops in 120 countries, manufacturing plants in Europe, Asia, the Middle East and India, and revenues of more than €2 billion. It has divested its sportswear brands and now focuses its interests on fashion clothing, mainly casualwear, with the key brands of United Colors of Benetton, Undercolors of Benetton and Sisley.

Much of Benetton's success until the 1990s could be attributed to its innovative operations techniques and the strong network relationships that it has developed with both its suppliers and distributors. Benetton pioneered the 'principle of postponement', whereby garment dyeing was delayed for as long as possible in order that decisions on colour could be made to reflect market trends. At the same time, a network of subcontractors (small to medium-sized enterprises) supplied Benetton's factories with the labour-intensive phases of production (tailoring, finishing and ironing), while the company continued to manufacture the capital-intensive parts of the operation (weaving, cutting, dyeing, quality control) in Treviso in north-eastern Italy. In terms of distribution, Benetton sells its products through agents, each responsible for developing a market area. These agents set up a contract relationship, similar to a franchise, with the owners who sell the products.

Benetton is now beginning to transform its business by retaining its network structure but changing the nature of the network. Unlike most of its competitors, it is increasing vertical integration within the business. As volumes have increased, Benetton set up a production pole at Castrette near its headquarters. To take advantage of lower labour costs, Benetton has located foreign production poles, based on the Castrette model, initially in Spain, Portugal (now closed), Hungary, Croatia, Tunisia, India, Turkey and, more recently, through its Asia–Pacific subsidiary production in China and South-East Asia through Hong Kong and Bangkok. Castrette produces the designs for production in the regional poles. These foreign production centres often focus on one type of product, utilizing the skills of the region.

In order to reduce time throughout the supply chain, Benetton has increased upstream vertical integration by consolidating its textile and thread supplies so that 85 per cent is controlled by the company. This means that Benetton can speed-up the flow of materials from raw material suppliers through its production poles to ultimate distribution from Italy to its global retail network.

The retail network and the products on offer have also experienced changes. Benetton had offered a standard range in most markets but allowed for 20 per cent of its range to be customized for country markets. Now, to communicate a single global image, Benetton is allowing only 5–10 per cent of differentiation in each collection. Furthermore, it has streamlined its brand range to focus on the United Colors of Benetton and Sisley brands.

The company is also changing its store network to enable it to compete more effectively with its international competitors. It is enlarging its existing stores, where possible, to accommodate its full range of these key brands. Where this is not possible, it will focus on a specific segment or product. Finally, it has opened more than 100 megastores worldwide to sell the full range, focusing on garments with a high styling content. These stores are owned and managed solely by Benetton to ensure that the company can maintain control downstream and be able to respond quickly to market changes.

9.3 Quick response (QR) and efficient consumer response (ECR)

The notion of time-based competition through just-in-time (JIT) and quick response (QR) principles was given further credence in the fast-moving consumer goods (FMCG) sector with the advent of efficient consumer response (ECR). QR was initiated in the fashion supply chain to reduce time to market, especially in the USA, where it was viewed as a survival strategy to compete against low-cost imports. In response to this situation, the American textiles, apparel and retail industries formed the Voluntary Interindustry Commerce Standards Association (VICS) in 1986 as their joint effort to streamline the supply chain and make a significant contribution in getting the in-vogue style at the right time in the right place with increased variety and inexpensive prices. With the basic fashion category, relatively steady demand is a feature of the market, therefore the US concept of QR places much focus on the relationship between retailers and the apparel manufacturers.

Quick response implementation, however, has been patchy, as evidenced from studies undertaken in the last decade. Birtwistle *et al.* (2003), in a study of quick response implementation in UK clothing retailing, noted the slow progress made towards external integration of the textile supply chain, with most gains being made in the introduction of technologies and internal processes. Even in the USA, the financial benefits of QR implementation are inconclusive. Brown and Buttross (2008) measured the financial performance of companies that had adopted QR compared with those that had not. They found that adopters did not achieve significantly better results on profitability, cost efficiency or inventory levels than non-adopters, and cited increased transport costs, carrying of more lines and corporate culture issues pertaining to collaboration as possible reasons for this outcome.

Having established many of the QR goals, VICS has implemented a collaborative planning, forecasting and replenishment (CPFR) programme to synchronize market fluctuations and the supply chain in a more real-time fashion. Through establishing firm contracts among supply chain members and allowing them to share key information, CPFR makes the forecasting, production and replenishment cycle ever closer to the actual demands in the marketplace (VICS, 1998). While the American practices have played a leading role in the QR and SCM initiatives in the apparel industry, much of the success is in the basic fashion segment, where the manufacturing phase is normally the first to be transferred offshore. In this sense, the philosophy of QR as the survival strategy of fashion manufacturing in the industrial economies has not been realized. While the US apparel industry mainly competes on a cost basis in the basic fashion segment, other countries have adopted a different approach. For example, Japanese firms have forged their success on bridge fashion with flexible specialization in a subcontracting network of process specialists in the industrial districts (*Sanchi*, or an agglomoration of small and medium-sized enterprises), led by the 'apparel firms' with design and marketing expertise. This is more akin to the Benetton model discussed earlier. Overall, QR initiatives have had limited application within the domestic apparel industry, with most success in the basic clothing sector supplying department stores. Even in this segment QR has been mainly implemented with offshore suppliers in South Korea and China.

Perry *et al.* (2011) show how QR initiatives have been implemented between firms in the Sri Lankan garment industry and US and European Union (EU) retailers. With the trend to offshore sourcing, fashion buyers have sought out markets with plentiful cheap labour resources to manufacture labour-intensive components of garment production. The relatively remote location of Sri Lanka to European and American markets has led to the country focusing on high-quality, casual garments with relatively long product lifecycles. Furthermore, the government's 'Garments Without Guilt' initiative (discussed in the previous chapter) ensures that suppliers meet strong corporate social responsibility codes of manufacturing. The research findings show that trading relationships of 10–20 years were common and that the full-package suppliers have dedicated product development centres where buyers could come and work alongside the production team to speed up the product development process and reduce lead times. By collaborating with buyers during product development or by integrating design and product development into the sourcing task, suppliers could reduce uncertainty as well as lead times, thereby reducing the likelihood of order changes or cancellations further down the line.

ECR arrived on the scene in the early 1990s, when KSA produced another supply chain report, *Efficient Consumer Response*, in 1993 in response to another appeal by a US industry sector to evaluate its efficiency in the face of growing competition to its traditional sector. Similar trends were discerned from their earlier work in the apparel sector: excessive inventories, long, uncoordinated supply chains (104 days from picking line to store purchase), and an estimated potential saving of US$30 billion, 10.8 per cent of sales turnover.

ECR initiatives have never been fully embraced in the USA compared with Europe. A European Executive Board was initially created in 1994 with the support of European-wide associations representing different elements of the supply chain: AIM, the European Brands Association; CIES, the Food Business Forum; EAN International, the International Article Numbering Association; and Eurocommerce, the European organization for the retail and wholesale trade.

It was in 1994 that initial European studies were carried out to establish the extent of supply chain inefficiencies, and to formulate initiatives to improve supply chain performance (see Table 9.2). ECR Europe defines ECR as 'a global movement in the grocery industry focusing on the total supply chain – suppliers, manufacturers, wholesalers and retailers, working close together to fulfil the changing demand of the grocery consumer better, faster and at less cost'.

One of the early studies carried out by Coopers & Lybrand identified 14 improvement areas whereby ECR principles could be implemented. These were categorized into three broad areas of product replenishment, category management and enabling technologies (see

Table 9.2 Comparisons of scope and savings from supply chain studies

Supply chain study	Scope of study	Estimated savings
Kurt Salmon Associates (1993)	US dry grocery sector	10.8% of sales turnover (2.3% financial, 8.5% cost). Total supply chain $30 billion, warehouse supplier dry sector $10 billion. Supply chain cut by 41% from 104 to 61 days
Coca-Cola supply chain	127 European companies	2.3–3.4 percentage points
Collaboration (1994)	Focused on cost reduction from end of manufacturer's line	Small proportion of category management of sales turnover (60% to retailers, 40% to manufacturer)
ECR Europe (1996 ongoing)	15 value chain analysis studies (10 European manufacturers, 5 retailers); 15 product categories; 7 distribution channels	5.7 percentage points of sales turnover (4.8% operating costs, 0.9% inventory cost). Total supply chain saving of $21 billion. UK savings £2 billion

Source: Fiddis, 1997.

Figure 9.4). Most of these improvement areas had received management action in the past; the problem was how to view the concepts as an integrated set rather than individual action areas.

As the ECR Europe movement began to gather momentum, the emphasis on much of the work conducted by the organization tended to shift from the supply-side technologies (product replenishment) to demand-driven initiatives (category management), and latterly an integrated approach. This is reflected in the early ECR project reports, which dealt with efficient replenishment, transport optimization and unit loads identification, then in the late 1990s and early 2000s projects focused upon consumer value, efficient promotion tactics, efficient product introductions, and collaboration in customer-specific marketing.

During the last ten years there has been a more holistic perspective, albeit with an emphasis on the sustainability agenda. Commensurate with this change in emphasis has been the topics under discussion at the annual ECR Europe conference. At its inception in Geneva in 1996, the concept was being developed and efficient replenishment initiatives were prominent on the agenda. Subsequent conferences have tended to emphasize demand-driven initiatives and emerging issues such as e- and m-commerce, new technologies, on-shelf availability, and product and packaging waste.

It can be argued that the early work focused upon improving **efficiencies** within the supply chain, and later collaborations have stressed the **effectiveness** of the supply chain. Thus, the focus now is on how to achieve profitable growth, as there is little point in delivering products efficiently if they are the wrong assortment, displayed in the wrong part of the store!

After the exceptional success of ECR Europe's annual conferences in the late 1990s/ early 2000s, a series of initiatives was promulgated which encouraged much greater

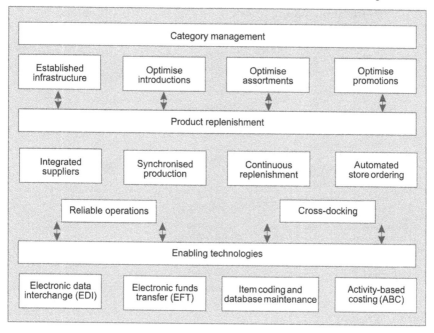

Figure 9.4 ECR improvement concepts
Source: Coopers & Lybrand, 1996.

international collaboration. ECR movements began to share best practice principles, most notably by bringing together the different versions of the US, European, Latin American and Asian scorecards to form a Global Scorecard. The scorecard was used to assess the performance of trading relationships. These relationships were measured under four categories: demand management, supply management, enablers and integrators (see Figure 9.5). Comparing Figures 9.4 and 9.5 shows how ECR has developed to accommodate changes in the market environment. It is not surprising that the Global Commerce Initiative (GCI) has been the instigator of the Global Scorecard in that one of its key objectives is to advocate the promulgation of common data and communications standards, including those pertaining to global web exchanges. The GCI has merged with CIES and the Global CEO Forum to create the Consumer Goods Forum.

Aastrup *et al.* (2008) have proposed a model that integrates the prerequisites for success to ECR activities and outcomes (Figure 9.6). The prerequisites are either industry-level or specific-company based. The industry-level prerequisites include the availability of applicable standards and tools, the existence of critical mass within the sector and consensus on norms. Firm-specific prerequisites include attitudes towards the ECR concept, degree of collaboration necessary to share information, and agreement on how costs/benefits are realized. Furthermore, the capability of companies to develop ECR initiatives is important – for example, top management commitment to ECR and the technical capabilities to carry out such initiatives.

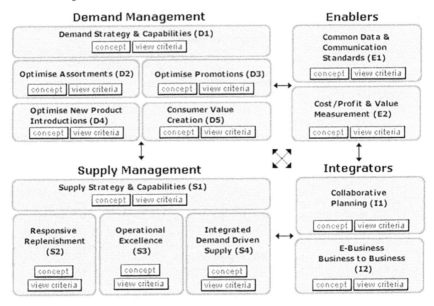

Figure 9.5 ECR concepts
Source: The Consumer Goods Forum, reprinted with permission.

On performing ECR activities, outcomes and performance measures can be evaluated through demand- and supply-related indicators. Demand-related factors are grouped into sales/store variables and consumer/shopping measures. The latter are strongly focused on consumer satisfaction, the former on 'hard' data such as category sales, sales per square metre, direct product profitability (DPP) or activity-based costing (ABC) indicators. Supply-related measures can be classified into three areas: logistics costs, logistics reliability (service levels, on-shelf availability), and administrative accuracy (invoice accuracy and master data precision).

9.4 The UK grocery retail supply chain

The implementation of ECR initiatives has been identified as the fourth and final stage of the evolution of grocery logistics in the UK. Fernie *et al.* (2000) classify this as the relationship stage which relates to a more collaborative approach to supply chain management after decades of confrontation. The UK is often mooted to have the most efficient grocery supply chain in the world, a key contributor to the healthy profit margins of its grocery retailers.

The four stages are:

- supplier control (pre-1980);
- centralization (1981–89);
- just in time (1990–95); and
- relationship (1996–the present).

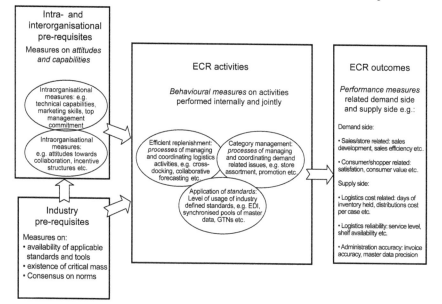

Figure 9.6 Structures of measures in efficient consumer response

The first stage, **supplier control**, is widespread in many countries today and was the dominant method of distribution to stores in the 1960s and 1970s in the UK. Suppliers manufactured and stored products at the factory or numerous warehouses throughout the country. Direct store deliveries (DSDs) were made on an infrequent basis (7–10 days), often by third-party contractors that consolidated products from a range of factories. Store managers negotiated with suppliers and kept this stock in 'the back room'.

Centralization, stage two, is now becoming a feature of retail logistics in many countries and was prominent in the UK in the 1980s. The grocery retailers took the initiative at this time in constructing large, purpose-built regional distribution centres (RDCs) to consolidate products from suppliers for onward delivery to stores. This stage marked the beginning of a shift from supplier to retailer control of the supply chain. There were clear advantages from a retailer perspective:

- reduced inventories;
- lead times reduced from weeks to days at stores;
- 'back room' areas released for selling space;
- greater product availability;
- 'bulk discounts' from suppliers;
- fewer invoices, lower administrative costs; and
- better utilization of staff in stores.

Centralization, however, required much capital investment in RDCs, vehicles, material handling equipment and human resources. Centralization of distribution also meant centralization of buying, with store managers losing autonomy as new headquarters functions were created to manage this change. This period also witnessed a boom in the third-party contract market as retailers considered whether to invest in other parts of the retail business rather than logistics. All of the 'big four' grocery retailers at the time, Sainsbury's, Tesco, Asda and Safeway, contracted out many RDCs to logistics service providers in the mid- to late 1980s.

In stage three, the **just-in-time** phase, major efficiency improvements were achieved as refinements to the initial networks were implemented. The larger grocery chains focused upon product-specific RDCs, with most temperature-controlled products being channelled through a large number of small warehouses operated by third-party contractors. By the early 1990s, temperature-controlled products were subsumed within a network of composite distribution centres developed by superstore operators. Composites allowed products of all temperature ranges to be distributed through one system of multi-temperature warehouses and vehicles. This allowed retailers to reduce stock in store as delivery frequency increased. Furthermore, a more streamlined system not only improved efficiency, but also reduced waste of short-shelf-life products, giving a better quality offer to the customer.

Whilst efforts were being made to improve secondary distribution networks, initial projects were established to integrate primary with secondary distribution. When Safeway opened its large composite in 1989 at Bellshill in Scotland, it included a resource recovery centre that washed returnable trays and baled cardboard from its stores. It also established a supplier collection programme that was to save the company millions of pounds during the 1990s. Most secondary networks were established to provide stores with high customer service levels; however, vehicle utilization on return trips to the RDC was invariably poor, and it was efforts to reduce this 'empty running' that led to initiatives such as return trips with suppliers' products to the RDC, or equipment/recycling waste from stores.

Although improvements to the initial networks were being implemented, RDCs continued to carry two weeks or more of stock of non-perishable products. To improve inventory levels and move to a just-in-time system, retailers began to request more frequent deliveries from their suppliers in smaller order quantities. Whiteoak, which represents Mars, and therefore suppliers' interests, wrote in 1993 that these initiatives gave clear benefits to retailers at the expense of increased costs to suppliers. In response to these changes, consolidation centres have been created upstream from RDCs to enable suppliers to improve vehicle utilization from the factory.

The final stage, the relationship stage, is ongoing but is crucial if further costs are going to be taken out of the supply chain. In the earlier third stage, Whiteoak had noted that the transition from a supplier- to a retail-controlled network had given cost savings to both suppliers and retailers until the just-in-time phase in the early 1990s. By the mid-1990s, retailers began to appreciate that there were no 'quick wins' such as that of centralization in the 1980s to improve net margins. If another step change in managing retail logistics was to occur it had to be realized through supply chain cooperation. The advent of ECR and its promotion by the IGD (formerly entitled the Institute of Grocery Distribution) fostered further cooperation between supply chain members.

The most radical initiative to impact upon grocery supply in the 2000s was the implementation of factory gate pricing (FGP) by the major multiple retailers. Initiated by Tesco and Sainsbury's, FGP is the price retailers are willing to pay excluding transport costs from the point at which the product is ready for shipment to the retailers' RDC. In essence, this is the next step on from 'ad hoc' backhauling and the consolidating of loads. In theory, FGP optimizes the entire transport network throughout the supply chain. Instead of a series of bilateral transport contracts between logistics service providers (LSPs) and retailers/ manufacturers, transport resources would be pooled to maximize vehicle utilization. The larger retailers and logistics service providers can see the major benefits of FGP. With increased international sourcing, LSPs have been keen to offer services in managing product flows across countries and continents. Technologies are now available to track such movements, and cost visibility should enhance openness in negotiations. Most of the major grocery retailers in the UK now have a network of inbound logistics and a fully integrated primary and secondary distribution network. It is interesting to note that Tesco's initial move to FGP was in collaboration with its frozen food suppliers. Tesco and its competitors subsequently began to build frozen food distribution centres and began to move from the initial composite idea to supply stores with RDCs and national DCs (for slower-moving goods). Commensurate with these changes was a trend by UK retailers to bring back these activities from LSPs to managing them in house.

9.5 Differences in logistics 'cultures' in international markets

ECR initiatives launched throughout the 1990s have done much to promote the spirit of collaboration. Organizations began to accommodate and embrace ECR, and to dispel inherent rivalries that have built up over decades of confrontation. The UK has been in the vanguard of implementing ECR, with Tesco and Sainsbury's claiming to have saved hundreds of millions of pounds in the late 1990s/2000s. The rate of adoption of ECR initiatives has varied between companies within international markets. Table 9.2 shows that the KSA report hoped for an improvement of supply chain time from picking line to consumer from 104 to 61 days in the USA. A comparative study of European markets by GEA Consulenti Associati (1994) showed that all of the major countries hold much less stock within the supply chain. In 1997, Mitchell argued that few of the largest European retailers (mainly German and French companies) were ECR enthusiasts. Many of those French and German retailers are privately owned or franchise operations, and they tend to be volume and price driven in their strategic positioning. By contrast, UK and Dutch firms are essentially publicly quoted, margin-driven retailers that have had a more constructive approach to supplier relations. Whilst accepting that there are key differences in European markets, in general there are differences between the USA and Europe with regard to trading conditions. Mitchell (1997, p.14) states that:

- The US grocery retail trade is fragmented, not concentrated as in parts of Europe.
- US private-label development is poorly developed compared with many European countries.
- The balance of power in the manufacturer-retailer relationship is very different in the USA compared with Europe.

- The trade structure is different in that wholesalers play a more important role in the USA.
- Trade practices such as forward buying are more deeply rooted in the USA than Europe.
- Trade promotional deals and the use of coupons in consumer promotions are unique to the USA.
- Legislation, especially antitrust legislation, can inhibit supply chain collaboration.

Although Walmart's penetration into new US markets and its growth in private label goods has been emulated by its competitors, many of these factors remain in force today. While legislation has imposed controls on US retailers in terms of pricing and competition policy, there are significantly fewer controls on location, planning and store choice issues (see Chapter 1). This has resulted in US retailers being able to operate profitably on much lower sales per square metre ratios than the higher-priced fixed costs associated with the more 'controlled' markets of Europe.

To understand how different country logistics structures have evolved it is necessary to understand the nature of consumer choice and the range of retail formats, prior to seeking explanations for the nature of logistical support to stores through supplier relations, cost structures and other operational factors.

9.5.1 Consumer choice and retail formats

US tourists coming to Europe are probably puzzled at store opening hours and the restrictions on store choice compared with their own country. Although liberalization of opening hours has occurred across Europe, the tight planning restrictions on store size and location have tended to shape format development. Furthermore, cross-national surveys of attributes influencing a consumer's choice of store have shown the strong influence of price in France and Germany compared with the UK, where price tends to be ranked behind convenience, assortment range, quality and customer service. The recession, the rise of discounters such as Aldi and Lidl, and Walmart's influence in the UK, have led consumers to revalue these store attributes. In the USA, price and promotion are also strong drivers of store choice; however, US consumers spend their food dollar in a variety of ways, including eating out, which has always been more common than in Europe. Indeed, the KSA survey on ECR was initiated because of the competition from warehouse clubs and Walmart into the traditional supermarket sector.

A partial explanation for the high inventory levels cited by KSA in their survey is that US consumers buy in bulk. With such an emphasis on price and promotion, consumers shop around and stockpile dry goods in garages and basements. Compared with their European counterparts, who have neither the space nor the format choices, US consumers have their own household 'back-room' warehouse areas.

In Europe, the pattern of format development did follow a broad north–south division. The southern Mediterranean and Eastern European markets continue to have a pre-dominance of small independent stores, despite the entry of the largest transnational retailers (see Chapter 5). In Northern Europe, retailers have developed large store formats, but in different ways. Germany has a strong discounter culture. This is reflected in its large number of hypermarkets and hard discounters, but the German consumer also shops at local markets. In France, the home of the hypermarket, large-scale formats coexist with 'superettes' and local markets, whereas in the UK and the Netherlands fewer formats are evident, with superstores and supermarkets respectively dominating their markets. Only in the 2000s has there been a greater emphasis on smaller retail formats, with the major companies moving into the convenience and even the discount market, for example Asda's takeover of Netto UK.

In these Northern European countries, different logistics networks have evolved in response to format development. As discussed earlier in the chapter, many of the largest supermarket chains in the UK that have a portfolio of superstores developed composite distribution to improve efficiency throughout the supply chain. Here all product categories – produce, chilled and ambient – are consolidated at a regional distribution centre for onward distribution to stores in composite trailers which also can carry a mix of products. In the Netherlands, Albert Heijn has utilized cool and ambient warehouse complexes to deliver to its smaller-sized supermarkets, whereas the German and French retailers have numerous product category warehouses supplying their wide range of formats (with hypermarkets, depending on spread of stores, products may be delivered direct by suppliers).

9.5.2 Manufacturer–retailer relationships

A major feature of retail change in Europe has been the consolidation of retail activity into fewer, large corporations in national markets. Many grocery retailers in Europe were small, privately owned family companies 30 years ago, and they were dwarfed by their multi-national branded suppliers. This is no longer the case. Some may remain privately owned, but along with their PLC counterparts they are now international companies that have grown in economic power to challenge their international branded suppliers. Although the largest companies are predominantly German and French in origin, a high degree of concentration also exists in the Netherlands and the UK. Indeed, the series of investigations by the Competition Commission throughout the 2000s into the operation of multiple retail grocery companies in the UK illustrates this shift in power from manufacturer to retailer.

An indication of the growth of these European retailers has been the way in which they have been able to dictate where and when suppliers will deliver products to specific sites. Increasingly, the product has been of the distributor label category. This is of particular significance in the UK, where grocery chains have followed the Marks & Spencer strategy of premium value-added brands that compete directly with manufacturers' brands.

The implications of these changes in power relationships between retailers and their suppliers have been that manufacturers have been either abdicating or losing their responsibility for controlling the supply chain. In the UK, the transition from a supplier-driven system to one of retail control is complete compared with some other parts of Europe. As mentioned earlier, most grocery retailers in the UK have not only centralized over 90 per cent of their products through regional distribution centres, but have also created primary consolidation centres further back up the supply chain to minimize inventory held between factory and store. The implementation of factory gate pricing and integration of primary and secondary networks has reinforced the trend to retail supply chain control. Although this degree of control is less evident in other European markets and in the USA, the spate of merger activity in the late 1990s/2000s and the expansion of retail giants (Walmart, Carrefour, Tesco) with their formats into new geographical markets is leading to internationalization of logistics practice.

Despite these shifts in the power balance, it is generally accepted that to apply ECR principles, the greatest challenge for European retailers is the breaking down of cultural barriers within organizations to move from a confrontational culture to one of collaboration. Organizations will change from a traditional functional 'internal' structure to that of a multifunctional 'external' structure. The changing organizational forms are shown in Figure 9.7, which depicts the traditional 'bow tie' and the new cross-functional team approach. To achieve the significant supply chain savings mooted in ECR reports, companies are having to change their attitudes, although the politics and inherent rivalries built up over the decades mean that it will take years for this cultural revolution to take place.

9.5.3 Logistics cost structures

A critical aspect of these organizational changes that have been evolving in response to ECR initiatives is how to share both the benefits and the costs of the initiatives. Until

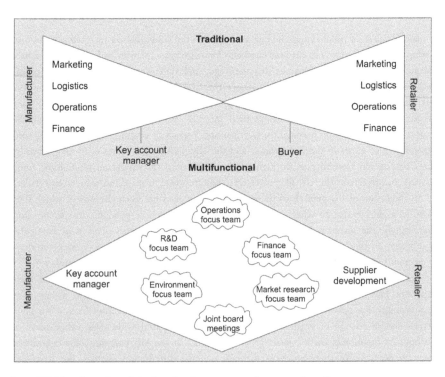

Figure 9.7 Transformation of the interface between manufacturer and retailer
Source: Fiddis, 1997.

the mid-1990s, much of the emphasis on logistics costs focused upon the company or industry channel costs rather than overall supply chain costs.

The advent of **activity-based costing** (ABC), one of the enabling technologies identified in Figure 9.4, has allowed for a 'process' approach to be taken to supply chain activities. For example, many of the initiatives undertaken on product replenishment had clear benefits for retailers but required extra work (i.e. extra costs) further up the supply chain. Thus, the cultural revolution referred to in the previous section is necessary for retailers to establish 'ground rules' on attributing costs as well as benefits when seeking supply chain efficiencies. Although the tools are being developed to improve existing practice, the question of a trade-off of costs within the logistics mix is appropriate at a country level. Labour costs permeate most aspects of the logistics mix – transport, warehousing, inventory and administration costs. Not surprisingly, dependence on automation and mechanization increases as labour costs rise (the Scandinavian countries have been in the vanguard of innovation here because of high labour costs). Similarly, it can be argued that UK retailers, especially grocery retailers, have been innovators in ECR principles because of high inventory costs, mainly as a result of high interest rates in the 1970s and 1980s. This also is true of land and property costs. In Japan, the USA and the Benelux countries the high cost of retail property acts as an incentive to maximize sales space and minimize the carrying of stock in store. In France and the USA the relatively lower land costs lead to the development of rudimentary warehousing to house forward buy and promotional stock.

9.5.4 Role of the logistics service provider

One area of collaboration often overlooked is that between retailer and professional logistics contractors. Historically, the provision of third-party services to retailers varied markedly from country to country. In the UK, where centralization of distribution occurred early, a major market was created for third-party providers to manage RDCs. In the rest of Europe, less enthusiasm for 'contracting out' was initially shown, with a tendency for companies to retain warehousing 'in house' and possibly contract out the transport. Financial conventions differ by country, and in Germany, for example, strong balance sheets were viewed more positively compared with the UK; also, the opportunity cost of capital (investing in logistics infrastructure compared with retailing assets) may result in retaining rather than outsourcing these functions.

In recent years, however, the role of logistics service providers has been enhanced. This can be attributed to the internationalization of retail and transport businesses and the need for greater coordination of supply chain activities. The supply chain is now more complex than before. Retailers are optimizing traffic loads to minimize empty running and are backhauling from suppliers and recovering packaging waste from recycling centres. As efficient replenishment initiatives are implemented, consolidation of loads is required within the primary distribution network. LSPs are better placed to manage some of these initiatives than manufacturers or retailers. Furthermore, the internationalization of retail business has stretched existing supply chains, and third-party providers can bring expertise to these new market areas. Some British companies utilized British logistics companies as they opened stores in new markets. Similarly, the world's largest retailer (Walmart) utilized the expertise of a British logistics company (Tibbett & Britten) to provide logistical support to stores acquired in Canada. Now many British companies including Tibbett & Britten have become part of global LSPs that provide consolidation of loads sourced in international markets in addition to distribution services to stores.

9.6 The internationalization of logistics practice

The gist of our discussion on differences in logistics cultures was to show that implementation of best practice principles has been applied differentially in various geographical markets. Nevertheless, the impetus for internationalization of logistics practice has been achieved through the formal and informal transfer of 'know-how' between companies and countries. ECR Europe conferences, their sponsoring organizations, and national trade associations have all promoted best-practice principles for application by member companies. Many of the conferences initiated by these organizations have included field visits to state-of-the-art distribution centres to illustrate the operational aspects of elements of ECR. At a more formal level, companies transfer 'know-how' within subsidiaries of their own.

The expansion of the retail giants with their 'big box' formats into new geographical markets has led to the internationalization of logistics practice. The approach to knowledge transfer is largely dependent upon the different models of globalized retail operations utilized by these mega groups. Wrigley (2002) classified these retailers into two groups: one following the 'aggressively industrial' model, the other the 'intelligently federal' model (see Table 5.3 in Chapter 5). In the former model, to which Walmart and, to a lesser extent, Tesco can be classified, the focus is upon economies of scale in purchasing and strong implementation of the corporate culture and management practices. Hence, Tesco's implementation of centralized distribution in Ireland, the incorporation of a chilled 'composite' facility and the use of best practice ECR principles developed in the UK. In developing markets such as in Eastern Europe and Asia, Tesco has had to instil discipline with regard to quality assurance for a very fragmented supplier base. Development programmes for a large number of small suppliers were necessary prior to the implementation of centralized distribution in these markets. Walmart, however, is the best example of the aggressively industrial model. In Europe, for example, it tried to integrate buying across the acquired chains in Germany and the UK. The problem here for Walmart was its size in the German market. It did not bring in sufficient volumes to warrant significant discounts from suppliers to justify central distribution (Fernie *et al.*, 2006). Clearly, Walmart had intended to acquire further stores in Germany to achieve such scale economies but its acquisition efforts came to nothing. The initial two acquired chains had a widely dispersed store network leading to high transport costs from the two distribution centres. Eventually, after eight years without breaking even, Walmart withdrew from Germany, selling to Metro in 2006.

In the UK, Walmart's impact on Asda's logistics has been mainly in enhancing IT infrastructure and reconfiguring its distribution network to supply the increase in non-food lines. Its plan to create 20 supercentres by 2005 was realized with 50 per cent of their space devoted to non-food (general merchandise, clothing, electricals, etc.). Furthermore, existing stores have released more space for such lines because of enhanced IT systems. Walmart revolutionized Asda's electronic point of sale (EPOS) and stock data systems in

Project Breakthrough, which commenced in 2000 and was rolled out to stores, depots and finally Asda House by late 2002. The incorporation of Walmart's Retail Link system allowed greater coordination of information from till to supplier, reducing costs and enhancing product availability.

Ahold, by contrast, adheres to the intelligently federal model. It has transformed logistics practices through its relationships in retail alliances and through synergies developed with its web of subsidiaries. In the USA, for example, it has retained the local store names post-acquisition and adopted best practice across subsidiaries. Furthermore, it shares distribution facilities for its own-label and non-grocery lines.

9.7 Future challenges

Clearly, there has been a transformation of logistics within retailing during the last 25 years. Centralization, new technologies, both in materials handling and information hand-ling, ECR and the implementation of best practice principles have resulted in logistics becoming a key management function within retailing. But what of the future? Are we about to experience evolution or revolution of retail logistics? Throughout the 2000s the ECR movement has focused upon areas such as on-shelf availability and a sustainable supply chain. Many of the initiatives discussed in this chapter should enhance product availability – for example, collaboration and technological improvements. Similarly, methods to reduce the carbon footprint include a better integration of networks to minimize empty running of vehicles and the construction of state-of-the-art, 'carbon-neutral' distribution facilities. The main areas that will continue to provide key challenges for logisticians will be the nature of international sourcing and the scale of international retail networks in addition to managing e-fulfilment in an ever growing online market. If the Chinese and Indian markets continue to grow and develop, the increased costs will lead to a gradual shift to sourcing markets closer to areas of consumption.

The biggest challenge facing retailers is how to respond to the market opportunities offered by e-commerce. As shown in Chapter 6, innovation in the ordering process has led to the order 'any time, any place' mentality and retailers have responded through offering a plethora of delivery (and returns) options for customers. This means that retailers offer tighter time windows for delivery, provide 'click and collect' choices (the customer incurs the transport costs!) and a range of collection/return points (mainly convenience stores). Some pure players such as ASOS offer free delivery as the cost is viewed as a marketing rather than a logistics cost.

Arguably, the greatest logistical challenges are faced by companies providing a grocery delivery service to the home. They must typically pick an order comprising 60–80 items across three temperature regimes from a total range of 10,000–25,000 products within 12–24 hours for delivery to customers within 1–2-hour time slots. For example, Tesco is currently picking and delivering an average of 250,000 such orders every week. On a peak day its Enfield dot.com store will pick 145,000 products. New logistical techniques have had to be devised to support e-grocery retailing on this scale. Online shopping for non-food items has demanded less logistical innovation. An order comprises a small number of items (often just one) and the order picking is centralized at a national or regional level. A large proportion of the orders are channelled through the 'hub-and-spoke' networks of large parcel carriers or mail order companies. However, around 30 per cent of non-food products delivered to the home are returned to e-tailers (in contrast to 6–10 per cent for 'bricks-and-mortar' retailers). This requires a major reverse logistics operation comprising the retrieval, checking, repackaging and redistribution of returned merchandise. Catalogue mail order companies have, after all, had long experience of delivering a broad range of merchandise to the home, while some major high street retailers have traditionally made home delivery a key element in their service offering. Online shopping is, nevertheless, imposing new logistical requirements. First, it is substantially increasing the volume of goods that must be handled, creating the need for new distribution centres and larger vehicle fleets. Second, many online retailers are serving customers from different socio-economic backgrounds from the traditional mail order shopper. As they live in different neighbourhoods, the geographical pattern of home delivery is changing. Third, online shoppers typically have high logistical expectations, demanding rapid and reliable delivery at convenient times (Xing and Grant, 2006).

Over the last decade there has been much discussion on the relative merits of the fulfilment models. Currently, there are two main logistics models for grocery e-commerce: the store-based order-picking and the dedicated order-picking models, The store-based system initiated by Tesco makes use of existing distribution assets, in that products pass through RDCs to stores, and their store staff pick and distribute orders to customers. The advantages of this system are the speed of implementation and the relatively low initial investment costs. This system offers customers the full range of goods available in the local store; however, 'out of stock' occurs because the online shopper is competing with in-store customers. It also permits the pooling of retail inventory between conventional and online markets, improving the ratio of inventory to sales.

Tesco's approach is interesting because it is reminiscent of Asda's late acceptance of centralized distribution. Asda's decision not to centralize in the 1970s like some of its regional competitors meant that it could achieve national penetration quickly (compared with the national leader of the time, J Sainsbury, which only opened an RDC in Scotland in 2000!). Tesco delivered 'direct' from stores rather than centralizing its e-commerce operation because it gave greater market penetration in the first decade of operation.

Conflicts between conventional and online retailing are likely to intensify at the back of the store as well as at the 'front end'. Back storeroom areas, where much of the assembly and packing of home orders is undertaken, will become increasingly congested. Over the past 20 years, the trend has been for retailers to reduce the amount of back storage space in shops as in-store inventory levels have dropped and quick-response replenishment has become the norm. This now limits the capacity of these retail outlets to assume the additional role of online fulfilment centre.

Furthermore, it has been estimated that 50 per cent of distribution costs are tied up in-store. Our discussion on delivery options has been the so-called 'last mile' problem. Out-of-stock on the shop floor was a major concern in the early 2000s, despite JIT replenishment techniques, because of the haphazard nature of back stores. Shelf stackers were having difficulty finding products and online fulfilment aggravated the problem (Fernie and McKinnon, 2003). Although Sainsbury's problems were often highlighted (see Zentes *et al.*, 2007), the out-of-stock issue was an industry problem at the time, and was the focus of research by industry bodies such as ECR UK and the IGD. The e-tail delivery problem was solved by allocating or building dedicated space within the store's warehouse for Internet orders (Fernie and Grant, 2008). The Dutch retailer Ahold has coined the term 'wareroom' to describe a dedicated pick facility co-located with a conventional supermarket.

The dedicated order-picking model utilizes e-fulfilment centres to pick and deliver orders to customers. The advantages of this system are that it is dedicated purely to e-commerce customers so 'out of stock' incidences should be low and delivery frequencies should be higher. These fulfilment centres can be designed specifically for the multiple picking of online orders, incorporate mechanized picking systems, and provide much more efficient reception facilities for inbound and outbound vehicles. However, they have less of a product range and they need to be working at capacity to justify investment costs. As their inventory is assigned solely to the online market, home shoppers can have greater confidence in the availability of products at the time of ordering. In non-food there are some highly successful operators of this model (e.g. ASOS.com).

Ultimately, the picking centre model will be the long-term solution to online grocery fulfilment. The problem is that the economics of order fulfilment and delivery is so poor in the short run that most companies have abandoned this approach or gone bankrupt – for example, Webvan in the USA. In the UK in the early 2000s Asda closed two picking centres in London and Sainsbury's developed a hybrid model. So why has the so-called least-efficient fulfilment model proven successful? The answer is simple. You need to create market demand before you invest in costly infrastructure. There is a break-even point where sales volumes justify investment in picking centres. Tesco reached this point in 2006 when it opened its first dot.com facility in Croydon, and by 2013/14 it had opened six other sites, all supporting the densely populated south-east of England where volume and order density was high. By contrast, Walmart is at the very early stage of online innovation partly because of the different nature of the US market from the UK; indeed, Asda, which lags far behind Tesco's operation in the UK, offers Walmart its best business practice on e-commerce. Nevertheless, the world's largest retailer announced plans in 2013 to make up lost ground. It intends to use its 4,000 plus stores in the USA as order fulfilment centres and is trialling a locker collection scheme in 12 stores to offer a 'click and collect' option. More radically, it is considering the use of store shoppers as a delivery mechanism whereby shoppers would deliver to web customers in return for discounts on their purchases (*Retail Week*, 12 April 2013).

9.7.1 Solutions to the last mile problem

In the UK, it has been estimated that the average cost of order processing, picking and delivery for groceries is around £13 per order. As the charge to the customer is normally £5 per order, it is clear that unless the order value is high, retailers will make a loss on every delivery they make.

The cost of the delivery operation is strongly influenced by time constraints, in particular the width of the 'time window' when an order is dropped at a customer's home. In deciding how wide a time window to offer online shoppers, e-tailers must strike a competitive balance between customer convenience and delivery efficiency. From the customer's standpoint, the ideal would be a guaranteed delivery within a very narrow time interval, minimizing the encroachment on his or her lifestyle. It is very costly, however, to provide such 'time-definite' deliveries. Nockold (2001) modelled the effect of varying the width of time windows on home delivery costs in the London area. The window was initially set at three hours. He then reduced it by 25 per cent, then 50 per cent, and finally eliminated this time constraint. These options had the effect of cutting transport costs by, respectively, 6–12 per cent, 17–24 per cent and 27–37 per cent. His conclusion was that by having completely open delivery times, cost savings of up to a third were attainable. Normally, to achieve this degree of flexibility, it must be possible to deliver orders when no one is at home to receive them. It is estimated that around 50–60 per cent of UK households have no one at home during the working day and that 12 per cent of home deliveries fail for this reason, incurring costs to carriers and inconvenience to online shoppers (IMRG, 2006).

Unattended delivery can take various forms. According to market research in 2000 the preferred option for around two thirds of British households is to leave the goods with a neighbour (Verdict Research, 2000), and it is likely that this is the preferred option for packages today. Because of their bulk and the need for refrigeration, few online grocery orders are left with neighbours. Instead, home-based reception (or 'drop') boxes were promoted as a technical solution to the problem of unattended delivery. These boxes can be divided into three broad categories:

- **Integral boxes**: generally built into the home at the time of construction.
- **External fixed boxes**: attached to an outside wall.
- **External mobile (or 'delivery') boxes**: moved to and from the home and secured there temporarily by, for example, a steel cable linked to an electronic terminal.

These boxes come in various sizes and offer different types of electronic access. Most are well enough insulated to maintain the temperature of frozen and chilled produce for 6–12 hours. In a comparison of fixed and mobile boxes, Punakivi *et al.* (2001) concluded that their operating costs are similar, assuming that the latter are only collected at the time of the next delivery. Mobile boxes, however, have a capital cost advantage because they are shared between many customers and can achieve much higher utilization rates.

In the USA, unattended reception was pioneered, unsuccessfully, by Streamline. Their Stream Boxes were generally located in customers' garages, which were equipped with keypad entry systems. Home access systems do not require the use of a reception box. Several home access and mobile reception boxes were trialled in the UK throughout the 2000s, but none has proven commercially viable.

A more practical means of cutting transport costs is by delivering to local collection points rather than to the home. These collection and delivery points (CDPs) can be existing outlets, such as corner shops, post offices or petrol stations, purpose-built centres or communal reception boxes. Few existing outlets have the capacity or refrigeration facilities to accommodate online grocery orders. This has led one property developer to propose the development of a network of specially designed collection centres (or 'e-stops') to handle a range of both food and non-food products. A much cheaper option is to install banks of reception boxes at central locations within neighbourhoods where orders can be deposited for collection. One company has adapted left-luggage lockers into pick-up points for home-ordered products. However, their size, shape and lack of refrigeration limits their suitability for the collection of online grocery orders. The use of collection points economizes on transport by sharply reducing the number of delivery locations and increasing the degree of load consolidation. It achieves this, however, at the expense of customer convenience, by requiring the online shopper to travel to the collection point to pick up the order. If the collection can be made in the course of an existing trip, say from work or to a petrol station, the loss of convenience may be acceptable.

It is likely that for the foreseeable future CDPs strategically located in or around transport terminals, petrol stations and convenience stores offer the best prospect of commercial viability. Collect +, a joint venture between delivery company Yodel and payments group PayPoint, was established in 2009. It utilizes a network of more than 5,250 convenience stores and petrol stations to which orders from retailers can be delivered, returned and tracked. This has proven popular with pure e-tailers such as ASOS and multi-channel retailers. These initiatives appear to strike a reasonable balance between the conflicting demands of customer convenience, delivery efficiency and security. They can also integrate flows of business-to-consumer (B2C) and business-to-business (B2B) orders to achieve an adequate level of throughput. This has been the approach adopted by Amazon to combat the last mile problem, with its Amazon lockers appearing in shopping centres and convenience stores in the USA and UK in the early 2010s. Asda has introduced lockers at railway and tube stations in the London region to target the working commuter. Waitrose also plans to implement temperature-controlled lockers both in store and in remote locations. This 'click and collect' approach has become extremely popular with UK consumers and has been embraced by retailers from all sectors, albeit through pick-up at a local store rather than at third-party locations. Indeed, in late 2013 Argos, the UK's long-standing multi-channel retailer, announced a pilot scheme to allow eBay merchants to collect goods from their stores.

9.8 Summary

This chapter has outlined the theoretical constructs underpinning supply chain management and their applications to the retail sector. It was shown that the notion of time as a driver in competitive advantage is reflected in concepts such as just in time (JIT) in manufacturing, quick response (QR) in fashion, and efficient consumer response (ECR) in the grocery sector. If the aims of ECR are to be realized by meeting consumer demand better, faster and at less cost, supply chain integration will be necessary between and within companies.

Considerable progress has been made to realize these objectives in the last few decades. Fashion retailers such as The Limited, Zara and Benetton have gained competitive advantage through efficient management of their supply chains. The traditional adversarial approach between grocery retailer and supplier also weakened as ECR initiatives were implemented throughout the 1990s/2000s. In the evolution of grocery logistics in the UK, this has been identified as the relationship stage since 1996.

What was clear from the discussion on international markets was that collaboration and the implementation of ECR are more advanced in the UK than in other countries. Differences in logistics networks across markets can be explained by factors other than the nature of manufacturerERRORretailer relationships – for example, the range of retail formats and their spatial distribution, variations in logistics costs in relation to land, labour and freight costs, and the relative sophistication of the logistics service provider market.

Nevertheless, the consolidation of retail markets throughout the world and further internationalization by the retail giants will result in more global sourcing and the adoption of logistics best-practice principles across international markets, as illustrated by the cases of Tesco, Walmart and Ahold.

Finally, the main challenge facing retailers in the future is how they unlock the potential of e-commerce. Chapter 6 shows how this market has developed, but most dot.com failures resulted from fulfilment problems. The two models discussed here outlined the pros and cons of the store-based model compared with the picking centre model for meeting consumers' orders. Although the store model is currently the most successful, the example of Tesco shows how picking centres are introduced once there is sufficient level of demand in a region to justify the required capital investment. The 'last mile' problem continues to pose challenges for retailers. The standard two-hour delivery window offered by most retailers does not maximize the utilization of their vehicle fleets. Thus, a variety of technical solutions, involving unattended reception boxes, have been trialled to reduce these costs. It appears, however, that collection and delivery points, including click and collect, are the favoured options for customers.

Review questions

1   Discuss the key concepts and theories of SCM and their application to fashion retailing.
2   Discuss the evolution of QR and ECR and their implementation in different geographical markets.
3   Evaluate the four stages of grocery logistics in the UK in comparison with other markets.
4   Discuss the various solutions to the 'last mile' problem of delivering goods to home shoppers.

References

Aastrup, J., Kotzab, H., Grant, D.B., Teller, C. and Bjerre, M. (2008) 'A model for structuring efficient consumer response measures', *International Journal of Retail and Distribution Management*, 36(8): 590–596.

Agarawal, A., Shanker, R. and Tiwari, M.K. (2006) 'Modelling the metrics of lean, agile and leagile supply chains: An ANP-based approach', *European Journal of Operational Research*, 173(1): 211–225.

Bhardwaj, V. and Fairhurst, A. (2010) 'Fast fashion responses to changes in the fashion industry', *International Review of Retail, Distribution and Consumer Research*, 20(1): 165–173.

Birtwistle, G., Siddiqui, N. and Fiorito, S.S. (2003) 'Quick response: perceptions of UK fashion retailers', *International Journal of Retail & Distribution Management*, 31(2): 118–128.

Brown, T. and Buttross, T.E. (2008) 'An empirical analysis of the financial impact of quick response', *International Journal of Retail & Distribution Management*, 36(8): 607–626.

Camuffo, A., Romano, P. and Vinelli, A. (2001) 'Back to the future: Benetton transforms its global network', *MIT Sloan Management Review*, Fall: 46–52.

Christopher, M. (1997) *Marketing Logistics*. Oxford: Butterworth-Heinemann.

Christopher, M. and Peck, H. (1998) 'Fashion logistics', in *Logistics and Retail Management* (Fernie, J. and Sparks, L., eds). London: Kogan Page.

Christopher, M. and Peck, H. (2003) *Marketing Logistics* (2nd edn). Butterworth-Heinemann, Oxford.

Coopers & Lybrand (1996) *European Value Chain Analysis Study – Final Report*. Utrecht: ECR Europe.

Cox, A. (1996) 'Relationship competence and strategic procurement management: towards an entrepreneurial and contractual theory of the firm', *European Journal of Purchasing and Supply Management*, 2(1): 57–70.

Drucker, P. (1962) 'The economy's dark continent', *Fortune*, April: 265–270.

Ferdows, K., Lewis, M.A. and Machura, A.D. (2004) 'Rapid-fire fulfilment', *Harvard Business Review*, 82 (11): 104–110.

Fernie, J. (1990) *Retail Distribution Management*. London: Kogan Page.

Fernie, J. and Grant, D.B. (2008) 'On shelf availability: the case of a UK grocery retailer', *The International Journal of Logistics Management*, 19(3): 293–308.

Fernie, J., Hahn, B., Gerhard, U., Pioch, E. and Arnold, S. (2006) 'The impact of Wal-Mart's entry', *Agribusiness*, 22(2): 247–266.

Fernie, J. and McKinnon, A.C. (2003) 'Online shopping: the logistical issues', in *The Retail Book* (Freathy, P., ed.). Maidenhead: Prentice Hall.

Fernie, J. and Perry, P. (2011) 'The international fashion supply chain', in *Case Studies in International Management* (Zentes, Z., Swoboda, B. and Morchett, D., eds). Wiesbaden: Gabler.

Fernie, J., Pfab, F. and Marchant, C. (2000) 'Retail grocery logistics in the UK', *International Journal of Logistics Management*, 11(2): 83–90.

Fernie, J. and Sparks, L. (1998) *Logistics and Retail Management*. London: Kogan Page.

Fernie, J., Sparks, L. and McKinnon, A.C. (2010) 'Retail logistics in the UK: past, present and future', *International Journal of Retail & Distribution Management*, 38(11/12): 894–914.

Fiddis, C. (1997) *Manufacturer-Retailer Relationships in the Food and Drink Industry: Strategies and Tactics in the Battle for Power*. London: FT Retail and Consumer Publishing, Pearson Professional.

Ford, D., Gadde, L.-E., Hakansson, H. and Snehota, I. (2011) *Managing Business Relationships*. Chichester: John Wiley.

GEA Consulenti Associati (1994) *Supplier-Retailer Collaboration in Supply Chain Management*. London: Coca-Cola Retailing Research Group Europe.

Harrison, A., Christopher, M. and van Hoek, R. (1999) *Creating the Agile Supply Chain*. Corby: Institute of Logistics and Transport.

IMRG (2006) 'E-tail delivery cost benefit analysis', www.imrg.org.

Lopez, C. and Fan, Y. (2009) 'Internationalisation of the fashion brand Zara', *Journal of Fashion Marketing and Management*, 13(2): 279–296.

Mason-Jones, R., Naylor, B. and Towill, D.R. (2000) 'Lean, agile or leagile? Matching your supply chain to the marketplace', *International Journal of Production Research*, 38(17): 4061–4070.

McKinnon, A.C. (1989) 'The advantages and disadvantages of centralised distribution', in *Retail Distribution Management* (Fernie, J., ed.). London: Kogan Page, pp. 74–89.

Mitchell, A. (1997) *Efficient Consumer Response: A New Paradigm for the European FMCG Sector*. London: FT Retail and Consumer Publishing, Pearson Professional.

Naylor, J.B., Naim, M.M. and Berry, D. (1999) 'Leagility: integrating the lean and agile manufacturing paradigms in the total supply chain', *International Journal of Production Economics*, 62(1): 107–118.

Nockold, C. (2001) 'Identifying the real costs of home delivery', *Logistics and Transport Focus*, 3(10): 70–71.

Perry, P., Fernie, J. and Towers, N. (2011) 'The impact of the internationalisation of apparel sourcing on fashion retail supply chain relationships: the case of Sri Lanka', European Association of Retail and Commercial Distribution Conference, Parma, July.

Porter, M. (1985) *Competitive Advantage: Creating and Sustaining Superior Performance.* New York: Free Press.

Punakivi, M., Yrjola, H. and Holmstrom, J. (2001) 'Solving the last mile issue: reception box or delivery box', *International Journal of Physical Distribution and Logistics Management*, 31(6): 427–439.

Retail Logistics Task Force – DTI Foresight (2000) *@Your Service: Future Models of Retail Logistics.* London: DTI.

Retail Logistics Task Force – DTI Foresight (2001) *@Your Home: New Markets for Customer Service and Delivery.* London: DTI.

Slack, N., Chambers, S., Harland, S.C., Harrison, A. and Johnson, R. (1998) *Operations Management*, 2nd edn. London: Pitman.

Tokatli, N. (2008) 'Global sourcing: insights from the global clothing industry – the case of Zara, a fast fashion retailer', *Journal of Economic Geography*, 8(1): 21–38.

Towill, D. and Christopher, M. (2002) 'The supply chain strategy conundrum: to be lean or agile or to be lean and agile?' *International Journal of Logistics*, 5(3): 299–309.

Verdict Research (2000) *Electronic Shopping, UK.* London: Verdict.

VICS (Voluntary Interindustry Commerce Standards Association) (1998) *Collaborative Planning, Forecasting and Replenishment Voluntary Guidelines.* Lawrenceville, NJ: VICS.

Whiteoak, P. (1993) 'The realities of quick response in the grocery sector: a supply viewpoint', *International Journal of Retail & Distribution Management*, 21(8): 3–10.

Williamson, O.E. (1979) 'Transaction cost economics: the governance of contractual relations', *Journal of Law and Economics*, 22, October: 223–261.

Womack, J.P., Jones, D. and Roos, D. (1990) *The Machine that Changed the World: The Story of Lean Production.* New York: HarperCollins.

Wrigley, N. (2002) 'The landscape of pan-European food retail consolidation', *International Journal of Retail & Distribution Management*, 30(2): 221–243.

Xing, Y. and Grant, D.B. (2006) 'Developing a framework for measuring physical distribution service quality of multi-national and "pure player" internet retailers', *International Journal of Retail & Distribution Management*, 34(4/5): 278–289.

Zentes, J., Morschett, D. and Schramm-Klein, H. (2007) 'Case study: Sainsbury's', in *Strategic Retail Management: Text and International Cases.* Wiesbaden: Gabler.

10 Adding value through customer service

Learning objectives

After studying this chapter, you should be able to:

- Define customer service in four different ways.
- Understand the role of customer service in raising service quality.
- Assess strategic options for managing customer service.
- Evaluate four key aspects of managing a consumer business.
- Plan and implement excellent customer service in a retail setting.

10.1 Introduction

There are two main roles in a retail organization: Daffy (2011) argues that directly serving customers, or serving the people who do, means that they can serve customers better. Definitions of customer service show the wide-ranging nature of a subject which many, if not most, customers equate merely with a positive and easy-to-use returns process and complaints procedure. In addition to the growing breadth of extra services offered by retailers, from bag packing to crèches, information to installation, customer service is also linked to customer perception of service quality. It is, in one definition, the reason for retailers' existence.

The intangibility of services together with other service characteristics – inseparability, ownership, heterogeneity and perishability – create challenges for retailers, especially in terms of delivering clear customer expectations and experience of service quality over time. These can be used for the purposes of organization or store brand differentiation in an intensely competitive market facing slow growth of the customer base. Where this is coupled with an ageing population, customer retention through customer service is deemed essential as the pool of new customers will decline over time (Rust and Oliver, 1994).

Service quality has been defined as the ability of the organization to 'consistently meet and exceed customer expectations' (Christopher *et al.*, 1991). If the main difference between service quality and customer satisfaction is that the former relates to managing the quality of the service and the latter to customers' expectation and experience of the quality of service delivery, then improving customer service means delivering service quality improvements that are customer defined.

The SERVQUAL model, a useful tool for retail managers to use in the quest for service quality improvement and enhanced customer satisfaction, explores the sources of the gap between service expectation and perceived service experience.

The management of consumer services involves:

- renewing the service offering;
- localizing the point-of-service system;
- leveraging the service contract; and
- using information power strategically.

It also involves planning, organizing, implementing and controlling customer service within the organization.

10.2 Customer service defined

Customer service can be defined in four ways (Baron *et al.*, 1991, p. 55).

10.2.1 The reason for the existence of a retail business

Retailers exist to provide service to customers – at a profit. All the functions of retailing – location, assortment, breaking bulk, providing inventory, marketing and so on – add value to the products purchased by customers. Each function, in adding value, provides a service to customers. It can be argued that it is the retailer's role in adding value which creates profit for retail organizations.

Efficiencies in supply chain management that can be generated by logistical streamlining through systems such as just in time (JIT) and electronic data interchange (EDI), can be passed on to customers in terms of better service at lower prices. However, few retailers would argue that investment in such systems is aimed at increasing profit margins. Generally, the higher the level of customer service provided, the higher the price customers are willing to pay, and the greater the profit margin made by the retail organization.

There is additional profit to be made through customer retention over time. There are sizeable incremental profits to be made (Reichheld and Sasser, 1990):

- From increased purchases over time: as individuals' families grow and as their income increases with age.
- From reduced costs of operation: as customers become more experienced in shopping with a retailer, they need less information or help with shopping and they recognize the retailer brand, have confidence in it and are more likely to shop there over time.
- From customer referrals: word of mouth is a powerful tool for recruiting new customers. Social media have enhanced this power.
- From price premium: while new customers often have to be recruited through introductory promotions or discounts, long-term, loyal customers are more likely to buy at regular prices.

10.2.2 The provision of facilities, activities, benefits, environments, etc., by a retailer as an augmentation of the fundamental exchange relationship between merchandise supplied and money taken

There is an enormous range of services and facilities offered by retailers today. They include:

- accepting credit cards;
- altering merchandise;
- trolleys;
- childcare;
- demonstrating goods;
- information services;
- offering credit;
- assembling merchandise;
- bag packing;
- changing rooms;
- merchandise display;
- financial services;
- offering cash back;
- delivering merchandise;
- bag carrying;
- restaurants;
- sampling of goods; and
- online order points.

The environments presented to shoppers by retailers diversified as successful retailers used the technique of market segmentation to identify target markets, to develop customer profiles, and to create merchandise mixes that suited the needs of target customer groups. This not only allowed major grocery retailers to tailor formats to different product and shopping needs, but also led to innovative retail formats such as forecourt retailing and airport retailing.

Box 10.1 Retailer profile: J Sainsbury plc

Many large retailers operate a number of formats under different names. For example, at one point J Sainsbury plc operated six store formats designed to appeal to various market segments:

Savacentres
Superstores
Supermarkets
Country Town
Sainsbury's Central
Sainsbury's Local

They also operated two trial formats:

Sainsbury's Assisting Village Enterprises
Orderline

Sainsbury's aim was to 'make the Sainsbury's brand accessible to as many customers as possible, and so maximise its value and achieve a competitive advantage' (J Sainsbury plc, 1999, p.15). The organization developed a variety of formats targeted at different market segments. The approach was 'driven by a combination of the desire to improve our geographical spread and to changing lifestyles ... we have introduced a variety of formats to meet different customer needs' (J Sainsbury plc, 1999, p.15).

With this in mind, Country Town stores were developed to suit the needs of shoppers in small towns, and Sainsbury's Central to suit the needs of city shoppers. Sainsbury's Local provided the group's convenience store format. The merchandise range and the range of services in each format were tailored to the demands of the target customer.

The first aim has been reinforced through Sainsbury's online offer, which has developed into a retail portal offering a wide range of goods. 'The trend continues for customers to shop across a range of channels – supermarkets, convenience stores and online, from home and on the go' (J Sainsbury plc, 2014, p.13). The plethora of store formats has been rationalized to two – convenience stores and supermarkets – although Sainsbury's supermarkets exist in a range of sizes, from so small they could be classified as convenience stores, to superstores of over 90,000 sq. ft. By 2014 the number of Sainsbury's convenience stores was larger than the number of supermarkets. The development of online formats complements these, while allowing the company to widen the product offer available to customers, as well as underpinning future development opportunities through expanding other services such as banking, mobile phone contracts, and pharmaceutical and learning centres.

The previous focus on segmentation and development of store formats has been replaced with a true multi-channel offer which offers customers choice in how and where they shop: 'Helping people shop where, when and how they want, across all channels, is a key driver of loyalty, and where customers shop all three channels their total spend is more than double the average of a supermarket-only shopper' (J Sainsbury plc, 2014, p. 13).

Source: J Sainsbury plc, 1999, 2014.

Profiling customer behaviour also led to the development of category management. For customers, category management reduces the time taken to make choices, while for retailers it rationalizes the plethora of products and brands available in the market (Molla *et al.*,

1997). If customer service is considered to be about augmenting the basic exchange relationships between retailers and customers, it becomes a key element in the way retailers
can differentiate themselves from their competitors – through the range and quality of
services and environments offered to customers.

10.2.3 The perception held by a (potential) patron of the likely provision of facilities, activities, benefits, environments, etc., by a retailer in support of the exchange relationship and its continuation, or a patron's experience of this 'total purchase package'

The expectations of customers will affect the service they receive from a retailer. For
example, a shopper in Sainsbury's will expect space; cleanliness; a welcoming, bright
environment; well-trained, helpful staff; and well-stocked shelves. They expect to be able to
park, have a trolley available and have their bags packed on demand. In return, they are
willing to pay a little more, but if the service is not up to standard the customer will be
disappointed, or even angry. A shopper in Lidl will have lower expectations. They will
expect to be able to park, but will be satisfied with a restricted range of goods, basic shop
fittings and services, and more restrictions on when or where they can shop.

A customer's perception of the service they receive is affected by several factors, including:

- previous experience of shopping with the retailer;
- experience of shopping with competing retailers;
- information from the retailer in the form of corporate image, advertising and other
  promotions; and
- word of mouth.

This means that retailers have to be careful to maintain or improve the standard of
service and merchandise over time to avoid disappointing customers. A good example of
what occurs when this does not happen is provided by Marks & Spencer, a well-established
UK retailer specializing in clothing and food merchandise.

Marks & Spencer had a reputation and premium pricing strategy built on quality merchandise and a popular, generous returns policy. After many decades of successful growth,
Marks & Spencer's reputation began to suffer when the quality of its clothing products
diminished. The company had a reputation for demanding the highest quality of goods at
competitive prices from mainly UK suppliers, and as goods began to be sourced abroad,
quality declined. This meant that customers were disappointed and began to shop elsewhere. Not only that, but there was extensive press coverage as some former supplier
companies struggled or went under, creating unemployment. Marks & Spencer also refused
to take credit cards long after other major retailers had adapted to this form of payment,
despite the rise in the number of people who habitually used them for shopping and
managing their cash flow, and the loss of custom from overseas visitors as credit cards
replaced travellers' cheques as the main means of spending money abroad. Despite being a
clothing retailer, Marks & Spencer also did not provide changing rooms in many stores,
relying instead on its generous returns policy. So, at the same time as product quality

declined, service quality fell behind that of competitors. As customers abandoned their favourite 'high street' retailer in droves, the company rapidly approached crisis point.

Customer perceptions of retailer quality also require that the image and promotion of the retailer give a true reflection of the quality of service and merchandise offered. Otherwise, again, customers will be disappointed. Until 1999, Marks & Spencer relied mainly on its image and reputation and word of mouth to convey the level of quality of the products and service offered. When the level of product and service quality declined and the corporate image was damaged, the retail organization had to take steps to improve the quality and range of merchandise but it also had to invest heavily, and for the first time, in marketing. A marketing director was appointed and the company finally started advertising, to get customers back into the shops. Changing rooms are now an essential feature for clothes shoppers and recognized as the place where the decision to buy is frequently made. There was outrage when Marks & Spencer closed them temporarily during the sales in December 2013.

10.2.4 The explicit provision by a retailer of: facilities for the alteration, customization, after care, etc., of products sold; and complaints-handling procedure.

Many people equate good customer service with a no-quibble goods returns policy. This type of policy encourages customer confidence in making the purchase decision, and will tend to increase repeat purchases.

Retailers may also give customers confidence in their purchase of larger items by offering a warranty, a fitting service (for example, in the purchase of kitchens, bathrooms, bedrooms), and a technical helpline (for example, in the purchase of computers). These retailers recognize that customer service does not end when the customers leave the store. By recognizing post-purchase needs and behaviour, retailers encourage the purchase decision, and profitably extend their relationship with customers.

For example, Dixons Retail, until its merger with Carphone Warehouse in August 2014, was the parent company of UK electronic and household goods retailers PC World and Dixons. The company recognized a growing customer demand for technical help with installation and set-up of complicated electronic goods and exploited it in the development of a dedicated service business called Tech Guys which provided a new income stream. Later this service was rebranded as Knowhow, simplified and merged with the activities of the previous insurance business Coverplan. The combined service provided customers buying more complex and expensive items with delivery, installation, extended warranty and technical help services. Their complaints-handling procedure extended the returns policy – both returns and other complaints were often handled at a customer service counter.

A customer-focused retailer should encourage customers to complain when they are dissatisfied. This is because it is a good way of finding out what customers think of the service offered. By listening to customers, retailers can generate improvements to merchandise mix, operations and service. Customer complaints, if handled politely and promptly, can also improve customer relations and generate customer loyalty.

10.3 Service characteristics and their implications for customer service

Services and products differ in a number of important ways which have implications for purchasers and for customer service itself. By understanding the characteristics of services, retailers can learn to overcome the problems they pose for service providers. Retailing is itself a service: retailers make a variety of goods available for the customer in a single location, offer information, display merchandise, and provide finance and an array of additional services. The characteristics of services include:

- intangibility;
- heterogeneity;
- perishability;
- ownership; and
- inseparability.

10.3.1 Intangibility

Intangibility means 'not being able to perceive by touch' (www.oxforddictionaries.com, 2014) – services cannot be touched or held. Retail customers buy tangible (touchable) goods, but the service of providing them, selling them, giving information about them and delivering them cannot be touched.

Whereas you can hold, eat and taste the shiny apple you have bought, and gauge its quality and value for money in that way, the quality of the service the retailer has provided in sourcing, displaying and selling the product is assessed through perception, observation and communication. That is why retailers provide a pleasant environment in which to buy the product, and why staff attitude and communication are so important in conveying the quality of service the retailer intends his or her customers to experience.

10.3.2 Heterogeneity

Heterogeneity is defined as 'diversity in character or content' (www.oxforddictionaries.com, 2014). Services are experienced in different ways on different occasions by the same consumer. Similarly, different consumers will have dissimilar experiences of the same service at the same time.

As a customer, when you go into a store, on different occasions, the experience will differ in terms of display, staff, goods, communication and so on, but also because you will be in a different mood, or may have had more or less difficulty in parking, and may be in different company. It is probable that every experience you have of service in the same store will vary in some way from all the other experiences. For example, consider how the same store may be more or less crowded, how stock changes, how shelves may be empty, the different waiting times for checkout, how you may be too warm or cold according to the season, how you may be in a hurry or at leisure, have friends or children with you or not, and so on.

Retailers, wanting their customers to experience quality customer service, will generally try to reduce the amount of heterogeneity by making every experience of their store a positive one. One of the means of doing this is by reducing heterogeneity through standardization of processes where possible. Equipment can be used to standardize selection and transactional processes, for example. Staff are often trained to use standard techniques in dealing and communicating with customers. Dress codes and décor standardize appearances to enhance corporate image and reinforce the retail brand.

It also can be argued that retailers have exploited this service characteristic in developing multiple channels – routes to market – so that customers can shop by phone, mail order, transactional websites, apps, social media and so on.

10.3.3 Perishability

Perishability can be defined as 'a brief life or significance, or transitory' (www.oxford dictionaries.com, 2014). The opportunity to experience or to provide a service, once passed, is lost forever. For example, as a customer you can buy a good and store it, use it and often reuse it. Not so with a service. If you go to a store to buy an apple, you occupy a **service experience**, in a certain location at a certain point in time. That opportunity will never recur. You cannot go in to buy the same apple at a different time, or go to buy another and experience exactly the same service. If you, or other customers, decide not to buy, or to buy elsewhere, then the retailer has lost these particular service opportunities forever.

Retailers deal with the characteristic of perishability through trying to maximize customer service opportunities. The time for providing service in a physical store is finite. Hence, longer opening hours provide more service opportunities, as do reducing prices at the end of the day and providing extra services such as delivery for customers who could not otherwise shop with them. Online and mobile retailing offer a 24/7 opportunity to provide customer service. Fast-fashion retailers like Zara exploited this perishability characteristic by developing logistical systems that allowed for providing popular fashion items for short 'seasons', which attracted people to shop for clothes more frequently; online deal providers like Groupon also offer 'when its gone, it's gone' opportunities for people to buy products.

10.3.4 Ownership

Ownership is 'the right, state or act of possession' (www.oxforddictionaries.com, 2014). Retailing, it could be argued, is an intangible service that provides people with the chance to buy physical, tangible goods, so in terms of retail service provision this means that although a customer can own a product, they cannot own the service provided in making the product available – or any of the other related services that retailing entails.

When you buy your shiny apple, you can take it away with you and do what you want with it. You cannot own the service with which the retailer provides you in sourcing and selling the apple. You cannot own the service provided by staff who have directed you to the display, or the information conveyed by the display.

The goods you take home, and sundry other associated items such as bags, receipts and guarantee documents (these are named 'peripheral evidence' when referring to the service marketing mix), represent the quality of service experienced. Retailers try reliably to provide goods that accurately represent the quality of service they want to provide for their customers. The peripheral evidence of purchase is also used to reinforce brand image. Reliability of goods and service quality is a key means of developing trust between customer and retailer. If the quality of either reduces over time, customers will be dissatisfied and shop elsewhere.

10.3.5 Inseparability

Inseparability is defined as 'a person or thing inseparable from another' (www.oxford dictionaries.com, 2014), and in terms of service it means that the service you experience as a customer is inseparable from the service being provided by the retailer.

When you buy your apple, the service you experience is intrinsically related to the people providing the service, most notably the personnel who communicate with you in the store, but also linked to the personnel who, though invisible to the customer, help to make the product and service available.

For retailers, this is why staff represent such an important cog in the wheel of service provision. Shop-floor staff's attitude and training improve the customer service experience, while the operational teamwork required in providing goods for sale to the customer needs to focus on the quality of service to the end customer. The characteristic of inseparability is the reason why customer service training is a key requirement for staff and management in retailing today.

It can be argued that this characteristic is even more important when the customer is distant from the retailer – shopping with a smartphone while on a bus, for example. The ease and confidence in shopping in such a situation is very closely related to the design and security of the website, in trusting the reliability of the delivery and returns services, and not least in being confident in the provision of good communication links with the 'customer service' staff to turn to if things go wrong.

10.4 Improving the quality of customer service

Customers' perception of the quality of service provided by retailers depends upon the level of satisfaction they experience in the process of shopping (Oliver, 1981). Their satisfaction is affected by both their **expectations** of the shopping experience and the **actuality** of the experience. If customers experience higher levels of service than expected over time, then they will perceive the retailer as offering a high quality of service. If the level of service is lower than expected over time, the retailer will be perceived as offering a low level of service quality (Bell *et al.*, 1999). The main difference between service quality and customer satisfaction is that the former relates to managing the quality of the service and the latter to customers' expectation and experience of the quality of service delivery. Therefore, improving customer service means delivering service quality improvements that are customer defined. The SERVQUAL model can be used as a basis for considering how to do this.

10.4.1 *SERVQUAL: a model for improving service quality*

The SERVQUAL model has been widely applied as a means to measure service quality (Parasuraman *et al.*, 1985). In this model, the **service gap** (gap 5) – that is, the difference between the level of service quality that customers expect and the level they experience – is the result of four main criteria (see Figure 10.1). These are:

- the gap between what customers expect and what managers think they expect – the **knowledge gap**;
- the gap between what managers think customers expect and the standards of service they specify – the **standards gap**;
- the gap between standards of service set by managers and standards of service delivered – the **delivery gap**; and
- the gap between standards of service delivered and those communicated to the customer (which create the customer's initial expectations of the level of service they will experience) – the **communication gap**.

The size of the service gap – between perceived and experienced quality of service – affects the level of satisfaction experienced by customers of a retail organization. According

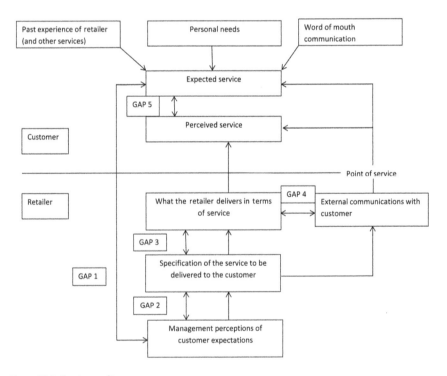

Figure 10.1 Service quality gaps
Source: After Parasuraman *et al.*, 1985

to this model, retailers can improve their service quality, and hence improve the level of customer satisfaction, by closing or reducing the four gaps. This theory has been criticized, not least because it:

- oversimplifies the relationship between customer and service provider; and
- does not allow for the relationship between customer and service provider, which is an integral part of the service experience.

However, SERVQUAL is a useful model for retail practitioners because it provides an easy-to-use framework for improving their customer service and overall service quality. It should be noted that SERVQUAL has been studied and applied widely for a number of years, and that other versions of the model have been developed, including a 7 Gaps Model (Luk and Layton, 2002).

10.4.2 Closing the knowledge gap

Retail managers very often overlook this potential gap because the measure of meeting customer needs lies directly in successful sales figures. If sales dip below expectations, the action taken is often to create economies in the organization by restructuring, reducing staff numbers, by sourcing cheaper suppliers or by creating further efficiencies in the supply chain.

In fact, the problem will frequently lie in the changing expectations of customers. These are affected by a range of factors, including:

- The customers' experience of the retailer over time – even if service quality is meticulously maintained over time, customers will become used to the level of service quality on offer. It will become the norm. The route to customer satisfaction is to raise the **experience** of shopping above the **expectation** of the experience of shopping, to maintain a state of **customer delight** (Piercy, 1997) with the retail offering. Then the retailer has to take care to substantially raise service quality levels periodically, or to improve service quality levels continuously. This may take the form of increasing the range of services on offer, of altering the product/service mix available, of changing the quality of the retail environment, or of raising the level of post-purchase service. Homebase, for example, offers an additional service to customers by having a list of tradesmen who can help with or install merchandise bought in store.
- The customers' perception of the level of product and service quality offered by the retailer relative to those of competing organizations. Service quality is very frequently used by retailers as a means of differentiating their retail offer from those of their competitors. Certainly, this was the case with Marks & Spencer and Sainsbury's.

The recent recession impacted enormously on customers' receptions of the product and service quality that they required. As unemployment soared, most people above all sought low prices. Many swapped to lower-priced retailers, a trend that benefited discount retailers and impacted on the profitability of others. Others swapped branded merchandise for lower-priced retailer brands. Retailers cut costs to support price lowering or maintenance over time. Staff numbers were cut, leading to less help for customers and less secure stores. In the UK there was a trend to zero-hours contracts, meaning staff had less secure incomes and were partly supported by state benefits. In turn, they were less likely to become skilled, loyal employees capable of producing great service. At the same time sales via Internet retailing were rising fast – shopping in massive out-of-town stores was growing less appealing – as goods could be bought online and groceries delivered to the door. As recession turned into recovery, it is unsurprising that some retailers suffered what appeared to be an identity crisis.

Morrisons is a good example of a large grocery retailer that was floundering as recovery took hold. Years of cost cutting led to low staff levels, cut many popular brands of merchandise, replaced them with very high levels of retailer-branded merchandise of lower perceived and actual quality. Associated services like bag packing and a customer service counter all but disappeared. Meanwhile low-service, low-price discounters were improving the quality of products. So Morrisons, with low-quality goods and low-quality service actually began to deliver less value to customers than discounters like Aldi and Lidl. This was compounded by their very late entrance into online retailing.

The recession years aside, customer expectations of service quality have generally risen over time. Shoppers are well travelled, media literate, and able not just to compare the product/service offerings of competing local retailers but also to compare these with the quality of merchandise and services offered online by national and international retail organizations. The raised expectations of sophisticated customers mean that in the future, high levels of customer care will be standard in retailing: to differentiate their service quality, retailers will have to be innovative in surprising or delighting the customer with the level of service quality.

Managers can learn more about customers' expectations and perception of service levels through market research, including analysis of customer service data. They can spend time on a daily basis in direct contact with customers and shop-floor staff. They can facilitate communication routes for shop-floor staff upwards through the organization. They also need to act rapidly to implement improvements suggested as the result of research and communication.

10.4.3 Closing the standards gap

Meeting the changing and increasingly sophisticated expectations of customers through the development of service standards can be difficult for retailers. Management training for retail managers is largely organizationally based or non-existent. In the first instance, there is an internal bias in the management techniques acquired; in the second, staff acquire management skills on an ad hoc basis. Under either circumstance, the development of performance standards for service quality that will deliver the service desired by external customers can be difficult for managers. In addition, many retail organizations have to deliver short-term profit levels to satisfy shareholders, which will preclude setting of levels of service that retail managers and customers desire.

To close the standards gap, therefore, there has to be a commitment from the senior management team towards service quality. Only then will the human, financial and material resources be made available for the development of a formal quality system. The quality system should establish the formal processes for setting service quality objectives, and should establish the roles of staff within these processes. Only if there is a visible commitment to quality service at senior level will managers be confident in setting and implementing the service quality standards within their remit. A reward system for service quality achievement will enhance staff and management commitment to implementing, meeting or exceeding the standards set (Zeithaml *et al.*, 1988).

The achievement of standards of quality can be made easier through the use of technology to standardize processes. Hard technology has been used widely in retailing in checking in, display and checkout procedures, whereas soft technology includes refinement of work methods – two examples are the use of teamwork to solve customer problems quickly, and bag packing by checkout operators.

10.4.4 Closing the delivery gap

The gap between standards set and those delivered arises for a variety of reasons – for example, unrealistic standards, lack of clarity in standards, poor communication of standards and their purpose, weak staff motivation, poor supervision, lack of human, financial or material resources. To reduce this gap, managers can focus on the following (Lovelock, 1991, 2001; Lovelock and Wirtz, 2011):

- clarification and communication of standards and staff roles so that staff understand the context of their work and know about customer expectations and perceptions;
- involvement of staff in setting standards so that they own and commit to quality;
- selection and training of staff so that they are capable of delivering the set standards;
- encouragement of teamwork, including cross-functional service teams, to deliver quality;
- motivation of staff through empowerment, moving customer responsiveness to lower levels in the organization;
- regular and spot measurement of performance so that staff become accustomed to performing and to being assessed to the set standards;
- making sure staff have the technology, materials and equipment to do the job to the required standards;
- putting in place good internal communications and internal customer service to support customer-facing staff; and
- balancing demand against productive capacity.

10.4.5 Closing the communication gap

The communication gap is the difference between the standard of service delivered to customers and that communicated by the retailer to customers through their external marketing communications.

The information communicated to customers should accurately reflect the quality of service to be offered. Merchandise should be accurately represented and available, prices accurate, delivery times adhered to. It is very easy to cause inadvertent dissatisfaction in providing for the disparate needs of customers in an online, national or international context. For example, at one point PC World offered some computers at one price in store, and a significantly different price online. Likewise, associated bundles of merchandise (security and other software and selected peripherals) were offered at different prices. At the same time, the company guaranteed to match any lower price found within seven days for identical merchandise. So one customer could come into store with a price printout showing the online price and purchase the merchandise at a much lower cost than another customer shopping at the same time in the same store.

The reason why the communication gap exists in many organizations is because promotion is undertaken by a marketing department or agency. Therefore, the staff drawing up promotional materials and messages are doing so in isolation from the realities of the shop floor. By reducing this internal communication gap, it is possible to portray the retail offering more accurately to customers. John Clare, the former long-term CEO of Dixons and PC World, was a strong advocate of identical pricing across multiple channels to simplify communication and reduce risk for customers shopping in different ways.

One way to reduce the internal communication gap is for shop-floor staff to be involved in the creation, content or approval of promotional materials. Another is to involve marketing staff in operational duties. A third is improved internal communication through internal marketing, cross-functional teams or shared training programmes. In the PC World example above, staff could easily check the online price quoted for computers and verify the reduced price. However, this was at a time cost to both the company and other shoppers waiting for service. There was a risk of dissatisfaction to both staff and customers as the former would feel time pressure from the extra task and the latter would have to wait longer for service.

Other ways to reduce the communication gap include focusing the content of promotional programmes on key aspects of the retail offering – those of most importance to customers; standardizing service levels across the retail organization; offering and promoting different levels of service for different price bands.

While the closure of the service gap between perceived and experienced service is a desirable focus for service quality management, it does not address the spiral of rising customer expectations of service quality. To compete successfully on the service quality front, exceptional service is required, which means the closure of a further gap: between what customers experience in terms of service quality and what they really want. For this, retailers have to listen closely and respond rapidly to customers' desires.

Box 10.2 Research focus

Bell *et al.* (1999) carried out a research study on service quality in food retailing, which appears to be just as applicable for stores today. Over 1,000 interviews were carried out with customers in two superstores in south-east England. Customers were asked to recall recent occasions when they had been particularly satisfied with service, and when they had been particularly dissatisfied with service. The incidents collected were categorized under the headings:

physical;
price;

interpersonal;
merchandise;
process; and
non-core services.

The researchers found that over 50 per cent of negative incidents were generated by the retail process. Process was divided into subcategories:

travel;
arrive and enter;
select items;
checkout;
leave with goods; and
appraisal.

They concluded that improvements in store design, together with a proactive focus on service delivery, could gain a retailer competitive advantage. Their conclusions included the following:

Since the shopping experience begins outside the store (travel), there needs to be a focus on entry roads, car parking, security and cleanliness.

On entry to the store, customers like to be greeted or acknowledged in some way. Also on entry, customers appreciate a 'decompression' area where they can relax into the shopping experience.

Extra space is needed round areas where customers congregate – e.g. special displays, in-store bakeries – so that the flow of customers is not impeded.

Poor product availability is a distinct problem for customers, and one which is recalled even after a long period of time. The authors suggested that products being out of stock corrupts sales data in JIT systems because replenishment is based on sales rather than demand.

Extended shopping hours created problems for high-volume replenishment during closed hours. Customers do not like trolleys and boxes blocking the aisles.

Switching staff from stocking to checkout activities to meet variable customer demand causes problems with a stocking backlog to the end of the day – again exacerbated through extended opening hours.

Customers really like quick, efficient checkout operation. Bag packing and help with bags are currently a route to 'customer delight', although it is liable to be accepted as standard in the future.

Whole-trolley scanning would be a means of speeding up checkout and replenishment, and therefore the expense could be justified.

Source: Bell *et al.*, 1999).

10.5 Managing customer service

10.5.1 Strategic options: standardization and customization strategies

While standardized methods and machinery can improve the efficiency and effectiveness of the service experience, customers want to feel special, and hence customization of service to the needs of the individual is seen as the route to building and maintaining a secure customer base. Standardization and customization of service can be viewed as a continuum (see Figure 10.2).

Many retail businesses are built on the premise of standardization. The main UK grocery retailers have developed standardized formats to build market share. Customers are guided round the store in a pre-set flow pattern, greeted and dealt with according to standardized procedures. Automation and standardization are fundamental to the high levels of service retail customers experience in their shopping today.

If standardization is the cornerstone of retail excellence, then customization is the key to retail differentiation. Customized services – service experiences customized to the needs of the customer – have always existed in retailing (for example, couture clothing and quality dining). In addition, the range of extra services available in some stores allows a degree of customization to be available to self-service shoppers – for example, dropping off the laundry in the grocery store, having a meal, buying petrol, childcare, bag packing and so on. With home delivery and online shopping in its various forms, the range of customization has expanded.

In recent years, supported by information technology and the integration of organizations in the supply chain, progress along the continuum towards mass customization has become more feasible for retail organizations because the costs of customization have been reduced. Mass customization means that every customer can receive a unique service tailored to individual needs. As information and communication technologies (ICTs) have developed and converged, and the number of ways to shop has increased, a mass-customization strategy has been made more feasible.

The concept of mass customization was first applied to products before being considered in service marketing. Gilmore and Pine (1997) discussed four approaches:

- Transparent customization: goods and services are customized by observing customer behaviour, for example Amazon suggesting books based on past purchase patterns.

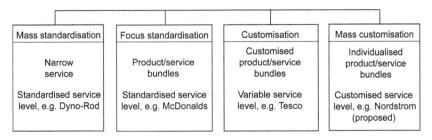

Mass standardisation	Focus standardisation	Customisation	Mass customisation
Narrow service	Product/service bundles	Customised product/service bundles	Individualised product/service bundles
Standardised service level, e.g. Dyno-Rod	Standardised service level, e.g. McDonalds	Variable service level, e.g. Tesco	Customised service level, e.g. Nordstrom (proposed)

Figure 10.2 Standardization and customization of service as a continuum

- Adaptive customization: standard, customizable goods and services can be customized by customers themselves. For example ethreads.com offers customers the chance to customize handbags; Nike lets customers customize a pair of trainers; service alternatives include selecting delivery times and places for online purchases.
- Cosmetic customization: standardized products and services are packaged specially for different types of customer, for example Sainsbury's Local stores are designed to appeal to shoppers who want convenience items and a quick and short shopping experience.
- Collaborative customization: there is a dialogue between customers and product and service designers. Apple Stores were one of the earliest retailers to invite customers into stores to interact with products and staff, to offer training, seminars and events to encourage deeper interaction with customers (see Box 10.3).

Among other shopping options, it is now possible for individual customers to scan bar-codes with a mobile phone, adding merchandise to a personalized shopping list, process the list at an online store and select a convenient delivery time; or they can shop via computer in the online store and arrange store pick-up; or they can visit one of a range of physical store formats depending upon the level of their shopping needs, and while there they can often also shop online for merchandise that is not available in-store, arranging convenient delivery. And so on.

The notion of collaborative customization underpins more recent retail concepts, including retail theatre, which introduces the concept of the store as a stage and customers as audience/participants; and of experiential retailing, in which retailers develop stores that foster and encourage customers to spend longer through encouraging interactions between individual customers and the store space.

Box 10.3 Retailer profile: Apple Stores, collaborative customization and experiential retailing

Apple was a manufacturer not a retailer, but the CEO had the good sense to hire retail experts to develop Apple Stores. A focus group comprising people from different backgrounds was also involved in the design of its retail offer. The group was asked about the best service (not retail) experience they had ever encountered. Almost all had experienced their best ever service in a hotel. The senior vice-president of Apple Retail commented:

> This was unexpected. But of course: The concierge desk at a hotel isn't selling anything; it's there to help. 'We said, "Well, how do we create a store that has the friendliness of a Four Seasons Hotel?"' The answer: 'Let's put a bar in our stores. But instead of dispensing alcohol, we dispense advice.'
>
> (Useem, 2007)

The Genius Bar proved an attractive innovation. Genius staff are especially trained to help Apple customers with the variety of problems they experience across the product range. Of course, visitors to the Genius Bar will be walking past the latest merchandise and tempted to try it out. Apple stores also provide training seminars and workshops, field trips and personal shopping to produce an experience for customers that can be highly customized – from going in to buy a new iPhone, to discussing the best software and hardware for a new business start-up – and then getting training in its use.

Apple has carefully combined three key service marketing elements in retailing: physical evidence, process and people, which have been integrated to produce an attractive environment for selling merchandise, engaging customers and maintaining relationships. However, the company took a manufacturing approach to developing the store format, building a prototype store and tinkering with it for months before the design was complete. The CEO of Apple at the time, Steve Jobs, commented:

> People haven't been willing to invest this much time and money or engineering in a store before ... 'It's not important if the customer knows that. They just feel it. They feel something's a little different.'
>
> (Useem, 2007)

Product designer Jesse James Garrett (2004) believes other retailers could learn a lot from the design of Apple Stores, which are organized around the context in which customers use the products. For example, digital cameras, photo printers and Apple's iPhoto software are set up together so customers can consider how these products can be integrated into and used in their own lives. Garrett also believes Apple got it right in creating a store experience that attracts customers into and round the store, interacting with the merchandise and staff and even (via spectacular glass staircases) upstairs. Garrett also praised Apple's consistency – creating a store that is aligned with Apple products and company personality. He was, however, critical that Apple had not got the human element properly aligned with the rest.

Alex Frankel, a journalist, carried out a two-year undercover project as a front-line employee for Gap, Starbucks and Apple Stores for a book on front-line employee experiences (Frankel, 2008). In a feature to promote his book he states: 'Staff don't appear to be selling too hard, just hanging out and dispensing information. And that moves a ridiculous amount of goods: Apple employees help sell $4,000 worth of product per square foot per month. When employees become sharers of information, instead of sellers of products, customers respond' (Frankel, 2007).

Despite this, Frankel claimed that sales staff were very carefully trained in selling techniques.

Unfortunately, Garrett's experience was that some staff were not customer orientated and that contrasted so much with the expectations raised during the rest of the store experience that it led to greater disappointment.

Apple's product innovation and design background formed the basis for its retail success. This meant the company approached the retail offer from the perspective, first, of designing innovative solutions to technical problems, second, compared the design of a store and associated services to the design of computer hardware and software, and third, Apple management were confident enough to look outside the company and its key market sector for ideas and advice. Attention to how customers shop, careful design of the customer/retail service interface, investing in techno-literacy of staff and facilitating exchange of customer/company information generated profit for the company. The Apple Store retail chain, with an aggressive store expansion strategy, grew annual sales at levels unprecedented in retailing, reaching annual sales of US$1 billion within just a few years.

Nevertheless, collaborative customization and experiential retailing, which necessarily focus on customer interaction, mean that trained and motivated staff are fundamental to customer satisfaction and retention.

10.5.2 Customer service strategies: key aspects of managing a consumer organization

Four key aspects of managing a consumer business are worth considering (Allen, 1991, p.145):

- renewing the service offering;
- localizing the point-of-service system;
- leveraging the service contract; and
- using information power strategically.

10.5.2.1 Renewing the service offering

In retailing, the need to revise and renew the service offering stems from the considerable investment in premises and infrastructure, which contrasts with the perishable nature of services. Therefore, the high fixed costs of premises and supply chain infrastructure contrast with the fluctuating flow and demands of customers. Even for retailers operating entirely online, considerable investment is needed in warehousing and distribution of goods.

Retail operators have to be creative in maximizing customer opportunities to shop, and both sensitive and responsive to changing customer and market demands. Service extension and enhancement are the means to consider in responding to opportunities offered by the changing marketplace. Retail examples of service extension include Internet information and advice provided by a retailer operating from physical premises; direct delivery; installation; and financial services. While these extend the service retailers provide, service is enhanced by associated services such as childcare, changing rooms, toilets, bag packing and credit. Online service enhancements include suggestions for complementary merchandise; making online shops easy and entertaining to use; providing fast and easy checkout; and multiple delivery and returns options.

The route to innovative service extension and enhancement lies in understanding consumers' problems through proactive market research, and in altering the service in response. This is because consumers are more able to articulate their complaints and problems than they are able to express the benefits they want from a service. Growth in the use of social media has been exploited by retailers as a way to promote and sell goods and at the same time has facilitated the influence of 'e-word-of-mouth'. Retailers have to be quick to exploit and respond to this. A simple example illustrates the power of e-word-of-mouth. UK menswear retailer Topman was forced to withdraw from sale two T-shirts with slogans intended to be light-hearted, but which many people found offensive. The outpouring of criticism on social media websites (highly visible on the retailer's promotional blog) drew traditional media attention and rapidly led to removal of the T-shirts from the retailer's website. Nowadays, retailers should not only deal rapidly with customer complaints and put in process the means for preventing their recurrence, but should also encourage customers to express their problems, as this can be the basis for enhancing and differentiating the service they provide.

If the development and revision of procedures for reviewing and upgrading service provision is the key to creative response in a changing market, then localizing the point of service is the means of increasing the rate of customer interception, which helps to increase numbers and the value of customers to the organization.

10.5.2.2 Localizing the point-of-service system

According to service management theory, if customers are intercepted at the time and place when a service is needed, they will purchase the service. Hence a convenience store will attract custom if it is located near the customer and open at the time the customer wants to shop, and so premium prices can be charged. Another example is fast-food delivery, in which the distance barrier to purchase is overcome through reliable and speedy delivery.

In the 1990s retailing polarized into **destination** and **proximity** formats (Dawson, 1995). The former is based on a merchandise mix, merchandise selection, and associated price quality and service levels that will attract customers from a distance – for example, Jenners, the Edinburgh department store, or IKEA stores. The latter is based on customer interception through locating where potential customers naturally congregate – for example, forecourt and shipping, rail and airport terminal retailing. Major grocery retailers successfully used forecourt outlets to localize their point of service and increase market penetration – for example, Tesco and Sainsbury's developed small convenience formats, Tesco express and Sainsbury's Local, that could provide groceries in smaller neighbourhoods or near major employers.

Direct mail, television and Internet retailers intercept potential customers at home or at work. More recently, mobile retailing allowed the ultimate in localizing point of service to customers, entering their home and mobile environment in an interactive mode. However, because services are consumed without ownership (see section 10.3 above, on service characteristics), this means that the service a retailer provides also has to incorporate the delivery of the goods. So, unlike the service provided within a shop, which is consumed within and close to the premises, the service provided by a retailer on the Internet cannot be focused entirely on website design and content, but has to focus on delivery of the goods.

In one study, website users rated convenience, reliability, content and responsiveness the most important factors in meeting their needs, but other significant factors were a user-friendly interface, marketing communication, and information management and maintenance (McGoldrick *et al.*, 1999). These factors, which enable customer interception, have been incorporated into website design and management. A more recent challenge is facilitating the retailing of goods via mobile phones and tablets, which requires development of a more specialized format, for example one that is appropriate to a small screen, restricted keystrokes and the shopping preferences of individual consumers. One study showed that 42 per cent of customers abandon a purchase on a mobile device because it is too complex. To localize the point of service through Internet and mobile channels, retailers also have to streamline logistics, delivery and returns services.

10.5.2.3 Leveraging the service contract

The third key aspect of managing a consumer service is leveraging the service contract, which means establishing the basis for retention of customers, and raising barriers against customers switching to competing service deliverers.

The large retail groups in the UK have extensively implemented leverage strategies. In order to retain customers and increase their spend, retailers in the competitive UK retail market have had to minimize reasons for customers to switch to competitors, and build and maintain barriers to defection.

Service extension and enhancement can build share and loyalty among customers, as can loyalty card schemes, and loyalty card scheme extensions such as catalogues, mailings and direct delivery. However, in areas with extensive coverage of competing retailers, customers tend to be promiscuous, with loyalty cards to many stores. In this case, managers have to focus on barriers to switching, such as extra point values, double points and bonuses. Other barriers include promotional activities – advertising and sales promotions – and partnerships with, or acquisition of, competing retail organizations.

Loyalty card schemes reward all members equally according to the amount spent. While this can increase customer spend, it is expensive to administer, and retailers also need to focus on finding and retaining those customers who spend the most – their key customers – and establishing retention strategies specifically designed for them. This type of strategy has been implemented successfully by airlines, which reward different levels of loyalty with different service contracts, such as executive and premier club membership.

It has been argued that loyalty schemes create loyalty to the scheme, not the retailer. They are costly to administer, and some retailers have withdrawn from them. UK grocery retailer Safeway (before its acquisition by Morrisons), for example, used the savings from abandoning their ABC card to fund their high/low promotional strategy. True loyalty exists when a customer remains loyal to the retail organization over an extended period of time, despite price and other incentives to change. This type of loyalty costs time, effort and expenditure. It was achieved by Marks & Spencer, for example, over decades, before dissipating in the late 1990s as product and service quality declined below the threshold offered by competitors and acceptable to loyal customers.

As more retailers track customers' on and offline shopping behaviour and habits, they can target customers with personalized messages designed to increase spend – according to one survey, most customers are likely to read messages from a brand they are familiar with, and about 50 per cent are likely to buy (*The Marketer*, 2014).

10.5.2.4 Using information power strategically

The characteristics of services – inseparability, heterogeneity, perishability and intangibility – are reasons why the quality of the customer's service experience is so closely allied with the quality of services provision and services personnel.

Feargal Quinn (former CEO of Irish grocery multiple Superquinn) and early practiser of customer-orientated retailing, thinks that retailers should encourage a listening culture using a variety of listening systems. Observing the customer's point of view is essential, and there are various ways of doing this, from market research to focus groups, comment forms and complaints procedures. Superquinn, for example, operated a rule that managers should do their household shopping there once a month to see the shops through the eyes of the customer, and there should also be encouragement of shop-floor staff to feed back information from customers. Other feedback routes include market research, focus groups, customer complaints and 'walking the floor'. In order to achieve service superiority, quick response should be applied not just to the supply chain but also to the implementation of customer-derived service improvements. (See the case study at the end of this chapter.)

The close relationship between customer and provider means that service businesses are well placed to benefit from the exponential growth of ICTs. These can be used to help personalize service, manage service quality and extend the service offering. Tesco, one of the first UK grocery retailers to go online in the mid-1990s, has over time offered an increasingly wide range of products and services through its Internet provision.

Some large UK retailers have had a presence on the Internet for nearly two decades and were in a good position to exploit the opportunities afforded by this new medium. At the same time they developed and implemented their loyalty card schemes, gathering personal and purchase information from their regular customers. On the one hand they developed the infrastructure and methods for quality service delivery to distant customers, and on the other they were developing their strategic use of information power to develop multiple channels that meant their customers could shop whenever and however they wanted.

The development of communication media is fast paced, offering diverse means and routes to communicate with customers. It is interesting to note, however, that dedicated online 'e-tailers' still use traditional media such as television, newspapers, magazines and even bus shelters to build brand awareness.

The large UK retailers with extremely strong brands before the widespread uptake of online shopping could concentrate on the use of new media in developing, customizing and communicating service and market extensions. In the USA, Walmart analyses the information shared by customers on social media after store purchase, in order to make better personalized product recommendations (Bolger, 2014).

ICT developments have also afforded opportunities to smaller retailers, allowing them to broaden the range of services offered and widening their market potential. Lacking the financial muscle to build brand awareness using traditional mass media, some smaller retailers instead are more focused in developing a dialogue with their customers. However, many small retailers still lack ICT skills, and many do not collect information on customers.

10.6 Implementing good customer service in retailing

The successful implementation of good customer service as a differentiation strategy requires recognition that it has to apply within as well as outside the organization. The previous section highlighted the importance of listening to customers and incorporating feedback routes within the organization, from customers and staff. Implementation of good customer service requires management to view staff as internal customers (and vice versa), and to give them the resources to meet customers' needs effectively and competitively.

Managing in a retail organization includes developing both the 'hard' factors – the formal structure, processes and procedures – that constitute the business, and managing the 'soft' factors – the informal style of doing business. The 'hard' factors include:

- formal statements of objectives and strategies, formal planning process;
- organizational structure;
- formal communication system;
- formal processes; and
- formal procedures.

The 'soft' factors include:

- shared norms and aspirations;
- organizational 'culture';
- informal networks of communication that modify formal policies and information flows;
- the established style of doing work; and
- the skills, knowledge and expertise of the workforce.

The soft factors are 'people related' rather than 'process related', and because customers' perception of good service is so closely related to their interaction with the workforce, it is especially important that retail managers recognize and manage the 'fit' of the informal culture of the organization with the formal strategy and structure. Where the 'fit' is poor – for example, when the workforce is faced with changed processes and procedures which conflict with the established style of doing work, or which undermine their skills and expertise – stress will occur, and workforce stress will impact on customer service. In the case of Apple Stores, referred to in Box 10.3, product designer Garrett (2004) had the unfortunate experience of encountering a disinterested member of staff in one of the stores he visited. This contrast with the look and feel of the store left him more disgruntled than had it occurred in a less carefully designed, upmarket and streamlined store.

Of course, good communication, training and involvement of staff in the development of plans and policies will tend to reduce conflict. Implementing the formal strategies, policies, processes and procedures (Stone and Young, 1994) requires managers to:

- communicate with staff – tell them your objectives and policies; not just what they are, but why they are;
- train staff – make sure they know what the processes and procedures are and how to do them;
- give staff the support they need to succeed;
- give them the right equipment and other resources to succeed; and
- give them adequate time to complete the set work.

Applying this framework within the organization requires excellence in customer service as an organizational priority. It has to be championed by the senior management team – embedded within the organization at the highest level. This should take a visible form: managers serving customers, interacting with customers and staff, listening to views and demands, implementing change as a result of their findings.

There should be customer service objectives set and strategies in place for these to be achieved. A written customer service policy and/or charter should be created. This needs to be shared with staff and customers to establish the level of service of the organization, to establish customer and staff expectations.

A formal planning cycle for customer service should be established (see Figure 10.3). The organizational structure for customer service has to be set up, establishing the roles and spans of control for dedicated customer service staff, and for the rest of the staff. Standards for key customer service tasks have to be developed and implemented through communication with the staff concerned. Indeed, communications regarding customer service – lateral, diagonal, up and down the organization – can help to implant a customer service philosophy throughout.

Training of staff in customer service processes and procedures should be arranged. Staff have to be clear regarding how and when their performance will be measured and controlled. In addition, a system of reward will help to embed the required levels of customer service throughout the organization. Feedback on performance should be used in the development of new objectives at the end of the planning cycle.

One of the leading fashion retailers in the USA is Nordstrom. The company's customer service is recognized for its excellence. The company believes in employing staff who are customer driven, entrepreneurial and motivated. Staff are then trained and empowered to make decisions that ensure every customer leaves the stores satisfied (see Box 10.4).

Plan customer service

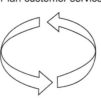

Control customer service   Organize customer service

Implement customer service

Figure 10.3 Planning cycle for customer service

Nordstrom has survived both the online revolution and the global recession with its customer service focus intact. John Lewis in the UK is a similar example.

Box 10.4 The Nordstrom route to exceptional customer service

In the last century, Nordstrom grew from modest beginnings to become one of America's foremost fashion retailers, with shops across the country selling clothing, shoes, cosmetics and accessories for the whole family, aimed at customers in middle/upper income levels. The company is committed to principles of service, quality, selection and value for money:

> The best Nordstrom sales associates will do virtually everything they can to make sure a shopper leaves the store a satisfied customer, carrying home the right item in the right size in the right colour at the right price ...
>
> (Spector and McCarthy, 1995, p. 25)

Value is created by the entrepreneurial style of buying. Strong negotiation secures best value, buyers work with manufacturers to secure a wide variety of styles which can sell at various price points, and quality is closely inspected. Buyers also have freedom to source stock close to the store, which allows for regional variations in taste, while buying for a limited number of outlets reduces the potential for large-scale failure of any item of stock. Buyers are also expected to spend time on the shop floor to keep tabs on customer-based market information.

Nordstrom's reputation for the depth and breadth of its inventory has grown out of the belief that customer service and satisfaction are related to the availability of stock for every customer. Therefore, a wide range of styles, from economical to expensive, needs to be available, and in a wide variety of sizes. If a customer likes a style of merchandise but it is not available in the right size, the customer will leave the store dissatisfied.

As a customer-driven organization there is a strong service culture, and employees are given freedom to make customer and stock-related decisions, to serve the customer throughout the store and to operate 'like entrepreneurial shopkeepers' (Spector and McCarthy, 1995, p.100). Store managers have the autonomy to employ staff and buy inventory. Nordstrom believes in a 'hands-on' management style in which managers are visible on the shop floor, serving customers and encouraging staff. All staff are expected to put the customer before the organization in making decisions, with the organization bearing the consequences.

Employee selection is regarded as crucial to the success of the organization. Employees need genuinely to like people, and to find satisfaction in serving people. Ideas and innovations are required from shop-floor staff, who must also be happy to work in an unconfined environment in which they are expected to take the initiative. Nordstrom believes that staff work best when there are few restrictions and bureaucracy is minimized.

Staff pay is based on commission to reward for ability, and success is further rewarded with more responsibility and promotion – the organization believes in promoting from within as a motivational tool. Sales targets are net of returns, and there is a generous returns policy, which guarantees that if a customer is dissatisfied with a purchase, for whatever reason, it can be returned to the store. This means that salespeople are not induced to hard sell to make targets, but to meet customers' needs so that returns do not occur. Successful staff build up a database and profile of customers they serve in order to serve them better over time. Therefore, staff stand to increase their own income through managing relations with their own customers. Staff who fail to meet sales targets, on the other hand, are given special coaching to help them achieve.

The culture is spread to new stores by involving established Nordstrom staff in new store openings. Acquisition or merger are rejected as expansion strategies because of the difficulties involved in culture change. The organization is structured like an inverted pyramid, with management supporting the sales associates who serve the customers.

The threat posed by discount and value retail competitors has been tackled in a number of ways. First, entrepreneurial buying enabled fashion items that cannot be replicated by discounters to be stocked. Second, Nordstrom used its private-label brands to achieve value for customers rather than higher profit margins. Third, the organization developed its own self-service value outlets to dispense clearance merchandise and special buys not carried in its normal stores: Nordstrom Rack. These stores also served to introduce customers and staff to Nordstrom, and provide entry-level training for staff. There has been strong growth in the number of Nordstrom Rack stores.

Further innovations are regarded as necessary to meet the needs of shoppers in the future. Nordstrom experimented early on with personalized interactive shopping in which customers using diverse communication media were dealt with directly by Nordstrom salespeople and given the same kind of service as in-store customers. Nordstrom Direct now includes the online store and mail-order 'store', with centralized headquarters, customer-contact centres and fulfilment/returns facilities. The online store offers live stylist advice for fashion, beauty and weddings, as well as live customer service help. Mail order, previously regarded as an additional means of advertising, was also extended as a direct sales medium. In 2011, sales growth via the Nordstrom Direct channels was higher than through the traditional store channels. The company maintained its customer focus through a time of deep recession and not only survived an economic climate that put many retailers out of business but expanded its store portfolio.

Source: Spector and McCarthy, 1995, 2012.

Management input to good customer service includes:

- **Adding value**: encouraging staff to add value to everything they do, and leading by example.
- **Giving ownership**: where possible, assigning responsibilities and ownership for offering customers excellent service to the relevant staff so that progress can be easily monitored by all.
- **Increasing staff creativity** by encouraging them to take initiative and by allowing mistakes in the pursuit of real progress and improvement.
- **Encouraging teamwork**, because it improves communication and harnesses the abilities and knowledge of staff to create synergy.
- **Investing in people**: in addition to dedicated customer service training, all staff, including managers, will benefit in terms of confidence and capability from constructive appraisal and self-development opportunities.
- **Communicating**: good formal and informal communication routes generate better relationships among staff, between staff and managers, and help staff to develop a better dialogue with customers. Use direct communication where possible because feedback is instantaneous.

Service excellence requires more than management dexterity, however. According to Zeithaml *et al.* (1990, p. 5):

> People in service work need a vision in which they can believe, an achievement culture that challenges them to be the best they can be, a sense of team that nurtures and supports them, and role models that show them the way. This is the stuff of leadership.

10.7 Summary

In retailing, customer service can be defined in four ways. First, retail organizations exist in order to provide products to customers, adding value to the products through bringing them together in one place, providing information about them and enabling customers to buy. Second, the wide range of services that retailers have put together to add value to the fundamental exchange relationship (money for products) has become an intrinsic part of customer service. Third, the customer's perception and experience of the service retailers provide affect the level of customer satisfaction. Fourth, customer service involves post-purchase facilities and services plus the complaints and returns policies.

The five service characteristics – intangibility, heterogeneity, perishability, ownership and inseparability – inherently frame the customer service experience. By considering each in turn, retailers can improve the customer service experience. The intangibility of the service means retailers have to focus on tangibilizing the brand – for example, by giving customers loyalty cards and carrier bags. The heterogeneity of the retail experience can be overcome through standardization of procedures, training and dress, although this can also be exploited through using new ICTs to customize the retail offering to individual or small group needs. The perishability of the service has led retailers to maximize the opportunities for their customers to shop. Ownership is a characteristic that means that retailers have to strive for consistency, in service terms and in reliable provision of products. Inseparability is the characteristic that requires retailers to ensure their staff have positive attitudes and behaviour and are well trained and informed, because the staff–customer interaction is so important in ensuring customer satisfaction.

The SERVQUAL model is a useful tool that retailers can use to focus on areas in which their service quality can be improved. By analysing the knowledge, standards, delivery and communication gaps in the service they provide, they can reduce the gap between what customers expect in terms of service and their perception of level of service they receive. In this way, they can improve the level of satisfaction their customers experience.

Customer service strategies range from standardization to mass customization – retailers have to decide which strategy to implement. However, as the costs of customization reduce with the convergence of ICTs, the opportunities for mass customization will increase.

There are four key aspects in managing a consumer business. First, retail managers should renew the service offering to generate customer interest and build customer relationships. Retailers do this through service extension and service enhancement. Second, retailers should localize the point-of-service system – that is, consider ways and means of intercepting customers beyond the confines of their traditional outlets, and making it easy for them to shop. Leveraging the service contract is the third factor. Retailers need to consider how to boost both loyalty and spend: focusing on delivering exceptional service to their key customers is one way of doing this. Finally, retailers are well positioned to make use of the ICT advancements in order to manage customer information to personalize services, develop service extensions/enhancements and manage service quality.

Implementing good customer service involves developing the formal structure, processes and procedures, the hard factors, and managing the people-related soft factors. Leadership is of key importance in this, creating the shared norms and aspirations, creating the desired organizational culture, managing the skills, knowledge and expertise of the workforce. A customer service planning cycle helps to embed customer service within the company and multiple communication routes are essential in implementing it. Hiring, training and retaining good retail staff is expensive, but pays off in getting the team to perform to the standard required. Look again at the management input to good customer service in section 10.6. The input is not necessarily expensive or onerous; it is simply good leadership.

Review questions

1   Consider the four key aspects of managing a consumer organization. Thinking of a retailer that you consider customer orientated, explain how the retailer 'renews the service offering' and 'leverages the service contract'.

2   Apply the service characteristics to a retailer you shop with frequently. How does the retailer exploit these characteristics?

3   'Retailing is about buying merchandise at one price and selling it at a higher price. The main reason for a retailer's existence is profit – pure and simple.' This is a statement made by the owner of two stores. With reference to the definitions of retailing, discuss the weaknesses of this statement.

Case study: Superquinn

Superquinn, a well-known and highly regarded Irish chain of grocery stores, grew from a single outlet opened in 1960 to 23 large stores and nine shopping centres in 2010. The owner, Feargal Quinn, was internationally known for his commitment to customer service and innovation as a route to service excellence, and has even written a book on the subject. The organization's mission – 'To be a world-class team renowned for excellence in fresh food and customer service' – therefore accurately summarized this entrepreneur's approach to his business.

Excellent service and innovation grew from Quinn's insistence that the organization would remain 'close to the customer', and this customer empathy laid the foundation for a series of initiatives that gave Superquinn an outstanding reputation for service quality and market leadership which were copied by other, larger retailers.

Feargal Quinn led by example. He preferred to hold meetings while 'walking the floor' of his stores, and his managers' offices were purposely small as he did not believe they should be used too much. Committed to the notion that business should be enjoyable and fun, he was given to issuing tangible motivational symbols such as tie pins shaped like boomer- angs to remind staff that customer retention was a key objective, or with the inscription 'YCDBSOYA', reputedly an acronym for 'You can't do business sitting on your ... armchair'. Customer views on service improvement were sought formally through holding two-weekly customer panels, and informally but actively through taking his turn at bag packing.

'Investing in people' at Superquinn did not just mean setting up a training and assess- ment programme for staff; it meant investing in staff levels to enable a quality of service that encouraged customers to return, and which drove up volume to pay for the extra costs involved. It was socially inclusive – the organization actively encouraged the employment and training of disabled staff, for example. Customer retention was also encouraged through a loyalty scheme which was the first of its kind in Ireland: SuperClub, a points- based system which was purposely kept simple for customers (points were registered on till receipts; bonus points called SuperCents had a value of 100 to the euro) and flexible (points could be increased on items, days or even for particular customers).

Source: www.superquinn.ie.

Note: The Musgrave Group bought Superquinn in 2011 and the acquired stores were rebranded as SuperValu by 2014.

1   Explain why Superquinn set a good example for successful implementation of good customer service as a differentiation strategy.
2   'Both of my sons had part-time jobs in Superquinn, and they got great training. One of my sons was sweeping the floor one day and Feargal Quinn came over and said "that's not how you sweep the floor", and he showed him how to. And my son loved it.' What does this quote from a Superquinn customer imply about Quinn's approach to implementing good customer service in his stores?

References

Allen, M. (1991) 'Strategic management of consumer services', in *Services Marketing* (Lovelock, C.H., ed.). London: Prentice Hall.

Baron, S., Davies, B. and Swindley, D. (1991) *Macmillan Dictionary of Retailing*. London: Macmillan.

Bell, J., Gilbert, D., Lockwood, A. and Dutton, C. (1999) 'Getting it wrong in food retailing: the shopping process explored', 10th International Conference on Research in the Distributive Trades, Stirling, August.

Bolger, M. (2014) 'Digital disruption', *The Marketer*, July/August: 30.

Christopher, M., Payne, A. and Ballantyne, D. (1991) *Relationship Marketing*. Oxford: Butterworth-Heinemann.

Clements, A. (2000) *Retail Week*, 21 January.

Daffy, C. (2011 [1999]) *Once a Customer Always a Customer* (3rd edn). Cork: Oak Tree Press.

Dawson, J. (1995) 'Retail trends in Scotland: a review', *International Journal of Retail Distribution Management*, 23(10): 4–20.

Frankel, A. (2007) 'Are your frontline employees going to save or kill your most important quarter? At Apple nothing is left to chance', www.fastcompany.com/60838/magic-shop (accessed 5 January 2015).

Frankel, A. (2008) *Punching In: The Unauthorised Adventures of a Front Line Employee*. New York: Harper Collins Publishers.

Garrett, J.J. (2004) 'Six design lessons from the Apple Store', *Adaptive Path*, www.adaptivepath.com/ideas/e000331/ (accessed 13 July 2014).

Gilmore, J.H. and Pine, B.J. (1997) 'The four faces of mass customization', *Harvard Business Review*, 75 (1): 41, 91–101.

Lovelock, C.H. (ed.) (1991) *Services Marketing*. London: Prentice Hall.

Lovelock, C.H. (2001) *Services Marketing: People, Technology, Strategy*. London: Prentice Hall.

Lovelock, C.H. and Wirtz, J. (2011) *Services Marketing: People, Technology, Strategy* (global edn). Upper Saddle River, NJ: Pearson, .

Luk, Sh.T.K. and Layton, R. (2002) 'Perception gaps in customer expectations: managers versus providers and customers', *The Service Industries Journal*, 22 (2 April): 109–128.

The Marketer (2014) 'How to perfect the personal touch', *The Marketer*, July/August.

McGoldrick, P., Vazquez, D., Lim, T.Y. and Keeling, K. (1999) 'Cyberspace marketing – How do surfers determine website quality?' Proceedings of the 10th International Conference on Research in the Distributive Trades, Stirling, August.

Molla, A., Mugica, J. and Yague, M. (1997) 'Category management and consumer choice', Proceedings of the 9th International Conference on Research in the Distributive Trades, Leuven, July.

Oliver, R.L. (1981) 'The measurement and evaluation of the satisfaction process in retail settings', *Journal of Retailing*, 57 (Fall): 25–48.

Oxford Dictionaries (2014) www.oxforddictionaries.com (accessed 7 July 2014).

Parasuraman, A., Zeithaml, V.A. and Berry, L.L. (1985) 'A conceptual model of service quality and its implications for future research', *Journal of Marketing*, 49 (Fall): 41–50.

Piercy, N. (1997) *Market-Led Strategic Change: Transforming the Process of Going to Market*. Oxford: Butterworth-Heinemann.

Reichheld, F.F. and Sasser, W.E. Jr (1990) 'Zero defections: quality comes to services', *Harvard Business Review*, October.

Rust, R.T. and Oliver, R.L. (1994) *Service Quality, New Directions in Theory and Practice*. Thousand Oaks, CA: Sage.

J Sainsbury plc (1999) *Annual Report and Accounts*, www.j-sainsbury.co.uk/investor-centre/reports/1999/annual-report-and-accounts-1999/ (accessed 1999).

J Sainsbury plc (2014) *Annual Report and Financial Statements*, www.j-sainsbury.co.uk/media/2064053/sainsbury_s_annual_report_and_accounts_13-14.pdf (accessed 4 July 2014).

Spector, R. and McCarthy, P.D. (1995) *The Nordstrom Way: The Inside Story of America's No. 1 Customer Service Company*. New York: John Wiley.

Spector, R. and McCarthy, P.D. (2012) *The Nordstrom Way to Customer Service Excellence: The Handbook for Becoming the 'Nordstrom' of Your Industry*, 2nd edn. Hoboken, NJ: Wiley and Sons Inc..

Stone, M. and Young, L. (1994) *Competitive Customer Care: A Guide to Keeping Customers*. Kingston-upon-Thames: Croner.

Useem, J. (2007) 'Apple: America's best retailer', *Fortune*, 6 March, archive.fortune.com/magazines/fortune/fortune_archive/2007/03/19/8402321/index.htm (accessed 13 July 2014).

Zeithaml, V.A., Berry, L.L. and Parasuraman, A. (1988) 'Communication and control processes in the delivery of service quality', *Journal of Marketing*, 52: 35–48.

Zeithaml, V.A., Parasuraman, A. and Berry, L.L. (1990) *Delivering Service Quality*. New York: Free Press.

11   Visual merchandising and retail selling

Learning objectives

After studying this chapter, you should be able to:

- Know the role of visual merchandising and selling in generating retail sales.
- Understand the relationship between visual merchandising and selling.
- Comprehend the main dimensions of visual merchandise management.
- Relate the amount and quality of time that retail salespeople spend actively selling to:
  - product classification;
  - types of buying decision; and
  - stage in the buying process.
- Discuss the various retail sales roles and activities involved in the retail sales process.
- Understand the role of retail selling within the promotional mix.

11.1   Introduction

Impersonal selling means that sales are generated without (or with minimal) human intervention. In retailing the multiplication of ways to buy online and the growth of mixed merchandise superstores means some customers rarely encounter a real live retail salesperson who is actively engaged in selling. Many retail textbooks discuss visual merchandising as part of the buying and merchandising function that deals with the acquisition and allocation of stock to stores. Here we discuss the role of merchandising in generating sales. Visual merchandising has been called 'the silent salesperson' in that it is used to attract customers into and through stores, and encourages them to make a purchase (Kaur, 2013).

In many stores, retail salespeople have a role in visual merchandising in terms of stock replenishment and tidying and cleaning displays together with a minimal, relatively passive sales role – they merely process the purchase. Nevertheless, retailers increasingly expect their salespeople to 'sell up' or actively promote items at checkout.

An increasingly competitive market means that retail selling is growing in importance for all retailers, not just retailers of high-value, complex products. This is especially so when 'bricks-and-mortar' stores and salespeople often physically represent a wider, valuable online retail offer and can be influential in generating online footfall and sales beyond the physical premises.

Retailing is a service, and retail selling is as essential a function as customer service. Indeed, the two are interlinked, not just because both functions are undertaken by the same staff in many retail organizations, but also because both customer service and sales staff have the prime role as an interface between the retail organization and its customers. The customers' interpretation of the organization's image and ethos are affected by the nature of their relationship and encounters with retail staff.

Retailers operating market-focused service businesses need to tailor their retail selling to the customers' requirements with regard to the type of product being bought and the type of purchase decision. They also need to take into consideration their customers' shopping motives and their stage in the process of making the buying decision (Merrilees and Miller, 1996). Retail selling requires, therefore, a good knowledge of the products being sold, an understanding of the profile of target customers and, further, comprehension of customers' needs, in terms of both merchandise being sold and the shopping experience.

The nature and depth of retail selling are related to a variety of factors, including type of product, the customer's understanding of its qualities, uses and attributes, the complexity and value of the product, brand loyalty and the extent to which the customer desires involvement in the buying process. Retail selling, as only one element of the retail promotional mix, is dependent on successful deployment of selected other elements, and should be integrated into a full promotional programme in order to nurture customer satisfaction.

11.2 The dimensions of visual merchandise management

Visual merchandising is concerned with the creation of a store environment which, on the one hand, consistently represents the values of the retailer and their brand to consumers and, on the other, satisfies the needs and expectations that the consumer has of the retailer. Indeed, as Lea Greenwood (1998) noted, the purpose of visual merchandising is at once both to convey the retailer's corporate positioning to the market and to reflect the aspirations of prospective customers.

The processes inherent to the creation and management of a store environment are many and complex. Indeed, a veritable science of store atmospherics has emerged which seeks to manipulate the visual, aural, olfactory and tactile dimensions of the store environment in order to influence customers' perceptions and subsequent behaviour (Kotler, 1973). As a result, a variety of studies have been undertaken by academics into this interesting dimension of retailing, and these include consideration of the psychological effect that store design has upon consumers' decision making in stores (Green, 1986), the role that store atmospherics has in relation to brand development and positioning (Sherry, 1998), and more recent studies which have suggested that a primary purpose of store atmospherics is to entertain consumers in a theatrical way (Kim, 2001). In an online context atmospherics can include elements such as the distinctive look and feel of the homepage and how it invites the shopper into the 'store'; layout of individual pages and the links between them; the display of merchandise, for example full product or tailored assortments, themed displays, links to sale merchandise; and the checkout process (Berman and Evans, 2010).

Prominence of the delivery and returns processes, availability of chat facility and the complaints process are further elements.

The development and implementation of a visual merchandise strategy is a costly activity and requires significant capital investment by retailers. For example, Mintel (1999) estimated that in the UK the store design and shop-fitting sector was worth £1.5 billion each year.

Given that the store design and visual merchandising functions are complex, a range of key elements are discussed in this chapter, including:

- the relationship between visual merchandising and consumer behaviour;
- the key business objectives of visual merchandising;
- factors affecting layout and display;
- the principles of store layout; and
- the common methods of in-store display used by retailers.

11.2.1 Visual merchandising and consumer behaviour

The investments made by retailers in store atmospherics are predicated upon a clear assumption: that the environmental context within which customers shop can have a significant impact upon their purchasing behaviour. Furthermore, it is based upon the assumption that significant and worthwhile proportions of customers' decisions are unplanned and are made at the point of purchase within the store.

A variety of studies, such as those undertaken by the Point of Purchasing Advertising Institute (POPAI) Dupont Surveys in 1977 and 1986, identified that two thirds of purchase decisions are actually made within the store. Their study classified purchasing decisions into four categories:

- **Specifically planned**: the customer knows which product and brand they want before entering the store and does not deviate from this position when buying.
- **Generally planned**: the customer knows which product they want, but has no specific brand in mind when they shop.
- **Substitute purchase**: the customer purchases a different product from their declared intention.
- **Unplanned purchase**: the customer buys a purchase without prior intention.

Based upon the results of the 1986 study, it was found that 33.9 per cent of purchases were specifically planned, 10.6 per cent were generally planned, 2.9 per cent were substitute purchases, and 52.6 per cent were unplanned purchases.

A number of models have been developed in order to explain consumer behaviour. Among the most important are those provided by Nicosia (1969), Howard and Sheth (1969), and Engel *et al.* (1990). Each of these models indicates that there is an opportunity for external agents, such as retailers, to influence the buying decision-making process, in terms of stimulating the buying process or influencing the final decisions that buyers make. Therefore, it is by virtue of their desire to affect positively customers' decision making that retailers decide to make considerable investments in the area of visual merchandising.

11.2.2 The key business objectives of visual merchandising

Lea Greenwood (1998) identified that the key business objectives of visual merchandising were to: attract customers' attention; encourage customers to increase the time and money they spend in store; differentiate the retailer from the competition; and reinforce the messages integral to the company's marketing communications strategy. Schimp (1990) maintained that the role of visual merchandising is to:

- create awareness among consumers about a product, and provide relevant information about it;
- remind customers about the benefits of a product and of its availability;
- encourage a customer to buy a particular product or brand;
- maximize reutilization of space, while making the buying experience as easy as possible for consumers;
- reinforce the retailer's communications campaign; and
- assist the customer in locating, evaluating and selecting a product.

Within this context, Harris and Walters (1992) identified that visual merchandising should serve to:

- reinforce the marketing positioning of the company within the competitive environment;
- encourage interest and comparison among customers, and prompt the customer to make a purchase; and
- coordinate the merchandise into a coherent proposition, which provides an integrated communications message.

Similarly, Varley (2006) suggests that visual merchandising has a crucial role to play in communicating and differentiating the retail offer to consumers, and maintains that the image that the visual dimensions of the store generates must be consistent with the retailer's overall positioning in the market.

11.2.3 Factors affecting layout and display

A variety of factors affects layout and display of stores (see Figure 11.1). Cost factors include the cost of layout and display and the cost of fixtures and fittings used in layout and display. These costs can be significant: consider, on the one hand, the time taken to design and install a stylish window display in a department store and, on the other, the gondolas, freezer and fridge units used to display merchandise in a superstore.

The layout of the store and the display of products for sale are normally intended to portray the store image and to reflect the desired corporate brand. Continuing the example above, the department store window display illustrates the quality of merchandise for sale in the store but also conveys store image through the level of display design and the quality of the display fittings, intended to attract the target market. The gondolas in the superstore are 'permanent' fixtures that not only display merchandise conveniently for self-service

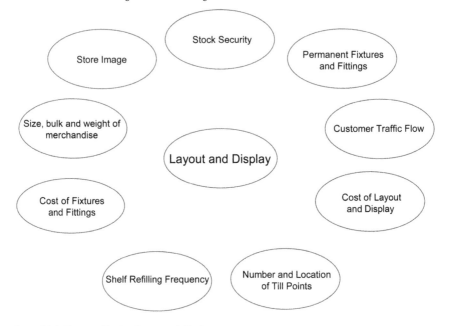

Figure 11.1 Factors affecting layout and display

customers but also guide customer traffic flow through the store, allowing customers to view the maximum amount of merchandise for self-selection and encouraging selection of own brands or those of preferred suppliers. The size, bulk and weight of merchandise also affect where and how it is displayed. In a superstore, for example, bulky, light items such as kitchen or toilet rolls can be stacked into special displays or stocked on high shelves in a way that would be inconvenient or even dangerous with heavy, breakable items such as six-packs of bottled drinks. Stock security is another significant factor – the display of valuable jewellery on a fitment designed for self-service of cheap, impulse-buy jewellery items would be unwise; valuable merchandise can be displayed in secure display boxes or, in the case of high-priced grocery items, under electronic surveillance, visual surveillance and/or the control of staff. The number and location of till points also affect layout and display. One of the main purposes of layout and display is to facilitate sales, so pay points have to be visible and sufficient for the number of customers anticipated at peak times – hence the banks of till points in a superstore, or well-signposted pay points in the different departments of a department store.

11.2.4 Layout and display starts at the entrance

The visual impact of the store begins before customers enter it. Consider, for example, the entrance to the Apple Store in Times Square, New York – a much-photographed glass cube attracting people to the underground store, which is accessed via a glass spiral stair-case. With most purchases being unplanned, it is important to intercept customers as they walk along a street or through a mall, as they drive along a shopping area or as they browse the Internet.

It can be argued, therefore, that visual merchandising starts outside the store. The design and situation of the physical store – on a prominent corner, at a road junction, among retailers offering brands to the same target customers – can be used to visually intercept potential customers. With physical stores, a variety of types of window (for example, parallel, corner, angled, bay) is used to display merchandise in order to attract attention and generate interest. The fascia of the store presents a 'summarized image' of the store brand using a recognizable logo, font, signage and colours. Lighting is a further element of store-front design. The store entrance, which should be accessible to all and can integrate window displays or be used for special displays of merchandise or planters, is designed both to communicate the image of the store and to facilitate the start of the shopping experience.

There are many types of store entrance. A standard door entrance separates window displays from the door. The door, which may be designed to open automatically, commits the shopper to browsing in the store. Sometimes an awning is used to draw attention to the entry. Awnings, of course, can also be used to protect window displays from the sun, to make window displays easier to see in sunny weather or to offer window shoppers some protection from rain or snow. A standard door entrance can promote exclusivity and is often seen in upmarket shopping areas of towns and cities. Open entrances, with minimal side display windows, are perhaps the most welcoming type of entrance, providing few visual barriers to entering the store, although they do present security issues. Also, they provide little or no space for window displays and the space available for the fascia is reduced, which makes presenting the store image problematic. Examples are commonly found in anchor stores of in-town shopping malls, where walkways through the mall 'carry straight into' the store, attracting customers browsing through the shops in the mall towards and into the store at the end. The mall security defence system complements store security to reduce the potential for theft. A semi-open entrance is one way of combining window display areas with a wide entrance to attract customers into the store, and this type of entrance is common on shopping streets and in malls. A funnel entrance combines one or two side window display areas with a covered 'lobby' that attracts customers to browse an extended range of merchandise while covered from the elements (where the store is on the street) but without committing to entering the store. An arcade store front presents a number of these 'lobbies' interspersed with display windows, which tend to slow down passing shoppers. Funnel entrances are sometimes designed with angled windows, displaying merchandise that 'leads' the customer into the store.

11.2.5 The principles of store layout

An important dimension of visual merchandising is the design of the store layout. The layout that the retailer adopts is dependent upon a number of factors, including:

- the sector in which the retailer operates – for example, a food retailer will adopt a different layout scheme from that of an exclusive fashion retailer;
- the architecture of the store itself; and

- the market positioning of the retailer – for example, a discount retailer will adopt a layout that maximizes the use of space and ensures that as much product as possible is available on the shop floor.

Like most aspects of retailing, most companies adopt a standardized approach to store layout which is managed and controlled by a visual merchandising team at their head office. This ensures that the layout plans used within a retail chain are consistently applied and that a corporate store format is developed (Lea Greenwood, 1998).

There are four principal store layout formats. The first is the **grid layout**. The grid layout is used primarily by food retailers, as well as retailers that operate large-scale, warehouse-style formats, such as DIY and electrical goods retailers. A grid layout involves the organization of gondola fixtures on a row-after-row basis. Merchandise rows are separated by aisles which allow for customer movement. At the end of each gondola, where customers enter from one row to the next, the selling areas are usually classified as 'hot spots', where promotional lines are displayed. These are described as 'hot spots' by virtue of the fact that a large number of customers are exposed to these areas. Furthermore, because of the widespread adoption of 'hot spot' areas by retailers, it would appear that customers are conditioned to expect that the merchandise displayed in these areas will be of particular interest.

According to Varley (2006), the grid layout maximizes the use of space available and provides a logical organization of the various product categories on offer. In many cases, the grid layout tries to expose customers to as much merchandise as possible. Within food retailing, this is achieved by placing high-demand products, such as bread and milk, in the centre of the store, at the middle of the aisle. This technique seeks to manipulate the movement of customers throughout the store, and ensures that they are exposed to as much of the store as possible.

However, this approach to store layout has some negative dimensions. For example, some customers can feel frustrated by the manipulation that the grid layout provides. Furthermore, this layout can also be criticized for being inflexible and a monotonous experience for shoppers.

An alternative approach to store layout is the **free-flow layout**. This layout is used within fashion stores and involves the presentation of merchandise fixtures on a more random basis. This approach enables the customers to move easily between fixtures and allows them to browse as they select merchandise. McGoldrick (2002) noted that while this approach was more visually appealing, a free-flow layout allows for a less intensive use of space, is cost intensive and, if the merchandise is not presented in a coordinated manner, then the overall effect may be of confusion.

Boutique layouts are similar to the free-flow layout, but departments or sections are laid out to produce the feeling of a 'shop in a shop'. This approach is often adopted by brands within department stores on the basis that it helps to promote a unified identity for the brand. For certain fashion brands sold under wholesale arrangements, the adoption of a boutique layout is a precondition to supply. This is because these fashion brands want to protect their distinctive identity and ensure that no other brand infringes on their business. While this layout approach allows for the targeting of specific groups of consumers and allows for a variety of different brand experiences for customers, it has to be acknowledged that it does not provide for an economical use of selling space.

The Swedish furniture retailer IKEA is famous for its adoption of the **controlled-flow layout**. This involves the creation of a layout that tightly controls the movement of customers through the store by creating a one-way racetrack system from which the customer cannot deviate. This system seeks to expose as many customers to as much merchandise as possible. Like all layout forms that seek to control rigidly the movement of people, customers can feel frustrated by the lack of freedom of movement that this approach involves.

Whatever the store layout method that a retailer adopts, it is clear that all must ensure that a balance is struck between ensuring the optimum use of space with the need to provide flexibility and interest for customers.

The design and layout of e-tail stores also plays a twin role in communicating corporate or store image (along with other elements of the promotional mix), and in generating sales. Dennis *et al.* (2004) argued that it is even more important and extensive in scope than the design and layout of physical stores because it also includes what used to be covered by interaction with the salesperson and because the customer plays such an important part in the purchasing process. Navigability is the most important component (see also Chapter 6), as customer traffic is guided in different ways through the merchandise towards purchase. Vrechopoulos *et al.* (2004) tested e-tail grid and free-flow layouts, finding that while the e-tail grid layout was easier to use, e-tail free-flow layouts were more useful for finding products, were more entertaining and engaged people for a longer time. Two other essential components of e-tail design, according to Dennis *et al.* (2004), are interactivity (between retailer and customer, and customer and customer), and web atmospherics (visuals, audio, offers, reviews and so on).

11.2.6 Methods of in-store display

Many retailers allocate considerable amounts of resource to the display and presentation of their products. Indeed, retailers such as the upmarket department store Harrods have developed such a reputation for innovative presentation that many customers are attracted to the store in order to view their latest displays. Window displays have been found to be a crucially important marketing communications device, and studies have found that the positive impact of a window display can serve as the primary reason why a customer chooses to enter a store for the first time (Lochhead and Moore, 1999).

Given the importance of window displays to the process of generating and communicating a brand identity, many retailers have decided to centralize the process of constructing, implementing and controlling window displays by vesting the responsibility with the visual merchandising team based at head office. As a means of ensuring the consistency of window display presentation, many retailers now opt to use large-scale photographs of their products, rather than the products themselves, in their store windows. An increasing number, however, now augment these photographs with actual products so as to avoid the impression of a display that is sterile, predictable and lacking in detail.

The display of merchandise takes two forms. Standard merchandise displays are used for the presentation of products en masse. Special merchandise displays are used to showcase specific products (which are perhaps either seasonal or are on promotion) within a discrete space within the store.

11.2.6.1 Standard merchandise displays

Every product that is offered for sale within a retail outlet is subject to some display principle. The method of display may be to use shelving, or it may be in the form of a hanging fixture. In most cases, the organization of display would exhibit some form of internal logic, such as in terms of price, size, colour or use. The organizational logic that retailers use is usually based upon an understanding of how the customer actually selects the product. As such, an understanding of the customer's principal selection criteria is crucial. If the retailer has no clear idea of how the customer interacts with a product, then there is every possibility that the manner in which they organize their display may hinder, rather than assist, the product selection process.

For example, the fashion retailer Next presents its men's formal shirt range on the basis of the product's primary feature. For example, all long-sleeved shirts are presented separately from short-sleeved shirts, and double-cuff shirts are arranged separately from their single-cuff range. The company also distinguishes between shirts that are made from 100 per cent cotton and those that are made from mixed fibres. Within each grouping, the shirts are presented in size order, from the smallest to the largest in their range. The underlying principle behind Next's approach to product display is to make product selection and eva-luation as easy for its customers as possible. By simplifying the display process, Next believes that it is providing an important and valued service to its customers.

11.2.6.2 Special merchandise displays

For merchandise that a retailer wants to highlight or promote in particular, there are a number of display options available:

- **Event displays**. This is perhaps the most commonly used display format. Merchan-dise that has some connection to an event, holiday or festival is displayed together in order to maximize the impact of the range. Events may include Christmas, Easter, Valentine's Day or Mother's Day. Often located near to store entrances, the purpose of these displays is to showcase the range of merchandise that the retailer has to support the event. These displays are often used as a means of giving ideas and inspiration to customers.
- **Table-top displays**. These involve the presentation of merchandise on table tops with the aim of encouraging customers to interact with the product range and, in some cases, to select for purchase from the display. The Italian knitwear retailer Benetton has successfully pioneered this technique.
- **Hot spots**. These are displays of promotional merchandise presented in areas of high customer density. Often the merchandise is 'blocked', one on top of the other, to give the impression of product availability and to ensure maximum promotional impact.
- **Lifestyle displays**. These sorts of displays utilize props that are associated with a particular lifestyle in order to create an association between the product range and a

lifestyle image. The American fashion retailer Ralph Lauren uses lifestyle displays of artefacts typically associated with English country living so as to connect his Polo brand with an English country lifestyle. Indeed, the Ralph Lauren flagship store in New York takes the lifestyle display to another level in that the store has the feel and aura of an English gentlemen's club.

- **Brand displays.** These present the goods that are included in a brand range collectively in order to showcase to customers the breadth of the range. For example, in Debenhams department stores, the company presents edited displays from their Designers at Debenhams range at the foot of escalators and at their stores' entrances.

Increasingly, retailers are recognizing the importance of effective visual merchandising as a means of generating differentiation within the market. Its importance is clearly evident in the observations made by the managing director of a major UK fashion chain:

> The reason for people shopping has changed in the past 10 years. It is not always just a chore but is for many an enjoyable leisure activity. For this reason, retailers need to invest in visual merchandising in order that the theatre and fun of retailing can be established. In the future, the visual dimensions will be as important as the products themselves.

11.3 Retail selling and product classification

The amount and quality of time a retail salesperson will spend actively selling depends first on the type of merchandise stocked by the retail organization. Merchandise can be classified as follows:

- Convenience goods: relatively inexpensive goods that are bought on a regular basis, without much thought going into the purchase, as customers are confident in product qualities, uses and attributes. Examples of convenience goods include items such as milk, eggs, bread, toilet rolls, cling film, floor cleaner and other 'everyday' items for which buyers tend to have low brand loyalty. The customer usually buys convenience goods at a supermarket or convenience store, and needs little help to buy from the retail salesperson. In this situation the visual merchandising plays an important part in generating sales within the store. The layout and displays within the store, together with freely available trolleys and baskets, encourage customers to choose the items they want to buy. At checkout, though, they can be encouraged to buy extra or associated items through suggestion and reminder. For example, cakes or pies can be suggested with bread, cream or cheese with milk, or the customer can be reminded of a special promotion on a larger size, or on two-for-one in a non-pressurizing manner.
- Preference goods: relatively inexpensive goods that are bought without much thought on a regular basis, for which the customer may have a reasonable amount of brand loyalty, but is less certain about desired product attributes. Goods such as tea, coffee, cigarettes, soft drinks and shampoos tend to fall into this category, and they are normally bought in grocery or convenience stores. Brand preference may have been

established over time through other promotional activities such as advertising and sales promotion, and branding makes such stock highly visible within the store. Again, little help is required from the salesperson, although brand extensions and associated items can be suggested or new alternatives demonstrated.

- Shopping goods: more expensive and normally more complex goods that the customer wants to compare and contrast with competing or complementing goods within and outside the store. The customer is normally relatively confident about the attributes, qualities and uses of these goods, but is not strongly brand loyal and therefore wants to 'shop around' to compare quality, price and features. Although customers are willing to spend time shopping for these goods, they are not always keen to travel to make comparisons. These goods are often bought from small specialist retailers. Goods such as clothes, shoes, accessories and cards often fall into this category. Visual merchandising is important in communicating the brand and salespeople can help customers to make a decision by giving information on comparative features, benefits and qualities for the price.

- Speciality goods: more expensive and complex goods, for example many electronic goods, in which customers experience uncertainty regarding attributes, qualities and uses, but for which they are willing to spend time and effort in shopping, including willingness to travel to buy from specialist retailers. Salespeople have an important role in helping customers to make a selection and come to a buy decision.

- Unsought goods: normally more expensive and complex goods that the customer would not necessarily think of buying, and therefore for which there is both uncertainty regarding attributes and low brand loyalty. Many unsought goods are sold door to door, although increasingly they are offered through traditional retail outlets. Examples are insurance, windows, conservatories and kitchens. Salespeople have a relatively important role in helping customers to make a buy decision. However, unlikely items that are occasionally juxtaposed with convenience and preference items also could be said to fall into the 'unsought' category. One example of this is the 'power aisle' in Tesco superstores where customers are encouraged to view a changing combination of popular electronics, household and seasonal goods on the way in to shop for groceries. In this case the buy decision can be encouraged through strong promotional pricing or by information given to the customer through the sales process. In both cases the decision process will be aided by assurance through guarantee/returns policy.

The classification above is general, and retail sellers need to understand how their target customers regard the products they are selling, something that is influenced by factors such as age, income, wealth and buying experience. Some buyers will have strong preferences for some convenience items, for example, and others will regard some shopping goods as speciality goods. Direct communication between customer and salesperson allows rapid determination of the amount of help needed.

11.4 Retail selling and types of buying decision

The complexity of the buying decision is related to the variety of factors introduced in the sections above. The range of buying decisions can be classified as follows:

- Routine decision making: tends to be associated with repeat buying of convenience or preference products, whether because of habit, low involvement in the purchase or because a strong preference for brand has been established, which aids decision making.
- Limited problem solving: in this situation the customer tends to have a higher level of involvement with the decision and will take more time to buy. Some information or incentive is needed to help make the buy decision. For example, a new brand or brand extension may have entered the market, or for a relatively simple, inexpensive item, the buyer may be new to the product category.
- Extensive problem solving: here the customer is willing to spend time and effort in shopping, perhaps because the product is complex or new to the market, or is expensive, or has high value to the customer in some other way, or the customer has little experience in the product category.

The role of the retail salesperson is closely related to the complexity of the buying process. The complexity of the process can vary for individual customers, and knowledge of the target segment customer profile will help to determine the degree of personal selling needed. For example, a computer is a complex and expensive product which many customers may need help to buy. However, many other people are now computer literate, confident in buying or have established strong brand preference.

11.5 Retail selling and shopping motives

People have a wide variety of motives for shopping:

- necessity;
- recreation;
- fun/entertainment;
- stimulation;
- socializing; and
- exercise.

This is why, though the merchandise being bought is the main reason for the shopping experience, for most customers the total shopping experience will affect customer satisfaction. Shostack, one of the early researchers into service design, maintained as far back as 1984 that companies should 'incorporate the orchestration of tangible evidence'. The retail service incorporates two types of tangible evidence: essential (experienced as part of the service) and tangible (owned as a result of the service). The total shopping experience includes essential aspects of the retail service including visual merchandising components such as atmospherics, store design, display, price, location, assortment and the dynamics of shopping. These will be experienced differently from customer to customer and on each shopping occasion. In addition to the variation of essential elements across shopping occasions there will exist differences in mood, staff encounters, number of other shoppers and so on. Customers also acquire tangible evidence of the retail service, not only in the form of the goods they buy but in terms of packaging, bags, receipts, store cards and so on.

The most successful retailers tend to be those that have 'orchestrated the tangible evidence' in a way that promotes the brand and intended level of product and service quality coherently and reliably to customers.

Even where the motive for shopping is necessity, it is widely recognized that the total shopping experience, rather than the merchandise itself, influences sales levels. Where shopping is for motives such as entertainment, recreation or social interaction, the dynamics of the shopping experience are more important, and the creation of a fun, exciting, interesting and diverting shopping environment is even more important.

Shopping motives vary from person to person and from occasion to occasion. Again, from a retail selling perspective, this illustrates the need to profile target customer groups. Almost every person who enters a store is a potential customer, however, and the role of selling in contributing to the total shopping experience should not be overlooked. Retail salespeople can quickly gauge shopping motives and respond accordingly. They can also help to create an 'exciting' shopping experience by exhibiting products or offering merchandise to customers to sample. Even if they only help in redirecting the customer to another store or destination, then they are contributing to the image of the organization as customer friendly, which may bring in future custom.

11.6 Retail selling and the buying process

Two models illustrate the buying process. The AIDA model is the simplest to remember and is useful to consider here because it is widely used in developing promotional campaigns that include selling as one contributory element:

Awareness Interest Desire Action

Potential buyers first become aware that they have the need for a specific product, brand or product group. Awareness can be stimulated by immediate lack of the product – running out of milk, for example – or by a growing awareness, such as a large car bill which heralds the onset of the need to start looking for another car. Awareness means that the potential buyer consciously or subconsciously begins the search for product.

The next phase is growing interest in finding the product required and is characterized by the search for and collection of information on the product. The type and extent of information looked for varies with product classification, with the type of buy decision, and even with the nature, confidence, experience and intelligence of the potential buyer. However, more information will be collected for shopping and speciality goods, which may include items such as product attributes, competing brands, competing outlets, prices, features and sources of finance. The potential buyer will collect information from the media, outlets, friends and family.

Studying the information and refining the data collected leads the potential buyer to gain a clearer picture of the product or brand required. One of the ways in which consumers reduce and refine the desired data from the plethora of information available is illustrated by a concept known as the evoked set. For each product category, consumers will develop over time a set of brands from which they are most likely to choose an alternative. Hence, for example, a consumer in the biscuit aisle of the supermarket may decide between

McVitie's Ginger Snaps, Rich Tea Biscuits or Hobnobs, Nestlé's KitKats and Traidcraft Geobars, automatically filtering out supermarket own brands and other varieties. Further, for each member of the evoked set, customers learn and compare the various features and benefits (price, calories, taste, size), so that choice of alternative is facilitated. **Desire** has been defined as need plus ability to buy – so for expensive products, sources of finance will have been found. This customer is ready to buy. There may still be some doubts regarding brand, model, alternative finance sources and product features.

Action is when the potential customer makes the buy decision. Payment methods, terms and contracts need to be settled, but the decision has been made.

The weakness of the AIDA model is that it does not recognize what happens after the buy decision. Later versions of the AIDA model added 'conviction' or 'satisfaction' as a fifth element (as AIDAS).

The consumer buying process addresses this by dividing the process into five steps, the first four of which are comparable with the AIDA model:

- problem recognition;
- information search;
- alternative evaluation;
- alternative choice; and
- post-purchase evaluation.

Post-purchase evaluation is the phase after the buyer has committed to the buy decision and seeks reassurance that the right decision was made through continuing to scan for alternatives, asking friends, checking items out in other shops and so on. **Post-purchase dissonance** is the term used for the vague unease regarding whether the right decision has been made, and post-purchase evaluation helps to reduce the dissonance until the buyer is certain that the buy decision was, if not correct, good enough in the circumstances.

One of the benefits of retail selling is the potential of the seller to take the potential buyer through all the steps of the buying decision process, sometimes in a single visit, speeding and facilitating the decision to buy. Depending, of course, on the type of merchandise being sold and the type of buying decision, the retail salesperson has a role to play at every stage of the buying process (see Table 11.1).

However, because retail selling is primarily a one-to-one activity, and therefore expensive, the most effective use of the salesperson's time is during the stages of alternative evaluation and alternative choice. In many selling situations the successful deployment of the other promotional mix elements can abbreviate the sales time spent on customers in the other stages of the buying process. For example, one study found that visual merchandising had a positive role in the buy decision for 75 per cent of respondents (Kaur, 2013).

It should be noted that the AIDA, AIDAS and buying decision process are old models that have been used for decades in sales training.

Table 11.1 Salesperson activities in relation to the buying decision process

Process stages	Salesperson activities
Problem recognition	Introduce new models or forthcoming product developments; can contact previous buyers to indicate current model is ageing or out of date; approach in-store customers to assess needs
Information search	Give information on alternative models, outlets; indicate sources of information
Alternative evaluation	Highlight particular features and benefits of alternative models, illustrations of satisfied customers
Alternative choice	Highlight particular features and benefits of alternative models, illustrations of satisfied customers; indicate special offers, finance, guarantees to help the decision to buy
Post-purchase evaluation	Telephone or write to check satisfaction; can invite back to exhibitions, previews and other special events; can remind the customer it is time to buy again

11.7 Retail sales roles

Retail salespeople have a major role to play in facilitating and enhancing the process of purchase decision making. Additionally, they can represent and reinforce store image, provide a dynamic shopping experience, and build immediate relations with customers and potential customers.

There are two main roles that retail salespeople undertake:

- order taking; and
- order getting.

Very many retail salespeople are **order takers**. That is, they process customers' decisions on products bought at the very simplest level, merely running the item through checkout. This tends to happen with convenience and preference goods, and in shopping situations where routine decision making is the norm. Nevertheless, these staff have an important role in maintaining processing speed, and can influence sales through efficiency (or lack of it). Other order takers may show customers the location of goods, get them from stock, or give some limited information to aid evaluation and choice.

Stores that stock shopping and comparison goods, but which specialize in providing value at the expense of customer service, often operate staffing levels that preclude any but the most basic order-processing sales activities. These retailers rely on discounting, price, sales promotions and value to stimulate the decision to buy.

Increasingly, order takers will be encouraged to increase sales through means such as suggesting additional items to buy at the checkout, offering delivery service or passing on information on deals and offers.

Order getters are retail salespeople who deal primarily with shopping and speciality goods where the decision to buy is not routine. This type of salesperson tends to sell higher-priced and/or complex goods, and is more actively involved in getting and giving information, in persuasion and in closing the sale (Berman and Evans, 2010). The great benefit of salespeople in this role is their capability for direct customer communication and for gauging a customer's shopping motive, relationship with merchandise and stage in the buying process. A salesperson in a clothes shop, for example, has to engage actively in the selling process to find out what shoppers really want in order to find solutions for them (Levy and Weitz, 2009).

These salespeople will engage potential customers in the selling process, informing them, guiding them and helping them make the decision to buy on the spot, or at some time in the future. Sometimes termed **sales associates**, order getters may be paid partly (or even wholly) in commission, which can lead to a pressurized selling environment that can conflict with customer preferences. One way around this is to relate commission not only to sales but to the value of returned products. Customer-orientated selling places customer focus at the heart of the selling process and aims at building a long-term customer relationship, which increases satisfaction with the product bought, salesperson, retailer and manufacturer (McGoldrick, 2002). Due to their more extensive involvement in directly communicating with customers, order getters have a prime role in influencing customer perceptions of the retail organization and levels of customer satisfaction.

11.8 The retail sales process

The selling process includes the stages summarized in Table 11.2. Although stages of the selling process are most actively engaged by 'order-getting' retail salespeople, they also form a useful checklist for core retail activities.

A **prospect** can be defined as any person who has the potential to purchase your goods or services. Sources include:

- previous customers;
- customer and employee referrals;
- lapsed customers;
- direct mail and other promotional methods;
- exhibitions and demonstrations; and
- centre of influence method – use of local/regional/national celebrities to endorse store/organization.

Preparation includes learning about the target customer group, and how to handle different types of customer, including difficult customers. It also includes learning about the merchandise, its make-up, uses, performance, care, background and associated services. Retail salespeople also need to know about store policies on opening hours, payment, returns and delivery (Dunne and Lusch, 1999).

Customers who ask for help, try to catch the eye or who are inspecting merchandise closely are the salesperson's best prospects, and a friendly, outgoing approach with a direct greeting is recommended. The salesperson has to determine the customer's needs quickly through open questioning, but should remember to allow the customer time to talk freely, while listening, understanding, responding and summarizing. During the approach the

Table 11.2 The buying process, the selling process and salesperson activities

Buying process stages	Selling process stages	Salesperson activities
Problem recognition	Prospecting	Develop a list of prospective customers
	Preparing	Learn customer profiles; learn features/benefits of products and other relevant information; match to profiles
Information search	Approach	Approach customer to determine shopping motives and needs; find out desired product(s), benefits sought
Alternative evaluation	Presentation	Present information on product(s) under consideration; show and, if necessary, demonstrate features and benefits
	Overcoming objections	Find out reservations and barriers to the buy decision for products under consideration; answer questions; attempt trial closes
Alternative choice	Close	Ask for a buy decision
Post-purchase evaluation	Follow-up	Suggest additional or complementary items; highlight future events; check customer's satisfaction with the product and service experience

salesperson has to indicate extensive product knowledge, show a genuine desire to meet the customer's needs, and show a positive service attitude.

Once the customer's needs and price range have been defined, the salesperson **presents** the merchandise. The AIDA model can serve as a structure for the presentation, as the salesperson outlines or demonstrates merchandise features, advantages and benefits to the prospect, relating these to the customer's specific needs. Allowing the customer to try or handle the merchandise helps to build desire, as does showing that a particular product will save money or exceed customer needs. Open questions allow the customer to express reservations or further needs, and closed questions allow the salesperson to determine understanding, facts and level of interest. The aim is not to 'sell' to the customer, but to help the customer buy the merchandise that will give most satisfaction.

Reservations and objections are barriers to the buy decision, and if they are genuinely important to the customer, they have to be overcome to make a sale. It is best to anticipate common objections early in the presentation to prevent negativity later in the process. Other means of handling reservations include:

- Pass up the objection: skirt around the issue. If it comes up again it is important and needs to be addressed.
- Ask questions: find out the prospect's concerns.
- Rephrase the objection: summarize understanding of the customer's reservation. This buys thinking time.

- Compensate for the objection: outline the features and benefits that make the product worth buying.
- Deny the objection: where the customer reservation is based on a misconception, acknowledge their views and concerns, then explain the correct situation.
- Use a testimony or third party: explain or demonstrate an instance in which the objection was previously made and the customer subsequently satisfied.

As each objection is answered, the salesperson should check that it has been overcome, using a closed question to determine the customer's agreement. This is sometimes called a trial close. Where the objection cannot be overcome, this has to be acknowledged, followed by an indication of how the benefits of the product outweigh the disadvantages or, if appropriate, presentation of an alternative product.

Closing the sale is the point at which the customer is directly asked whether they want to buy. Buying signals are those behaviours that indicate genuine interest in purchase, such as reading the warranty or user manual, trying the product, examining the item in detail, asking questions about colours, styles, delivery, accessories, and making positive comments about the product. If the buying signals have been misinterpreted and the customer refuses to close, it is possible that there is a further reservation that needs to be determined and met. Alternatively, there may be another product or model that will meet their needs. It is, however, important not to pressurize the customer into buying.

Following up the sale can lead to extra sales in a number of ways: supplementary and complementary items can be suggested to the buyer; a discount can be offered for the next purchase, or for a referral; the buyer can be added to a list of future prospects. It is good practice to enquire by telephone or card about customer satisfaction with any expensive or complex purchase.

11.9 Retail selling and the promotional mix

Retail selling should form part of an integrated promotional plan, encompassing a variety of promotional mix elements and clear promotional objectives that need to be communicated to those undertaking sales roles. Integration is required due to the nature of the consumer buying process. Consumers engaged in the 'information search' and 'alternative evaluation' stages of the buying process will be consciously or unconsciously acquiring and absorbing information put out by the retailer in the form of advertising, publicity, sales promotions and/or sponsorship (in addition to information from other agencies such as the media, competitors and friends). This information feeds into their expectations regarding the product(s) sought, the retail experience and the sales experience. Where there is a divergence between expectation and actuality, there is likely to be dissatisfaction. For example, where an advertisement indicates a price reduction, the buyer will expect the salesperson to know about it and to offer it. Where a retailer advertises certain products for sale, the buyer will expect them to be in stock. When a retailer advertises in a magazine associated with high-quality, high-price merchandise, the buyer will expect an equally polished retail and sales experience.

The other promotional tools act together to form the foundation of the sales experience – they will bring in the potential customers, and the more successful they are, the less 'selling' will be required. However, the sales role undertaken by staff, the selling process itself, has to be tailored to accommodate the customer expectations raised through other promotional efforts. The knowledge salespeople have, their sales targets, the way they dress, the way they act and how they sell all have to be related to the other elements of the promotional mix and to the overall promotional objectives of the retailer. For example, sophisticated retailers apply elements of visual merchandising, from window displays to layout and store atmospherics, to promote their desired brand not only across their store portfolios but also in their online formats. In physical stores, sales staff interact with customers within a carefully constructed store environment. Their dress, manner and the way they act and sell to customers should be controlled through selection and training, through good leadership, through communication of clear sales objectives, and through application of suitable evaluation and reward systems.

11.10　Retail selling and the Internet

In virtual stores, the selling process takes place without the involvement of staff; there is potential for a selling role only at the point where the customer contacts the company, for example to question, complain or follow up an order. However, many people shop in physical stores after searching for information online and developing an understanding of the required product, and sometimes a preference for a particular brand or brands. They then come into stores to buy the product. With potential customers already at the alternative evaluation stage of the buying process, salespeople can focus on presenting suitable merchandise, illustrating features and explaining benefits to facilitate choice and the buy decision. Online information speeds up the selling process and helps to make more efficient use of sales staff.

According to Grewal *et al.*(2002), some product groupings traditionally demanded limited personal selling. These include commodities such as groceries and hardware, and quasi-commodities with strong brand identities such as office supplies and computer products, CDs, DVDs, books and music. Selling many such commodities demanded that salespeople spent (expensive) face-to-face time with customers, giving information and filling orders. The Internet and related technologies increased the productivity of salespeople not only by shortening the selling process but by allowing them to access customer details to personalize and focus the presentation and to give customers information about what was in stock but not in store. Of course, many such quasi-commodities, such as books, music, DVDs and software, are now downloaded directly by customers. The personal selling role is more important for selling products that customers like to touch and feel, or unique products. Here, salespeople have a consultative role, explaining the benefits and overcoming objections leading to a successful sale and reduced post-purchase dissonance. The selling of such products is also facilitated via the Internet, for example through building one-to-one relationships and deployment of personal promotions. It can also be used to communicate trends, out-of-stock products and customized orders to buyers and suppliers. The selling of such merchandise was successfully pioneered through transactional online retail outlets such as Net-A-Porter and ASOS, companies which have virtualized the consultative selling role by providing online fashion and style advice.

11.11 Summary

This chapter reviewed the relationship between visual merchandising and selling. The processes inherent to the management of the visual presentation of goods within retail outlets were considered together with the relationship between visual merchandising and consumer behaviour, and it was noted that a sizeable proportion of consumer decisions are made within the store.

The key business objectives of visual merchandising were introduced, as were the principles relevant to store layout decisions. The most popular methods of managing displays within a retail setting were also outlined.

There is a strong relationship between retail selling, customer service and customer satisfaction. Retailers operating market-focused service businesses need to tailor their retail selling to customers' requirements with regard to:

- the type of product being bought;
- the type of purchase decision;
- customers' shopping motives; and
- the stage in the process of making the buying decision.

The nature and depth of retail selling required are related to the type, complexity and value of the product, the customer's understanding of its qualities, uses and attributes, brand loyalty and the extent to which the customer desires involvement in the buying process.

Merchandise can be categorized into convenience, preference, shopping, speciality and unsought goods, although the category for any one product may vary according to the customer's attributes, such as age, wealth and buying experience.

The role of retail salespeople and the nature of the selling process will vary according to merchandise category and target customer profile.

The nature of retail selling also varies according to the extensiveness of the customer decision-making process. Less involvement is required in selling convenience items, or those for which a strong brand preference has been established. More extensive selling is required for complex and expensive products that engage customers in extended problem solving.

The role and activities of retail salespeople also depend on the shopping motives of customers; where shopping is for social reasons, or for fun and entertainment, salespeople can contribute to a dynamic and changing retail experience.

The customer buying process can be summarized within the AIDA model, or more commonly within the five stages of the buying process. The speed at which customers proceed through the stages depends on individual characteristics such as age and background, merchandise category and type of buying decision. The role of retail salespeople as direct communicators with customers allows them unique capability in rapidly determining, through simple questioning, which stage any individual customer has reached. The activities of retail salespeople will vary according to each stage of the buying process, but the most effective use of salespeople's time is to contribute to alternative evaluation and choice.

Most retail salespeople have an order-taking role – processing customers' orders once they have selected the merchandise. However, these staff can increase sales through their own efficiency and by suggesting supplementary and complementary merchandise to customers. Order getters have a more extensive sales role, usually associated with more complex and expensive merchandise, and these salespeople will engage potential customers in the selling process, informing them and helping them make the decision to buy.

The sales process undertaken by order getters includes seven stages: prospecting, preparing, approach, presentation, overcoming objections, close, and post-purchase evaluation and follow-up. These can be linked to the stages of the buying process so that the salesperson has a more informed basis for the activities to be undertaken during each stage.

Retail selling is one element of the promotional mix and contributes to the achievement of promotional objectives. The integration of selling and other promotional mix elements is required to meet in-store customer expectations built through promotional activities during the information search stage of the buying process. The growth of online stores means a reduced role for personal selling; however, it also affects the selling process in stores, increasing the efficiency of sales staff who can focus on presentation and facilitate choice, because many customers have already had the opportunity to find and evaluate information relating to their purchase before coming into the store to make a final decision.

Review questions

1   Identify how visual merchandising may assist retailers in the achievement of their key business objectives.
2   What are the various options that retailers have when it comes to the selection of a layout for the store? Identify the factors that may influence their layout decision.
3   Describe the options that retailers have available to them for the display and promotion of their merchandise.

Case study: Conways

A privately owned upmarket British grocer, Conways, with 35 stores, had sales of £250 million. Growing both in size and sales, the company's owners decided to initiate a project they called 'Success through Sales'. This project meant a move towards a more sales-orientated environment, making the company – according to Chairman John Conway – 'more of a retailer and less of a stockholder'.

Spearheading 'Success through Sales' was the move to a sales-based ordering system, with software being rolled out across all stores. The owner felt that this, being orientated towards customer demands, should bring a higher volume of sales, although at the risk of dissatisfying customers by terminating the stockholding of products for which there was low demand. The objective was to improve the retailer's range and customer service.

The project also involved initiating a sales culture among the company's staff through training them to take a more active role in selling. This training would mean staff would have more product knowledge, give better customer service and be more aware of service quality issues.

1 Examine the links between customer service and retail selling and explain how the establishment of a 'sales culture' would inevitably involve training in both personal selling and customer service.

References

Berman, B. and Evans, J.R. (2010) *Retail Management: A Strategic Approach* (11th edn). Upper Saddle River, NJ; Prentice Hall.

Dennis, C., Fenech, T. and Merrilees, B. (2004) *e-Retailing*. Abingdon and New York: Routledge.

Dunne, P. and Lusch, R.F. (1999) *Retailing* (3rd edn). Orlando, FL: Dryden Press.

Engel, J.F., Blackwell, R.D. and Miniard, P. (1990) *Consumer Behaviour*. Orlando, FL; Dryden Press.

Green, W.R. (1986) *The Retail Store: Design and Construction*. New York: Van Nostrand.

Grewal, D., Levy, M. and Marshall, G.W. (2002) 'How does the Internet and related technologies enable and limit successful selling?' *Journal of Marketing Management*, 18: 301–316.

Harris, D. and Walters, D. (1992) *Retail Operations Management – A Strategic Approach*. Hemel Hempstead: Prentice Hall.

Howard, J.A. and Sheth, J.N. (1969) *The Theory of Buyer Behaviour*. New York: John Wiley.

IGD (1997) *A Guide to Category Management*. Watford: Institute of Grocery Distribution.

Kaur, A. (2013) 'The effect of visual merchandising on buying behavior of customers in Chandigarh', *International Journal of Engineering Science and Innovative Technology (ISJESIT)*, 2(3), May.

Kim, Y. (2001) 'Experiential retailing', *Journal of Retailing and Consumer Services*, 8(5): 287–289.

Kotler, P. (1973) 'Atmospherics as a marketing tool', *Journal of Retailing*, 49(4): 48–64.

Lea Greenwood, G. (1998) 'Visual merchandising – a neglected area in UK retail fashion marketing', *International Journal of Retail and Distribution Management*, 26(8): 324–329.

Levy, M. and Weitz, B.A. (2009) *Retailing Management* (7th edn). New York: McGraw-Hill Irwin.

Lochhead, M. and Moore, C.M. (1999) 'A Christmas fit for a Prince's Square', in *European Cases in Retailing* (Dupuis, M. and Dawson, J., eds). Oxford: Blackwell, pp. 247–256.

McGoldrick, P. (2002) *Retail Marketing* (2nd edn). London: McGraw-Hill.

Merrilees, B. and Miller, D. (1996) *Retailing Management: A Best Practice Approach*. Victoria: RMIT Press.

Mintel (1999) 'Retail store design', *Retail Intelligence* (August): 1–112.

Nicosia, F.M. (1969) *Consumer Decision Process*. Upper Saddle River, NJ: Prentice Hall.

POPAI (Point of Purchasing Advertising Institute) (1977) *The 1977 Supermarket Consumer Buying Habits Study*. New York: POPAI.

POPAI (Point of Purchasing Advertising Institute) (1986) *The 1986 Supermarket Consumer Buying Habits Study*. New York: POPAI.

Schimp, T.A. (1990) *Promotion Management and Marketing Communications*. Orlando, FL: Dryden Press.

Sherry, J.F. (1998) 'The soul of the company store', in *The Concept of Place in Contemporary Markets* (Sherry, J.F., ed.). Chicago, IL: NTC Business Books, pp. 109–146.

Shostack, G.L. (1984) 'Designing services that deliver', *Harvard Business Review*, 62(1): 133–139.

Varley, R. (2006) *Retail Product Management – Buying and Merchandising* (2nd edn). Abingdon: Routledge.

Vrechopoulos, A.P., O'Keefe, R.M., Doukidis, G.I. and Siomkos, G.J. (2004) 'Virtual store layout: an experimental comparison in the context of grocery retail', *Journal of Retailing*, 80: 13–22.

12 Retail security

Learning objectives

After studying this chapter, you should be able to:

- Define shrinkage and identify its main causes.
- Discuss the main types of retail crime.
- Evaluate the scale and nature of retail crime in the UK.
- Know how to deal with shoplifters.
- Analyse security issues and develop a strategy for retail crime prevention.

12.1 Introduction

Retail crime has long been trivialized in the eyes of the general public. The stereotypical shoplifter is envisaged as a 'naughty teenager' enacting a dare, a poor pensioner lifting a few items, a poorly paid member of staff supplementing a low income or a drug addict looking for goods to sell on quickly. The general view is that retail theft is a minor misdemeanour at the expense of organizations making large profits from their customers. This perception is enhanced by low levels of reportage and conviction. For example, according to a 2004 study, less than 50 per cent of thieves apprehended by retailers were even handed to the police. The main reasons cited include (Bamfield, 2004):

- it takes up too much staff time (particularly in owner-operated stores);
- low prosecution rate;
- low level of conviction;
- poor deterrence by fines/penalties; and
- reluctance to prosecute the elderly, juveniles or the mentally ill.

Further, retailer confidence in successful prosecution of customer thieves appears to be decreasing over time. According to the Office of National Statistics (ONS, 2013) only 12 per cent of customer theft was reported to police, while according to a British Retail Consortium (BRC) study in 2013, the rate was even lower at 9 per cent.

Low level of conviction is a key reason for low reportage and this is compounded by the staff time needed to pursue a shoplifter to successful conviction. Less than half of apprehended customer thieves in the UK were found guilty in court in 2001 (BRC, 2001). In 2004 fines (fixed penalty notices) were brought in for those apprehended for shoplifting for the first time and for low-value shoplifting offences. Retailers protested at the time that this would not do enough to discourage repeat offending. Indeed, many offenders ignored the fines: in the five years from 2008, half of fines were unpaid and most unpaid fines were unchallenged (Whitehead, 2013). While conviction rates (in England) later improved for shoplifting offences, most convictions relate to serial offenders (Ministry of Justice, 2010).

Retailing is a key economic sector in advanced economies, but it is only relatively recently that retail security has been highlighted as a major issue for the retail industries. This is because reliable and comparative data on shrinkage, crime and security measures are needed to underpin increased, coordinated action in combating crime. This is easier where the retail sector is mature and ownership concentrated – that is, where large businesses control a high proportion of outlets. Such businesses also have the economic and political influence needed to underpin initiatives designed to improve security across the retail sector.

Retail shrinkage and retail crime are often confused. Retail shrinkage is the term used to describe stock losses due to genuine administrative error in addition to losses from criminal activity such as employee and customer theft and supplier fraud. Shrinkage is normally expressed as a percentage of turnover. The shrinkage rate is calculated as the recorded value of inventory at retail prices, based on purchase and receipt of inventory, minus the value of inventory at retail prices in stores and distribution centres, divided by retail sales during the period of calculation.

Not all retailers define shrinkage in the same way, however. For example, when surveyed, all retailers included external and internal theft plus loss due to process failures; however, only about 50 per cent included supplier and courier theft (BRC, 2009). In the various surveys referred to below there are substantial differences in levels of shrinkage and crime reported (these relate to survey methodology and measures used); nevertheless, they offer an overview of the extent and causes of retail shrinkage, and of the main sources of retail crime.

Nowadays it is easy to compare patterns of retail loss across not only stores owned by one company, but across store types and sizes, and across retail sectors. The collection of retail shrinkage and crime data originated in the USA, which has a highly developed retail sector. The first National Retail Crime Survey was published in 1992 (Hollinger and Hayes, 1992). The following year, the Retail Crime Initiative was set up by the BRC in the UK, financed by a number of major UK retail companies. The first of the annual BRC surveys into retail crime was carried out the same year.

As with Hollinger and Hayes's publications in the USA, the BRC surveys would establish and publicize the scale of retail crime, raising the profile of the subject, and forming a basis for analysis and action. The sharing of information on retail crime informed retailers themselves, government, police and the justice system of the scale of the retail crime problem. These annual surveys can be used by retailers as a benchmark against which to measure shrinkage and crime in their own operations, and to influence sector-wide schemes for crime prevention. More recently, the BRC turned its attention to retailing e-crime, conducting a survey of members engaged in a range of retail sectors including supermarkets, department stores, fashion, health and beauty, and mixed retail (BRC, 2012b).

In 2002, the first European Retail Theft Barometer was published, with a view to establishing European-wide comparison of shrinkage, crime statistics and crime prevention. The first of these six-monthly studies of retail crime within Europe was based on a survey of 424 major European retailers across 15 countries (CRR, 2002a). Later surveys included central European countries such as Poland, Hungary, the Czech Republic, Slovakia and the Baltic states. In 2007, the Centre for Retail Research (CRR) published the first Global Theft Barometer, surveying over 900 of the largest retailers in North and Latin America, Europe, Africa, Asia and Asia–Pacific (Bamfield, 2007). These efforts to highlight the extent and nature of retail crime, to involve related agencies and share information across the retail industry have had a role in reduction of shrinkage rates, which fell relatively steadily from 2003 until the start of the recession in 2008 (which brought an increase in shoplifting) as retailers developed integrated security programmes and invested in a variety of measures to reduce crime.

12.2 Shrinkage rates and causes

In Europe, the average shrinkage rate reduced in the six-year period from 2001 to 2006 from 1.42 to 1.23 per cent of turnover, with the UK rate declining from 1.76 to 1.33 per cent (the highest rate in Europe). Shrinkage in the USA was 1.52 per cent, slightly higher than the previous year (Bamfield, 2007). Post-global recession shrinkage rates in the UK and USA were higher at 1.37 and 1.59 per cent, respectively (CRR, 2012).

Among major retailers the shrinkage rate of a store is a key performance indicator for the effectiveness of store management. For example, UK department store retailer Debenhams has target shrinkage rates of 1–1.5 per cent, depending upon store size and location.

As well as management policy and practice, shrinkage is affected by retailer sector and size. For example, top sectors for shrinkage include clothing and textiles, food specialists and department stores, while those with the lowest rates include shoes and leather retailers, supermarkets and hypermarkets, and general/discount stores (CRR, 2005). The level of theft experienced (and the amount spent on crime prevention) is also related to the size of store. In the UK, larger formats such as department stores and grocery superstores attract more and more organized thieves (CRR, 2009).

The CRR defined four main causes of retail loss in its national survey of retail crime and security:

- customers;
- employees;
- vendors/suppliers; and
- administration (internal error).

Most loss is due to crime linked to customers, employees and vendors, with administration accounting for just over 15 per cent of overall shrinkage (Bamfield, 2007; CRR

2012). Vendor (supplier) fraud accounts for another 6 per cent, with the rest related to employee and customer theft. Large multiple retailers experience both higher administrative error and higher levels of staff crime than small and medium-sized multiple retailers.

During one British Retail Crime Survey, retailers were requested to give a value for unexplained stock losses that were attributed to unrecorded crime (excluding unexplained losses due to administrative error, breakages and vendor (supplier) fraud). That survey found that 50 per cent of unexplained stock loss was attributed to customer theft and 39 per cent to staff theft.

Undoubtedly, all the surveys highlight that the major source of shrinkage experienced by retailers is crime – by customers and by employees. However, according to the Global Theft Barometer, the amount of customer and staff crime differs from country to country, with the USA, Canada and Australia attributing most crime to staff, and the rest of the world to customers (Bamfield, 2007). Clearly, collusion between staff and customers to steal from retailers exists, although the extent of this is unclear.

It has been found in both the UK and the USA that high shrinkage is associated with:

- low rates of pay;
- non-existence of profit-sharing schemes;
- high staff turnover;
- high proportion of part-time staff; and
- poor store management.

All are widespread features of the retail industry, and therefore it would seem apparent that human resource management in retailing is as important an issue as increasing security measures. Staffing was an issue raised by Hollinger. His research showed an increase in crime during the early recession in 2008. As retailers struggled to remain profitable, lower staffing levels offered greater opportunity for staff and customer theft, while under-availability of staff to check in stock coming into the store from vendors meant there was a higher risk of vendor crime (Goodchild, 2009).

12.3 Types of retail crime

12.3.1 Customer theft

Customer theft is a major (in the UK *the* major) type of retail crime. In order to display goods in a way that is conducive to attractive and easy self-service, they have to be accessible, which attracts shoplifters along with buyers. In a time of economic turbulence with high unemployment, as happened after the banking crisis in 2008, shoplifting tends to rise. This was compounded by a competitive and pressurized retail market in which retailers were tempted to reduce staffing to cut costs. In many countries economic crisis meant less spent on public sector employment, reducing the policing of retail crime, and making it more difficult for retailers to report and prosecute criminals successfully.

The pattern of customer theft in the UK retail market indicates that this type of theft is persistent, although it fluctuates according to both economic and political conditions. After a sharp rise of 56 per cent from 1999 to 2000, customer theft continued its relatively steady rise even after the increased industry efforts to raise the profile of retail crime and share best practice, and despite the use of increasingly sophisticated anti-crime measures. Of course, some of the rise in customer theft could be attributed to an increase in reportage as a result of the development of retail security as a focus for the industry. Investment in security systems such as chip & PIN (explained below) did not stem the rise, but changed the ways in which some customers steal.

A decrease in customer theft was finally reported in the Retail Crime Survey 2008; however, the decrease was short-lived and the following recession brought a sharp rise in shoplifting. A rise of 59 per cent in the number of thefts per 100 stores was reported in one year alone (BRC, 2013). There are likely to be multiple reasons for such a rise. Apart from general recessionary pressures on individuals and retailers referred to above, this happened during an ongoing economic squeeze to generate recovery that lowered incomes, raised unemployment and produced welfare reform resulting in a rise in poverty. At the same time many retailers altered employment conditions for many staff. For example, zero-hours contracts meant job and income uncertainty from day to day and week to week, generating flexibility in terms of human resources, but in a way likely to lower the training, skills and motivation of the workforce to prevent retail crime. Declining police levels meant that conditions were favourable for shoplifters.

The amount of detected theft, where retail criminals are caught and prosecuted, is far less than theft that goes reported, or where criminals are not caught and prosecuted. In 2012, it was estimated that only 12 per cent of customer theft was reported to the police; half of customer theft was undetected. It is interesting to note that in the same year there was a decrease in recorded crime in England and Wales (ONS, 2013).

Shoplifters tend to target merchandise for their own consumption or for quick conversion to cash. The items most frequently stolen tend to be high-value/high-demand items such as perfumes, alcohol, brand-name clothing and small electronic items like laptops, software, MP3 players and mobile phones (CRR, 2006).

Thieves are more likely to be male than female, and merchandise stolen tends to be gender related, with males, for example, stealing electronic hardware, and women perfume and cosmetics (Bamfield, 2005). In the UK in 2000, 22 per cent of thieves were minors (17 and under); in Scotland the figure was 31 per cent, similar to that in the USA. Youth crime accounts for an even more disproportionate amount of theft because of the low percentage of the population under the age of 18. One study showed that most adult theft was also committed by young adults (under age 30), and 90 per cent of UK offences are carried out by people aged 16–40 (CRR, 2007).

One of the important underlying causes of retail theft is drug addiction. The 2000 BRC study established that drug-related crime accounted for the majority of retail and other crime in city centres, with drug addicts needing to steal £22,000–£44,000 per year to fund an average £11,000 per year drug habit. In 1998, a Home Office study showed that 80 per cent of people arrested tested positive for at least one drug, while 47 and 30 per cent tested positive for opiates and cocaine, respectively. However, a more recent study of convicted retail thieves estimated that only 24 per cent stole from shops to fund drug use (Sentencing Advisory Panel, 2004). Handling of drug abusers by drug courts with the power to impose drug treatment orders and regular drug testing of offenders is a potential means of reducing drug-related crime.

Customer theft is frequently planned by professional shop thieves, who steal to order, operate in gangs and move from town to town. Targets are carefully monitored, with lunch times, tea breaks and shift changes noted, and the layout of the store investigated. Sometimes a group of thieves will enter a store at a time when there is low staffing, fanning out through the store to prevent apprehension.

Stock near the entrance to stores is at most risk of theft, with the displays used to attract customers into the store proving the most vulnerable to shoplifters. Many professional shop thieves dispose of the items to their customers almost immediately on leaving the store, exiting the scene by prearranged routes and transport.

A further influence on customer theft is the size of the market for stolen goods. Although the buying of stolen goods is also a criminal act in the UK, customer thieves find a ready market for their goods through commercial and residential intermediaries (fences) or through 'hawking' – that is, selling stolen goods direct to consumers. The market for stolen goods is age and gender related in the UK. One study found that over half of young males had been offered or bought stolen goods over a five-year period, while 18–24 year olds were four times more likely to buy stolen goods than older people (Sutton, 1998; Sutton *et al..*, 2001).

12.3.2 Employee theft

The level of employee theft in the UK is difficult to determine for a number of reasons. First, both theft and fraud were dealt with under the Theft Act 1968 and there was some ambiguity between the two; one of the purposes of the UK's Fraud Act 2006 was to clarify and extend the difference (see section 12.3.3 below). In the USA, where levels of loss attributed to employees has always been much higher than in Europe, the term 'employee fraud' is used. Second, it can be difficult to establish the level to which employees are colluding with customers stealing from retailers. Third, employees caught stealing are frequently dealt with internally by dismissal, with no further action taken (and they are free to take up employment with other retailers). According to the Global Theft Barometer, 35 per cent of shrinkage globally was attributable to employees. In the USA, employee fraud accounted for 44 per cent of shrinkage (CRR, 2009; Euromonitor International, 2013). In the UK employee theft accounted for 33 per cent of shrinkage (Euromonitor International, 2013).

It is clear that employees, with inside knowledge of retailer weaknesses, are able to steal more per theft. For example, according to the BRC, employees stole £538 per incident compared with just £74 for customer theft in 2000 (by 2012, the cost of employee theft had increased to £1,577 per incident). The amount of undetected employee theft has fallen with heavy investment on the part of large retailers in crime detection equipment such as closed-circuit television (CCTV) at point of sale, and in the use of data mining to uncover systematic theft and fraud.

Risk of employee theft varies according to type of retailer. For example, pharmacists experienced the highest degree of employee theft, both in terms of number of incidents and in value of goods stolen. Department stores and DIY/hardware stores are also sectors that experience a high number of employee thefts (BRC, 2001).

Internal theft is difficult to detect and deal with because of the wealth of opportunity for theft and the degree of trust that must rest with employees; this is particularly the case where managers or security staff are involved. There is a wide variety of ways employees can steal from retailers, including:

- under-ringing sales at the till;
- taking cash from the till;
- taking a cheque without registering the sale, later taking out the equivalent in cash so the till balances;
- throwing merchandise into waste bins and returning to remove it later;
- collusion with customers – handing out merchandise to relatives or friends, or by including free items with legitimate purchases;
- collusion with suppliers – for example, fraudulent deliveries made with forged slips;
- retention of receipts to gain fraudulent refunds or voids;
- stockroom theft;
- display theft; and
- delivery theft, including use of company vehicle for personal use, false declaration of mileage and overtime.

Where retailers are using their staff and store to fulfil online orders and deliveries, there is the additional risk of collusion among store-based and delivery management and staff.

The market for stolen goods increased rapidly with the growth of eBay in the early 2000s. The onus was on retailers to prove that goods sold on the auction site were stolen, which meant monitoring hundreds of sales. Retailers both invested in software to detect and close down auctions of stolen goods, and collaborated to lobby eBay to make it harder to sell stolen goods on the auction website.

Retail theft exists beyond the confines of the store. For example, in 2007 one distribution depot manager was charged with stealing £40,000 worth of goods to sell on eBay (King, 2007).

Many employers condone small infringements of their code of employee conduct, such as appropriation of small items like pencils and pens for personal use, and personal use of the photocopier, e-mail, phone or Internet, all of which can foster a culture in which daily theft by employees is regarded as acceptable and the level of acceptable theft is difficult to determine.

12.3.3 Fraud

Retail fraud is the largest source of non-theft retail crime and the amount of loss to fraud has increased rapidly since the start of retail crime studies in 1992. Theft means that property is taken without the owner's consent. With fraud, the owner consents to part with the property (under the 1968 Theft Act); however, the consent is obtained by deceit, falsehood or other fraudulent means.

The 2006 Fraud Act extended and clarified provision for prosecuting fraud in the UK, defining the three major ways in which fraud is committed:

- by false representation;
- by failing to disclose information; or
- by abuse of position.

New fraud offences created within the 2006 Act include: obtaining services dishonestly; possessing, making and supplying articles for use in fraud; and fraudulent trading by non-corporate traders.

Payment card fraud includes credit and debit card fraud. There are different kinds of payment card fraud including card-present fraud (where the card owner presents the card for payment); card-not-present (CNP) fraud (where card details are given by phone, mail or Internet); stolen card fraud; mail-non-receipt fraud (where the card is intercepted by fraudsters en route to the owner); and counterfeit card fraud.

The level of card fraud varies according to retail sector. For example, the mixed retail, furniture and carpet sectors experience three times the UK retail average payment card fraud (BRC, 2001).

As the use of payment cards developed, the level of payment fraud caused so much concern that a nationwide chip & PIN initiative was rolled out across the UK retail scene in 2006. This initiative required customers to key in a unique PIN number when paying by card, and led to the halving of card-present fraud losses on retail transactions in the first four years. Other types of card fraud also declined, except for counterfeit and CNP fraud. The growth of Internet, catalogue, telephone and TV shopping increased the number of CNP transactions, exposing both retailers and customers to fraud on a larger scale. According to the Association for Payment Clearing Services (APACS), CNP fraud rose steeply after the chip & PIN initiative and in 2009 accounted for 54 per cent of all card fraud losses. However, the strong growth of online retail sales in the previous years was not matched by similar growth levels in CNP fraud (APACS, 2010).

Counterfeit money, another common type of fraud, accounted for 17 per cent of retail fraud in the UK in 2001. There was a marked increase in the year after a quarter of banknotes were removed from circulation between 2006 and 2007, particularly among notes of larger denominations such as £20 and £50 (BRC, 2001; Serious Organised Crime Agency, 2010).

There are two further common methods of fraud:

- fraudulent refunds: for example, claimed by staff who have retained receipts, or by customers who claim refunds for merchandise that has been bought and used; and
- price switch: in which the price of a lower-priced item is switched to a higher-priced item, the lower price being paid.

The 2009 BRC survey reported the type of fraud in the UK by value. According to its respondents, over 80 per cent of fraud was attributed almost equally to refund fraud and card-present fraud. CNP fraud was the third significant form of fraud experienced, accounting for 14 per cent of losses attributable to fraud (BRC, 2009). Supplier fraud and supply chain theft are also a significant issue for retailers.

12.3.4 External threats to retail security

The key external threats to retail security include burglary, criminal damage and robbery, which cause significant costs to retailers in terms of stock losses, repairs and staff time. Arson and terrorism pose a much lesser threat in terms of number of incidents although, like robbery, this class of incident poses a significant danger to retailers, as does violence. Verbal abuse and threats of violence, like robbery and some shoplifting incidents, pose real psychological and confidence problems for staff and can contribute to raised staff turnover, leading to higher recruitment, training costs and lower productivity. In the UK the annual retail crime survey tracks the trends (BRC, 2001, 2006, 2009).

12.3.4.1 Burglary

In the UK, nearly a fifth of all retail outlets are burgled per annum, and another tenth are subject to attempted burglary. However, the DIY and hardware sector, and food and drink stores experience much higher levels of this type of crime, with over 50 per cent of outlets burgled per annum. In 2006, electrical and electronics stores were also very susceptible to this type of crime: one fifth had experienced an increase in burglaries over the previous year. Although burglary is much less common than theft, the amount of loss per incident is much higher – in 2000 this was £1,800, with an extra £1,200 average repair costs per incident. Burglary also causes loss due to staff time and loss of trade during investigation and repairs. The number of burglaries decreased in subsequent years, although value of stock stolen increased substantially (2008/09 was an exception: the number of burglaries increased substantially, but value of stock stolen per incident was much lower). Burglary and attempted burglary are higher than average for small retailers in terms of the number of incidents and stock loss per incident, with small food and drink outlets most at risk.

12.3.4.2 Criminal damage

In 2000 this was a declining form of retail crime but nevertheless it accounted for a significant external threat to retail security, particularly for small retailers. Twenty-four cases occurred per 100 outlets, but the level for small retailers was nearly double that. Again, small food and drink outlets are most susceptible, with more than double the average rate. The 2006 BRC report classified arson with vandalism under the criminal damage crime category and indicated that this type of crime was increasing sharply at that time, particularly in convenience stores, DIY and hardware, and electrical and electronic stores. Between 2000 and 2008/09, the number of incidents nearly doubled. Nearly a third was damage through anti-social behaviour, with the rest the result of attempted burglary and robbery.

12.3.4.3 Robbery and till snatches

Food and drink retailers are most at risk of these crimes, with small food and drink outlets almost twice as likely as other retailers to experience robbery and till snatches. By 2006, this category of crime had doubled in terms of number of incidents per year. Violent robbery was also on the increase. 2008/09 brought another surge of robbery – like burglary, there were more incidents but less value stolen per incident.

12.3.4.4 Arson and terrorism

Incidents in these categories of crime are surprisingly numerous. In 2000, 2.5 cases of arson and 3.0 cases of terrorism occurred per 100 outlets. The cost per incident in these two categories doubled within a year from 1999. Terrorism includes use of explosives, hoax calls and evacuations. Arson was reclassified under criminal damage by 2006.

12.3.4.5 Violence and threats

Retail staff are at risk of physical violence, threat of physical violence and verbal abuse, which can injure them physically and psychologically. The main cause of physical violence to staff is theft. On average, five in every 1,000 retail employees experience physical violence, and a further 14 experience threats of violence. Staff in small retail organizations, and in large food and drink retail outlets, are much more at risk. For example, it is estimated that 195 out of 1,000 supermarket employees experience violent incidents per year (BRC, 2006).

12.4 The scale of retail crime

The scale of retail crime has been highlighted by various studies conducted since the early 1990s. The important factor to understand is that not only do stock losses impact on retail profitability, but there are significant costs involved in the various measures used to prevent retail crime.

The British Retail Crime Survey assesses such costs annually for UK retailers based on a survey of members of the BRC which include 44 retailers employing 1.4 million staff and accounting for 58 per cent of UK retail turnover annually (BRC, 2012a). The cost of crime to retailers in the UK was assessed as £1.6 billion in 2012.

The European Theft Barometer posted the results of a survey on retail crime statistics of retailers across Europe (including the UK) until 2006. From 2007 the Global Theft Barometer presented results of a global survey that included over 1,000 retailers across 43 countries. The results were grossed to represent the size of each national retail market. When the research was taken over by Euromonitor International the scale of the research was reduced. However, the interviews and survey still included 157 companies with 160,000 stores generating over US$1.5 trillion sales across 16 countries (Euromonitor International, 2013).

It is important to note that the European and Global Theft Barometers attributed sources of retail crime differently from the BRC, and that the results of both surveys have to be viewed with caution, not least because retailers can be reluctant to highlight security issues that can be perceived as weakness. Nevertheless, both surveys concurred that coordinated efforts to highlight retail industry crime as a political issue, to share data and best practice, effectively lowered the costs of crime for retailers during the early years of the twenty-first century leading up to the global recession (BRC, 2006; CRR, 2006).

In 2009, the Global Theft Barometer reported shrinkage of $114,823 million from the 1,000+ retailers surveyed across 41 countries. Some $24.5 billion was spent in retail crime prevention. A downward trend in shrinkage was evident until the year 2008/09. One of the impacts of the recession was a sharp increase in shoplifting across almost all countries. Figure 12.1 shows key sources of shrinkage according to the Global Theft Barometer in 2009. Customer theft continued to increase in the following years, accounting for 43.2 per cent of shrinkage in 2011 despite an increasing spend on prevention ($28 billion) (CRR, 2012).

In addition to customer theft, staff theft and fraud, the BRC now breaks down retail crime into the following categories: burglary, criminal damage and robbery. Figure 12.2 displays losses attributable to the various forms of retail crime in the UK. Customer theft, staff theft and fraud are the three key sources of crime, with customer theft the most troublesome for retailers, accounting for 83 per cent of incidents. A new category of crime was surveyed in 2012 – e-crime, involving card and CNP fraud, identification-related fraud

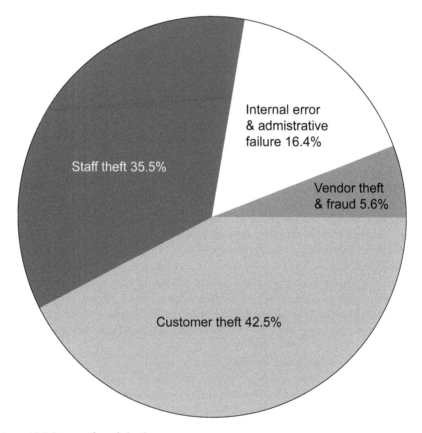

Figure 12.1 Sources of retail shrinkage
Source: CRR, 2009.

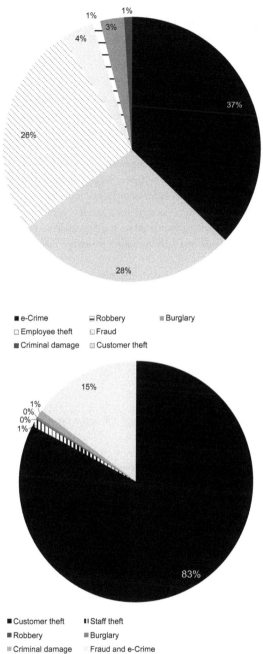

Figure 12.2 UK retail crime by cost and number of incidents, 2011/12
Source: After BRC, 2012a.

such as account takeovers and refund fraud. According to the BRC survey in 2012, e-crime cost retailers more than any other single category of crime.

12.5 Factors affecting retail crime

In section 12.2 it was shown that retail shrinkage was affected by management policy and practice, by retailer size and by retail sector. As the major component of retail shrinkage is crime, low levels of shoplifting, staff theft and fraud are indicators of good store management and retail leadership.

Retail crime is linked to catchment composition and location of stores. In a simple example, a store located in a catchment featuring high population density and high levels of unemployment might be expected to experience higher levels of shoplifting than a store in a prosperous area. Similarly, a store located on a corner with entrances on two sides is more exposed to risk of shoplifting than a store in a pedestrianized shopping area with one entrance. Therefore, for a large retail group, target shrinkage rates for managers will reflect this.

The risk of retail crime also varies with the size and category of store and occasional studies highlight these issues. For example, one BRC survey published risk rates by retail category of the various forms of crime. Some types of retailer in the UK faced above-average risk of customer theft, such as (BRC, 2001):

- department stores;
- food and drink retailers; and
- mixed retail businesses.

The risk of staff theft was also above average for some types of retailer, such as:

- department stores;
- booksellers and CTNs (confectionery, tobacco and newsagents);
- chemists;
- DIY and hardware; and
- food and drink retailers.

The level of theft experienced (and the amount spent on crime prevention) is related to the size of store. In the UK, larger formats such as department stores and grocery superstores attract increasing numbers of organized thieves (CRR, 2009).

In 2006 the BRC focused especially on risk rates for small and medium-sized enterprises (SMEs) in the UK. SME retailers, which employ up to 250 staff, were particularly at risk of customer theft if they operated book, stationery and entertainment stores. The cost of customer theft in this category was twice as high as that of SME retailers operating department and mixed goods stores. On the other hand, the latter category experienced the highest losses from staff theft and fraud, followed by DIY and hardware retailers, and book, stationery and entertainment retailers. This type of data is useful in helping SME retailers to make decisions on what type of measures to take to combat crime.

Fraud can be considered theft by deception, and is sometimes categorized under theft, so estimates of the scale of retail fraud vary. The results of a 2006 study into financial and retail fraud (Bamfield, 2006) indicated that retailers should be concerned about employees with links to organized crime; corruption and coercion of employees; call centre and CNP fraud; and large-scale theft of personal consumer and card data.

As the use of payment cards developed, the level of payment fraud caused so much concern that in 2006 a nationwide chip & PIN initiative was developed, as described above. Face-to-face card fraud was halved in a year, and there was a reduction in the overall level of plastic card fraud. However, retailers selling online were faced with a different challenge. In the same year, CNP fraud, which had been growing strongly since the advent of transactional websites, accounted for more than half of all card fraud losses.

Again, risk of payment card fraud varies with retail category. An early survey of payment card fraud indicated that mixed retail businesses, furniture textiles and carpets, department stores and footwear and leather goods retailers were at particular risk (BRC, 2001).

The proportional costs of other important causes of UK retail crime are shown in Figure 12.2. All these categories of crime declined between 2003 and 2005, although for each category, some types of retailer experienced the opposite trend. The most volatile category is criminal damage. Falls in the cost of damage to some types of retailer (such as electrical and entertainment) where online purchase of merchandise has risen strongly have surpassed strong rises in damage to convenience stores. Convenience stores also experienced a rise in robbery rates, while robbery from clothing, footwear and supermarkets declined. Although there was a fall in the cost of till snatches, convenience stores, DIY and hardware and electrical retailers all experienced rises in this category of crime.

The rise in overall plastic card fraud as use of plastic cards developed can be seen in Figure 12.3. This includes all the main forms of fraud related to plastic cards, including lost/stolen and counterfeit card fraud, CNP fraud, mail-non-receipt fraud and identity theft. The UK experienced high growth in online shopping in the first decade of the

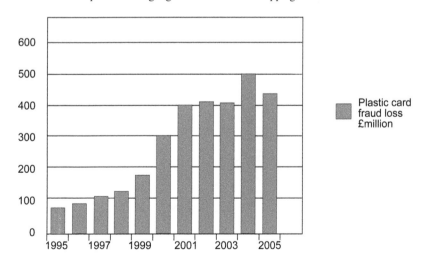

Figure 12.3 Plastic card fraud – UK-issued cards

twenty-first century but focus and publicity on dealing with card fraud led to a decline in all forms of CNP fraud from 2008 to 2011. This was followed by a surge in fraud the following year (see Figure 12.4) (The UK Cards Association, 2013).

A rapidly developing online retail market that includes multiple ways to shop online and multiple payment technologies brings opportunity for fraudsters, which requires multi-party cooperation in developing defensive solutions to deter criminals. Figure 12.5 gives a picture of the complexity of the 'ecosystem' surrounding mobile payment for goods.

12.6 Dealing with store theft (UK)

12.6.1 Definitions of theft and powers of arrest

Due to differences in legal systems, there are variations in definitions of the crime experienced by retailers, and in how retailers and the legal process interpret and deal with crime. For example, even within the UK, the crimes most commonly suffered by retailers are defined and dealt with slightly differently in Scotland from in England.

In England, theft is dealt with by statute under the Theft Act 1968. It is defined as 'dishonest appropriation of property belonging to another with the intention of permanently depriving the other of it'. In Scotland, theft is a common law (law based not on statutes, but on precedent set by judgments in cases) offence, defined as 'the felonious

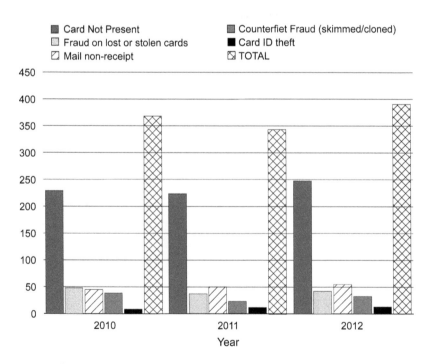

Figure 12.4 Plastic card fraud, 2009–12 (£ million): UK-issued cards

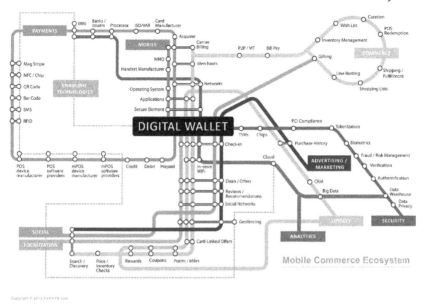

Figure 12.5 The mobile commerce ecosystem
Source: Payments Cards and Mobile, 2013.

taking or appropriation of the property of another without the consent of the owner and with intent to deprive him of that property'.

Both definitions, however, include the same basic elements:

- the thief acted dishonestly;
- the property was appropriated by the thief;
- the property belongs to another; and
- the intention was to permanently deprive the owner of the property.

In both England and Scotland the law allows ordinary citizens the power to arrest anyone who has committed an offence for which they may be sentenced on first indictment to five or more years in prison. Theft belongs in this category of offence, and therefore ordinary citizens have the power to arrest any individual who has committed a theft.

Power to arrest is slightly different in each country. In England, the Police and Criminal Evidence Act 1984 states that 'any person may arrest without warrant anyone who is, or whom he with reasonable cause suspects to be, in the act of committing an arrestable offence'. In Scotland, the power of arrest is provided under common law and under the Civic Government (Scotland) Act 1982, section 7: 'any citizen witnessing a crime may apprehend the criminal, but must not do so on suspicion or information'.

In Scotland, therefore, the power to arrest is more limited than in England. Whereas in England a citizen's arrest for theft can be carried out of anyone whom the arresting person 'with reasonable cause suspects to be in the act of committing an ... offence', in Scotland only persons who have actually *witnessed* the offence being committed can make an arrest.

Box 12.1 Penalties for theft

Both definitions of and penalties for theft vary from country to country. The information below portrays the range of penalties for theft experienced by retail thieves in England and Wales.

Of 61,670 adult offenders (aged 18 and over) sentenced for theft from a shop, the majority (97 per cent) were sentenced in a magistrates' court. Of those sentenced:

- 16,448 (27 per cent) were given an absolute or conditional discharge;
- 13,519 (22 per cent) a fine;
- 16,613 (27 per cent) a community sentence;
- 13,135 (21 per cent) custody; and
- 1,955 (3 per cent) were otherwise dealt with.

Of those sentenced to a community sentence, 56 per cent received a community rehabilitation order, 19 per cent received a drug treatment and testing order, and 15 per cent received a community punishment. Only 22 offenders received sentences of over two years and only one was sentenced to more than four years in prison.

Source: Sentencing Advisory Panel, 2004.

12.6.2 Dealing with a shop thief

Larger retail organizations have clear guidelines for staff on what to do when dealing with a person suspected of shoplifting, and train staff how to deal with this type of situation.

General UK guidelines include:

- Be sure the person has the item(s) still with them.
- Be sure you witnessed the theft and kept the suspect under continuous observation.
- Be careful to have a second member of staff there to assist, and to act as a witness to what is said and done when you deal with the suspect.
- Wait until the suspect has passed all points of payment and/or left the store.
- Tell the suspect who you and your witness are. State your job title and show an ID if possible. Take care that the suspect is given no reason to complain about assault.
- Say 'I am employed by ... I have reason to believe that you have goods in your possession which you have not paid for. Will you please return to the store'. Describe the article(s) and clearly state the name of the store.
- If he/she refuses, you can carry out a citizen's arrest. Tell the suspect you are 'making a citizen's arrest for theft'.

- If the suspect tries to escape you can use the minimum amount of force necessary to restrain him/her.
- Note that if you do not inform the suspect of the citizen's arrest and the reason, he/she could bring a charge of assault against you.
- Return to the store. One member of staff should lead the way, and the other follow the suspect to make sure that the merchandise (evidence) is not thrown away.
- Take the suspect to an office or room. Make sure that there is a member of staff of the same sex as the suspect with him/her at all times.
- Ask the suspect to declare goods he/she has not paid for and to empty pockets and/or bags. If he/she refuses you have no power to search him/her.
- If the suspect asks you to search him/her, do not comply.
- Call the police to prosecute. Keep the suspect under observation all the time to make sure that the stolen articles are not dumped.
- On arrival of the police, outline the circumstances to them in the presence and hearing of the suspect.
- Keep a record book to record details of all incidents in a locked cupboard. Record all details of the offence, including date, time, names and offices held by witnesses, name, address, age and full description of suspect, full description of stolen items, full description of the arrest and the numbers of police officers present.

Do not:

- Leave suspect on his/her own.
- Lock suspect in a room.
- Let suspect take pills or medicine, or smoke.
- Let suspect get between you and the door.
- Get into conversation with the suspect.
- Accept payment for any goods.
- Accuse the suspect.
- Question the suspect in public.

If there are any doubts regarding theft, it is recommended that no action is taken because if a person is arrested wrongfully they may take legal action. If the suspect is physically threatening it is wise to let the suspect escape and to inform the police, who are able to arrest a person on suspicion of theft, and both to search and detain the suspect.

12.6.3 Statements and evidence

Evidence, which is the means of proving or disproving the truth of a matter under judicial examination, is used to prove whether or not a crime has been committed, and also whether the accused committed the crime. Evidence must prove that the person is guilty of theft 'beyond all reasonable doubt'. Therefore, to make a prosecution, the person who saw and heard the theft has to give direct evidence, sometimes on oath in court.

There are three types of evidence:

- oral evidence from an eye witness;
- documentary evidence – for example, a written statement of events, photograph or official records; and
- real evidence, which is any article involved in a crime, including goods stolen.

For example, in Scotland, under common law, there has to be corroboration of evidence – two pieces of evidence that support each other. (Please note that at the time of writing, in 2014, the need for corroboration was under review.) This can be provided by two or more direct eye witnesses or by one eye witness supported by indirect or circumstantial evidence, such as goods stolen or CCTV evidence, or supported by sufficient indirect evidence to conclude the guilt of the accused.

In England, under the Police and Criminal Evidence Act 1984, the rules for evidence are similar to those in Scotland, except that it is not always necessary to have corroboration. However, corroboration does strengthen the case.

Box 12.2 Dealing with young people

Young people have to be deterred from retail theft. A young shoplifter is very likely to turn into a law-abiding adult and a criminal record will affect their job and career prospects. In both England and Scotland it is rare for children under the age of 14 to be prosecuted for shoplifting. However, in Scotland, the age at which a child can be found guilty of an offence is eight years old; in England it is ten years old. In Scotland, children under 16 years charged with a criminal offence will have their case dealt with by a special Children's Panel, which can order custodial and other types of sentence. Children have the right of appeal to a higher court.

In England, the penalty for theft ranges from a verbal or written caution to ten years' imprisonment; the range of penalties is shown in Box 12.1. In Scotland, all arrests and their circumstances are referred to the Procurator Fiscal's Office by the arresting officers. At this level lies the decision to proceed further, to issue a caution, to send a report to the Reporter of the Children's Panel or to prosecute in court.

12.7 Retail loss prevention

Retail crime in the UK costs well over £1 billion a year. This figure includes both losses and expenditure on crime prevention. Investment in prevention measures has been increasing. Figure 12.6 shows the breakdown of expenditure.

The 2009 BRC survey assessed the crime prevention measures receiving increased investment among UK retailers. These included: CCTV (live and hidden); shoplifting deterrence signage; plain-clothes detectives; secured display fittings and radio-frequency identification (RFID) tagging (used by about half of all retailers).

This true cost of crime prevention also includes other measures required to reduce crime, such as employee recruitment methods and screening, investment in staff retention,

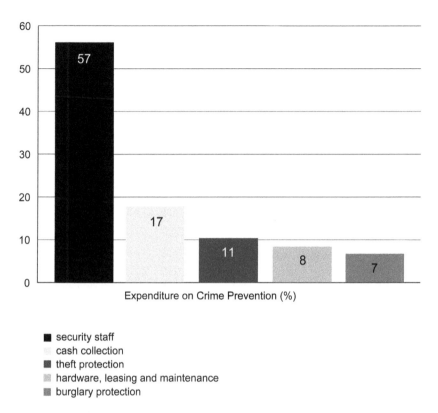

Figure 12.6 Expenditure on crime prevention
Source: BRC, 2001.

reduction in employment of part-time staff, and training in retail crime and security plus supervisory and management skills. Retailers know that motivated, trained and retained staff can reduce customer and staff theft, in addition to spotting and dealing efficiently with external threats to security.

There are three main categories of methods for retail crime prevention that retailers can employ to combat customer and staff theft, fraud and external threats to security:

- human;
- mechanical; and
- electronic.

A range of examples of each category is shown in Table 12.1.

A wide variety of methods of deterrent is available within each category, and many are used to counteract a range of crimes. Many of the human deterrents (for example, store layout; policies, procedures and audits; display security; credit and employment checks during recruitment; staff awareness; and training in security) are no more than good retail

Table 12.1 Human, mechanical and electronic loss deterrents

Human	Mechanical	Electronic
Employee screening	Mirrors	Loop alarms
Honesty testing	Screens and grilles	Electronic article surveillance tags
Security training	Shutters	Scanners
Supervisory and management training	Cages	Lighting
Security staff and plain-clothes police	Locks	CCTV
Staffing levels	Lockers	Dummy cameras
Procedures for storage/disposal of risk items such as invoice/receipt pads, delivery details and addresses, scrap credit card vouchers	Bells	Radio links
Staff alertness and reporting procedures	Security cases	Secure payment applications (online fraud)
Audits	Chains	Burglar alarms
Public posting of loss levels	Display cabinets	RFID tags
Monitoring averages, shortages and voids	Security doors/glass	Data mining
Design of unit and shop layout	Shoplifting deterrence signage	
Cash collection and routing methods		
Banking procedures		
Exit and alarm procedures		
Integrity shoppers		
Goods reception and display procedures		
Searches		
Risk assessments		
Rewards		
Drug courts		
Cooperative efforts such as retail crime		
Partnerships and retail crime conferences		

management practice, and are cheap to deploy. One research study found, for instance, that regular public posting of loss levels reduced crime (Oliphant and Oliphant, 2001). According to a later industry survey, retailers concur (BRC, 2009).

Other deterrents require retailers to act together to drive down crime through the sharing of crime/criminal information and security best practice. For example, Retail Crime Partnerships encourage retailers to identify local criminals through photographs, radio links and CCTV.

A different level of deterrence involves retailers joining with other local, regional and national agencies. For example, Retailers Against Crime (RAC) was set up in Scotland in 1997 to share information on crime and detection of criminals; information is shared among members, UK Police and Retail Crime Partnerships. RACs were later launched in the north-east and north-west regions of England. Liaison with crime-prevention agencies from outside the regions is essential in tackling organized criminal gangs operating in multiple regions. Getting involved with tackling the underpinning reasons for crime is also helpful. In Scotland, it is estimated that 50 per cent of retail crime is drug related (in some areas the proportion is much higher), and the frequency of drug-related crime, together with its potential for associated violence and threats, further impacts on one of the generators of staff crime – poor recruitment procedures and high staff turnover: 'There is a direct link between drug use, theft from shops and violence and intimidation towards employees, which poses problems for the recruitment and retention of staff' (Clarke, 2001).

Charities such as Drug Abuse Resistance Education are aimed at reducing drug usage and associated crime, and Drug Courts provide an alternative way to deal with drug-related offenders.

Civil recovery is an initiative widely used in the USA and Canada, in which retailers obtain compensation from those who commit crimes such as theft, fraud and criminal damage. Commitment of any crime also involves a tort, or wrongdoing under civil law, for which the person or organization affected by the crime can claim damages. Shortly after the offender is arrested, the retailer sends out a civil demand, which includes the circumstances of the crime, legal position and a claim for damages. These can include the cost of goods, investigation, security relating to the arrest and costs of the civil demand process itself. The offender also faces criminal prosecution. Civil recovery seems poised for growth in the UK as a means of deterring retail crime. The Proceeds of Crime Act 2002 provided for civil recovery in the UK. There is a retailer-run National Civil Recovery Programme in England and Wales, while in Scotland a national Civil Recovery Unit was set up.

There is a ready market for products stolen from retailers, and many otherwise law-abiding people will purchase tagged merchandise, fraudulently branded merchandise and branded merchandise sold at unrealistically low prices from market stalls, informal markets or online. In 2001 a Market Reduction Approach was put forward by the Home Office, aimed at reducing the market for stolen goods. This proposed measures such as more vigorous prosecution of those handling stolen goods and a marketing campaign to change public thinking that the buying of stolen goods is a victimless crime (Sutton *et al.*, 2001).

New shopping centres and new retail units have the opportunity for customized security solutions. Secured by Design is a scheme intended to provide adequate security based on police crime prevention experience of the particular locality of the retail development, with architectural liaison officers charged with approving developments to the Secured by Design standard. Considerations include boundary definition through walls, fences, landscaping or psychological barriers such as changes in road surface, rumble strips and use of colour to delineate 'private' areas. Landscaping can be used to enhance security, for example through densely planted thorny bushes to deter entry to certain areas. Physical security of doors, windows and locks can be designed into the plan, and higher levels of lighting applied to areas such as loading bays and fire exits, where security is especially important. There are also basic specifications for burglar alarm wiring that should be incorporated into all commercial premises.

Over half of intrusions occur via doors and another third via windows. Mechanical deterrents include the wide variety of grilles, shutters and screens that can be used to bar entry to the unit or sections of the unit where high-value stock is located. Mirrors can be used to enable staff surveillance of the shop floor, or management/security staff surveillance of staff and customers, and bells can be used to warn of theft or emergency. Security can be built into new units in the form of secure locking systems for external doors, laminated glass used in glazed doors and glazed panels adjacent to door locks, locking handles and opening restrictors to accessible windows (Scottish Office, 1996).

According to Hollinger (2008), the use of technological solutions to manage shrinkage, including electronic tagging and surveillance, has been instrumental in lowering shrinkage levels. Electronic deterrence devices, such as mobile wireless systems, allow discrete messages to be sent between stores and security staff to warn of shoplifters or secure emergency help. In addition to combating crime, these contribute towards staff confidence in their own security. CCTV and point-of-sale closed-circuit television (POSCCTV) allow retailers and security providers to monitor customer, staff and stock movements. If live monitoring is not feasible, it enables investigation or proof of theft on stored film. That this is an effective means of combating retail crime is indisputable, with benefits in terms of detection and evidence of crime and in terms of enhancement of customers' perception of security. However, concerns regarding the infringement of civil liberty and misuse of information were addressed through The Data Protection Act 1998, which established eight principles of data protection with which controllers of CCTV have to comply:

1   Personal information shall be processed fairly and lawfully.
2   Personal data shall be obtained only for one or more specified and lawful purposes and shall not be further processed in any manner incompatible with that purpose or purposes.
3   Personal data shall be adequate, relevant and not excessive in relation to the purpose or purposes.
4   Personal data shall be accurate and, where necessary, kept up to date.
5   Personal data processed for any purpose or purposes shall not be kept for longer than is necessary for that purpose or purposes.
6   Personal data shall be processed in accordance with the rights of data subjects under this Act.
7   Appropriate technical and organisational measures shall be taken against unauthorised or unlawful processing of personal data and against accidental loss or destruction of, or damage to, personal data.

8   Personal data shall not be transferred to a country or territory outside the European Economic Area unless that country or territory ensures an adequate level of protection for the rights and freedoms of data subjects.

As a result of this Act, controllers of CCTV had to take care of:

- assessment of the purpose of its usage;
- notification of its usage with the Office of the Information Commissioner;
- establishment and documentation of security and disclosure policies;
- location of cameras;
- notification of usage;
- access to data by data subjects;
- retention of images;
- access to and disclosure of CCTV images; and
- quality of the images.

Online retailers have to consider carefully how customer data are stored and used. Guidance is available via The Privacy and Electronic Communications (EC Directive) Regulations 2003 and their later amendments. Online customers are also protected via Distance Selling Regulations (2000) and Electronic Commerce Regulations (2002).

A variety of electronic tagging devices have been developed to combat theft. Sale items are tagged with tags removed or deactivated on purchase. Pedestals are installed at exit points that trigger an alarm should an item be taken through that has not been 'de-tagged'. Electronic data tags, or intelligent tags, which support storage of article information, can provide further applications aimed at improving retail and supply chain efficiency. Although there is a range of technologies involved (including electromagnetic, radio-frequency and acoustic magnetic), they are all devices that signal their presence and transmit data. Both retailers and electronic article surveillance (EAS) suppliers envisage a future in which items for sale are data-tagged at source or integrated during manufacture, and packaging tagged, using a range of low-cost tags containing information about the merchandise – for example, product and batch number, price, date and so on. The amount of source-tagged merchandise is increasing, with over 20 per cent of all merchandise in the USA and Europe that is tagged, being tagged at source (CRR, 2012).

Intelligent tags perform multiple functions in controlling retail and distribution operations. These include not only combating theft for a wide range of merchandise but also controlling movement of goods, controlling inventory and providing customer information, for example for household inventory and reordering.

There are a number of technological issues to be considered in developing tags with the potential to transmit significant amounts of data, but a basic specification includes four key requirements:

- data must be accessible consistently, accurately and from a distance;
- control of data/interface/communications;
- data storage; and
- energy source.

Other issues include tag security (elimination of mistakes in reading tag data), tag value (the added value to retailers provided by investment in electronic data tagging), and standardization. As technology issues were addressed, and more (and larger) organizations entered the electronic data tagging market, prices were expected to come down to the level where they are applicable to fast-moving consumer goods organizations (CRR, 2002b).

RFID is regarded as the key to visibility and hence security in the supply chain because tags are embedded in the products and inappropriate movement of products can be traced. For example, Tesco used RFID, CCTV and a smart shelf system run with Gillette to track stock movement of a type of product that experiences high levels of theft (Fernie and Sparks, 2009).

Online fraud is also being tackled through a variety of screening devices and electronic deterrents. In the pre-payment phase measures include checks on the payment card, including authorization, address verification and card security check data (Growcott, 2009; BRC, 2009). One measure is the secure payment application, which is the equivalent of a cardholder signature in which a pop-up window appears on screen where the buyer enters the password. This scheme, introduced by MasterCard, requires cardholders, retailers and banks dealing with the card to work together within an integrated system.

A similar system is in use by MasterCard's rival, Visa. Called Verified by Visa, this was first used in the USA, before being introduced to the UK. With this system, the buyer types a password into the website, then the card-holding bank verifies the identity of the cardholder and notifies the retailer to go ahead with the sale.

Card verification devices are already in use by some banks and may well come into use by online retailers in the future. Here customers are issued with a card reader. They enter their PIN number and the reader issues a unique code authorizing the transaction. However, retailers may be reluctant to introduce an extra barrier to online transactions. Digital signatures are a third means of authorizing payment, and there could also be potential to exploit an online version of authorization by thumbprint, which was a precursor of chip & PIN.

In the payment phase fraud deterrents include real-time authorization, in which credit card information is sent to the processor for approval; a check is made that it is not lost, stolen or has inadequate funds, and authorized or rejected within seconds. There is no proof that the card belongs to the person using it, so a further deterrent is required in the form of an address verification system that checks the address of the cardholder is correct (Growcott, 2009). Nearly 60 per cent of retailers use the card verification method to verify that the card (not just the number) is in the hands of the purchaser; this involves entering the three- or four-digit security code on the back of the card during the checkout process (BRC, 2009).

12.8 Summary

Retail crime has developed as a major issue for collaboration within the retail industry only relatively recently, during which retailers and associated agencies such as (in the UK) the BRC and the Scottish Grocers' Federation have developed collaborative initiatives to combat crime. Retail crime and shrinkage statistics are published annually, which retailers can use as a benchmark for their own levels of crime and security.

Customer theft accounts for a high proportion of retail crime. Drug use, youth and male gender are three factors closely associated with customer theft, and most customer theft could be classified under three headings: organized gang theft, opportunistic theft and peer-related youth theft. Staff theft is a second significant form of retail crime. Staff theft, including staff collusion with customer and supplier thieves, is also a fast-growing sector of retail crime, and is associated with inadequate management, poor pay, high staff turnover and high rates of part-time staff – all features of many retail organizations. Fraud is the third largest source of crime in retailing, with CNP fraud particularly fast developing as technology and the ways of shopping online multiply. External sources of crime including burglary, robbery/till snatches, criminal damage, arson and terrorism constitute a small percentage of overall retail crime.

The BRC publishes data on types of crime by retail sector and size of organization. Customer crime, for example, constitutes a much higher proportion of retail crime for small retailers than for large multiple retailers, whereas the latter experience a much higher level of employee crime. Department stores and mixed retail businesses experience higher than average customer and staff theft, whereas the furniture, textiles and carpet sector experienced lower than average customer theft but more than average levels of fraud. Retailers that diversify their merchandise ranges and multiply the ways their customers can shop, therefore, have to be prepared for changes in the nature and level of retail crime they experience.

Retail loss deterrents can be classified under three main headings: human, mechanical and electronic. While many security measures are easy and cheap to deploy, a high proportion of expenditure on retail security in the UK is directed towards security staff and cash collections. The published spend on deterrence does not include investment in most of the other 'human' methods of combating crime, although, given the rising levels of employee crime, retailers should give consideration to measures including stricter pre-employment screening, management and security training, and boosting staff loyalty. Collaboration is a growing feature of retail security, both in securing, publishing and sharing information on retail crime, and in developing a wide variety of preventative measures.

Review questions

1 Explain to the operator of a small local multiple retailer the reasons why it is essential to cooperate with other retailers and agencies in combating crime.
2 Discuss the reasons why a retailer should consider multiple categories of loss deterrent.
3 Why should retailers and the retail industry become involved in tackling the underlying causes of retail crime?
4 Discuss the restrictions on use of CCTV for a retailer.
5 Explain the multiple functions performed by intelligent tags in controlling retail and distribution operations.
6 Discuss the reasons why employee theft is so difficult to detect and prevent.

Case study: Games4kids

Games4kids is a well-established Midlands-based growing retailer of toys and games with ten outlets in large towns (over 100,000 population) across the Midlands. Originally the organization specialized in toys and games for early years and primary school children. The range was extended over time to include adult and executive games and toys, electronic toys and then video games and consoles. Internet kiosks were set up in the two largest outlets, and at the same time a section of each store was set aside to try out the sale of mobile phones and accessories. More recently, Games4kids had developed a click-and-collect facility for online customers.

Store sizes are between 200 and 400 sq. metres and most are located in corner 'high street' positions close to the centre of central business districts. Generally there are two entrances, which helps to generate footfall and allow display windows on two sides of each store. None of the stores is more than 200 metres from a bus station or car park, and several are near railway stations. The population is many millions with the necessary infrastructure to enable population movements. For example, there is a dense road, motorway, bus and train network. The aim of Games4kids' owner is that every potential customer can reach an outlet by car, bus or train within 30 minutes of starting their journey. Car parks lie next to three of the outlets. The development of out-of-town retail parks have adversely affected three of the towns with Games4kids stores – there has been a cycle of town centre deterioration, leaving many shops empty and reducing footfall and turnover in these outlets.

For the last ten years or so, an increasing number of customers have shopped in Games4kids' online store, which can be accessed via computer and mobile technology. Goods are delivered within 48 hours, using a regional express delivery firm. The online store is well maintained, with a growing turnover despite intense competition from Amazon and Argos.

The retailer's customers are primarily young: 70 per cent are between 18 and 30; 65 per cent are male, 35 per cent female. In addition, the stores attract parents and young children looking for pocket-money toys.

A few years ago, Games4kids set up a loyalty card scheme, offering a store card to all customers over the age of 16. This lets customers gain points that can be used to purchase goods or discounts on goods. The information collected has been used to set up a customer database and special promotions are offered to loyal customers several times a year. They are also invited to the launch of major new lines and services.

Games4kids is careful about staff recruitment and focuses on retention. John and Joan MacIver, the owners until retirement last year, took great pride in developing and motivating their workforce and employed an internal promotion scheme. A thriving social club arranged walking and cycling trips. More recently the club has been arranging outings to clubs in Birmingham and Manchester. There is high unemployment across most of the region. Although low, salaries are similar to those offered by other small multiple retailers. Staff are given the opportunity to supplement their basic wage by attaining predetermined sales objectives. Staff also gain an extra day's holiday for every two years of service for the first six years of their employment. After ten years they can take a six-week unpaid holiday. There is also a bursary scheme available to support further education.

The retailer is committed to social inclusion, racial and gender equality. Recently, two long-term unemployed people have been trained and offered full-time jobs and the company tries to ensure an equal balance of male and female employees. Most staff belong to a variety of ethnic minority groups. No employee is over 40 – most are between 16 and 30 years old. Employees are encouraged to recommend friends or relations for vacancies. Staff turnover at 17 per cent remains high, but it is actually less of a problem for Games4kids than for other regional retailers.

Training is 'on the job' by staff and supervisors, but a checklist has been carefully devised so all staff receive the same training. Completion of basic training is marked by the Games4kids Retail Certificate. For some staff this is their first ever qualification. One of the early jobs taken by new staff is picking for online orders. As staff are promoted from within, supervisors and most managers have been promoted people who joined the company as new recruits. Recently, however, the McIvers' son Ian, who took over the business on his parents' retirement, employed two of his friends as managers of the largest outlets. Naturally, those staff aiming for promotion were not very pleased.

The company cannot afford dedicated security staff. It is the job of all staff to be vigilant for shop thieves. The stores are included in ring-around systems in their local town centres, which means they inform and are informed about the movements and presence of suspected thieves. Games4kids feel their recruitment and retention policy makes staff crime unlikely. In order to promote quick sales, in Games4kids stores all games and toys are physically displayed. This means there is some opportunistic shoplifting by schoolchildren; however, the owners felt that the extra volume sales generated more than compensated for the losses sustained, and that loss was minimized anyway by staff vigilance.

Until recently, Games4kids' shrinkage rate was reasonably steady and certainly in line with the average for this type of retail business. In the last year or so the situation has changed, however. Two members of staff in separate stores have been attacked on their way to the bank with money, and one member of staff has been off ill since being assaulted by a gang of shop thieves who made off with thousands of pounds' worth of stock. There have been several break-ins and one store was broken into repeatedly. Losses from three of the stores have risen by 6–8 per cent. Staff turnover has also doubled in a short period of time.

The development of a new regional shopping centre within the Midlands has led to much discussion among the previous owners, their son and the managers of the two largest stores about consolidation of a number of units into one large unit within the new shopping centre. Meanwhile, stock loss has increased to the level where the owner now feels a full investigation is needed into the real and potential causes of the increase in levels of loss.

1   If you were investigating the increased shrinkage rates experienced by this organization, what are the potential causes you would suggest?

References

Association of Payment Clearing Services (APACS) (2010) 'New card and banking fraud figures', www. theukcardsassociation.org.uk/media_centre/press_releases_new/-/page/922/.

Bamfield, J. (2004) 'Shrinkage, shoplifting and the cost of retail crime in Europe: a cross-sectional analysis of major retailers in 16 European countries', *International Journal of Retail & Distribution Management*, 32(5): 235–241.

Bamfield, J. (2005) 'The gender offenders', Centre for Retail Research, www.retailresearch.org/downloads/PDF/female_offenders.pdf (accessed 3 August 2014).

Bamfield, J. (2006) *Sed quis custodiet? Employee Theft in UK Retailing*, Nottingham: Centre for Retail Research.

Bamfield, J. (2007) *Global Retail Theft Barometer*. Nottingham: Centre for Retail Research.

British Retail Consortium (BRC) (2001) *8th Retail Crime Survey 2000*.

British Retail Consortium (BRC) (2006) *Retail Crime Survey 2005–2006*.

British Retail Consortium (BRC) (2009) *Retail Crime Survey 2009*.

British Retail Consortium (BRC) (2012a) *Retail Crime Survey 2011/12*. www.brc.org.uk/ePublica tions/BRC_Retail_Crime_Survey_2012/index.html#/9/zoomed (accessed 2 December 2013).

British Retail Consortium (BRC) (2012b) *Counting the Cost of e-Crime*, www.brc.org.uk/downloads/Counting_the_cost_of_e-crime.pdf (accessed 11 November 2013).

British Retail Consortium (BRC) (2013) *Retail Crime Survey 2012*, www.brc.org.uk/downloads/brc_retail_crime_survey_2012.pdf (accessed 6 January 2013).

Browcott, S. (2010) 'Retail fraud and recommended defensive measures', *Internet Business Law Services*, www.ibls.com/internet_law_news_portal_view.aspx?s=sa&id=1819 (accessed 11 November 2013).

Card Watch (2007) 'The cost of card fraud', www.cardwatch.org.uk/default.asp?sectionid=5&pageid=123&Title=Cost_Of_Card_Fraud (accessed November 2007).

Centre for Retail Research (CRR) (2002a) www.retailing.uk.com/report2.html.

Centre for Retail Research (CRR) (2002b) 'Electronic data tags', www.retailing.uk.com/report6.html.

Centre for Retail Research (CRR) (2005) *The European Retail Theft Barometer*.

Centre for Retail Research (CRR) (2006) *The European Retail Theft Barometer*.

Centre for Retail Research (CRR) (2007) *The European Retail Theft Barometer*.

Centre for Retail Research (CRR) (2009) 'Key findings from the global theft barometer', www.reta ilresearch.org/global_theft_baromter/2009keyfindings.php.

Centre for Retail Research (CRR) (2012) 'Global retail theft barometer 2011', www.west-info.eu/files/www.retailresearch.org_grtb_currentsurvey.php_1.pdf (accessed 11 November 2013).

Clarke, M. (2001) 'Dealing with users', *Retail Week Crime and Security Report*, October.

Euromonitor International (2013) 'The new barometer', globalretailtheftbarometer.com (accessed 2 December 2013).

Fernie, J. and Sparks, L. (2009) *Logistics and Retail Management* (3rd edn). London: Kogan Page.

Goodchild, J. (2009) 'Q&A Richard Hollinger on shoplifting and retail shrink', *CSO*, www.csoonline.com/article/461365/Richard_Hollinger_on_Shoplifting_and_Retail_Shrink?page=1 (accessed 2009).

Growcott, S. (2009) 'Online retail fraud and recommended defensive measures', *Internet Business Law Services*, www.ibls.com/internet_law_news_portal_view.aspx?s=sa&id=1819 (accessed 2009).

Hollinger, R. (2008) *National Retail Security Survey Final Report*. Gainesville: University of Florida.

Hollinger, R.C. and Hayes, R. (1992) *National Retail Security Survey: Final Report (with Executive Summary)*. Gainesville: University of Florida.

King, L. (2007) 'Going, going, gone', *Supply Chain Standard*, April, www.orisgroup.co.uk/documents/0704SupplyChain.pdf.

Ministry of Justice (2010) 'Ministry of Justice Statistics Quarterly Update to December 2010', *Ministry of Justice Statistics Bulletin*, www.gov.uk/government/uploads/system/uploads/attachment_data/file/217704/criminal-stats-quarterly-dec10.pdf (accessed 20 June 2013).

Office of Public Sector Information (2006) 'Explanatory notes to Fraud Act 2006', www.opsi.gov.uk/a cts/acts2006/en/ukpgaen_20060035_en_1.

Oliphant, B.J. and Oliphant, G.C. (2001) 'Using a behavior-based method to identify and reduce employee theft', *International Journal of Retail and Distribution Management*, 29(10): 442–451.

ONS (Office of National Statistics) (2013) 'Crime in England and Wales, year ending September 2012', www.ons.gov.uk/ons/rel/crime-stats/crime-statistics/period-ending-sept-2012/stb-crime-in-engla nd-and-wales–year-ending-sept-2012.html#tab-Summary (accessed 6 January 2013).

Payments Cards and Mobile (2013) 'UKFraud seeks to reduce mobile wallet payment risks', www. paymentscardsandmobile.com/ukfraud-seeks-reduce-mobile-wallet-payment-risks/8November2013 (accessed 16 December 2013).

Scottish Office (1996) *Secured by Design – Commercial*. Edinburgh: HMSO.

Sentencing Advisory Panel (2004) 'Consultation paper on theft from a shop', *Sentencing Council*, www. sentencing-guidelines.gov.uk/docs/cons-annex-theft-0806.pdf (accessed 25 March 2010).

Serious Organised Crime Agency (2010) 'Counterfeit currency', www.soca.gov.uk/threats/counter feit-currency (accessed 24 February 2011).

Sutton, M. (1998) 'Handling stolen goods and theft: a market reduction approach', Home Office Research and Statistics Directorate: Research Findings No. 69.

Sutton, M., Schneider, J. and Hetherington, S. (2001) 'Tackling theft with the market reduction approach', Crime Reduction Service Series Paper 8, Home Office, www.homeoffice.gov.uk/rds/p dfs/r69.pdf (accessed 2001).

The UK Cards Association (2013) 'Card fraud type – on UK issued debit and credit cards', *Fraud: The Facts*, www.theukcardsassociation.org.uk/plastic_fraud_figures/index.asp (accessed 16 December 2013).

Whitehead, T. (2013) 'Half of fines for shoplifting ignored', *The Telegraph*, 25 December, www.telegrap h.co.uk/news/uknews/law-and-order/10518776/Half-of-fines-for-shoplifting-ignored.html (accessed 11 June 2014).

Wilson, D., Patterson, A., Powell, G. and Hembury, R. (2006) 'Fraud and technology crimes: findings from the 2003/04 British Crime Survey, the 2004 Offending, Crime and Justice Survey and administrative sources', *Home Office Online Report* (accessed September 2006).

Index

Entries in **bold** denote tables and boxes; entries in *italics* denote figures.